FIGHTER GENERAL
The Life of Adolf Galland

FIGHTER GENERAL
The Life of Adolf Galland
THE OFFICIAL BIOGRAPHY

Col. Raymond F. Toliver, USAF *(Ret.)*
& Trevor J. Constable
Foreword by General James H. Doolittle, USAF (Ret.)

Schiffer Military History
Atglen, PA

Dustjacket and profile artwork by Steve Ferguson, Colorado Springs, CO.

HARD BARTER FOR GLORY

Depicted on the dustjacket is JG 26 *Kommodore Oberstleutnant* Adolf Galland in his *Friedrich*, W.Nr.6413, intercepting the "Circus" Blenheims on that fateful mid-day sortie of June 21, 1941. The artist takes license here to suggest this fighter, a duplicate of a similarly marked aircraft, W.Nr.6414, had by this date had the infamous cigar smoking Mickey Mouse logo painted beneath the cockpit, as well as having heavy mottled RLM grey applied over the garish yellow cowling (also see profile on page 214). Whatever the image, the *Friedrich* was lost and nearly so was its pilot – and it was only the first of two horrendous sorties for the *Kommodore* that day. In exchange for the loss of a borrowed second fighter and a critical head wound, he would have his 59th and 60th aerial victories confirmed, and inevitably, be commended with the first ever Swords citation to enhance his Knight's Cross with Oak Leaves.

DEDICATION

This book is dedicated to the ground crews of all air forces, in both war and peace, the unsung heroes of air power.

NOTE TO THE READER

The Bf 109 fighter is known throughout the world as the Me 109, or the Messerschmitt 109. The German pilots themselves never refer to it as the Bf 109, but as the Me 109, pronounced "May 109." In America it is pronounced "me."

Bf stands for *Bayerische Flugzeugwerke*, a mouthful to say the least. Professor Willy Messerschmitt and his design team began the design of the Me 109 in 1934 as a part of the Bayerflugzeugwerke Company, which was re-named Messerschmitt A.G. in July 1938.

The authors prefer to call this outstanding fighter the "Me 109" and have done so throughout this book.

The original German language edition of this book was published by,
Verlag Herbig GmbH, Munich.

Book Design by Robert Biondi.

Library of Congress Catalog Number: 98-86787.

Printed in China.
ISBN: 0-7643-0678-2

We are interested in hearing from authors with book ideas on military topics.

Published by Schiffer Publishing Ltd.
4880 Lower Valley Road
Atglen, PA 19310
Phone: (610) 593-1777
FAX: (610) 593-2002
E-mail: Schifferbk@aol.com.
Please write for a free catalog.
This book may be purchased from the publisher.
Please include $3.95 postage.
Try your bookstore first.

Contents

Foreword

The largest single obstacle to the success of the strategic daylight bombing of Germany was the German fighters. The name of General Adolf Galland was directly associated with that force.

I took command of the United States Eighth Air Force in early January 1944. At first we had a shortage of long-range fighter planes, and our bomber losses were heavy. As we got more long range fighters, our bomber losses were reduced. Finally, we had enough fighters to risk putting part of them directly against the German fighters. This greatly displeased the bomber commanders, but delighted the fighter pilots and the fighter commanders.

Events soon proved, nevertheless, that free-hunting fighter sweeps ahead of, and sometimes far afield from, the bomber boxes resulted in serious and irreplaceable losses to the Luftwaffe Fighter Arm. This in turn allowed daylight strategic bombing to reach its full potential. Mortal damage was then inflicted not only on German air power, but also upon their industry, through destruction of fuel supplies, transportation, and other key targets.

General Galland foresaw these developments as early as 1942, including the eventual strangulation of German war potential. Repeatedly he warned his superiors. He urged strong fighter reinforcement of the Western Front so that decisive losses could be inflicted on the Americans before daylight bombing found its feet. His warnings went unheeded.

By one of those strange parallels that often occur on opposite sides in war, the measures I took with Eighth Air Force fighters were essentially identical with those that Galland had urged on Goering during the Battle of Britain. As a successful fighter ace and leader, Galland believed that free-hunting fighter sweeps were tactically essential against RAF Fighter Command. Goering insisted instead on close fighter escort of German bombers, thereby robbing his fighters of both battle initiative and flexibility.

Galland's rise to General of the Fighter Arm at age 30 was truly meteoric. History acknowledges now the broad accuracy of his tactical insights, and his gifted understanding of fighter aviation in the overall structure of modern air power. In my view, these wider attributes mark him larger than do his high decorations. The Luftwaffe produced many outstanding aces, but only one Adolf Galland.

Frequently it has been borne in on me how fortunate it was for the Allies that General Galland did not have full operational authority over the Luftwaffe Fighter Arm. In the event, the years of war between our countries were mercifully brief. The decades of friendship since, extending over the whole range of constructive human activity, have brought us all closer together than we ever were in the past.

General Galland became a peacetime businessman, like myself. Through the years we have met in friendship on this common ground, as well as having our memories of the past when we were opponents in war. This authorized biography gives us new insights into the forces that shaped Adolf Galland, built his character, and gave him the strength to face his unusual military challenges. Written by two respected American historians, this book is not only a worthy addition to the history of air power, but also contributes to the mutual understanding of our two nations.

James H. Doolittle
General, USAF Ret.

Acknowledgments

Numerous kind people have contributed in various ways to the compilation of this book. Their knowledge, experience, and capabilities have provided the authors with invaluable help and guidance. General Galland's former Luftwaffe comrades saw him from many different angles and perspectives, in a wide variety of military circumstances. Most of them have known him well in postwar times, adding to their insights.

Former foes who became peacetime friends with General Galland have added their special contributions. We are grateful as well to have had access to General Galland's war diary. The German fighter pilot community as a whole has been most helpful.

Detailing the aid we have received would require many pages. We are therefore listing alphabetically all those who have helped with technical and research assistance. For any unintentional omissions, we apologize. We have been helped by:

Sir Douglas Bader*
Cajus Bekker
Hermann Boschet
Hans Heinrich Brustellin
Joseph Buffer
Harley Copic
Robert T. Crow
James H. Doolittle*
Wolfgang Falck
James J. Finnegan
Erich Hartmann*
John H. Kirby
Walter Krupinski
Gerhard Meyer
Nathan Miller
Johannes Mohn
Eduard Neumann
Heinrich Olemotz
Douglas Pitcairn
Hans Schmoller-Haldy*
Werner Schröer*
Eduard Schroeder
Robert H. Stanford-Tuck *
Johannes Steinhoff*
Ray Waddey
Anton Weiler
Dr. John M. Whitten
Frank Wootton

**Deceased*

The authors also owe a special measure of gratitude to Frau Heidi Galland, the general's widow, for her steadfast support in ensuring that his official biography come to fruition.

In their totality, the contributions of the people named above have been indispensable, and the authors are duly grateful.

Colonel Raymond F. Toliver, USAF *(Ret.)*
Trevor J. Constable

A SPECIAL NOTE FROM GENERALLEUTNANT ADOLF GALLAND

Many opportunities and offers came to me through the decades for the preparation of an official,authorized biography.None of these proved appropriate or timely, until my friends Colonel Raymond F. Toliver and Trevor "Sailor" Constable proposed this biography to me several years ago.All the necessary elements were present at this time.

These American authors know personally all the successful Luftwaffe fighter leaders who survived the war,and have earned their respect for integrity and fairness.The Toliver-Constable literary team has been able in past works,to capture the inner spirit of the Luftwaffe Fighter Arm and make it comprehensible to future generations.They have told history what happened,minus the biases and distortions of wartime propaganda.

Many years of research by the authors into Luftwaffe WW II records,secret wartime code decrypts and Allied interrogation reports,material declassified just a few years ago,has gone into the assembly of this new book.Such official documentation was not available to me thirty years ago,when "THE FIRST AND THE LAST" was published.I must admit that through the authors I learned things about WW II history and also the Luftwaffe,that were new to me despite my central involvement.Additionally my close friends were indeed under my skin for a long time. Most of the photographs in this book furthermore,are from my private collection,and have never previously been published.

ADOLF GALLAND
Lt. General (ret.)

BONN, WEST GERMANY
September 1989

ONE

The Guns of Adolf Galland

Personal property of enemies may be confiscated by the State,
but never by individuals.
– Winston Churchill, 1940

The luxurious former home of screen star Joan Crawford in Brentwood, California, was the scene of a dramatic ceremony on 16 October 1980, centered on General Adolf Galland. The guests present and awaiting his arrival were aware of what was about to happen, but not Galland. Thirty-five years after the end of World War II, the leader of Germany's wartime fighter pilots was about to receive the surprise of his life.

The Joan Crawford mansion belonged now to Robert T. Crow, son of the Dallas-based Trammel-Crow Corporation family. Several of Crow's friends eagerly awaited the arrival of General Galland and his party. Mr. and Mrs. C. Allen Colley, Mr. and Mrs. Joe Buffer, Ronald Cox, the Hayden C. Eaves, and author Ray Toliver and his wife, Jen, were among the welcoming group.

Just as the second round of drinks was being served, Galland arrived in characteristic style – a lady on each arm. Virginia Bader and Norma Bert were both radiant. Galland nevertheless became the immediate focus of attention, a human magnet automatically establishing the center of any gathering.

Screenwriter and historian Joe Buffer introduced everyone, while Bob Crow stood quietly beside a long leather chest. A brass plate mounted on the chest was inscribed with the Luftwaffe eagle and the number 12. Crow made sure that Galland had a drink, figuring that he would soon need one. Then Crow rapped the table and called for attention. As conversation faded out, he made his announcement.

"General Galland, I have something here that belongs to you. I want to take this opportunity to return it to you now, to the rightful owner."

Shoving the case towards Galland, Crow motioned to the general to open it up. Galland stood transfixed, staring at the brass plate with its number 12. He was like a man magically teleported to another time and place.

Hands trembling with excitement, Galland slipped the catches and swung back the lid. Eyes wide, mouth open with astonishment and wonder, he stared down at the matched pair of Merkel trap shotguns. Inside the lid was the original, yellowed paper with the numbers of the guns and the owner's name: First Lieutenant A. Galland. The guns had been presented to him by the Luftwaffe at Suhl in 1936 – forty-four years previously.

In the surrender maelstrom of 1945, these guns had been stolen from storage by a Lieutenant Colonel of the U.S. Army. They had been "liberated," in the parlance of the times. Galland had lost hope of ever seeing them again. Still without a word, he scooped up the first gun and assembled it as though he had done so daily for decades. Aiming along the barrel over the sights, he swung the gun as though tracking a skeet pigeon, then dropped the weapon to his side.

"My God! My guns! My guns! My guns!"

"Yes sir, General" said Bob Crow, "your guns once more. They are hereby finally returned to you with my compliments, sir."

The following evening, Galland was entertained at a dinner in Santa Ana, California, hosted by former naval aviator Wilbur F. Bettis, at the latter's famous *Nieuport 17* restaurant. Present also on this memorable evening was General James H. Doolittle, one of America's most famous flyers and Galland's chief wartime adversary as the 1944 commander of the mighty 8th USAAF. General Curtis E. LeMay of B-29 fame, General Kirk Armistead of the U.S. Marine Corps and Midway Island action, and General Jay Hubbard of U.S. Marine Corps note completed the array of distinguished air generals.

American fighter aces James L. Brooks and Robert M. DeHaven represented the U.S. fighter pilot fraternity. Other notable guests included aircraft designer and aviation artist R.G. Smith, James T. Burton of McDonnell-Douglas, former Luftwaffe interrogator Hanns Joachim Scharff, Colonel Al Osequerra USMC, screenwriter Joe Buffer, and author Raymond F. Toliver. Virginia Bader and Norma Bert were again in the company of the guest of honor – Generalleutnant Adolf Galland.

Before this glittering assembly, financier Bob Crow once more presented the long-missing guns to Galland. This time there were two other enthusiastic shooters and hunters on hand – Doolittle and LeMay. Throughout the evening, these two historic personalities could be seen picking up the guns, sighting them at imaginary targets, and hefting each weapon to admire its balance and workmanship. Both American generals were intrigued by these exquisite examples of the gunsmith's craft. Equally intriguing to them was the chain of events by which the guns had been returned to their rightful owner – 35 years later and half a world away in California.

The guns dated from early 1936, when Galland was a member of the Luftwaffe clay pigeon shooting team. World War I ace Ernst Udet, a passionate hunter, gun enthusiast, and master marksman, had organized the team to help improve marksmanship and morale. Each of the ten young officers on the team was presented with a matched pair of Merkel shotguns as a personal gift. Their cost was out of reach for all save the wealthiest sportsmen.

Trap and skeet shooting was not a 1936 Olympic discipline. Parallel with the Olympic Games in Berlin, nevertheless, a World Shooting Championship was organized at excellent new facilities in Berlin-Wannsee. Using these superlative guns, the Luftwaffe team surprisingly outscored the best German civil teams. The exultant Udet presented every team member with a season pass to the entire Olympiad.

Galland kept the guns with him during the war. In April of 1945, he placed these guns and others from his extensive collection in the care of Mr. Erich Vollmer at Hohenpeissenberg in Bavaria. He was Galland's wartime cigar manufacturer, and also a Major of the Reserve in JV 44, the jet fighter unit that was Galland's last command. U.S. Army occupation forces after the surrender compelled Vollmer to hand over all Galland's guns. The Merkel pair were personally appropriated by a Lt. Colonel. Galland in the meantime had become a prisoner of war at the surrender.

He learned of his loss when his principal American interrogator, Captain John M. Whitten of the U.S. Army, escorted him on a clandestine visit to Mr. Vollmer. Whitten and Galland had become fast friends, and it was relatively easy for Whitten to learn the identity of the officer who had stolen the guns. He had already returned to America, guns and all. In the temper of the times, nothing could be done. Galland had to accept losing the guns and all his other personal property as part of the price of defeat.

Many years later, the former Lieutenant Colonel tried to sell the guns in America for an exorbitant price. Galland's 1953 memoirs "The First and the Last," had in the meantime made him internationally famous. This automatically boosted the value of the guns, although they were not sold at this time due to the excessive price. Galland made every effort to get his guns back, but there was no response of any kind from the man who now claimed ownership. A resident of the southeastern USA, he ignored all correspondence.

The guns were eventually sold to Dr. Frank Hannon, a physician residing in the state of Washington. Through a friendly female employee of the American Consul General in Frankfurt, Galland learned of the sale. He also obtained the name and address of the "new owner." Contacting Dr. Hannon by letter and telephone, Galland made him a substantial offer for the guns, which was turned down. Dr. Hannon argued that Galland had offered him only one third of the present value of the guns, and the physician had his eye on tomorrow.

"The price will triple" he said, "when you pass away in the near future, General Galland."

After the doctor himself died, leaving Galland still in this world but minus his guns, the weapons passed into Hannon's estate. Advertising for the estate sale caught the enterprising eye of Joe Buffer, of Malibu, California.

A collector himself, and a German arms and collectibles investment expert, Buffer knew he had a find. A former U.S. Marine Corps Master Sergeant who had voluntarily served in both World War II and Korea, Buffer had equipped himself with a detailed knowledge of German history. That left him in no doubt about the potential value of the Galland guns. He bought the guns from thc Hannon estate for his own collection, at a price he described as "a little staggering."

Shortly after Buffer's return to California, he told his friend Ron Cox about his purchase of the historic guns. A few days later, Cox was lunching with Robert T. Crow, then president of the Los Angeles Division of the Trammel-Crow Corporation. Crow turned out to be a longtime admirer of Adolf Galland, with a burning desire to meet personally the former General of the Fighter Pilots. When Cox told Crow about the Galland guns, the executive knew that he finally had the key to meeting with the German general – provided he could get Joe Buffer to part with his prize. Bob Crow made Buffer an offer that he could not refuse. The price this time was more than a little staggering. The guns thus began the final phase of their journey back to Galland. Crow returned these irreplaceable weapons to their rightful owner with absolutely no strings attached. Such a gift places Crow among the most big-hearted of men. The authors asked Crow why he performed this generous act, which could not possibly bring him any material return – the acid test of a true gift.

"These guns were looted property of a man of honor and integrity. If they had been picked up by an agency of the State, then the law would dictate that they should be returned to their rightful owner.

"A deeper motivation was to do something proper, honorable, and nice for a man of his stature. It has always pained me to see the way that the German people have flagellated themselves over the acts of a few. General Galland was a man of destiny, placed in a point in time of great events. His qualities as a man and a warrior served his people very well.

"He never allowed his duty as a soldier of Germany to force him to violate those higher principles of mankind that the German people – in the overwhelming balance – hold dear

THE RETURN OF GALLANDS SHOTGUNS
Joe Buffer (1) noted gun collector located and bought the guns from an estate. Robert T. Crow bought the guns and gave them back to Galland on 16 October 1980. Buffer and Crow watch as Galland expertly reassembles the guns as if he had never lost them 35 years earlier.

and exemplify in their lives as well as any other people on earth. These principles of truth, compassion, and mutual respect among people, are based upon belief in the inherent goodness of man.

"I believe that a generation of self-flagellation for the heinous acts of a few, by the German people as a whole, is penance enough." Bob Crow's action is perhaps the ultimate expression of a phenomenon that was evident internationally for several decades. Adolf Galland brought out the best in people. Their qualities of goodwill and unconditional admiration appeared kindled by him, despite his being a former enemy general. He generated their warmest respect.

Drawn to him in social groups, at seminars, and in similar settings, they wanted if possible to speak with and to touch this most famous of all German aviators. Those able to receive a handshake sometimes walked away holding up their hand and looking at it as though it were something holy and blessed. Many such gatherings contained numerous famous aces and aviation personalities from several nations, but it was to Galland that people gravitated. Even the heroes crowded around him. All this occurred with no effort on his part, as an automatic reaction to his presence.

Charisma is the modern, overworked buzzword for what Galland exuded, but the word explains nothing. Adolf Galland was a man of body, soul, and spirit, who brought all three principles into high function in a life of drama and challenge. How he directed his talents and gifts, developed his character and abilities, and survived his triumphs and tragedies, is the subject of this narrative. Those who stay the course will agree at the end that he certainly deserved to get his guns back.

TWO

Roots

The retired Luftwaffe general and fighter ace who criss-crossed planet earth into the 1990s was a combination businessman and international ambassador of the world fighter pilot community. He dealt with high technology in the aerospace epoch, but he began in the era of helmet and goggles. Adolf Galland was already six years old when Baron von Richthofen was shot down, but he remained involved in matters of aerospace seventy years later. Like a towering old German oak, it was his roots that enabled him to endure.

When he was growing up during and following World War I, there was no "counter culture" to menace his orderly development. Anything of such a nature thrusting into his boyhood would have faced a hostile and aggressive opponent – his father. Adolf Felix Galland ruled his household and his sons with an iron hand, in the fashion of that age. Permissiveness was unknown. The senior Galland's goal was to raise men of character and integrity, who would become capable and effective citizens. Adolf Galland, the younger, was raised in accordance with the trusted principles of tradition.

The presence of the Galland family at Westerholt in Westphalia, where the future General of the Fighter Pilots was born on 19 March 1912, was itself a tradition. Galland is a French name. The first Galland in Westerholt was a Huguenot refugee from France, who sought a new life in Germany in 1742. Appointed bailiff to the estate of Count von Westerholt, the immigrant Galland began a tradition that handed down the office of bailiff continuously from father to son.

Americans are accustomed to the term bailiff almost exclusively in the sense of a minor court official. The bailiff of the Westerholt estate held a far wider range of responsibilities. Adolf Galland's father supervised and administered the work of more than 100 persons, carrying out agricultural, mechanical, domestic, and maintenance pursuits, as well as the functions of forestry.

Management of such vast holdings today would classify the bailiff as an "agri-business executive." His authority on the Westerhold estate was unquestioned. So, also, was it unquestioned in his own home, located just outside the gates of Count von Westerholt's castle.

Galland's mother came from a successful business family in Bochum. Both parents were from the upper middle class of their own day. They were devout Roman Catholics, and the family was run along completely traditional lines. Young Adolf would live his own life and raise his own children, under basic Christian principles, but would never consider himself a religious man. In his boyhood home, an authoritarian father was accepted unquestioningly by everyone. Equality of the sexes would never have been accepted in the Galland home, even if anyone had dared suggest such a thing eighty years ago. Discipline for boys was a central family principle. Young Adolf and his elder brother Fritz caught the main force of their father's convictions about discipline. He drove all this home to his sons with stinging blows of a stick. They were sternly warned to avoid even minor infractions of their father's rules. Adolf and Fritz were afraid of their father.

Frau Galland, by contrast, embodied and exemplified the feminine principles of giving, softness, and caring. Consoling her sons after their thrashings, she would also gently remonstrate with their father against excessive severity. Until his final days, Adolf Galland remembered his mother with abiding fondness and warmth. A man rarely given to superlatives, he was lavish with them regarding his mother. "She was absolutely the best mother in the world. I loved her very much."

Two younger brothers came after Adolf, named Wilhelm-Ferdinand and Paul. Papa Galland had pet names for all family members. His wife he called "Anita" instead of Anna. Fritz was "Toby," Adolf was "Keffer," Wilhelm-Ferdinand was nicknamed "Wutz," and Paul was called "Paulinchen," or sometimes "Paula." When he arrived as the youngest family member, everyone was expecting a girl.

The arrival of Wutz and Paul diminished, through thinning out, the disciplinary pressure their father could exert. Perhaps mother Galland's importunings for more leniency had an effect as well, but life was easier in a disciplinary sense when there were four boys instead of two. Wutz and Paul had things relatively easy.

Papa Galland was not all severity and discipline. A hunter and outdoorsman of consummate skill, he had spent his life on the Westerholt estate. He made sure that his knowledge and skills were passed on to young Adolf – an eager pupil. He was taken on his first hunting trip at age 5. He shot his first hare at age 6. Safe gun-handling and correct shooting technique became part of him. Opportunities were provided for the steady practice that is essential to the development of a master marksman.

All the great fighter aces of the air wars have been excellent marksmen. Those among them who learned to shoot under expert guidance early in life almost invariably found quick success in aerial combat. Galland's training as a woodsman developed another crucial component of his success. Less ponderable than the ability to hit the bullseye, this faculty was developed by having a game preserve at his back door in boyhood, plus numerous invitations to the hunt. Galland had a fine "hunter's nose" – the ability to smell out his quarry. Open cockpit aces of World War I claimed it was literally possible to "smell out" the enemy. In World War II, the hunter's nose was an intuitive capacity to find the enemy, in the absence of radar control and direction. Years of hunting game honed this talent in Galland.

When he arrived on the Channel Front in June of 1940 to take command of III/JG 26, he was already a widely-known ace. He brought with him from the woods of Westerholt that all-important hunter's nose, at a time when German radar was not sufficiently sophisticated to control Luftwaffe fighters. Leading his units down to lower altitudes, he located RAF aircraft with uncanny consistency. His hunting talent, and the success that sprang from its wartime use, changed the fortunes of III/JG 26 and boosted their morale.

The Great War, later to be known as World War I, made only a superficial impression on the young Galland. He was six years old when it ended. The only glory emerging from the war's horror seemed to be the heroic status of ace fighter pilots. He read about Max Immelmann, Oswald Boelcke, and Ernst Udet. He learned who Hermann Goering was, and would find out in decades yet to come what he was really like. Von Richthofen was an ace young Adolf could identify with, because the immortal Red Baron was also a hunter and woodsman. From this beginning, Galland's interest in aviation expanded to admiration of the great international pioneers of the twenties, conquering by air the oceans and continents.

Bored stiff by classical academic subjects at Westerholt Public School, and later at the Hindenburg Gymnasium in Buer, Galland's boyhood interests were almost exclusively technical. Studying only enough Latin, Greek, and other deadly dull subjects to scrape through his grades, he educated himself in the subjects of his own interest. Fascinated by electricity, he rigged up numerous experiments to demonstrate its laws and capabilities. He built radios and rockets and became an expert motorcycle mechanic.

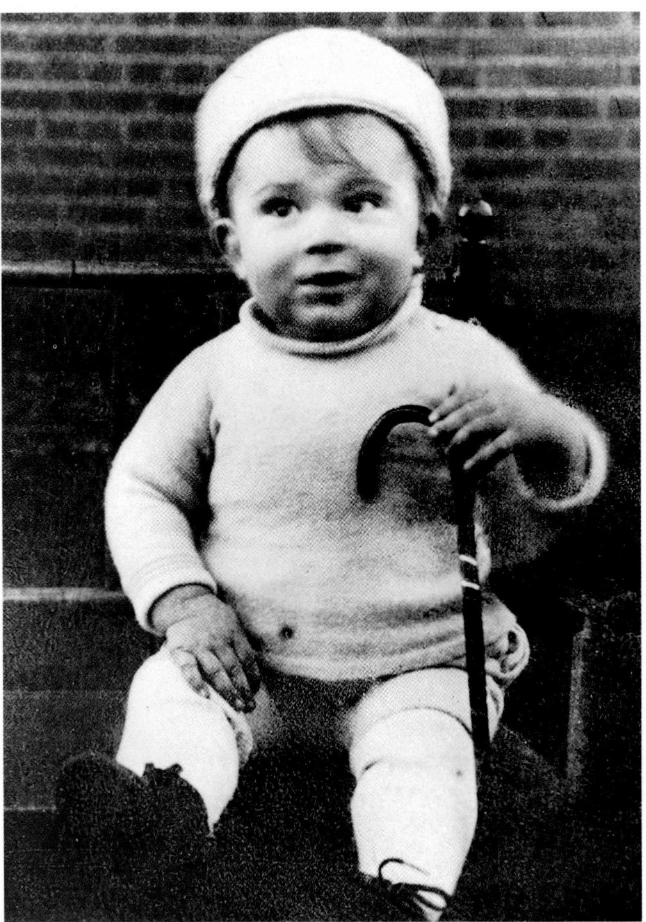

ADOLF "KEFFER" GALLAND
At home on Christmas eve, 1912, young Adolf was just 9 months old and had yet to light his first cigar.

Energetic involvement in athletics, especially sprinting and the high and broad jumps, ensured the development of a sound and healthy body. Trap shooting sharpened his marksman's eye to the point where he would later easily qualify for the Luftwaffe's first trap shooting team. Motor cycles, car driving, and girl chasing were all part of his versatile youth. Model aircraft rapidly turned his interest toward the burgeoning sport of sailplaning, and in a short time the air and aircraft became the dominant passion of his life.

Papa Galland had been watching his second son's technical abilities developing. He took a sort of gruff interest in the youngster's enthusiasm for sailplaning. Part of the vast Westerholt estate was the Borkenberge, a sprawling heath east of the Haltern-Munster railway. The Gelsenkirchen Flying Club had set up a camp on the Borkenberge for sailplaning about twenty miles from Westerholt. Papa Galland stunned Adolf by buying him a small motorcycle. A tremendous unfoldment would result from this act of paternal generosity.

While his brothers were enthusiastic horsemen and cantered about the Westerholt estate, Adolf sped over to Gelsenkirchen on his motorcycle and continued his chosen education. Classes were held by the flying club in aeronautics, including practical training in the design and construction of sailplanes, the theory of flight, meteorology, and kindred subjects. Galland absorbed this knowledge eagerly.

His relationship with his two younger brothers was one of fraternal love and respect. Different feelings were evoked by his elder brother. These feelings hovered between bare tolerance and dislike. Fritz then made the mistake of seeking to woo away from Adolf an exceptionally attractive girl who had attached herself to the would-be sailplane pilot. Outright antagonism awoke in Adolf toward Fritz. This antagonism was to have far-reaching consequences in shaping Adolf Galland's character and his whole approach to life.

Surging up from his depths came an intense drive to excel his brother. He told himself repeatedly that he would always be better than his brother and that no matter what sacrifices were necessary, he would make himself excel by sheer merit. This resolution went deep. Long after he had won back his girl from his brother, the drive to be number one remained. Minus any objective connection to his brother, the resolution came to apply to his life as a whole. He would find it impelling him to achievement and sustaining him through the darkest times of his life. He had tapped a profound wellspring of his will.

Sailplaning became a passion. Every weekend he was out on the Borkenberge toiling with the launching and retrieval of sailplanes. With other boys who shared his passion, he would haul the precious and fragile birds up with heavy catapult ropes, and then stand open-mouthed with wonder as they went rushing away on the bosom of the wind. He dreamed of the day that he would go aloft. Hard physical work improving their rough encampment, hacking out roads with picks, shovels, and wheelbarrows, hardened his resolve even more.

Galland made a rocky beginning as a pilot in 1927. His first sailplaning effort ended in a crash shortly after he became airborne. His second start went better; and, with thumping heart, he experienced for the first time the magical solidity of air when penetrated by a wing at the proper angle. Each flight saw his skill improve. He was hooked for life on the adventure of flying.

Life's proudest moment up to this time was passing his sailplane pilot's "A" license. The treasured lapel badge he was now entitled to wear showed a white gull on a dark blue field, and it would remain the most exciting of all the pilot's badges he would ever earn. He had stayed aloft 34 seconds to win the right to have the badge on his lapel.

Five more flights qualified him for the "B" test. The coveted "C" test was now within reach, but required five minutes of sustained flight. That was difficult to achieve on the Borkenberge, before the physics of thermals – vertical air streams caused by temperature differentials – were understood by scientists and airmen. The Borkenberge soaring record was 47 minutes 45 seconds at that time. Galland assaulted this record after a detour to the Mecca of German sailplaning – the Rhoen.

ADOLF GALLAND'S PARENTS
Anne (nee Schipper) and Adolf Galland, mother and father of Lt. General Adolf Galland posed for this photo on Christmas day 1949.

His Rhoen trip almost slipped from his grasp. His interest in soaring brought about a nosedive in his classical schooling. His father was furious to learn from the gymnasium in Buer that young Adolf did not meet the standards of his class. An ultimatum was issued: school work up to standard, or there will be no more flying.

The 19 year-old maintained himself in school by a bare margin. He was therefore able to attend the Easter soaring meet at the Rhoen in 1931. The Rhoen mountains lie about 25 miles north of Frankfurt-on-Main. Highest among them is the legendary *Wasserkuppe* – the "water hill" – so named because its top is frequently swathed in wet clouds. The view from the crest in good weather is among the world's most spectacular. Gliding had begun there before World War I, developed into soaring, and by the middle nineteen twenties the Rhoen had become a famous international soaring site.

A luminary of the twenties on the Rhoen was a tall, dark, gaunt-looking designer of sailplanes and soaring machines – Willy Messerschmitt. Half-designer and half-artist, he learned and applied well the lessons of the Rhoen. Messerschmitt was famous as a sailplane designer long before he created his first fighter aircraft. His later creations would figure significantly in the life of Adolf Galland.

The legendary stars of German soaring had all made their names and records at the Rhoen. Galland now rubbed shoulders with some of these personalities, watched them in action, and took the course that would lead to his Pilot's Certificate. Enthusiasm and fellowship at the Rhoen were like champagne, bubbling and irresistible.

Galland was back at the Rhoen in the autumn, with members of his own club, participating in the International Soaring Competition. They had hauled their own best sailplane, designed as Meyer II, to the meet. The elated young Galland stayed aloft for an hour, thus qualifying for his Pilot's Certificate. Only two other men in Westphalia held this certificate. The honor was sufficient to warrant its presentation to Galland by the President of Westphalia. This presentation was the first of numerous similar ceremonies that would mark his life as a pilot.

He could now make cross-country flights, perform at air shows, and instruct other sailplane pilots. He was excelling his brother Fritz, but nearly crashed educationally as a result. As his *Abitur* loomed, he had to literally force himself into familiarity with all the classical knowledge that did not interest him.

Count von Westerholt now provided special incentive. He had watched young Galland's progress as a pilot with interest. He offered him a sailplane of his own as a reward for successfully passing his final examination at Buer. Young Adolf knew how to take advantage of an opportunity. His final composition described the design and construction of a trailer for sailplane transportation to soaring sites. The trailer was designed to provide overnight shelter for the soaring team, including their food supply, and the unit also provided storage for the sailplane when it was not in use.

Galland passed his finals. He had won his heart's desire – a brand-new sailplane built to his specifications at the factory. His choice was the Grunau Baby, a popular and durable craft that enjoys classic status today among sailplane enthusiasts. Excitement ran high at the Gelsenkirchen Flying Club as Galland drew up his specifications and sent them to the Grunau factory.

"TOBY" and "KEFFER"
Father Galland gave each of his sons a nickname. The eldest was called Toby and the future General was called Keffer.

Galland began to notice something about himself that was a portent of his military future. The sailplaners all pitched in to help build the trailer he had designed. He became aware that his comrades were increasingly looking to him for leadership, and came to him with ideas for his approval. When he spoke, they listened receptively, as though intuitively aware that he knew more than they. The entire group worked naturally and efficiently under his direction in memorable harmony. All necessary discipline came from within them. Galland was their naturally chosen leader, without any election or badges of rank.

Years later with the Condor Legion in the Spanish Civil War, Galland would again encounter this phenomenon. As a squadron commander in his middle twenties, he had more than 140 men under his authority. The squadron ran smoothly and successfully. All his life he would remember with pride that he never had to punish even one member of his Condor Legion squadron, despite his own youth and operations in a foreign country.

Club members on the trailer project contributed both labor and their savings. When they were still short of funds, they borrowed from parents, relatives, and friends to push the job through to completion. Practical idealism in action, the venture was crowned by the arrival of the sailplane by rail. The proper craft was in their hands to prove the merits of the Borkenberge as a soaring site, and for Galland to make his attempt on the Borkenberge record of 47 minutes aloft.

"Calvary" was the nickname given to the high launch point on the Borkenberge, since it always involved heavy loads and sacrificial labor. Labeled Rauher Hang on the map, the site was wreathed in freezing murk on the morning of 27 February 1932. Club members struggled the precious Grunau Baby into position in zero visibility. Galland was strapped in, already frozen to the bone by a biting northeaster.

Visibility lifted slightly. Galland gave the starting signal, and his comrades launched him into the soup. He immediately vanished from sight. The near-blizzard was as bad as it looked. He felt the frigid pinch of ice on his face. His goggles fogged. The sailplane's wings quickly developed an ominous frosty mantle. A lull in the wind decided the issue. The would-be record breaker crunched back down on the icy heather. With diminished enthusiasm, the freezing ground crew stiffly hauled the craft back up to the launch point.

By 9:25 am, in better visibility he was catapulted up again, rejoicing at the responsiveness of the new sailplane. Higher and higher he rose in a series of steep turns. Facial detail of the dancing figures below disappeared as he passed the 30-minute mark. Navigating carefully to catch the upwind, nursing his kite through air pockets, he felt as though born to the air. Surviving 47 minutes, he smashed the old Borkenberge record and swept on. He was determined to make it a decisive improvement.

Turbulence amid the fresh breeze jarred the Baby, pushing Galland to the limit of his piloting skill. Far below, his comrades were in an ecstasy of delight – distant pygmies prancing and waving sheets in salute. He reached a triumphant two hours aloft. Part of him wanted to continue the intoxicating majesty of his victory over the air. Intellect nevertheless ruled emotion. He could feel the slackness that had worked into the aileron cables from more than 300 turns.

When he landed back on the Borkenberge, he had been aloft for 2 hours, 6 minutes and 5 seconds. He had not only shattered the old Borkenberge record, but also had established a new regional soaring record for northwest Germany. The legend of Galland the pilot had begun. His feat was hailed and he became famous in soaring circles, a success that would continue until he became the most famous German pilot of his time.

The Borkenberge was now established as an excellent soaring location for good sailplanes. Local enthusiasm boomed. The Westerholt Soaring Club, affiliated with the DLV (*Deutscher Luftsport Verband*), was formed to give this enthusiasm a focus. At the foundation meeting of the Club, Galland's record-breaking sailplane was christened The Imp (*Strolch*). He had proved that he could make things happen through his resolution always to be number one – the best.

His father was enthusiastic over this success, but highly skeptical about aviation other than as a sport. He was taken aback when, in a fatherly interview about the direction of young Adolf's future, the latter said immediately that he wanted to become a commercial pilot. Such an ambition would be normal in today's world, but Westerholt in 1932 was another world.

Europe was then served by numerous air-taxis. Small aircraft transported businessmen and were used in medical emergencies and in similar functions. Hermann Goering had run an air-taxi in Scandinavia. Galland senior equated commercial piloting with taxi-driving. He could not envision an airline operating like a steamship line, even though Lufthansa already operated on long international routes.

Papa Galland had been born in the nineteenth century. Expectation on his part that young Adolf would follow him as bailiff was normal and natural. Galland senior would have been fully in character had he tried to persuade his son to follow some orthodox and recognized profession. He showed instead a practical wisdom by urging his son to choose the profession for which he truly felt the call. Funds were available to young Adolf for any higher education he needed.

When his son still came out unswervingly for a career as a commercial pilot, Galland senior stilled his misgivings and supported his son fully. Papa could do little in a practical way, but he provided plenty of moral support, which earned him young Adolf's warm respect. Moral support was vital in such a discouraging situation. Chances for a young man to become a commercial pilot in Germany in 1932 were near zero.

Germany's social scene in the big cities bordered on anarchy. The most populous, energetic, and technically skilled nation in Europe was shabby, starving, and down-at-heel. Massive unemployment, soup kitchens, and the street riots of warring political factions exemplified Germany's desperate plight. Most of Adolf Galland's contemporaries would go from Germany's schools directly to swell the ranks of six million unemployed.

Qualified, mature, and capable men – the citizenry that should have been making the country prosperous – were living desperate lives. The German nation was a gaunt shadow of itself. The National Socialist Party led by Adolf Hitler daily drew attention to the monstrous irrationalism of a great nation in degradation. Hitler's unrivaled oratory, and the social situation itself, swept him onward toward political mastery of Germany.

With the German economy in low gear, 20 year-old Adolf Galland wanted to be an airline pilot. His chances were approximately the same as a young American today wanting to be an astronaut. The supply of human material grossly exceeded the demand. The national popularity of soaring had made German youth air-minded, and all the country's best young men wanted to fly.

The German Air Line Pilot School (*Deutsche Verkehrsflieger Schule*) had branches at Braunschweig, Warnemuende, Schleissheim, and at List on the island of Sylt. There were 20 vacancies for beginners. 20,000 applications inundated the school. Odds of 1,000 to 1 against Galland dropped steeply when the school itself weeded out all save 100 exceptional young men.

This elite would be privileged to sit for a grueling ten-day examination. Galland was among them. A battery of exhausting physical, academic, psychological, and technical tests was applied at Braunschweig with relentless thoroughness. Galland's sailplaning experience was a substantial help. He was among the 20 survivors of the ordeal. He was keeping his resolution always to be the best. The spirit in which he was approaching life at this time is exemplified in the following excerpt from a sailplaning article that he wrote in 1932:

"The dashing sailplane is flying like an arrow into the ether. Moments before, it was indifferent, heavy on the earth. Now it is in its element and flies noiselessly, carried by a magic force, climbing to enormous heights with entrancing boldness, obedient to the will of its master, the pilot.

"One is affected by the beauty of Nature, the grandeur of soaring, the almightiness of our Creator. Flying is foolproof, but it must first be learned thoroughly. There is always a way for a healthy person to become a pilot – when there is will power, consistent direction, and love and idealism for flying."

Fortified by this spirit, he was about to begin living his boyhood dream.

THREE

The Black Luftwaffe

The grueling tests that selected twenty elite young men from an application list a thousand times larger, characterized life at the German Air Line Pilot School in Braunschweig. Issued blue civilian clothes and quartered in modern barracks, the future airline pilots found themselves under tight discipline. They did not know it at the time, but Galland and his fellow students were becoming part of the "Black Luftwaffe."

Generaloberst Hans von Seeckt had laid the basis for this shadow air arm more than ten years previously. An air service for the Army was regarded as essential by the planners working under von Seeckt's direction. While there was no vision of a massive, completely independent Air Force such as the Luftwaffe later became, the secret aviation section within the War Ministry remained abreast of world aviation developments. This section also set in train clandestine design and engineering work on the military aircraft denied Germany under the Versailles Treaty.

Preparations were also made to produce a new generation of military aviators and aviation specialists. Under a secret clause of the Treaty of Rapallo in 1922, a German Army aviation training program was set up at Lipetsk in the Soviet Union. This program operated from 1926 until Hitler came to power. More than 200 German officers, including such later Luftwaffe luminaries as Albert Kesselring, Hugo Sperrle, and Hans Juergen Stumpff were given aviation training at Lipetsk.

The German Air Line Pilot School, to which Adolf Galland had now won entry, became later a part of the Black Luftwaffe. Creation of a cadre of excellent pilots, around whom the new air service could be built when open rearmament began, was a major goal of the shadow force. The rigid discipline at Braunschweig had little to do with flying an airliner. A crushing scholastic load and the demanding physical and practical training drew out of the young Galland the best that he could produce. Fear of failure was used to spur on the students to maximum effort.

Instructors repeatedly told the students that anyone who did not measure up would be dismissed from the school, and unceremoniously put aboard the first train to his home town. Thousands were waiting to jump into any vacancy. The stern, military-style training was supervised by a famous military aviator, retired Colonel Alfred Keller. His background for training airline pilots was flying bombers in World War I. Keller had been in London bombing raids, and had won the coveted "Blue Max." Keller and all others wore civilian clothes, but his war hero's aura shone right through.

Galland had personal contact with Keller after a couple of incidents involving aircraft damage and the loss of a Klemm training plane. The young man from Westerholt broke the undercarriage of an Albatros L 101, and this caused him acute anxiety due to the school's tight discipline. Visions of the humiliating rail ticket back to Westerholt swam before his mind's eye. Shortly afterward, a flying accident increased the tension. Galland was leading a three-plane formation of Klemm trainers, and the other two fledgling pilots collided. One got home and the other bailed out.

The ensuing investigation and fuss upset Galland mightily. Investigators attributed the collision to unordered formation changes. The inference was that Galland was to blame – or so it seemed to him at the time.

Fearing expulsion, he moved to cover himself by applying for officer-cadet training with the 18th Infantry Regiment at Paderborn. Passing the necessary entry examinations without missing any schooling at Braunschweig, he was further depressed when the Army people were pessimistic about an opening, and his application went into a pile of similar papers. Hundreds of applicants were available for every officer-cadet vacancy.

To his astonishment, loss of the Klemm trainer seemed to be gradually forgotten at Braunschweig. He had expected the incident to be held against him. Things had completely cooled down at flying school when the Army suddenly summoned him to officer-cadet training in the autumn of 1932. Taking the Army order to Colonel Keller, Galland explained his predicament to the bomber pilot, who had become a school principal, and asked his advice.

Keller made it clear that Galland's flying career was in no danger. Training young pilots necessarily meant some crashes and losses. His school record was good and the school would support and assist him. Seeking refuge in the Army was out of the question. Keller would not release him.

Galland now knew that he was going all the way as a pilot. Gone was the dark impression that his stay at Braunschweig was marginal. He would encounter Alfred Keller many times in coming years, as Generaloberst Keller, an Air Fleet Commander in World War II, and also as Chief of the National Socialist Flying Corps (NSFK), but his first meeting with Keller was the most memorable one. He withdrew his Army application immediately.

The school handled not only beginners, but also part-time released Army officers who were taking courses on special aircraft. These were a more obvious element of the Black Luftwaffe. Friction arose between Galland's group of blue-clad but authentic civilians and the Reichswehr officers who acted as though they had never been discharged. The civilians stoutly resisted being ordered about.

Powered flight was the focus of Braunschweig activities. The school had a sailplane available, but no soaring program, even though all the students had interest and experience in the national aeronautical sport. Galland used the school sailplane to keep his soaring skills sharp. Word had come through the mails that his old soaring mates were busy building an all-new sailplane.

His comrades christened the new sailplane "Keffer" – his own nickname. The flattered Galland was invited to make the maiden flight at the 1932 autumn soaring meet on the Borkenberge. Fashioned by the hands of his comrades, the sailplane had been designed by Georg Ismer, their instructor. The new craft looked enticingly beautiful and sleek. Galland climbed aboard in a fever of happy anticipation.

Galland's excited companions hauled the sailplane aloft manually, using heavy rubber catapult ropes. At altitude Galland slipped the tow. His eagerness turned to alarm. The tail dropped heavily, as though there were a sandbag in the rear fuselage. No pilot could have done anything to correct the imbalance at such a moment. Sir Isaac Newton took over, with the law of gravity.

Spinning in rapidly, the sailplane crashed. Dizzy and bleeding from facial cuts, Galland was pulled from the wreckage in the first of his several crashes as a pilot. Cuts on his face spoiled his dark good looks for the time being, and he had suffered a mild concussion. Resting for only a few days, he went back in the air at the controls of his own trusty "Imp" sailplane and took second prize. Then it was back to the grind at Braunschweig.

By Christmas of 1932, half of the elite twenty who had begun the course with Galland had been dropped by the school. By securing his B-1 pilot's certificate in the summer, he had acquired the necessary 150 hours for his B-2 certificate at New Year 1933. Aerobatic training at Schleissheim, near Munich, had revealed his talent and passion for the art of acrobatic flying. His piloting expertise now included looping, diving, spinning, rolling, and inverted flying.

After a 25-hour course in seaplane piloting, combined with instruction in naval procedures and terminology at Warnemuende, Galland and four comrades were told to report to the Central Air Line Pilot School in Berlin. Officials there "invited" them to take part in a "secret training course for military pilots." All five accepted. This meant flying fighter aircraft and learning the skills required to handle high performance machines. He was in the Black Luftwaffe.

Maintaining external pretenses, Galland and his comrades reported to Schleissheim still in civilian clothes. Training was under Major Beyer, an Army officer who had received aviation training under the Lipetsk project in Russia. The Schleissheim course was a poorly organized mixture of lectures and flying training. Oral material concentrated on military affairs, Great War air tactics, and aviation history. Galland enjoyed 25 hours in Albatros and Heinkel biplanes, including mock aerial combat and formation flying. The high point in the course for the marksman from Westerholt was firing with live ammunition at ground targets.

All this activity was strictly prohibited under the Versailles Treaty, but in Germany things were changing fast. While Adolf Galland had been developing his piloting skills, men who would bulk large in his life and career were busy shaping 20th century history. Hermann Goering had developed high skills as a political manipulator. These skills, combined with his status as an ex-officer and highly decorated war hero, were used on Germany's aging President, Field Marshal von Hindenburg, inducing him to appoint Adolf Hitler as Chancellor.

Hitler's first coalition government promoted development of the Black Luftwaffe. Goering was now not only President of the Reichstag, a post he was entitled to legally and electorally, but also Prussian Minister of the Interior. Through this latter office, he controlled the police. Hitler also made him National Commissioner of Aviation, a euphemistic title for Germany's first Air Minister. Behind the facade of civil aviation, Goering immediately began strengthening the Black Luftwaffe.

Goering wisely secured at this time the services of Erhard Milch as Secretary of State at the Air Ministry. An observer flyer who had finished the Great War in command of a fighter squadron, Milch had taken over the organization and direction of Lufthansa in the early nineteen twenties. Proving himself an outstanding organizer and administrator, Milch also had business acumen and vision. Lufthansa became one of the world's most progressive and innovative airlines, despite the aviation restrictions of the Versailles Treaty. Milch's achievements were accomplished despite numerous high-level intrigues against

Lufthansa within Germany. He was both capable and tough.

While building Lufthansa, Milch hired Goering as a lobbyist when the latter was serving in the Reichstag. Milch knew all about the Black Luftwaffe. He had seen to it that military aspects of aviation had been woven subtly into the courses at the German Air Line Pilot School. Airliner design and procurement kept military needs in mind. Milch had been reluctant to work for Goering – his former hireling – but the mind of the Lufthansa boss was changed by a personal interview with Hitler.

As State Secretary, Milch now became a sort of operating head of the Black Luftwaffe and all its workings. Adolf Galland, the pilot trainee at this time, would get to know Erhard Milch well during World War II, and he would also see more than he wished of both Goering and Hitler. The rise of the Black Luftwaffe accelerated almost by the month, as Milch increased production of the Ju 52 and many types of training aircraft. More obviously, old Goering flying comrades from the Great War began surfacing in significant posts.

Already prominent in national aviation was Goering's war comrade Bruno Loerzer, with whom Goering had broken in as an aerial observer prior to becoming a pilot. Loerzer had long been head of the DLV, the national body governing soaring. Goering would certainly put Loerzer in high rank in the new Luftwaffe.

Germany's most successful living ace, Ernst Udet, was appointed a consultant to the Air Ministry. He was told that big things were coming. Goering's former adjutant Karl Bodenschatz, who had loyally served him the Richthofen Circus, again became his liaison officer. Other famous ace pilots of the Goering era were already serving in the Black Luftwaffe and would hold commands in the new air force.

Official energy and resources pouring into clandestine preparations were much in evidence when Galland completed his Schleissheim course in May of 1933. Orders came to attend a meeting of some seventy young pilots, called by Goering at the Behrendstrasse in Berlin. Galland and eleven others were civilians. The rest were Army officers and NCOs, summoned from branches of the German Air Line Pilot School and from various secret training facilities. Goering promptly made clear that the purposes of the meeting were military.

Goering's official title of National Commissioner of Aviation seemed as harmless as calling him Lord of the Isles. His secret orders from Hitler nevertheless portended much harm. Civil aviation was to be aggressively developed, and Goering was ordered to create a new German Air Force. The latter massive task was to be accomplished in minimum time. Goering's public speaking style was forceful and inspiring. Combined with his fame as an ace and war hero, Goering's oratory and the plans he outlined left Galland and the other pilots with a positive impression. Goering was also a cultivated man, in contrast to some of the coarser personalities in the Nazi hierarchy. Goering therefore appeared to Galland, in the context of May 1933, to be a man worth following.

Goering told them that the shackles of Versailles were about to be removed forever. Training German pilots in the Soviet Union would soon become politically impossible. Hitler's friendship with Mussolini had provided an alternative. The fortunate young men present would be able to train as fighter pilots in Italy. This project was politically sensitive. Tight secrecy and camouflage were essential to preclude adverse international reaction.

Goering had made all necessary arrangements through his friend Marshal Balbo, head of the Italian Air Force and an old fighter pilot. Galland found all this translated into orders to rendezvous at Frankfurt-on-Main in civilian clothes. After three boring days of security lectures and other instructions, the pilots split into two groups. One was assigned to Udine in northern Italy, while Galland's unit was headed for Grotaglie in the south. They would train at an Italian Air Force base.

Crossing the frontier at Brenner as South Tirolean recruits, Galland's party detrained at Bari on the Adriatic coast. Italian civilians greeted them. Army motor transports were waiting, thinly disguised as civilian buses. After several miles, the convoy stopped at a remote olive grove, and their Italian greeters piled out and went behind some trees. They reappeared in elegant white uniforms of the Italian Air Force, and clambered back aboard the buses with an air of superiority that did not sit well with the Germans.

Jolting on to the Grotaglie airfield, which dated from the Great War, Galland and his fellow students were herded into a barracks and actually locked up. Frayed and worn-out uniforms of Italian Air Force officer-candidates were issued to them, and they were placed under close surveillance, almost like prisoners. Following this came recruit-style barrack drill, as though they were raw newcomers to military and aviation life.

Goering's way of doing things, combined with the language barrier, had misled the Italians. They failed to realize at first that they had three dozen fully-trained pilots on their hands, most of them German Army officers. These newcomers had expected to go to work immediately, flying modern fighters and shooting live ammunition. Galland's aerobatic skill helped clarify the situation.

An Italian pilot had just set a world record for inverted flight. His feat had been headlined in the press, and was the subject of some Italian boasting around the air base. The new record stood at about an hour and a half. When Galland's turn came to take up the flimsy Breda biplane trainer, he put the aircraft upside down and flew back and forth for about 45 minutes.

The deflated Italians ordered him down, and they were peeved. Their world record had been endangered before their eyes. The visitor from Westerholt never tried for the inverted flight record, mainly because he deemed this kind of flying only slightly less pointless than flagpole sitting. His inverted flight exhibition nevertheless served to convince the Italians that they had excellent pilot talent among their visitors.

The entire Grotaglie scene now improved. For hunter Galland, using machine guns was an exciting new dimension to marksmanship. For the entrenched Italians below, holding out strings of target balloons for the strafing pilots, things were also exciting – in a different way. There was too much metal whizzing through the air for comfort.

Despite the enjoyable flying and shooting, Grotaglie began to drag after a couple of weeks. There was no social life. No girls brightened the evenings of the secret visitors. Galland was glad to return to Germany in the autumn of 1933. He rated his Italian experience of minimal value, either to him as a pilot, or to the building of the new Luftwaffe.

Back in school at Braunschweig, he learned instrument flying and the special techniques of piloting required in handling heavy transport aircraft. After 50 additional hours of training, he passed his final examination and became a qualified airline pilot. Assigned as voluntary second pilot on Lufthansa's Stuttgart-Geneva-Marseilles-Barcelona route, he began his long love affair with the Spanish way of living.

Twice a week, he would fly a Rohrbach-Roland or a Junkers G-24 over the route that terminated in Barcelona. Layovers in the balmy Spanish city were idyllic interludes, but Galland's career as an airline pilot was itself little more than an interlude. Hermann Goering was galvanizing German aviation, and in January of 1934 Galland was again ordered to a Berlin meeting, this time at HQ of the German Air Line Pilot School.

The civil pilots who had trained in Italy were present. They were asked if they would like to go on the Active list of the new German Air Force. Galland wavered inwardly when he thought about giving up his hard-won civilian job. The happy days drinking and loving in Barcelona would have to be sacrificed. Going on the Active List also meant a period of recruit training, with its monotonous "square bashing" drills and loss of personal freedom.

Galland reasoned that by the time recruit training was over, and had been followed by a War Academy course, Goering's new Luftwaffe would be out in the open. He would be in on the ground floor. Weighing his chances for promotion in a new, rapidly expanding Luftwaffe against the relative stagnation of civil aviation, he decided to volunteer. The señoritas in Spain would have to wait.

When the 21 year-old Galland reported to the 10th Infantry Regiment at Dresden in February of 1934, he was the youngest man in his group. His pilot comrades included Army veterans in their late thirties, ex-Lufthansa pilots, flying club pilots, ex-instructors, and weather research flyers. Three months of basic infantry training instilled in them the importance of following orders, and gave them a basic orientation to military life.

Promotion to officer-cadet (*Fahnenjunker*) marked completion of the infantry course. Subsequent War Academy instruction exemplified the basic conservatism of the German Army toward aviation. Air power as a potentially dominant tactical and strategic instrument was not even contemplated. An air force as an independent service arm was never projected or discussed. The presumption throughout was that aviation would remain under the Army.

Goering was busy changing all this, even as Galland was taking the Dresden course, which he completed on 1 October 1934 with a commission as a lieutenant. The brand-new officer was then immediately discharged from the Army. In the waning days of the Black Luftwaffe, he went back into civil aviation. In uniforms that foreshadowed the coming new force, they wore birds on their lapels as badges of rank. He was now Kettenfuehrer Galland.

The Schleissheim branch of the German Air Line Pilot School was being transformed into the new Luftwaffe's first fighter pilot school. Still under camouflage, the facilities became steadily more militarized, along with the courses. The Black Luftwaffe was being phased out. An urgent need developed for instructors – many instructors – to train the hundreds of new pilots and mechanics who would man the coming fighter squadrons.

Realizing that his present Schleissheim course was not alone a modernization course, but also a means of selecting fighter pilot instructors, Galland took evasive action. Subtly fumbling every test, he made himself appear unsuitable for instructor duty. He had no intention of getting stuck in such a rut. He was duly passed over. Assignment to a fighter unit within a short time was now certain.

Goering came in February of 1935 to inspect the personnel and facilities at Schleissheim. At a subsequent meeting in the officers' mess at Mittenheim Castle, Goering outlined the plans and preparations of the past two years for the new Luftwaffe. Included was Goering's design for the new blue pilot's uniform, modeled for those who would shortly wear it by Rittmeister Bolle – late of the Richthofen Circus and a *Pour le Mérite* winner.

Goering told the eager pilots that all pretense would soon be dropped. The real Luftwaffe was about to be born. One month later, in March of 1935, the world public was shocked to learn that Germany's new Luftwaffe was an accomplished fact and not a paper proposal. Much was made of this in newspapers outside Germany, with emphasis on the clandestine preparations, as though it was somehow dirty of the Germans to do such things in secret.

The Black Luftwaffe had never been either a mystery or a secret to the intelligence services of the nations most concerned. No responsible leader in France, Britain, or Russia could honestly say that the Luftwaffe was a surprise. French intelligence had for years assembled a catalog of Versailles Treaty violations by Germany. The Russians had been hosts for over six years to German airmen training at Lipetsk.

Hitler had received, in February of 1934, a personal visit from F.W. Winterbotham, the remarkable British spy who won the confidence of top Nazis. Winterbotham was also destined later to oversee the distribution, to top Allied commanders and to Churchill, of the closely-guarded Ultra intelligence throughout the war. Hitler told the German-speaking Winterbotham almost casually in the course of their talk that the Versailles Treaty was dead. The Fuehrer added that his new Luftwaffe was growing rapidly. He expected that by the end of 1934 or early 1935, the Luftwaffe would have 500 operational aircraft. Winterbotham duly passed this information on to his British superiors.

All such political factors and machinations were well beyond the ken of Lt. Adolf Galland in April of 1935. He had achieved his immediate goal – assignment to a fighter squadron. Posted to the first official new fighter Geschwader, JG 2 *Richthofen*, he was a proud member of that formation's I Gruppe. HQ was at Doberitz, near Berlin, and Galland found life in JG 2 to be heady stuff, an exhilarating reward for all his toil.

Hitler and Goering and all the rest of the things going on in Germany were even less important to him when he was reposted to the newly-formed II/JG 2 as a foundation member. The unit was established at Jüterbog-Damm, and Galland was assigned as training officer – an honor for a pilot just out of school. The Luftwaffe was providing the opportunities for which he had hoped.

Flying the red-nosed He 51B-1 fighters, with their salty link to the Red Baron, was like riding in the stratosphere. The latest fighter type in the Luftwaffe, the Heinkel biplanes had a top speed of over 200 mph. Able now to indulge his personal passion for flying, thrilling to the joy of a powerful machine aloft, Adolf Galland thought about little else in 1935 but his own good fortune. Only a handful of young men in all the world could revel in the thrills – and spills – of flying.

FOUR

Crackups and Condors

Aerobatic flying was encouraged at Jüterbog-Damm. Assigned to specialize in aerobatics, and to train himself for appearances at air shows, Galland turned all his talent and energy to becoming an expert. Ernst Udet was at this time considered the greatest aerobatic pilot in Germany, and Galland modeled himself after the famous fighter ace.

"Aerobatics gave me great satisfaction," he recalled of this period. "After my earlier success in soaring, I realized for the second time in my flying career that I was better than most of the others."

His urge to be number one, combined with a natural talent for aerobatics, soon produced results. He became the kind of flyer that his fellow fighter pilots would gather to watch, dropping whatever they were doing to revel in his spellbinding skills. He became a pilot's pilot, yet still he reached for more.

He modified the carburetor of the Focke-Wulf *Stieglitz* (Fw 44) biplane that he flew aerobatically. His aim was inverted flight without fuel starvation. Seeking a further performance gain, he modified the horizontal stabilizer for more negative maneuverability – to help keep the tail down and nose up in inverted flights. This modification was strictly against regulations and changed the spin conditions of the Fw 44, but Galland did not know how much.

On a radiant October day in 1935, he took the modified aircraft up near noon for a tryout. Giving himself an extra margin of altitude, he took the little bird up to 2,500 feet and put it through a sequence of maneuvers he had accomplished many times previously without incident. He intended to make three turns of a spin and pull out handily. This time his illegally modified horizontal stabilizer had significantly changed the spin characteristics.

Spinning quickly, the kite lost altitude far more rapidly than before modification. Galland had the aircraft under control as he came out of the third turn, but his sink rate was extremely high. There wasn't sufficient altitude left for him to complete recovery to level flight. Knowing exactly what had happened, yet unable to do a thing about it, he sat transfixed – awaiting the imminent, unavoidable crash.

Hurtling into the ground at nearly a 45-degree angle, the biplane shattered into bits in a shower of dust and turf. Impact and unconsciousness were for Galland mercifully merged. Squadron mates, watching his aerobatics from the terrace of the officers' mess, groaned in horror as the biplane disintegrated. Jumping off the terrace, the shocked pilots went sprinting to the crash, certain that their comrade could not have survived.

A ghastly sight awaited. The pilot's seat had separated from the fuselage upon impact, slamming Galland's head into the instrument panel. His face was a bloody mask. Gently they pulled him clear and stretched him out on the grass. Medical personnel took over. A pall of sadness permeated the officers' mess that night, as the young pilot teetered between life and death.

For three days and nights he lay in a coma. Summoned from Westerholt in the emergency, his parents kept a round-the-clock bedside vigil. When he finally surfaced through the darkness, Galland heard his mother's voice, soothing, consoling and encouraging him. He felt the wondrous touch of her hand holding his. His father's voice was reassuring. Slowly he realized that he had survived, and that his head was swathed in bandages. He was alive, but only just.

Galland was under a lucky star. The finest German surgeon of that time, Professor Dr. Sauerbruch of Berlin, happened to be at the Jüterbog hospital on military duties, together with another Berlin specialist. Their skills and devoted labor were largely responsible for Adolf Galland's survival. He had suffered multiple skull fractures of a critical kind. Three months were needed for his injuries to heal.

Galland's face was permanently altered. When his nose was mashed flat against the instrumental panel, it was not only broken, but flattened and broadened beyond restoration. He had been a handsome young man before this crash, as contemporary photographs show. His visage was now different, and as the British put it in a preface to one of their postwar interrogation reports, ''He is not entirely a pleasant-looking man.'' The Jüterbog crash of 1935 gave the world the Galland face it came to know.

Serious for a pilot was the damage to his left eye. Severe cuts and glass splinters in the cornea drastically weakened this organ. His final hospital discharge report certified him as physically unfit for flying duty. According to the doctors, as a pilot he was finished.

The C.O. of II/JG 2 was Major Rheitel, a pilot from the Great War who had also trained at Lipetsk. He understood another pilot's problem. Galland was a gifted young airman of rich potential who had been in a crash. His abilities would be lost to the Luftwaffe if the doctors had their way.

Rheitel was one of the good old eagles from an earlier era who were not overawed by regulations. He conveniently shunted Galland's medical grounding report under other papers, and then claimed he could not remember seeing the report. "In the meantime, Lieutenant Galland," he said, "try to return to your normal flying duties until your medical report turns up."

At Jüterbog-Damm, two technical eras came together when Galland got his first look at the new Me 109. A developmental prototype of Professor Messerschmitt's widely-heralded new baby landed at Damm en route from the Augsburg factory to the Rechlin Test Center. The Me 109 was an all-metal, low-wing monoplane with an enclosed cockpit. This was the new aerial epoch.

Milling around the new aircraft were curious pilots of two generations. In addition to Major Rheitel, all three squadron commanders in II/JG 2 were Great War veterans: von Schoenebeck, Osterkamp, and von Kornatzki. The first two had been combat pilots. Theo Osterkamp had been a famous ace with 34 aerial victories and had won the Blue Max. These men carried enormous prestige because of their war experience, but they were highly suspicious of the Me 109's enclosed cockpit.

Arguments arose about the high wing loading of the Me 109, which meant that it was not ideal for a turning dogfight. Although he would later fly the Me 109 to glory and immortality, Adolf Galland was only slightly impressed by his first look at this historic aircraft. He would look back in his seventies and admit frankly that at Jüterbog in 1935, he was not able to recognize the extensive technical progress embodied in the Me 109. He could not then discern the new machine's virtues, despite an aeronautical background that already covered ten years.

The Me 109 test pilot was not permitted to demonstrate this developmental model. None of the II/JG 2 pilots was allowed to fly the machine. Similarly prohibited were comparison test flights against the He 51 biplane. Evaluations of the new bird therefore remained theoretical as far as Galland and his comrades were concerned.

HERMANN GÖRING
In 1918 Göring was a dashing fighter ace who had won the Pour le Merité, often called the Blue Max. He played a major role in the future of Adolf Galland.

His medical grounding report remained concealed for nearly a year. A disastrous test flight in an Ar 68 changed everything. With a misfiring engine, Galland swung around 180 degrees for a quick, downwind landing directly into the setting sun. Tall light masts at one end of the Bernburg airfield marked a row of fruit trees between the end of the runway and a nearby parallel street. Galland failed to clear one of the masts.

His left wing slammed into the light post and was shorn off. Slewing down in what was left of the Arado, he crashed thunderously. Cutting his head and face yet again, splintering his shin, and bruising himself all over, he was carted off to the hospital. Doctors pulling his personnel file were aghast to find – from almost a year previously – his medical grounding report.

This time, the medical authorities intended to make his grounding order stick. His latest crash proved that he was a menace to other pilots, aircraft, and himself, according to the doctors. He was to be grounded permanently, and there was

FOCKE-WULF 44 "STIEGLITZ"
This was the primary trainer airplane in the mid-1930s. Galland wrecked this airplane and altered his profile in a crash while doing aerobatics.

GALLAND'S FIGHTER BOMBER IN SPAIN
Adolf Galland flew the Heinkel He 51 during his tour in the Spanish Civil War. This artists rendition of the airplane was painted by Ray Waddey.

talk of a court martial for Major Rheitel for allowing a half-blind man to fly.

Galland took the offensive against this medical attack. Exemplifying his own later credo that a fighter pilot who does not at all times attack loses the initiative, he put on an energetic campaign to survive as a pilot. He lobbied and politicked with superior officers and comrades who visited him in hospital, seeking their assistance and support. Insisting from the outset of this campaign that his left eye vision was normal, he never stopped repeating this lie.

Prevailing upon a medical orderly to obtain for him the sequence of lines, letters, and numbers on the military eye chart, he lay for days in his hospital bed committing the chart to memory. Every line, every possible sequence of letters and numbers was burned into his memory so that he could run them back and forth like a movie film. His doctors, meanwhile, scheduled him for a complete physical at the town of Magdeburg, where nothing would be overlooked.

His general physical condition was satisfactory, but the medics at Magdeburg had his personnel file and they quickly zeroed in on his damaged left eye. They found the glass splinters in the cornea and other indications of damage. He was asked to read the standard eye chart with his right eye covered. He could see the chart, but the letters were blurred. Seeming to perceive them clearly, Galland began reciting them from memory.

As the dark-haired young pilot reeled off the numbers and letters with precision, the doctors stood gaping. On down the chart he went, reaching the final row without a single error. An incredulous examiner swallowed hard.

"Read the letters again, please. This time from the bottom row to the top, and backwards, please."

Out of Galland's mouth came the sequences. Making a slight pause here and there for effect, he made it sound as natural as possible. Even the doctors themselves could hardly boast of such eagle vision. They certified him fit for flying duty. He would enter the eighth decade of his life with the glass splinters still in his left eye, but by then he had hundreds of combat missions behind him. His return to the pilot roster of II/JG 2 was duly celebrated.

The period between Galland's two crashes with JG 2 was a time of signal international events in Europe. Hitler overrode the advice of his Army generals in 1936 and German troops reoccupied the demilitarized Rhineland. France and Britain enjoyed a marked superiority in every military category at this time. Only one Gruppe in JG 2, out of all the new Luftwaffe fighter formations, was thus far equipped with machine guns and ammunition. When the Allies backed down before Hitler's bluff, the Fuehrer gained a psychological edge over his highest generals that was to set the pattern of the years immediately ahead.

GALLAND IN THE LEGION CONDOR
In the Spanish Civil War, Galland and Gotthardt Handrick loved the warm weather and the beautiful señoritas. Handrick had been a famous Olympian in Berlin in 1936.

WHAT? NO MUSTACHE?
In 1938 Galland was a first Lieutenant (Oberleutnant) and had not grown the mustache he is so well known for.

In July of 1936 the Spanish Civil War broke out and further darkened the European scene. The political background to the Spanish conflict remains to this day one of the most complex and thorny sequences in modern European history. Contemporary political biases furthermore make it even more difficult to view the Spanish Civil War dispassionately and objectively.

The final general election of the Second Spanish Republic was held in February of 1936. Socialists of all shadings united with anarchists, separatists, syndicalists, and the communists to form the so-called Popular Front against a coalition of Rightist parties and factions. With a large majority of the seats in the Spanish parliament, but an extremely narrow margin in the total vote, the Popular Front nominally had complete control of parliament.

Street violence, massive property damage, and political murders erupted almost as soon as the votes had been counted. The extreme Rightist Falangists and the extreme Left Communists are generally credited with the main responsibility for the violence. By the time this savage scene degenerated into Civil War, more than 250 political murders had been committed, in a country riven by factionalism in mind-boggling complexity.

General Francisco Franco finally emerged as the strongest personality on the Right after the Civil War broke out, and he became the rallying point for the Nationalist, or Rebel, forces. Franco sent a three-man delegation to appeal directly to Hitler on 26 July 1936, and the Fuehrer received them personally at Bayreuth. He agreed to their immediate request for air transport.

That same evening, Special Staff was established in Berlin to manage and expand the aid program in secret. Soviet aid to the Spanish Left on a large scale was also secretly going forward. The British, German, Italian, and Soviet governments nominally all subscribed to a French proposal that other powers maintain a policy of strict non-intervention in Spain.

Air power was the cutting edge of German aid. In history's first major military airlift, German-flown Ju 52s ferried 2,500 Moroccan soldiers from North Africa to Spain early in August 1936. The sudden appearance of these troops at the front, and their professional capabilities, probably saved the Nationalists from defeat. Further aerial participation in the war was also being organized in Germany, in a project under General Wilberg.

An impenetrable factionalist tangle to most people even today, the details of the Spanish Civil War were certainly incomprehensible to Adolf Galland in 1936. He was 24 years old and had grown up without any interest in politics. The idealism that permeated the soaring sport had touched him, and National Socialism had seemed like its political expression.

MICKEY MOUSE IN SPAIN
Galland's He 51 sported the logo of Mickey Mouse in 1938. It became his signature throughout World War II.

His passion nevertheless was planes and piloting, not politics.

Galland had pursued his passion in difficult times for aviation. Conditions had required him to be single-minded, and so politics had no soil within him in which to take root. This was true of his own country, and it was certainly true of his attitude toward the Spanish Civil War.

When Galland's flying comrades in late 1936 began here and there to disappear suddenly from squadron life, as though swallowed into black holes, rumors soon abounded that they had gone to Spain as volunteers. Fighting in Spain against Communist takeover provided the conditions for military adventure. When some of these pilots reappeared six or eight months later, with sun-tanned faces and large rolls of money, the existence of the Condor Legion was no longer secret. Everyone wanted to volunteer. Adventure beckoned with the chance to test themselves in real combat.

Galland knew Spain well enough from his Lufthansa days to want to return. Experience and high pay that went with such service were added incentives. He also wanted to get to grips with the realities of aerial warfare after so much training, theory, and mock combat. He appeared at Special Staff W in Berlin, where Condor Legion volunteers were processed.

Civilian clothes, credentials, and money were provided, and Galland joined a "Strength Through Joy" tourist group of the Union Travel Society. This "excursion" group of 370 young Germans was ostensibly bound for Genoa. Embarkation was at Hamburg, where they boarded a battered 3,000-ton tramp steamer flying the flag of Panama.

Romantic ideas about tramp ship voyaging were soon dispelled by the overpowering stench aboard the vessel. Franco's navy had captured the wreck when she was running guns to the Loyalists. There had been only minimal conversion for carrying troops. Makeshift bunks had been hammered together out of old dunnage and roughly secured in the holds and tweendecks. Luftwaffe men accustomed to decent living conditions at their new bases in Germany found the ship a devastating blow to their pride.

As the senior officer present in terms of service, Galland was assigned by the ship's master, Captain van Ehren, to take command of the troops on board. The crude accommodations and facilities, heavy seas, and confinement below decks in stale air, created disciplinary problems. Civilian clothes contributed to disciplinary breakdown. Galland ordered officers and NCOs to wear colored armbands.

LEGION CONDOR PARADES IN BERLIN
In uniforms borrowed from the Reich Labor Service, the Legion Condor paraded before Hitler on their return to Germany.

Bad weather and engine trouble extended the voyage from seven days to twelve. Short rations followed by exhaustion of the water supply brought the volunteers to the brink of mutiny. Several violent characters had at times to be tied to the mast until they cooled down. This reality was a far cry from the Red propagandists' versions of the Condor Legion's arrival in Spain. When the hulk finally wallowed into El Ferrol on 7 May 1937, Galland gladly laid down his first command assignment with the Legion. Life ashore in Spain could not be other than an improvement.

Condor Legion personnel were issued distinctive olive-brown uniforms similar in design to those of Germany's National Socialist Labor Service. Fur boots were a special feature of the Legion garb. German officers were promoted to the next grade above their Luftwaffe rank, so Galland wore the three stars of a captain. Placed in command of the Staff Company of the Condor Legion's Fighter Group in Avila, Galland became unhappy. He was flying much less than if he had stayed in Germany. The adventurous life in Spain that he had visualized was proving elusive.

FIVE

First Combat

Soon acquiring the nickname of "Capitano" among his brother officers, Captain Galland was in charge of maintenance and repair for the Condor Legion's three fighter squadrons. A fourth squadron was to be added early in 1938. His responsibilities included assembly and testing of new aircraft from Germany, repair and testing of combat-damaged aircraft, major overhauls, vehicle maintenance, repair and improvement of ground support equipment, and provision of spare parts and tools to the squadrons. He had essential and time-consuming tasks, but they were unexciting.

The Staff Company was quartered in an ancient monastery, with Galland and his staff living in a small nearby hotel. In due course he discovered the Parador de Gredos, a stylish hotel some 60 kilometers distant in the Gredos mountains. The Parador became a beloved retreat for Galland and other pilots. He hunted ibex and partridge and went horseback riding. In the evenings he lazed with his comrades around the open fireplace. They drank red wine with young Spanish girls, who sang folksongs happily for their German companions. Relations with the Spanish villagers and the Spanish military were warm and affectionate, and deepened Galland's enchantment with the Spanish way of life.

The Condor Legion was a relatively small force. Flying units consisted eventually of four bomber squadrons, four fighter squadrons, and a strengthened reconnaissance squadron. Four heavy and two light anti-aircraft batteries, signals units, and miscellaneous support detachments completed a force that never exceeded 5,600 men. Communist propaganda nevertheless tried to convince the world that half the Luftwaffe was in Spain. By the time Galland arrived on the scene, the Legion had proved itself highly effective, and its command had significant influence on military decisions.

As the first C.O. of the Legion, Lt. General Hugo Sperrle set the tone for the unit. He celebrated his own arrival in Spain in dramatic fashion. On 15 November 1936, he personally led three squadrons of Ju 52s in a massive strike against Loyalist ships and port installations in Cartagena. Leadership of this forceful style impressed Franco's generals profoundly. Sound cooperation ensued between the Legion command and the Nationalist leaders. The Germans were called upon like a fire brigade when Franco's forces ran into difficulties.

An emergency situation gave Adolf Galland his first taste of combat. Both formally and informally he had applied for transfer to a fighter squadron, but the Legion command had taken no action. He organized his maintenance and administrative duties so well that he was occasionally able to fly on operations. When the Battle of Brunete was joined in July of 1937, the Condor Legion had a critical task, and every available pilot was needed for combat.

The Loyalists under General Miaja timed their Madrid offensive well, because Franco's main strength and virtually all his air power were absorbed in northern Spain, at Bilbao and in preparation for an attack on Santander. Miaja's goal was to free Madrid from the besieging Nationalist forces, which would have been a psychological if not a strategic catastrophe for Franco's armies.

The Red thrust resulted in a breakthrough past Brunete to a point near Navalcarno, shattering the Nationalist front. The gap in the Nationalist line continued to widen. Alarmed at this sudden reverse, Franco halted his northern offensive and ordered his able Navarre Brigades to the Madrid front immediately.

The Condor Legion was ordered to redress the aerial balance on the Madrid front, in the fire brigade fashion to which the Germans had become accustomed. The Reds enjoyed solid air supremacy around Madrid, due to their possession there of about sixty modern fighters – mostly Russian Rata and American Curtiss types. These aircraft were effectively harassing Nationalist troops in the breakthrough area when the Condor Legion arrived. Included in the Legion's combat pilots was the eager Adolf Galland, temporarily assigned to flying duties.

The Loyalists had moved numerous flak weapons into the

breach in the Nationalist line, ready to punish the slow Ju 52 transports assigned to bomb Loyalist troops in the breach. The Legion's 3.J/88 Squadron under Captain Harro Harder was to silence Loyalist flak weapons. Lumbering Ju 52s could then bomb without prohibitive losses.

Flying with Harder's squadron, Captain Galland got his baptism of fire in one of the most intense battles of the Spanish conflict. Their He 51 biplanes were no match for the Red fighters, but they were highly effective against small ground targets like flak batteries. Such close support attacks, combined with Ju 52 bombing strikes, halted the Loyalist attack on 12 July 1937.

The way for Franco's counter attack was open. The struggle continued as Franco sought to evict the Loyalists from the breach and re-establish his lines. In the ensuing two weeks, Franco's counter attacks were repulsed, and every He 51 in Harder's squadron was riddled with bullet holes. Galland knew the hair-raising experience of flying through hails of bullets that punched into his biplane.

On 25 July 1937, the Condor Legion again struck strongly against the Loyalist forces, targeting reserve units grouped in narrow valleys near Brunete ready to enter the battle on Loyalist call. Galland was in the thick of repeated attacks driven home against the brave and stubborn Loyalist troops. All available artillery was simultaneously directed on the same targets, including the 88mm flak guns of the Condor Legion.

The Loyalists collapsed. Abandoning their positions, they retreated in a rabble. The He 51s strafed the retreating troops, and frustrated their efforts to dig in and form a new front. The Loyalists suffered 30,000 casualties and Madrid was again besieged by Franco. The Condor Legion was decisive in the Battle of Brunete, in which it has been said that Franco actually won the Civil War without being aware of his victory.

Numerous missions in the Brunete struggle had provided Galland with an intense and indelible introduction to combat. Return to maintenance and repair duties with the Staff Company was now out of the question. The young captain's outstanding flying skill had shown up vividly in close support strikes, and his further urgent request for transfer to a fighter squadron was approved. He was given command of the Condor Legion's 3rd Fighter Squadron.

He took over command from Captain Douglas Pitcairn, one of the officers at Jüterbog-Damm who had witnessed his near-fatal aerobatic crash. When Pitcairn had helped pull the unconscious and bloody Galland from the wreckage of that biplane, he never expected him to survive more than a few more hours, let alone emerge as a combat leader in Spain. The two men would remain friends right through into the 1980s

Galland's new unit was the "Mickey Mouse" squadron. Their aircraft had the pistol-waving Disney character painted on the fuselage. Galland continued painting this insignia on all his personal aircraft in World War II. He believed that it always brought him luck. His fighter squadron was now the only one in Spain still equipped with He 51 biplanes. The long-awaited Me 109 had come on the Spanish scene, but the new era had thus far reached only the other two squadrons.

COLONEL GENERAL ERNST UDET
Generaloberst Udet was well-known world-wide as a famed stunt and racing pilot. On a visit to the USA before WWII he bought a military dive-bomber.

Captain Joachim Schlichting and Captain Guenther Luetzow were the fortunate commanders of the two Me 109 squadrons. They were soon cleaning up the skies with their new machines, which were superior to all Loyalist fighters. Both officers became fighter aces in Spain, with 5 aerial victories apiece, and both would also later fight in the Battle of Britain. Galland formed a friendship with "Franzl" Luetzow that was to endure until 1945. Luetzow was killed flying the Me 262 jet in Galland's elite JV 44, less than two weeks before the end of World War II. Luetzow had a lifetime score of 108 aerial victories.

Galland's admiration for the tall, haughty-looking Luetzow was never to dim from its beginning in Spain. Both were dedicated to their profession with the utmost seriousness. Both nevertheless had a fine sense of humor. This attribute prevented them from losing their humanity amid the often inhuman challenges of the war that was to come. Galland came to regard Luetzow as the finest leader in the Luftwaffe.

During the Spanish adventure, Galland found it a little frustrating that his friend Luetzow in an Me 109 was winning air-to-air combats, while he was on close support missions in a biplane. The Mickey Mouse squadron was due to receive Me 109s. They were promised, but never seemed to arrive from Germany. Galland had no option but to keep flying his number 78 biplane through hails of lead and explosive hurled up from the ground, while the Me 109s went off hunting for Loyalist aircraft. A hunter from infancy, Galland was sure that he would be able to find his quarry aloft.

The Me 109B and the Me 109D – the latter a longer-range variant that came to Spain in due course – outclassed any Loyalist aircraft. The Me 109s quickly dominated the aerial scene. An invaluable lesson was thus provided to the Luftwaffe on the importance of technical superiority in tipping the balance in the air. Two squadrons of Me 109s shifted the balance in Spain. Galland absorbed this lesson and never forgot its significance. In later years he would fight for technical advances against officers and leaders who either failed to learn the lessons of Spain, or forgot those lessons for political reasons.

In the overall development of Adolf Galland as an air force officer, he benefited immensely from his close support operations in the He 51. He probably learned more in Spain this way than he would have flying the Me 109, which he later rapidly mastered in World War II. The He 51, by contrast, was an obsolescent machine unable to contend with Loyalist fighters and thereby restricted to close support operations. Many significant lessons were thus learned about tactical air power, and Galland's analytical talents and experience allowed him to make substantial contributions in this area.

While the Condor Legion was effective in Spain, the propagandist idea that they went there already knowing what to do and how to do it is completely erroneous. The Spanish Civil War has often been described as a "curtain raiser" for World War II, but in the history of air power it is more accurate to say that the conflict was a *transition* from World War I to World War II. Galland's experiences provide an illustration.

When their slow biplanes were occasionally intercepted by Rata and Curtiss fighters, the Germans would form a Lufbery Circle in the pattern of World War I. Each He 51 would protect the tail of the He 51 immediately ahead. In this protective circle, the slower biplanes would gradually work their way back to their own territory. There was no radio communication between the aircraft in Galland's Mickey Mouse squadron. Visual signals were the means of control and command in the air. In these and other respects, World War I was repeated, but the new epoch loomed in the way the Germans learned to use tactical air power in close support. The Ju 52 and He 111 bombers used by the Condor Legion were both unsuited to such pinpoint tasks as eliminating enemy artillery, mortar, or flak positions, or for attacking troop columns – especially in the absence of accurate bomb sights. The sluggish Ju 52 was vulnerable as well as ineffective on such operations. The He 51s, by contrast, could *punish* such targets accurately at low level with machine guns and bombs, and yet were fast enough to avoid too heavy an attrition from ground fire.

Adolf Galland as a boy had always been interested in finding out how things worked. Examining cause and effect in electricity, gasoline engines, rockets, sailplanes, and motorcycles had developed his analytical abilities. These talents were turned in Spain to developing the new era of close support flying. The Great War had provided a slender tactical legacy because of the static nature of that conflict. Unimaginative generalship and the butchery of millions of men in the mud had been a poor scenario in which to comprehend the tactical importance of air power.

Spain was a vastly different military milieu. Ground warfare was much more mobile and open. Air power came into its own as a new military dimension that could control and dominate the ground – provided that correct tactics applied air power effectively. Modern tactical air power had its birth in Spain, and Adolf Galland was one of the midwives.

THE FEARED STUKA DIVE BOMBER
The Junkers Ju 87 "Stuka" served in every front during WWII. They fared well as long as the Luftwaffe had air-superiority.

FIESELER Fi 156 "STORCH"
This STOL (Short takeoff and land) airplane was successful in a myriad of war duties, one of the most important being the rescuer of pilots downed behind enemy lines.

Flying in his battered No.78, often wearing only swimming trunks in the hot weather, he flew more than 300 missions as a squadron leader. Quickly he saw the crucial importance of coordinating his strikes in time space with the ground forces he was assisting. Lack of radio communication, both air-to-air and air-to-ground, heightened the need to know the exact time and place to put in a strike. A target bombed and strafed could be rapidly overrun and captured with minimum losses if the ground forces moved in immediately. If stunned enemy troops were allowed to recover, or given time to bring up reinforcements, the air strikes were wasted.

A pilot hurtling through the air at around 200 mph, with bullets perforating his aircraft, had little chance of telling friend from foe on the terrain below. Marking of the most advanced lines and troops with colored cloths therefore became a fundamental principle. Marking the direction of strongest enemy resistance became another basic stratagem. As techniques of timing and control improved, the tactical value of the aging He 51 increased. Their power was being focused instead of scattered.

Galland encouraged his pilots and ground crews to suggest and try out innovations that would make their aircraft more effective. His squadron was a smooth-running unit with high morale and strong spirit. Everyone seemed infected by and committed to their young C.O.'s continuing drive for excellence. His mechanics devised a fire bomb that was a precursor of the napalm weapons that appeared in World War II.

Filling a 25-gallon drop tank with a mixture of old crankcase oil and aviation fuel, his mechanics then attached a fragmentation incendiary bomb. When dropped from a He 51, the inflammable mixture spread widely, ignited by the incendiary bomb. While the results did not compare with those later obtained from napalm, in Spain they contributed to the air power that helped Franco decisively. Galland wrote numerous reports on his tactical experience, innovations, and findings, sending them through official channels to Berlin.

He would live to regret this diligent reporting. The Luftwaffe was now fully committed in its doctrine and constitution to being an essentially tactical air force. Galland's reports from Spain were like a running commentary on the actual development of modern tactical air power. They fell into eager hands at the Air Ministry in Berlin. His expertise and experience in close support were almost to cost him his career as a fighter pilot.

Mobility is essential to modern military success. Galland made his squadron the most mobile air unit in Spain. The former sailplane pilot was appalled by the amount of labor expended in their frequent shifts from one operating base to another. The accompanying administrative turmoil reduced efficiency. The Spanish war was fluid compared with the 1914-1918 slogging matches. Galland conceived the idea of putting his entire squadron aboard a train, complete with sleeping quarters, offices, kitchen, repair facilities, and recreational space. His squadron could then move itself rapidly on rails.

Galland acquired the necessary coaches through the Nationalist army. Franco's officers and troops were fond of the airmen who protected them and were glad to provide the rolling stock. In the spirit of No.3 Squadron, everybody waded into the task of conversion. In a few days the needed modifications were completed, and thereafter the squadron rolled from base to base behind a locomotive, The aircraft flew to each new base, and in a matter of hours complete ground facilities and personnel were available.

This lesson learned in Spain was later applied in World War II on the Eastern Front. The Luftwaffe had only one night fighter Geschwader, NJG 6, available in that vast war theater. As with Galland's pioneering effort in Spain, NJG 6 assigned one squadron to each train. The resultant mobility multiplied the effectiveness of NJG 6 by rapid movement of its squadrons to sectors where they were needed. The units were able to go into action immediately, with complete administrative and command continuity.

The volunteer beginning of the Condor Legion was soon replaced by a more systematic rotation of personnel. New arrivals were still volunteers, but tours of duty were limited in duration. Berlin wanted to give combat experience to as many future Luftwaffe leaders as possible. When Galland's time was up, a replacement arrived that he knew would not work well with the efficient squadron he had shaped. The officer was sent back to Germany.

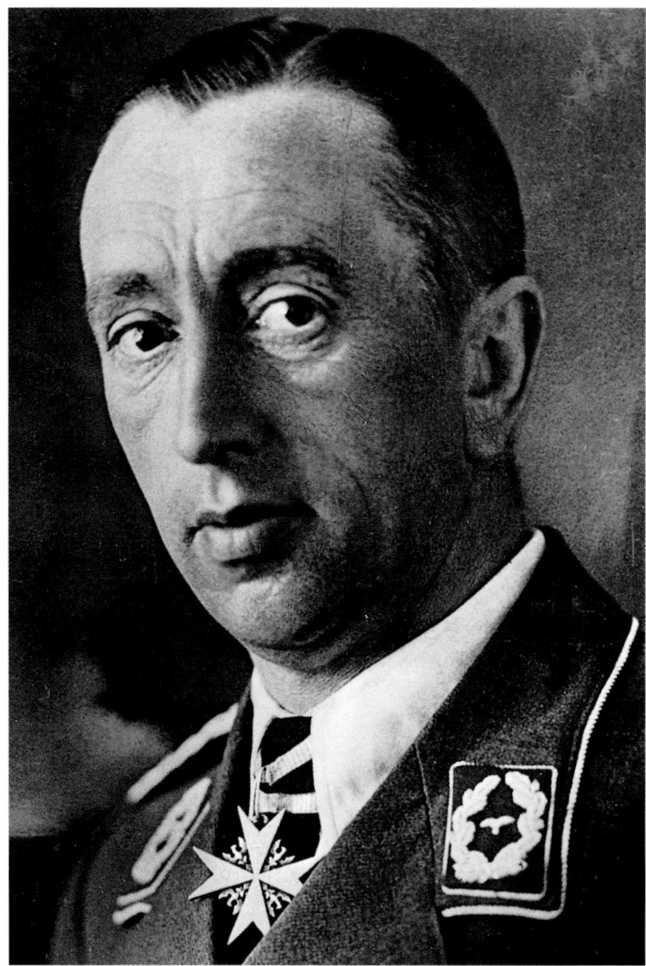

Generalleutnant "Uncle Theo" Osterkamp, Pour le Merité holder in WWI with 32 victories and Knights Cross holder in WWII with 6 victories. Osterkamp was a favorite of everyone who knew him.

A second replacement was assigned. Berlin sent an elderly pilot that Galland promptly disqualified. Before this officer could be returned to Germany, he collided in mid-air with one of the squadron's best pilots, killing both of them. Busy preparing for the Sudetenland challenge, the Luftwaffe High Command urgently needed its experienced leaders from Spain. Galland's return was overdue. The Condor Legion command received a curt teletype from Berlin: Galland's relief was on the way. This replacement was the best man they had. Galland was expected to accept him and hand over command promptly.

A lull in hostilities shortly afterward allowed Galland some days of relaxation in Seville. He shared this interlude with his C.O., Gotthard Handrick. Also in the party was Galland's close friend, Eduard Neumann, together with some other Condor Legion comrades. They were enjoying some glasses of wine in the bar of the Hotel Christina when a slender, dark-haired young man approached and asked to speak to the C.O. He also wanted to speak with "the squadron commander, Adolf Galland."

There was something steely and serious about this man. He exuded an aura of authority far beyond his years. He introduced himself as 1st Lieutenant Werner Moelders, the new commander of Galland's No. 3 Squadron. Galland felt himself stiffen. A sudden current of resentment rose within him, which he immediately had to suppress. He was attached to his squadron and concerned for their welfare.

Galland felt himself challenged, as a man dedicated to being number one, by Berlin having rated this man Moelders so highly. Could this slender newcomer handle the important responsibilities of squadron command in this foreign land, with all its complexities? Galland was slightly apprehensive when he shook the hand of Werner Moelders for the first time.

In the ensuing days, Moelders showed all the qualities of leadership and flying skill that made him one of Germany's immortal air heroes. Their instructional flights together quickly convinced Galland that his squadron and his men would be in highly capable hands. With Moelders came the long-awaited Me 109s. The old He 51s became No. 4 Squadron, commanded by Captain Eberhard d'Elsa, and carried on their tactical tasks until the end of the Spanish Civil War.

Moelders in the Me 109 soon started downing Loyalist aircraft. By the end of the war he had 14 aerial victories, the top score of the Condor Legion. His tactical innovations with the Me 109 laid the basis for the wide open "finger four" fighter formation, with much separation in altitude between aircraft. This formation was adopted eventually by both the RAF and the USAAF.

The fighters now flew in two elements (*rotten*) of two aircraft each. All four made up a *schwarm*. The combat flexibility and mutual protection provided by this formation were a tactical quantum jump that lasted until the jet age. Moelders was unsurpassed as a tactical innovator.

Galland missed out completely on the Me 109 in Spain. He was not finished with Werner Moelders by any means, and he would walk into history with him both as a rival and as a friend. For the moment, Galland was a young leader with fifteen months of Condor Legion service, and that made him invaluable. The possibility of war over the Sudetenland was the impelling force behind his gloomy return to Germany, where new challenges impended. He would have been even gloomier had he known that certain people in Berlin were planning to have him fly a desk.

SIX

Storm Clouds and Lightning War

By August of 1938 when Adolf Galland returned to Germany from Spain, Hitler had acquired more political and psychological momentum than any European leader since Napoleon. Announcing the new Luftwaffe and military conscription in 1935, the Fuehrer followed up on 7 March 1936 with his daring occupation of the Rhineland. He set up the Rome-Berlin Axis, intervened in Spain, and in March of 1938 – a scant two years after his Rhineland bluff – Hitler took over Austria and brought its 6,750,000 people into his Third Reich. The stage was thereby set for the dismemberment of Czechoslovakia, with Hitler now both head of state and supreme commander of the armed forces. Feverish propaganda detailed the alleged sufferings of 3,500,000 Sudeten Germans under Czech rule. This was the crisis scenario when the dashing young close air support specialist from Spain arrived back home.

Vigorous military preparations attending all Hitler's ploys automatically involved Luftwaffe expansion. Experienced leaders were sorely needed, and this was also one reason why Luftwaffe HQ had gone to such lengths to bring Galland home from Spain, despite the imminent end of that conflict. His detailed reports on close support tactics and techniques, written by an operational pilot and squadron commander, reinforced the current service-wide emphasis on tactical air power. His expertise had entrained him with the march of events in Europe.

Reporting in with the Air Ministry in Berlin, he was sent home for two weeks leave. The contrast between renascent Germany and war-torn Spain was staggering to the young officer as he crossed Germany. Newspapers from home, which he had devoured in his off-duty times in Spain, could convey no real impression of the physical and spiritual changes in Germany. People were vigorous and busy. Financial difficulties for industry had seemingly evaporated. New factories had appeared everywhere. Even the landscape seemed to reflect a new and vital beauty. He was drinking in these good aspects of his country when an abrupt telegram ended his leave four days early. He was ordered to report to the Air Ministry in Berlin immediately.

Assigned to help work out directives for the raising and training of new close support Gruppen (Schlachtgruppen), he found himself flying a desk in the Air Ministry building. Goering had erected this edifice at the corner of the Leipzigerstrasse and the Wilhelmstrasse in Berlin, as the power center of the Luftwaffe. Designed by the famous architect Dr. Sagebiel, the building had a cathedral-like entrance hall and contained 1,500 rooms and suites.

The place seemed to Galland like a vast formicary. He was just one of hundreds of officers who crawled in and out of and through the building every day. The elevators did not stop and start to let people out, but were run instead on a continuous basis. Passengers waited by an opening and stepped into the moving elevator car, stepping out again when they reached their desired floor.

Gone was the uplifting comradeship of his squadron. Absent also was the freedom of action he enjoyed under the distinctive operating procedures of the Condor Legion. He yearned for the cozy functionality of his HQ in the converted Spanish railroad car. Sadly missed also was the front line informality with which he had run his efficient unit of war.

Nobody in Spain paid the slightest attention to oil spots on their trousers – not even the squadron commander. Stained trousers were irrelevant in a fighting squadron. Trousers were important in Berlin. Staff types wore knife-edge creases in their distinctive crimson-striped trousers, as they scurried from office to office and braved the hazards of the elevators. All of them were much older than Galland. Some of them were so perfectly attired and immaculate they looked as though they had been varnished. Luftwaffe uniforms were nevertheless among the most attractive and fashionable of all services worldwide.

Many of these staff officers professed interest in his war experiences in Spain. Galland repeatedly got the impression, nevertheless, that when this experience ran counter to their own ideas from the past, they simply turned off mentally. His own tendency to informality in personal contact also contrasted sharply with their rigidity and consciousness of rank. The intellectual atmosphere of the Air Ministry was stifling.

Galland's boss at this time was Lt. Colonel Dr. Gnamm of the General Staff, who had flown as an observer in the Great War. In the interim he had been a doctor of dentistry, without intimate contact with aviation. While Gnamm was a correct and hard-working officer, he exemplified a practice of Goering and the General Staff that Galland was to find all too common: unqualified officers in leading positions. This was Galland's first direct experience of this phenomenon, but he would encounter it frequently as he worked his way up into the Luftwaffe hierarchy.

Together Gnamm and Galland buckled down to writing the necessary directives, infusing into them all the most recent experience from Spain. The work went well for a few days. The real world then intruded on their labors. They were ordered to stop writing about it and actually go out and raise and train two brand-new *Schlachtgeschwader*. These formations were needed immediately.

The Sudetenland crisis was putting heavy pressure on the armed forces. Every available combat aircraft had to be incorporated into a unit that could help support the Army. Galland put away his papers with glee. Cutting through peacetime red tape was to his liking, and short-cuts had to be made to raise the new *Schlachtgeschwader* in minimum time.

Improvisation had characterized life in the Condor Legion, and Galland now found this experience invaluable. Raw young recruits and obsolescent aircraft had to be transformed rapidly into operational close support units. The aircraft were second class performers, but still useful in close support. He 51s, Hs 123s and He 45s were assembled from all over Germany by ransacking secondary bases and training units. Pilots came straight from flying school. Recruits were whipped into a semblance of efficiency by NCOs who were themselves inexperienced. Flying accidents and crashes were frequent, but by the scheduled day the two Schlachtgeschwader were available for operations.

Lt. Colonel Gnamm was transferred from his steady desk job in the Air Ministry to become Kommodore of one of these units. Fully aware now of Galland's abilities, experience, and expertise, Gnamm had him assigned as his adjutant and operations officer. Galland protested, but to no avail. The ex-Condor Legion expert wanted to be a fighter pilot more than anything else in life, but he could not escape the close support involvement. A major war was coming, whether over Czechoslovakia or otherwise, and Galland hated the thought of flying in such a war exclusively in direct support of the Army. He felt trapped.

The new Geschwader was moved into Silesia at full mobilization tempo. They were to provide close support for an airborne operation near Jägerndorf, should Hitler give the order to invade the Sudetenland. Czechoslovakia was dismembered at Munich, and the Sudetenland was occupied without a shot being fired.

After Munich, the scheduled operation was nevertheless carried out as an exercise. Confusion reigned in the new Geschwader, and Galland thanked heaven that the operation was not taking place in anger. Instead of strafing the Czech front lines, he was able to watch Germany's elite paratroops landing with precision. Examination of the massive Czech fortifications close up was sobering. He wondered about the outcome had Britain and France stood firm with the Czechs.

Persistent requests by Galland for transfer to a regular fighter unit were finally answered, in a compromise fashion, in the autumn of 1938. He was assigned to a fighter formation called Jagdgruppe Böblingen, with its preliminary HQ at Ingolstadt. Unfortunately, the Gruppe did not yet exist. As a squadron leader in this new unit, he would help raise and train it from zero. His recent experience in creating two Schlachtgeschwader almost out of thin air was going to be useful.

The Gruppenkommandeur was Captain Count von Pfeil, who soon fell ill. As the oldest of the three squadron leaders, Galland therefore temporarily took command of the non-existent new unit. When Captain Count von Pfeil recovered from his illness, he got married, which further extended his absence. Working initially with 1st Lieutenant Alfons Klein and Lieutenant Wolfgang "Pequeño" Ewald, Galland soon had a harmonious situation with his subordinates. Klein was unfortunately killed in a flight crash, and was replaced with 1st Lieutenant Kuehle, but the organizational work continued. Galland got tremendous satisfaction from seeing the Gruppe arise from nothing.

At last he was involved with a real fighter unit. Jagdgruppe Böblingen, to which village near Stuttgart the formation soon moved, was equipped with the Me 109D. Here was a fighter pilot's dream come true, and Galland was living through it as an acting Gruppenkommandeur. He led the unit's formation in mock combat, squadron against squadron. His early doubts about the Me 109, the first time he saw the prototype, seemed an odd memory as he thrilled to the flying qualities of Professor Messerschmitt's gift to the Luftwaffe. Here was a machine to revolutionize aerial combat.

The new squadrons were gradually worked up into an efficient fighter Gruppe. Galland taught them what he knew about ground attack operations, and in full Gruppe strength, they made mock assaults on bomber formations provided by the Bomber Arm. Ammunition was now plentiful, so the pilots got all the air-to-ground firing practice they needed. In March of 1939, when Hitler occupied the rest of Czechoslovakia, Galland's formation sat with full gunbelts and engines warm on the Böblingen airfield. Bad weather socked in the field, and they never did take off. They were not needed. All Europe, and Russia as well, sat still for the final absorption of Czechoslovakia.

With the return of the last Condor legion personnel from Spain, a Decorations Commission was set up at Döberitz to judge the order of merit of the recipients. Galland was ordered to join this commission. An 8-day "Victory Festival" began with the award of these decorations, and was followed on 6 June 1939 by a march past in front of the Technical High School – with the Fuehrer on the reviewing stand.

In appalling early summer heat, the parade went through the Brandenburger Gate and up to the Lustgarten in Berlin. Former Condor Legionnaires were known in the Luftwaffe as the "Spaniards," and they were drooping badly at the end of this ordeal. In order to assure similarity in uniform, Galland and others long home from Spain had to wear thick and stifling uniforms borrowed from the Labor Service. These abrasive garments resembled Condor Legion olive-greens. In this makeshift garb, Galland was part of a small group received by the Fuehrer in his new Chancellery.

Galland's first meeting with Hitler was confined to hearing a short speech and receiving a perfunctory handshake. The Fuehrer drank tea with the "Spaniards," but they were all forbidden to smoke by the ascetic Hitler. This annoyed Galland profoundly. He had long cultivated a taste for large, black Brazils, which he used to enhance both his working power and his times of relaxation. He was destined to see Hitler many more times in the future – far more than he wished – and the Fuehrer always found time to chastise him about his cigar smoking. "You could approach him with a pistol as part of your uniform" said Galland, "but never with a cigar in your hand."

The Condor Legion parade also brought Galland into reunion with Werner Moelders, who had relieved him as squadron leader of 3.J/88 in Spain. Moelders had become the most successful of the new generation of Luftwaffe fighter pilots, with 14 aerial victories in the Spanish war. Like Galland, he had written reports on his experiences. When Moelders returned to Germany on 5 December 1938 he also was given an Air Ministry desk to fly. His assignment was to write parallel directives for the Fighter Arm, to those Galland was commissioned to prepare for the close support units. They were able after the parade to commiserate about desk flying, as well as joke about the decorations they had just received.

Chief among these decorations was the Spanish Cross in Gold, which was a German decoration. They also received the Medalla Militar and Medalla de la Campana from the new Franco government of Spain. Goering considered that the Decorations Commission on which Galland had sat had been stinting in its awards. Two weeks after the victory parade, Galland was summoned by Goering to the island of Westerland, together with his Condor Legion friend Wilhelm Balthasar. Goering awarded them the Spanish Cross in Gold with Diamonds, the highest order of the decoration and much more impressive in appearance. Goering took their plain Spanish Crosses from them as he handed over the diamond-encrusted variant. He put the plain crosses in his pocket.

Only nine participants in Condor Legion campaigns were given this special Spanish Cross in Gold with Diamonds. Galland, Moelders, Balthasar, Luetzow, Schellman and Oesau were all fighter pilots. Martin Harlinghausen was the lone bomber pilot recipient. The other two crosses went to Hugo Sperrle and Wolfram von Richthofen, both Commanders at different times of the Condor legion. In years ahead, Galland would find that Goering's passion for diamonds would eventually provide him with a dinner story, on which he would dine out around the world. Goering, at this moment in Westerland, was at his paternal best, exchanging new Spanish Crosses for old.

Busy training days with Jagdgruppe Böblingen continued, and were a happy fulfillment for Galland. This was what he wanted to do, right in his core – to be a fighter pilot and be the best. Relentless training improved efficiency. By mid-summer of 1939, Galland would have put them in the air against any fighter formation in the world, confident that they would operate effectively.

His father took great pride in Keffer, his second son. His mother never ceased urging him to take more care of himself, and his brothers Wutz and Paul were themselves eager to become pilots. Wutz received a bonus out of his older brother's Spanish adventures. The money from Spain was substantial, and while with the Condor legion he had spent relatively little. Now he splurged on a special new BMW cabriolet for himself. Wutz got Adolf's old Opel sportscar and could hardly have been happier.

The charming fighter pilot with the typically bent nose, thick black hair and magnetic personality was already attractive to women, and the attraction was mutual – especially with beautiful women. With the BMW cabriolet thrown in, Galland could hardly go wrong. Summer of 1939 was an idyll of satisfying work and happy leisure times. Early in August, the roof fell in.

A teletype advising him of his transfer back into the ground support flying units was something that Galland had to read repeatedly in disbelief. Fury rose in him. All he had built up with this superb new fighter Gruppe was to be torn from his grasp. He was being denied the fruits of his labors – the opportunity to lead the fighter unit he had raised and trained into the clearly imminent war.

He was being drawn again into the professional backwater he had created for himself through his expertise in ground support flying. Assigned to replace a squadron commander in II/SLG 2, he made his way to Tutow where the unit was stationed. Major Werner Spielvogel was the Gruppenkommandeur. Galland was transferring from the Me 109D to the Hs 123, another open cockpit biplane, designed as a dive bomber. He stepped out of the future and back into the past, like a man trapped in a time warp.

Galland took part in a massive exercise east of Cottbus in mid-August, an obvious rehearsal for the invasion of Poland. In command of air units was a familiar face from Spain, tough and energetic Lt. General Wolfram von Richthofen, destined to become the Luftwaffe's premier close support general. The most noteworthy event in this exercise was the loss of thirteen Ju 87 Stuka dive bombers, which flew into the ground en masse in a deceptive fog. Twenty-six of the Luftwaffe's best-trained airmen were killed in this disaster.

Amid these feverish August days, Galland was ordered to Rechlin to test two new types of ground attack fighters. The Air Ministry Technical Department had requested his services. They had seen his detailed reports from Spain. The Hs 129 had the luxury of a bulletproof cockpit, and the Fw 189 was a sturdy gun platform.

Both were twin-engined machines. Testing them was interesting, but that was no consolation. Galland felt like a youngster whose favorite toy had been confiscated by his parents. His most cherished plaything at age 25 was the Me 109D.

Diplomacy over Poland climaxed with the signature of the German-Soviet trade agreement, and four days later the German-Soviet Non Aggression Pact was signed. Hitler thus secured his rear while he absorbed Poland and dealt with Britain and France. The Soviets signed with Hitler largely because their protracted efforts to form an alliance with Britain and France, and earlier on with Czechoslovakia, had been rebuffed. Stalin was in no doubt that Hitler would eventually attack Russia. He bought a little time, intending a preemptive strike against Germany. Despite the mortal differences between Naziism and Communism, a secret additional protocol to the 1939 Pact divided between them not just Poland, but also the Baltic states. Germany invaded Poland on 1 September 1939, and France and Britain declared war on Germany two days later. The Soviet Union invaded Poland from the east on 14 September, four days prior to the end of Germany's Polish campaign. World War II was a reality.

At dawn on 1 September 1939, Adolf Galland was among the first German pilots to go into action in World War II. A successful strike was made against Polish Staff HQ, about 85 miles east of the German-Polish border. Weeks of tension before the invasion had adequately warned the Poles, and they had moved their important air units away from normal bases to makeshift and emergency airfields. When the Germans made their initial strikes against Polish airfields and hangars, with great success against Polish aircraft on the ground, the latter were obsolescent types left behind by the Polish Air Force. The Poles had concentrated on preserving their better fighters and bombers.

Initial German air attacks caused such wide disruption of Polish communications, nevertheless, that the Polish Air Force could not be properly directed and controlled. Polish fighters scored some successes against Me 110s on 2 September 1939, and Polish bombers and ground attack aircraft harassed the German XXI Army Corps later that same day as the invaders moved against Graudenz. Polish air strikes on 3 September against the 1st and 4th Panzer Divisions at Radomsko caused heavy losses.

The Luftwaffe was called on to suppress this Polish air activity. These efforts in combination with the hopeless state of Polish communications, ground down Polish air power in the ensuing week until it was reduced to a handful of bombers. Even these units were shortly withdrawn to Rumania. The Polish Air Force could not cope with the Luftwaffe. The Poles fought their best but were overwhelmed.

Galland's perspective from the cockpit of his He 123 allowed him to see airborne Polish machines only a few times. His squadron had no contact or combat of any important kind with Polish fighters. They were part of a fast-moving campaign that linked highly mobile ground forces and air power together on a scale not seen before. Galland had experienced it in miniature in Spain.

General von Richthofen applied with great skill the lessons learned with the Condor Legion, amplified now to the scale of Army Corps operations and all the more deadly because of their larger scope. Fighting for their native soil, Polish Army soldiers were individually brave and valiant, but the modern, well-integrated war machine that came thundering over the German border needed more than brave infantrymen and horse cavalry to halt its advance. Five Polish armies were overwhelmed. Ground attack units contributed significantly to this German success.

The Polish Army capitulated on 18 September 1939, although the Poles continued to defend Warsaw and Modlin until 27 September. In the course of ceaseless air action by his unit, Galland flew 87 missions in his Hs 123. These operations included bombing and strafing airfields, 9 bridges, troop concentrations, and trains. Where Polish flak appeared, it proved effective and accurate and much more dangerous than in Spain. Galland's Gruppe lost ten pilots, including Major Spielvogel, the Gruppenkommandeur.

During the campaign, Hitler visited Galland's squadron. The young pilot got his second close-up impression of the Fuehrer. Hitler was subdued and somewhat withdrawn amid the unit's personnel. He took a meal with them in the field, vegetable soup without meat. Galland's reaction to the visit was to wonder if this small and normal-looking man was really possessed of the leadership qualities claimed for him by Dr. Goebbels. Galland was unaware at this moment that his own life would soon include numerous encounters with Hitler, or that he would have abundant opportunity to experience the quality of the Fuehrer's military knowledge. On an airstrip in Poland in 1939, Hitler did not impress Galland as someone who could rock the world.

Blitzkrieg, or lightning war, was already a part of international language by the end of the Polish campaign. German propaganda made extensive claims for *Blitzkrieg*, and Galland could reflect that he had made a substantial contribution to its development in the close air support sphere. He was nevertheless unhappy with trends that he saw developing amid this climate of staggering military triumph and success.

The tendency became marked in Poland for the German Army to use air power to attack the enlarged enemy front line. Aircraft were being employed like concentrated airborne artillery. When his squadron had driven home attacks against bridges and railroad junctions, Galland could see from his perspective in the air that such targets behind the front were the nervous system of the enemy army. When a rail junction was made unusable, enemy supplies and ammunition would soon be found backed up behind the blockage, and these could then be destroyed.

If a bridge was knocked out, enemy transport would shortly be involved in fording operations and could be attacked and destroyed while in this vulnerable state. With his analytical faculties, he began having some critical thoughts about the growing tendency to substitute close support aircraft for field artillery. His mind was developing a strategic turn, reaching out for the broader canvas of war.

After Poland, Galland's unit was transferred to Braunschweig, and he was awarded the Iron Cross, Second Class, for his efforts in the recent campaign. On 1 October 1939, he was promoted to Captain, and amid his thoughts on strategy and tactics there dawned a means for him to free himself from close support flying and get back in a fighter unit.

During operations in the summer heat of Spain, he had flown the He 51 naked except for swimming trunks. From a health point of view this had been most unwise. Drastic temperature changes and the blasts of air in the open cockpit had afflicted him with periodic bouts of rheumatism, one of which hit him at Braunschweig. He was sent down to Wiesbaden to take the cure. When he returned to his squadron he had an interview with the medical officer, explaining to him his Spanish medical legacy.

"Doktor, you see that every time I fly now in these open cockpits, this rheumatism gets worse. The pain this last time was intense. Doktor, could you recommend my transfer to a Me 109 fighter unit, so that I do not have to fly any more in open cockpits?"

Galland was at his charming and persuasive best, to which most people were inclined to succumb. The doctor was not really fooled, but he was an understanding fellow. He took up the young pilot's medical dossier.

"Captain Galland is not to engage in any more flying activities in open cockpits, on account of rheumatic complaints" wrote the doctor.

Wheels within the Luftwaffe bureaucracy were set in motion by these few words. Captain Galland was transferred to JG 27, a fighter Geschwader at Krefeld, as Operations Officer. The close support nightmare was finally over. He would be henceforth, and for all his remaining days, a fighter pilot.

The Polish campaign contained one crucial element that was to bear heavily on Germany's subsequent war fortunes, and was also destined to bedevil Galland's future career. He would not be aware of its existence or its full implications until more than thirty years later. Colonel Gwido Langer, head of the Polish Cipher Bureau, had escaped to Rumania along with Major Maksymilian Cieski and the complete Polish cryptographic team. Years of dedicated labor by these men had produced an operating replica of the 3-rotor military Enigma coding machine used by the German forces since 1926. Six weeks prior to the invasion of Poland, the Polish General Staff presented French and British Intelligence each with a 3-rotor Enigma replica.

The escaping Polish cryptographers took with them to Rumania two additional Enigma machines that they had assembled at the Ava radio factory in Warsaw. These machines, and the union of the Polish experts with their Allied colleagues, had incalculable influence on the prosecution of the war. The most secret German codes were eventually broken.

By ensuring Allied possession of these Enigma machines, the Polish General Staff would inflict more damage on Germany than any army that Poland could have fielded. Luftwaffe radioteletype traffic would soon be read regularly in England. In the Battle of Britain, it would provide the narrow margin between victory and defeat for the RAF.

SEVEN

Nexus

Captain Adolf Galland regarded his return to a fully-fledged Me 109 fighter unit as a redemption. As operations officer for JG 27, he nevertheless became immediately involved with a problem that greatly expanded his nominal responsibilities. Lt. Colonel Max Ibel was in command, a pilot veteran of both World War I and the Lipetsk program. At the beginning of 1940, such experienced fighter pilots were commanding at both Gruppe and Geschwader levels. These valiant older men labored physically and mentally to keep pace with the new fighter epoch.

The Me 109 was a quantum jump in three major ways: design, performance, and demands upon the pilot. None of these veteran World War I pilots was really equal to leading a Geschwader of Me 109s in the air, where they were expected to fly into combat against men young enough to be their sons. When Galland joined Max Ibel, bringing with him the combat experience of Spain and Poland, plus the invaluable administrative experience gained in raising two Schlachtgeschwader, followed by Jagdgruppe Böblingen, he became especially important to his veteran Kommodore. Ibel was functioning at the limit of his abilities.

Galland was required to stick close to Ibel, both in the air and on the ground. This cramped his opportunities for combat and buried him in hated paper work. Further useful experience ensued for him when he was assigned to command each of the JG 27 Gruppen in turn, while their C.O.s went on leave. These assignments compressed considerable experience into minimum time. Each Gruppe had its idiosyncrasies and personalities. Knowing such things helped him in his later high responsibilities.

The warring powers were now engaged in the so-called "Phoney War," or "Sitzkrieg." Armies were not yet in conflict, but everyone grew more jumpy as the massive struggle kept brewing. Fighters scrambled after sometimes imaginary intruders. Stray reconnaissance aircraft were pursued by each side. When an Fw 58 Weihi piloted by JG 27's own Jafü was downed by German fighters, the incident put the impatient combat pilots' nerves on edge. The Jafü was the *Jagdfliegerführer*, or fighter pilot leader. A Jafü was usually a Colonel or a Major General, and served as liaison between Fighter Arm combat units and the Air Corps or Air Fleet of which they were a part. The downed Jafü was not happy at being shot from the sky by his own side.

Since the Fw 58 was an innocent-appearing aircraft, known in its ambulance version as "the sticking plaster bomber," the nervous pilots had to justify their attack. The situation was the same as if the RAF fighters had downed one of their lumbering all-purpose Avro Ansons. "How can a Jafü fly around in such a ridiculous plane?" said Galland's pilots, in self defense.

Higher directives at this time instructed Luftwaffe fighters to stay strictly on their own side of the border. Only intruders were to be engaged. The frontier became indistinct at 15,000 feet and over 300 mph, and sometimes was obscured by clouds. Along this border in an echo of World War I, aerial jousting occurred. French and German fighter pilots tested each other's machines and mettle. Most combat was joined in the "four borders" area, where France, Germany, Luxemburg, and Belgium came together.

Werner Moelders was there in the thick of the action. Now a Gruppenkommandeur with JG 53, and recognized as the leading German fighter pilot in every respect, he was adding to his score. Moelders was also implementing the tactical innovations that he had just codified during his Air Ministry assignment. This was unbearable for Galland. Moelders was adding to his aerial victories, while Galland struggled with the JG 27 paper mill and used ruses to get away on operations.

Galland wanted action, too. He also wanted to pick the fertile brain of Werner Moelders. Arranging through channels for a temporary transfer to JG 53, he soon found himself flying into action with Moelders, and taking factual and practical lectures from him on the lethal art of shooting down aircraft in air to air combat.

Moelders covered the full spectrum of fighter combat knowledge. Tactics, flying approaches, firing, angles of approach, seeing and distinguishing friend and foe, pressing home attacks, and separating enemy units after the attack were all covered by Moelders.

"Everything was given to me by my admired friend, Werner Moelders" said Galland of this time. "He was one year and one day younger than I, but I respected him as the superior tactician. Later we had strong competition in the number of aerial victories."

The basis for Galland's own later success in aerial combat was thus laid during this fortunate association with Moelders during the lull before the storm. Flying with the gifted pilot who was to be his great rival, Galland found that Moelders had a secret weapon – his eyesight. Moelders had phenomenal vision. He could pick out enemy aircraft in the sky before anyone else in the formation. Even after Moelders called out their location, most of the other pilots still could not spot the enemy aircraft. As Erich Hartmann, the greatest fighter ace of all time, would say in later years, "He who sees the enemy first already has half the victory." That was certainly true of Moelders. Galland envied his friend's visual gift, sharply aware all the time of the splintered glass and corneal scars in his own left eye.

Impressive also was Moelders's ingenuity in planting a small spotting unit on the ground near the border. The unit maintained radio contact with Moelders in the air, reporting recognized types, numbers, course, speed, and altitude of any incoming or passing enemy aircraft. This aided Moelders in making his remarkable interceptions, and exemplified his talent for innovation and planning. His border ground unit was probably one of the first efforts at fighter control in the Luftwaffe – a function in which the Germans woefully lagged behind the RAF. Little further was done along this line, because in 1940 German political authorities still considered their country safe from air attack. In those days, Germany was safe.

Galland and Moelders were temperamental opposites. Moelders was an extremely serious young man who smiled but little and rarely laughed. Galland's affability, sense of humor, and penchant for the good life made him a typical fighter pilot. Moelders tended by contrast to concentrate intensely on his duties, and on the larger functions of fighter aviation.

Moelders's bearing and demeanor evoked instant obedience, as though he were a mature general instead of a major in

"THOSE PESKY SPITFIRES!"
Meeting at Le Touquet on the Channel Front the Geschwader Kommodores discuss fighter tactics. Major Dr. Wenzel (Mölder's aide and only survivor of Mölders fatal crash on 22 November 1941), Adolf Galland (JG 26), Werner Mölders (JG 51), Theo Osterkamp (Jafu), and back to camera Gunther Lützow (JG 3).

his twenties. His subordinates nicknamed the old-young man "Daddy" Moelders in consequence. Galland got to know Moelders well during their historic four borders association in 1940. If Moelders was the master tactician and teacher, then Galland was the more enthusiastic hunter, and the teacher when it came to the good life – to the art of staying human amid inhuman events.

Galland chided Moelders about his monkish lifestyle and his abstinences. Galland's young pilots prepared a lavish "girl party" at a special suite in Paris. Galland persuaded Moelders to attend. Probably stung by Galland's chidings, Moelders was the first pilot to make his choice. Galland followed him immediately with his own choice, leaving the room with his famous ear-to-ear grin that appeared on such occasions. Moelders had unbent.

When the German offensive moved forward on 10 May 1940, JG 27 went into action, providing air support for the Army's successful crossing of the Maas River and the Albert Canal. On the third day of the campaign, Galland was leading a Rotte – a flight of two aircraft – five miles west of Liege at 12,000 feet, when he spotted eight Hurricane fighters 3,000 feet below him. He had not been seen.

He had the classic advantages of higher altitude and surprise in initiating a bounce. He was flying a superior aircraft, and was the recipient of a long and careful training, crowned by over 300 combat missions. He had all the advantages a fighter pilot could possess.

The bounce had been practiced in mock combat until it was part of him. No hunting fever rose in him as the Hurricane in his gunsight grew larger by the second. The instant he pressed his firing buttons, Galland knew that he had opened fire too far out. All that competition trap shooting still paid off. His bullets went right to their target. Taking evasive action immediately, the victim flew right into the fire of Galland's wingman as the Hurricane formation split in all directions.

Pressing a second attack on his now rattled quarry, Galland saw his foe's rudder break off. The Hurricane went spinning down, shedding debris and parts of its wings. Leaving the stricken machine to fall, Galland raced after another Hurricane in a diving chase. Closing in to 100 yards, he was about to fire when the Hurricane half-rolled and disappeared into the clouds.

Mentally calculating what the enemy pilot might do, Galland followed suit in his Me 109E. Seconds later he was behind the Hurricane again – but closer. A short burst sent the Hurricane into a stall, followed by a vertical dive from 1,500 feet directly into the ground. He shuddered at the impact, remembering his own near-mortal aerobatic crash at Juterbog before the war.

A third Hurricane fell to his guns near Tirlemont later that same day when he bounced a formation of five machines. Despite his having spent ten years preparing himself as a combat pilot, these first three victories brought him no elation. There had been none of the thudding excitement that seized him when storms of Loyalist lead ripped into his biplane in Spain. His

FRENCH MAPS ARE CONFUSING
Werner Mölders and his adjutant try to make heads-or-tails of a map in French.

conscience pricked him over the ease with which these first three victories had been won. Excited congratulations from his fellow pilots and the ground crews after he landed somehow sounded hollow.

His duties as operations officer precluded for a time any more missions. JG 27 moved forward with the Army. Numerous base changes, and the paper chase and administrative turmoil that came with these moves were absolute anathema to Galland. He fought to get back in the air, and on 19 May 1940 scored his fifth aerial victory. He was an ace.

He ran his victory tally to eight on 20 May, and was awarded the Iron Cross, First Class, by General Erhard Milch, Goering's Inspector General and deputy. As Milch pinned the decoration on him, Galland was not to know that he would be seeing plenty in the next few years of this captain of industry turned Luftwaffe General. Milch was freshly returned from commanding the Luftwaffe in the successful Norwegian campaign.

Battle lust was at an all-time peak among the JG 27 pilots, riding above a tremendous ground victory by the German Army. Colonel Ibel kept flying with his young pilots. Nothing daunted the crusty World War I veteran. Galland's duty when Ibel flew was to be his wingman, and this limited Galland's opportunities for further victories. The gallant Ibel evoked the admiration of his pilots, and Galland took good care of him in the air, except for one time when Spitfires caught them unawares. Ibel was shot down amid battlefield smoke and combat confusion. Galland was grateful when his haggard Kommodore trudged into their St. Pol HQ late that night, after a long and exhausting hike.

While operating out of Charleville, Galland tangled repeatedly with both Hurricanes and Spitfires of the RAF. He immediately realized that he was battling against high quality pilots. Courage and skill characterized these British pilots, but these qualities were undermined by their outdated tactics. They clung to their clumsy three-fighter "Vic" formation. The Spitfire was a hot performer and a hard hitter, but Galland was certain at this time of the superiority of his Me 109E compared to the Spitfire variants he was fighting.

The RAF was not hard to find. They usually flew fighter patrols over British and French troops who were being compressed toward Dunkirk. High above the historic beaches, Galland and his pilots were in daily savage combat with the RAF. The gentlemanly games of the Sitzkrieg period against the French were gone. Combat was for keeps. Every attack was driven home fiercely.

Galland could count on finding RAF fighters over the Dunkirk beaches. The British were wading into the German bombers and Stukas with telling effect, especially when Luftwaffe fighters had to withdraw to refuel. This happened often, due to the bombers arriving late for rendezvous with their fighter escort. The fighters sometimes missed their rendezvous with the bombers due to their involvement in dogfights with the RAF.

The Luftwaffe attempt to destroy the escaping British Expeditionary Force, without major participation by the German Army or Navy, had been undertaken with impulsive enthusiasm by Goering personally. He believed that he could achieve this Douhet-style triumph of air power. Goering had some support for this in high Luftwaffe circles.

Galland's perspective on the battle was simple and direct. Too much was being expected of the available German air strength. RAF fighter opposition was ferocious, and the Spitfire a nasty surprise. 350,000 Allied troops escaped, and the Luftwaffe lost about 250 aircraft. German air strength that had been held out of the Dunkirk battle to participate in the ongoing battle for France could have provided a decisive margin,. A Douhet-style air campaign demanded overwhelming strength. *The Luftwaffe had been warned.*

When Dunkirk passed into German hands on 4 June 1940, JG 27 turned its squadrons on to remaining French air units. The French Air Army was to be finally smashed through Operation Paula, conceived with strategic overtones. Paula was planned to destroy French aircraft factories in the Paris area. No aircraft and no usable airfields meant the end of the French Air Army. The Germans prepared inadequately, but still destroyed about 100 French aircraft for the loss of 30 of their own. Leading a small unit, Galland got into a wild dogfight with a Morane squadron. In downing one Morane, he almost came into full collision with another. Shearing off his own antenna mast and damaging his vertical stabilizer, it was as close as he cared to come to a mid-air collision. Even after Operation Paula there were still brave French air units to be hunted down. The French claimed that Paula was a failure, but little attention was paid to the operation amid a continuing string of German triumphs. The coming terrible years would prove that it takes a mighty Air Force to stop aircraft production.

After Dunkirk Galland was suddenly promoted to Gruppenkommandeur of III/JG 26 – a substantial upward leap. Goering was giving scope to the best of his younger fighter pilots by retiring to less demanding assignments the World War I veterans still in combat commands. Galland's Gruppe was transferred to Munchen-Gladbach for rest and refit at the end of the French campaign. The unit was then ordered to Doberitz, familiar to Galland from his fledgling days with JG 2. This was a special mission. JG 26 *Schlageter* – named for a National Socialist martyr who had been shot by the French in the Rhineland – had performed brilliantly against France. JG 26 had earned the honor of flying fighter cover for a spectacular investiture of Germany's highest commanders in Berlin.

OBERST WERNER MÖLDERS (1913-1941)
Mölders had 115 victories, including 14 in the Spanish Civil War. Before his death on 22 November 1941 he had been awarded the Knights Cross, The Oakleaves, the Swords and was the first to be awarded the Diamonds. He was Galland's great rival and friend.

Hollywood is the only place to stage spectacles more impressive than the investiture in the Kroll Opera House on 19 July 1940. Hitler made an impassioned speech, culminating in a last, hopeless attempt to offer a peace agreement to Britain. With Adolf Galland leading his fighter Gruppe in salute overhead, Hitler promoted twelve German generals to Field Marshals. Nineteen more became full generals. Amid the lavish pomp, the Luftwaffe was well represented.

Milch, Sperrle, and Kesselring became field marshals. Udet, Stumpff, Keller, Weise, and Grauert became colonel-generals. Jeschonnek, von Richthofen, Geissler, von Greim, and Goering's old squadron mate Loerzer were all raised to full generals *(General der Flieger)*. Goering rose above them all, boosted to grandiose heights as Marshal of the Greater German Reich. An exalted new grade of the Iron Cross was instituted exclusively for Goering. No one else in Germany would ever wear the Grand Cross of the Iron Cross, and that briefly satisfied the Reich Marshal's pathological vanity.

All these leaders moving up a rung or two all at once resulted in a promotional shockwave throughout the Luftwaffe. Galland said it was caused by the "common upward pressure for promotion." He was promoted Major at the age of 28, in recognition of his bravery in the French campaign, his 17 aerial victories, and his many aircraft destructions by strafing. Celebrations had hardly subsided when JG 26 was transferred back to the Pas de Calais. The war was still on.

Violent days lay ahead. Virtually all Galland's youth and adult life had been a preparation for this challenge. Leading an efficient fighter Gruppe in an historic operation of war completely filled his life. The award of the Knight's Cross, in addition to his promotion to Major, left him overwhelmed. All this had begun back at the Borkenberge, in those simple days when he had first strapped himself into a sailplane.

Service with a top fighter unit, with the comradeship and spirit that made life zestful, was all he wanted professionally. When off duty, the rest of the good life beckoned, and he was off in the woods and fields hunting. There were always birds and hares for the pot. An active social calendar saw him indulge his taste for attractive women.

Overriding everything was the sense of being involved in something bigger than himself. Petty individual concerns withered away for lack of worthy dimension. Had it been left entirely to him, Adolf Galland would have added nothing more than he now had at the beginning of the Battle of Britain. He was where he felt he belonged, doing what he knew best.

Seemingly unrelated chains of events, of which he was oblivious, were nevertheless moving into a remarkable confluence. A historian's perspective of more than fifty years makes these connections readily discernible. Such insight is not granted a man while he is living his life at full throttle. In Galland's case, policies and decisions of human beings outside his sphere would soon saddle him with problems and pressures that would make a fighter cockpit seem by contrast a peaceful sanctuary.

Other human beings that he would not even know about until he was 65 years old would eavesdrop on his troubles. Information thereby gained would be used to make his way harder. Then there was one human being looming on his horizon who would put his tolerance, self control, and soldierly fidelity to their limits.

In order to understand fully the high command career of Adolf Galland, the three main elements mentioned need to be outlined before dealing with the Battle of Britain – the Luftwaffe's most crucial encounter. Decisions and policies of the Luftwaffe General Staff and High Command, and of the Luftwaffe Supreme Commander himself in the development of Germany's new air arm, profoundly influenced the outcome of the Battle of Britain. Luftwaffe fighter pilots caught hell, not only in the air in combat, but also on the ground, where they were blamed for many gross, high level failures. Galland's combat career in the Battle of Britain, and his later career in high command, circulated around the omissions and errors of others – mistakes that can best be described as techni-political.

While Galland had been an eager participant in the growth of the Luftwaffe from its birth, he was a young pilot and a junior officer. He was never privy to questions of policy, doctrine, or the structuring of the Luftwaffe. His contributions to the development of modern tactical air power had been considerable, but the Luftwaffe had been fashioned by Goering and the mature leaders he had selected to work under his authority.

Fighter aircraft had always occupied a secondary role in the Luftwaffe. Luftwaffe policy was to acquire a Bomber Arm rapidly that would be sufficient to deter outside interference with German rearmament. The Fighter Arm was to receive attention only in a secondary way. The Bomber Arm thus enjoyed from the first days of the Luftwaffe both doctrinal and developmental primacy. Some officers in high Luftwaffe posts would persist in Bomber Arm primacy even when Allied bombers were laying Germany in ruins – that is how deeply this principle became ingrained.

Bombers as a key strategic weapon were understood and accepted by Generalleutnant Walther Wever, Chief of the Air Command Office. While the actual title of Chief of the Luftwaffe General Staff did not then exist, he was in all essentials the first Chief of the Luftwaffe General Staff. A former Army General Staff Officer who had been General Ludendorff's adjutant in World War I, Wever was extremely capable, well-trained in military affairs, and gifted in his grasp of air power fundamentals. His leadership qualities and initiative included learning to fly at age 46. This allowed him to speak with the added authority afforded him by his pilot rating.

Wever flew his own aircraft on visits to his troops. Galland met him and was impressed by Wever's dynamism when the latter made a visit to I/JG 2 at Doberitz in 1936. Wever was progressive, with great vision, clearly discerning the 4-engined bomber as the most important air weapon of the future. Only by this means could Germany strike strategically at Hitler's avowed enemy, Bolshevist Russia. Strategic blows against the Soviet Union required a 4-engined machine able to reach the Ural mountains and the main sources of Soviet material power. Wever intended to structure the Luftwaffe around this strategic air weapon, supported by the General Staff.

Presaging the coming epoch of the 4-engined bomber was the giant Junkers G 38, completed in 1930. A 4-engined passenger monoplane with a 150-foot wingspan, the G 38 also had copious freight and fuel space inside its wings. The machine flew a grand tour of Europe, including London. The famous editor of *The Aeroplane*, Charles Grey would later call this aircraft the father of all big bombers. Germany had the aeronautical know-how to build strategic bombers.

General Wever's appreciation of the form that German air power would have to take – if Russia were the adversary – was based upon the Luftwaffe having time to build to full and balanced strength. A fatal plane crash on 3 May 1936, during one of Wever's routine troop visits, removed his vision and drive from the strategic bomber program. General Staff advocates of the program were thereafter unable to maintain its momentum against economic and political expediencies.

Political considerations virtually eradicated strategic considerations from Luftwaffe planning. Hitler's political goals required construction of the largest possible number of aircraft in minimum time. Although Dornier and Junkers built promising prototypes under Air Ministry contracts, Goering was persuaded by Milch and the Technical Office to abandon the long range bomber. By the spring of 1937, German development of strategic air power had ceased.

With the strategic bomber dead, productive capacity was mainly concentrated on other bombers. Aside from the later innovations of Werner Moelders, only relatively minor resources and precious little vision were invested in the Fighter Arm. Dive bombing became a ruinous obsession of the Luftwaffe High Command – a veritable military neurosis – after Udet imported the dive bomber idea from America.

Udet gave up his cosmopolitan, carefree life and became Head of the Technical Department at the Air Ministry for the sake of the dive bomber, his passion. Small and relatively cheap, dive bombers could be built quickly and in large numbers. They delivered their bombs accurately. No adequate weight was given by the Luftwaffe hierarchy to the dive bomber's vulnerability to fast, modern fighters. Dive bombers meshed with Germany's political goals and purposes. Dive bombers were "in."

Amid shortages of raw materials, a stream of enthusiasm for dive bombers soon became an all-consuming flood. All bombers had diving capability written into their specifications, including the 4-engined Heinkel 177. This edict had serious consequences. The speedy, twin-engined Ju 88 medium bomber, for example, underwent extensive structural strengthening for diving. Up went its weight, down went its payload. More powerful engines to compensate for the diminished payload were not forthcoming.

This diving orgy soon permeated the whole bomber program. Carpet bombing, as developed by Galland in Spain, was abandoned in favor of pinpoint bombing. Cancellation of the strategic bomber in April of 1937 began the shrinkage of the Luftwaffe's horizons. Concentration on dive bombing shrank what remained down to a pinpoint.

A serious fighter procurement error influenced disastrously the fighter-to-fighter struggle that decided the Battle of Britain. The Me 109's competitor was the Heinkel He 112, marginally slower, but more maneuverable. The He 112 also had a wide track landing gear, the narrow landing gear of the Me 109 being a weakness that eventually led to thousands of wrecked and damaged aircraft. The He 112 had a 680-mile range, against 360-480 miles for the several Me 109 variants.

The short-winded Me 109 would never be able to stay more than ten minutes over London. Galland would have bitter experiences with this crippling handicap. The Air Ministry chose not to produce both fighters, to the chagrin of Ernst Heinkel. The incensed professor then created the He 100, a faster and more advanced fighter that would be cheaper to build. Udet personally set a new world record – 100 km circuit record – in the V2 prototype, at 394.6 mph.

On 30 March 1939, the He 100 in the V3 version was flown to a world speed record of 463.93 mph by Hans Dieterle. The Air Ministry had authorized a series of prototypes, but despite the imminence of war and the obvious supplementation of Me 109 deficiencies provided by this aircraft, mass production was never authorized. On the contrary, six prototypes were actually sold to Russia. Three more went to Japan. Luftwaffe fighter pilots were thereby denied the 559-mile range of the He 100 in their mortal clash with the RAF.

MÖLDERS ADJUTANT HARTMANN GRASSER
Grasser flew Mölders wing against the RAF. He was awarded the Knights Cross on 4 September 1941 and the Oakleaves on 31 August 1943. Grasser also served on Galland's staff. A businessman after the war, he passed away on 2 June 1986.

Adolf Galland was an extern to all these high level decisions on policy, doctrine, procurement, production, and planning. The command arrangements and personalities who were responsible for creating the Luftwaffe as an exclusively tactical air force – like airborne artillery and minus any significant strategic capability – were also beyond his sphere as a young pilot. He would, nevertheless, have to cope with all the consequences arising from neglect of the Fighter Arm, and for numerous mistakes made by senior officers and planners in the nineteen thirties.

The massive tactical Luftwaffe assembled at the beginning of the Battle of Britain had brought Hitler and Goering the greatest succession of victories in modern times. Success seemed to make everything right. The Luftwaffe's very existence had bulked large in the bloodless prior diplomatic triumphs, as well as in the victories over Poland,

Norway, Holland, Belgium, and France. Victories are insidious. They conceal the weaknesses of the victor – especially from the victor himself. Top Luftwaffe leadership had an insufficient sense of weakness in July of 1940.

British conquest of German military Enigma ciphers was the second vital chain of events affecting Galland's war career. Even as the young Gruppenkommandeur prepared for the Battle of Britain, British cipher teams at Bletchley Park near London were beginning to read regularly the radioteletype cipher traffic of the Luftwaffe in France. Immense and ingenious labors by the British, based on the advantage given to them by the Polish cipher team and their smuggled Enigma machines, produced this breakthrough. Inadvertently aiding them was the Luftwaffe itself, through slackness in its enciphering practices and procedures.

Before the Battle of Britain started, the Luftwaffe Order of Battle was known to the RAF. The British knew the status of every participant Luftwaffe unit, including pilots, aircraft, spare parts, and fuel. This intelligence was protected by maximum security and given the classification Ultra Secret. Security was tight enough to protect the secret by all involved until the middle nineteen seventies – a marvel of both security and fidelity.

Extreme security measures were essential with Ultra during the war to preclude German realization that their ciphers had been broken. The high Allied officers who were authorized to receive Ultra decrypts remained tightly limited in numbers throughout the war. British master spy F.W. Winterbotham, the RAF Group Captain who had moved in high Nazi circles before the war, played a major role in the distribution of Ultra intelligence, including getting crucial decrypts to Fighter Command in the Battle of Britain. His experiences are recounted in *The Ultra Secret*, his 1974 book published by Harper and Row.

Winterbotham set up Special Liaison Units (SLUs) with the various high commands to which the Ultra intelligence was distributed. Part of Winterbotham's job was to brief high commanders on the origin of this remarkable intelligence, so that they, in turn, could guard the secret. Winterbotham also was responsible for passing Ultra information personally to Churchill.

GRASSER IN 1943
Hartmann Grasser reports his 100th victory to Major Forel, the Geschwader administration officer.

Early in August of 1940, Winterbotham established a small SLU at Fighter Command HQ at Stanmore. Ultra material relevant exclusively to the air battle that was about to begin could thus be sent directly to the SLU's soundproof, subterranean cell in "The Hole" at Stanmore. SLU personnel would give German signals personally to Air Chief Marshal Sir Hugh Dowding, AOC Fighter Command. SLU personnel ensured that the written information was thereafter removed.

When Winterbotham also briefed Air Vice-Marshal Keith Park, AOC No. 11 Fighter Group, on the Ultra intelligence, the RAF was set for its historic aerial battle with the Luftwaffe. Park would know throughout the battle that orders emanating from Dowding were taking into account actual German radio traffic, crucial information that would reach Dowding almost as rapidly as it reached Goering, his Air Fleet chiefs, and lesser operational commanders. Park's fighters were based in south-eastern England. They would take the brunt of the Luftwaffe assault. Ultra thus became a subtle higher dimension of the Battle of Britain, through which the considerable qualities of Dowding's mind were further magnified. Galland, across the Channel, would have little authentic information on the RAF other than what he gleaned in action.

On the morning of 8 August 1940, when the HQ teleprinter at III/JG 26 on the Pas de Calais punched out an order of the day from Goering, Dowding was a recipient, as well as Major Galland:

CAMOUFLAGED HANGAR AT MALDEGHEM
II/JG 26 received its first Fw 190 in August 1941. First combat in the Fw 190 against the RAF took place on 27 Sept. 1941.

"From Reich Marshal Goering to all units of Air Fleets 2, 3, and 5. Operation Eagle. Within a short period you will wipe the British Air Force from the sky. Heil Hitler."

From this time on until the end of the war, virtually every important radioteletype message addressed to Galland would be simultaneously in the hands of the Allies. The losses suffered by the fighter units he would command in the coming battle would be known in Britain whenever he sent them via radioteletype to HQ. Constant possession of such information by his opponents would increase their ability to outwit him, multiply his difficulties, and partly nullify his bravery in action.

Allied air commanders opposing Galland would always have this beneficial intelligence when making their own decisions. Luftwaffe commanders like Galland would have nothing comparable concerning Allied leaders and their plans. The weight of Ultra gave unprecedented advantages to the Allied high commanders.

The vain man behind the Operation Eagle order of the day was the third force coming to confluence in Adolf Galland's life in 1940. Hermann Goering was Galland's direct superior when he rose to his highest responsibilities. The Reich Marshal was remote now from the young Gruppenkommandeur, but it was "his" Luftwaffe in which Galland held his commission. Soon it would be "his" Fighter Arm that Galland would command. Goering's authority in the Luftwaffe was unquestioned. There were no congressional committees to ensure that the Reich Marshal did not go too far.

Their relationship was to be a clash of strong men, strange in its many shadings. Goering stretched all the way from paternal mentor to abusive tyrant, and swung unpredictably between these extremes. His bulky shadow would fall across everything Galland would seek to do in the years ahead. You had to go through Goering in the Luftwaffe, and nobody ever went around him, except Adolf Hitler.

Common historical impressions of Goering are disastrously simplistic. Galland was not to deal with this entrenched caricature of Goering, but with Germany's number two man, whose authority was almost unlimited. Goering denied direct operational authority to Galland when he ushered him into the Luftwaffe hierarchy. This stricture, and the clash of character that was inevitable between Goering and Galland, was to influence the course of the air war. Before following Galland into the Battle of Britain, a realistic look at Goering is appropriate.

EIGHT

The Fat One

Four days after taking command of the Richthofen Circus in July of 1918, Lt. Hermann Goering summoned all leading pilots for a dressing down. He rebuked these aces for their sloppy flying discipline, but he also had an unspoken reason for blasting them. Even in 1918 Goering had a flair for personal politics, and a determination to get his own way – if need be by browbeating.

Goering was an outsider from Jagdstaffel 27, who had been given command of the elite Flying Circus in preference to aces already serving with the unit. Living legends like Ernst Udet, Carl Loewenhardt and Lothar von Richthofen – brother of the recently slain Red Baron – were all passed over for command. Naturally, they resented Goering's appointment. He provoked a face-down with the veterans to assert his leadership. "Plucking the peacocks before they fall over their own feathers" was how Goering described his action to Lt. Karl Bodenschatz, his adjutant.

Twenty-two years later on the French coast, Goering as Supreme Commander of the Luftwaffe would again assail one of Germany's greatest aces. This time it would be Adolf Galland, Kommodore of JG 26. This confrontation took place in a new epoch, but it was the same old Goering, tough, forceful, and with his actions politically motivated.

Clashes between the two men were to continue, with increasing acrimony on Goering's part, until Galland's controversial dismissal from high command in January of 1945. These encounters were to be the most unpleasant in Galland's life. Antagonism between these two powerful personalities cannot be judged solely from a military standpoint. There was a characterological gulf between them that influenced profoundly their professional relationship.

With Galland's formative years already described, a survey of Goering's early life is warranted. He was at once Galland's sponsor and main antagonist. Goering was behind Galland's meteoric rise to high responsibilities, but as his direct superior, blocked most of the capable young man's recommendations. Sponsor and protegé were almost always at loggerheads.

Goering survives in public memory as an overweight poseur, a flamboyant lover of uniforms, pomp, and personal adornment. Everyone knows he was a drug addict, but few know how his addiction began. He enjoys posthumous fame for plundering art works. As Hitler's closest associate and heir to the Fuehrer's power, he is stained by the excesses of the regime he helped create, engineered into place and served to the end.

Goering was all these things, but to view him exclusively as a shallow sybarite is highly misleading. His capabilities were exceptional. One of the most formidable German personalities of the twentieth century, his native brilliance and intellectual gifts were regained when the Allies weaned him from drugs at war's end. At the Nuremberg trials, the world saw the real Goering. Unrepentant, eloquent, fearsomely logical, and armed with a photographic memory, his defense put the best Allied legal brains to their limits in coping with him. This was as a defeated captive, with all the legal rules and procedures drawn up by the victors in trials under their total control.

Adolf Galland as a young general in his early thirties had to deal with this same personality on military issues. Goering was then in power – his direct superior. "Der Dicke" – the Fat One – was a heavyweight in more ways than one.

Galland developed in a solidly-based family. Nothing disrupted the development of his character. From his boyhood interests, he phased smoothly into his flying career, armed with a strong character, sharp intelligence, and the personal equilibrium that stems from a sound upbringing. Hermann Goering, by contrast, had an emotionally rough childhood. He was disastrously influenced by his godfather, Dr. Hermann von Epenstein.

Right after Goering was weaned, he was placed with surrogate parents, while his mother went to join his aging diplomat father in Haiti. In his maturity, Goering would often complain to friends about the cruelty of such separations. His formative years were overshadowed by his mother's love affair with his godfather, while his aged natural father descended into senility. Hermann von Epenstein was the major influence in Goering's formative years, and he largely shaped the character of the man destined to become one of the lords of the Third Reich.

Von Epenstein was a lover of medieval pomp, and his example would induce Goering to live on a grandiose scale in the twentieth century, while keeping one foot in the Middle Ages. Young Hermann Goering had a natural affinity for the folklore of chivalry, knighthood, and medieval splendor. Von Epenstein was so situated and disposed in life as to infuse all these boyish fantasies with an overwhelming reality, a fairy tale translated into the here and now.

Acquiring a castle at Mauterndorf in Austria, von Epenstein moved the Goering family into lodges on the grounds of this romantic edifice. Von Epenstein had an arrogant, commanding method of speaking, with which he overpowered people in ordinary life. As the adored exemplar of all that young Goering admired and fantasized, von Epenstein was undoubtedly responsible for the way in which the adult Goering handled his military subordinates and his contemporaries in politics.

Von Epenstein introduced young Hermann to flamboyant manners and dress, which the youngster sought to emulate. All this was carried through into Goering's adult life. As Reich Marshal, he could indulge these tastes. Medieval grandeur sprang back to life at Mauterndorf. Uniformed retainers bowed and curtsied at von Epenstein's approach, surrounding him with groveling deference. Meal times were signaled with a hunting horn blast. Banquets in the great hall were laid on amid the trappings of bygone ages, including musicians playing in the gallery. This bizarre scenario sank into the receptive psyche of

GALLAND AND HIS DOG
In July 1940, Galland was Kommandeur of the third Gruppe of JG 26. His Me 109 sports the third squadron insignia, the red "Hollenhund."

STRATEGY MEETING AT LE TOUQUET
On a bright and sunny day in 1941, Luftwaffe fighter leaders met to review operations against the RAF. Left to right: Adolf Galland, Gunther Lützow, Werner Mölders, Carl Viek, General Theo Osterkamp, Günther von Maltzahn and General Teichmann.

Hermann Goering like a draught of regal wine, evoking dreams in which he himself would swagger as the royal master. No atmosphere could be conceived that was less conducive to humility.

Von Epenstein was not content with one castle. He acquired Castle Veldenstein, 25 miles north of Nuremberg. Within its walls, decades later, Goering would thunder at Adolf Galland and be heard in the village below. Von Epenstein moved the Goering family into the old fortress, which he restored and refurbished. A suite was reserved for von Epenstein's exclusive use when he was in residence. At those times, Hermann Goering's mother was in von Epenstein's bed. Her husband Heinrich and the Goering children were aware of these arrangements. Alcohol deadened the old diplomat's feelings. The children got used to it all, and Hermann continued to idolize his godfather.

Goering was shattered at age 11 when his school authorities informed him that von Epenstein was half-Jewish. Young Hermann had made the mistake of writing about his godfather in an essay assignment, "The Man I Admire Most In The World." Summoned to the headmaster's office, Goering was shown the listings in the semi-Gotha, which catalogued all titled Germans of Jewish blood – and there was the name of his hero. His fellow students added to his miseries by frogmarching him around the school grounds with a placard around his neck, advertising the Jewish origin of his godfather. He bolted from school. Jew or no Jew, Goering's loyalty to his godfather never wavered, and nor did his desire to model himself after his hero.

Von Epenstein's arrogant, domineering ways, his tastes, flamboyance, and assertiveness, impressed themselves on young Hermann like a behavioral matrix. The boy would carry these impressions into adult life, and find full expression when he rose to political power. All of it was, nevertheless, engrafted, and tended to obscure his high native intelligence and outstanding intellectual capacity.

He was first class across the board in the elite Karlsruhe military academy, to which he was admitted through von Epenstein's influence as an ex-cavalry officer. His stellar performance at Karlsruhe got him an appointment to the cadet college at Lichterfelde, near Berlin, which trained officers for the German Army. Here he wrote a record of sustained brilliance, emerging with top honors and a commission in the Prinz Wilhelm Regiment.

Goering went into action as an infantry officer within a few hours of the outbreak of World War I. Fighting the Fatherland's wars was to Goering at 21 the highest challenge to his manhood. He proved himself resourceful, courageous, and capable, with plenty of initiative and daring. Rheumatic fever took him out of the trenches just before the Battle of the Marne.

While in hospital at Freiburg, his former regimental comrade Bruno Loerzer visited him. Loerzer was a pilot trainee for the new air service of the German Army. He was going to be flying over the mud of the battlefield, instead of wallowing in it as Goering had been doing. Fired by the adventure of flying, Goering immediately applied for transfer to the Freiburg flying school. While awaiting approval, he took some hops with Loerzer, and thereafter was utterly determined to become an airman.

ALERT PILOTS AT PLAY
Recreation for the alert pilots sometimes consisted of playing soccer. This mascot dog wouldn't let them have the ball. Feldwebel Nocker is at left and other pilot is not identified.

HEINKEL 111 ALL-PURPOSE BOMBER
Used as a transport, a bomber, a night fighter, a courier, etc. this speedy airplane served the Luftwaffe well throughout the war.

Goering's historic association with German air power began at this moment. His ambition was almost stillborn when his request for transfer was refused. Ignoring the order to return to his regiment when fit, he wrote fake transfer orders for himself and haunted the flying field. He went aloft at every chance to learn the task of observer-photographer, from which beginning he would later transition to pilot.

When his regimental authorities learned of his self-discharge from the hospital and his self-transfer to the air service, he was ordered to report for duty immediately. Any ordinary officer would have been frightened into compliance, for he had already committed court martial offenses. Goering was no ordinary officer. He reacted by telegraphing his godfather, who was well connected in royal circles in Berlin. Von Epenstein pulled strings.

Instead of a court martial, Goering was ordered by Crown Prince Friedrich Wilhelm, son of the Kaiser, to join the German Fifth Army's air detachment at Stenay in northern France,

LUFTWAFFE HANGAR IN FRANCE
During the Battle of Britain, the Luftwaffe used barns as airplane hangars in their efforts to disperse their fighters. This shows a Me 109 with just its nose visible in the doorway.

Loerzer along with him. Goering was to be a flyer for the rest of the war. As Loerzer's observer, Goering demonstrated an almost mystical quality of bravery. In the field he won the Iron Cross, First Class.

The Albatros in which Goering and Loerzer flew was not well suited to aerial photography. Goering compensated for that by hanging down out of the cockpit with his camera, taking photographs of fortifications and other targets. Stowing his camera after completion of photography, he would lean out again with a machine gun, hosing bullets into the entrenched troops below.

Nicknamed "The Flying Trapezist" for these exploits, his bravery made him into a legend in the German air service. Wild derring-do was in keeping with his extravagant tastes. Memories of these days undoubtedly colored his judgments of Luftwaffe fighter pilots in World War II, when he berated Galland with accusations of their cowardice. Goering's combat courage was of the highest order. Only in Hitler's presence would he ever appear awe-struck.

After unflawed pilot training in 1915, Goering was sent to the squadrons. By mid-1917 he had shot down 17 aircraft, and earned two more medals, including the coveted Blue Max. He was not just a successful fighter ace, but proved himself an excellent administrator. His all-around capabilities won him command of the Richthofen Circus after the death of the Red Baron in action. At the armistice, Captain Hermann Goering led the most famous aerial unit of the war.

From chivalry, fame, and glory at the zenith of his flying career, Goering went tumbling into the social maelstrom of defeated Germany. His descent from life among the gods was sickening to his soul and spirit. Evidence of revolution and social disintegration was everywhere visible. Socialists and communists on the left and numerous factions on the right locked themselves in verbal and physical combat all over Germany. War heroes were humiliated and spat upon.

Goering was revolted by what he saw. Soldiering and flying were all he knew. The winter of 1918-19 became for him a personal nightmare. Anarchy threatened to engulf the country. Misery, poverty, and street violence were symbols of political chaos. Goering had not fought for four years for this. He began living a pillar-to-post life as a peacetime pilot, testing and promoting for Anthony Fokker, barnstorming and operating an air taxi.

The socio-economic soil in postwar Germany was perfect to stimulate the growth of communism. The Communist Party was on its way to controlling Germany. A traditionalist and professional officer like Goering could only react with rage toward these elements, until in November of 1922 the angry Goering found Hitler.

A spellbinding orator who articulated with precision the wrongs and shames of German life, Adolf Hitler seemed to be roaring out Goering's own thoughts. Hitler also laid out the pathway back to world respect for Germany. The Red betrayers, Jews, and Marxists would be eradicated. A new Germany would be built, proud and strong enough to tear up the humiliating Versailles Treaty. Goering was hooked. He had found a hero to supplant in his own maturity, the godfather he had idolized in childhood. Hitler was a rising star to which Goering hitched his energy and ability.

Goering brought prestige to the Nazis, striving as they were for a respectable image. He was a member of the officer caste, a celebrated war hero and winner of the Blue Max. Hitler welcomed him and put him in charge of his 10,000 storm troopers, the SA (*Sturmabteilungen*). Goering turned them from a uniformed mob into dependable, smooth-working commandos. He infused them with high morale. Their public parades made good impressions. Their street operations against the hated communists became highly successful.

Goering had entered a world not normally invaded by German officers – politics. Goering's high intelligence quickly grasped the intricacies of this new milieu, with its maneuvers and parlance. He was beside Hitler in Munich in November of 1923, when the Nazis tried to take over the government of Bavaria. This was a pivotal moment in Goering's life, because he took two bullets in the skirmish with the German Army.

One bullet in the hip was of no great significance, but the second shot entered his groin. Protracted, excruciating pain ensued, and led him eventually to morphine addiction. Wounded, wanted, and hunted, the ex-hero was smuggled into Austria and thereafter led a desperate existence outside Germany. Hitler meanwhile languished as a prisoner in Landsberg Fortress, writing *Mein Kampf.*

Goering was sustained in his ordeal by his wife Karin, whom he had met and married while operating his air taxi into Sweden. They returned now to Sweden, where Goering had to face his unfortunate morphine addiction. At a hospital, his therapy was bungled and he became violent. Doctors straitjacketed him and committed him to Langbro Insane Asylum.

"Cold turkey" withdrawal followed in a padded cell, an ordeal guaranteed to weed out the non-survivors among drug addicts. Three months saw the return of his impressive mentality, and he was released, only to become re-addicted and recommitted. Two trips to hell and back nearly broke Goering's morale and spirit. Within his structure he now carried a weakness, a mental wound as a counterpart to the gnawing presence in his groin. He would not be free of dabbling with drugs again until dried out by the Allies after his surrender in 1945.

Goering returned to Germany under a 1927 general political amnesty, overweight, limping, and wasted. Hitler unenthusiastically told him to make a place for himself in commercial life, as a prelude to any further Nazi Party involvement. Goering bootstrapped himself up from zero in an epic comeback that verified his will power and gumption.

Landing a job as Berlin representative of BMW, he exploited every wartime friendship and connection. Bruno Loerzer gave him access to both Heinkel and Lufthansa. By energy and the shameless use of influence, the former Flying Trapezist was soon again riding high. He became a Nazi Party candidate in the 1928 Reichstag elections.

By studying Hitler, Goering had learned how to excite a mob through oratory. He put on a fierce political blitzkrieg in Berlin and was elected. Only eleven other Nazis, including Hitler and Goebbels, sat in the Reichstag with him. Goering was on his way to the top.

GALLAND IN HIS TRUSTY FIGHTER
Adolf Galland during the Battle of Britain. The "S" was the insignia of JG 26. Mickey Mouse logo is just below the cockpit. The telescopic gunsight was scrapped after only a few sorties.

Hitler put him on the Nazi Party payroll and sent him all over Germany as a spokesman and recruiter. Record crowds met him everywhere, and they started joining up. His hard financial times in exile faded behind him as his fortunes soared. Hanging on to his BMW agency despite his other responsibilities, Goering also became a paid political lobbyist for Lufthansa – courtesy of Erhard Milch.

Goering's background enabled him to influence the nobility in the direction of the Nazis. His aristocratic wife Karin, and his own social graces, gave the Nazis a respectability they needed. He promoted the Party with industrial and financial magnates. When the Nazis won 108 seats in the Reichstag in September of 1930, most of the credit for the party's 96-seat gain belonged to Goering.

Despite the mortal illness of his wife, Goering maintained the pressure. His oratory repeatedly drew crowds in excess of 40,000 people in the bloody elections of 31 July 1932. Scores of people were killed in street battles, and hundreds were wounded as Reds and Nazis clashed all over Germany. When the dust settled, more than thirteen and a half million Germans had voted for Hitler, 38 percent of the vote. The Nazis now held the balance of power.

In the machinations that followed to make Hitler Chancellor of Germany, Goering played a masterful role. His personal friendship with Germany's aged President von Hindenburg, dating from the war, allowed him access at will to the former Field Marshal. Von Hindenburg was opposed to appointing Hitler. Goering worked subtly on the old gentleman.

As President of the Reichstag Assembly, Goering first organized the ouster of Chancellor Franz von Papen through a Reichstag vote of censure. Goering then manipulated the Army and von Hindenburg's son on to the side of the Nazis. The old Field Marshal himself thereafter acceded. Hitler was appointed

Chancellor. Goering had completed a masterpiece of political engineering.

Goering's achievements up to this time were anything but dilettantism. He had become a master of politics. Once Hitler took office, Goering, as Prussian Minister of Interior and President of Police, ruthlessly purged the bureaucracies of all known anti-Nazis. He set up the *Forschungsamt*, the innocuous-sounding "Research Bureau," with monopoly control of wiretapping. Eventually to employ a force of more than 3,000 persons, the *Forschungsamt* eavesdropped on everything likely to be of use to Hitler and Goering. Foreign diplomatic traffic continuously in Hitler's hands contributed enormously to his pre-war triumphs. Goering received daily digests of wiretapped information, ranging from foreign embassy intercepts to the scandal being traded by Nazi officials' wives. Goering used all this to protect his political position and consolidate his grip on the vast range of offices that he assumed.

Under Hitler's first government, the new office of Commissioner of Aviation was created, with Goering in charge. He used this office to initiate the birth of the new German Air Force, which he had long envisaged as a separate, independent service arm. As has been previously related, Adolf Galland met Hermann Goering for the first time during this period, and was impressed by the new Commissioner's vision of Germany's aerial future. As he sat in that May audience in 1933, Galland was not to know, or even dream, that his professional life and fortunes would be so directly and drastically influenced by this man.

ADOLF GALLAND IN 1940
"Dolfo" leans on one of the cannon mounted on his Me 109 fighter.

Goering initiated Luftwaffe development, but an Air Force could not be built with his enthusiasm alone. The actual work of creating the Luftwaffe from near zero was the responsibility of other men, far more technically capable than Goering. The prime mover was Goering's deputy and State Secretary, Erhard Milch, the tough ex-boss of Lufthansa. Goering wanted a Luftwaffe fast, and when Milch obliged, Goering became jealous and acted to limit his power.

Several major reorganizations in the 1930s failed to prevent a destructive rivalry between Milch and the Luftwaffe General Staff. Instead of insisting on harmony, Goering allowed the friction to become chronic. The Luftwaffe suffered from these squabbles, but Goering obviously preferred that his main subordinates waste energy in rivalry. That way, there were no rivals for Goering.

His authority and political influence in Nazi Germany placed maximum resources behind the developing Air Force. Goering's ruthless energy smashed through bureaucratic barriers, securing priorities and precious raw materials for the Luftwaffe. This enabled the new Air Force to be created in minimum time, despite its inner weaknesses. Since Goering's numerous offices included Minister of the Four Year Plan, finance ceased to be a problem for the building Luftwaffe.

Goering had no technical knowledge. Tuning in a broadcast radio taxed him technically, by his own admission. He nevertheless made himself Commander-in-Chief of the most highly technical of all the armed services. He made technical decisions of far-reaching consequence, such as shelving the long range bomber, and he allowed the dive bombing obsession to get out of hand. At critical wartime junctures, he brushed aside the advice of capable generals and sometimes took personal charge of operations for which he had no training. His high command career is a catalog of miscalculation and disaster. Due to the nature of his upbringing in the shadow of Ritter von Epenstein, he was intoxicated by his desire to command.

Glory he regarded as his divine right. He demanded and basked in all the credit for the creation of "my Luftwaffe," and for its stunning early successes. Others were shut out. In defeat, he sought scapegoats, with unscrupulous zeal. He played favorites, and was ill-served by the favorites he chose.

Envy often motivated him. Able subordinates in key posts were likely to find their authority and powers circumscribed by Goering. This was done with Galland. Goering once confided to Colonel Josef "Pips" Priller, a successor to Galland as Kommodore of JG 26, that he envied Galland's leadership talent, and his ability to get the best out of subordinates. Yet in his own circle, Goering surrounded himself with toadies and sycophants of total transparency. They gave him poor advice. A realist like Galland, making recommendations based on logic, fact, and experience, usually found Goering's reactions entirely based on politics. His chief political goal was self protection – the maintenance of his position.

Goering's emotions swung back and forth like a weighted cord. He could pass in seconds from friendly interest to abuse and invective, and had done so since childhood. Drugs amplified this trait, causing clouding of his superb intelligence. News of heavy aircraft losses could make him weep openly, yet he would persist in the unwise stratagems that caused numerous combat deaths.

Goering was cultivated with an appreciation of fine art and a taste for elegant living, yet he associated politically with members of the Nazi hierarchy whose grossness revolted him. Goering was one of the most ruthless men in the most ruthless state of modern times, but he loved and protected animals and wild life. He was a conservationist of the first rank, a practical yet visionary ecologist many decades before that word ever became fashionable. The steps he took to protect German wildlife and forests showed both foresight and insight, and were an enduring legacy to his people.

Goering was happily married. After his great love Karin passed away, he found marital peace with his second wife, Emmy, and he was a loving and tender father. He sent many men to their deaths, and yet insisted on the chivalrous treatment of captured enemy flyers. His lifestyle was supported by many sources, including clandestine payoffs from industrialists seeking his influence and favor. Fully awake to the spiritual magic of great paintings and art, still he could not resist the corrupt impulses that drove him to plunder such works for his own collection.

Goering on social occasions was a man of great charm and charisma, and a lavish host. He could rise to towering rages and bellow threats to Galland, and afterward in cooler days he would apologize humbly for his conduct. From this brief but realistic overview of Goering, his forcefulness will be seen as permeating all his errors and as the character trait that produced his grossest mistakes. Goering was something much more than the posturing clown whose portrait propaganda has left in the world.

JG 26 RITTERKREUZ AWARDEES
Gerhard Schöpfel, Adolf Galland and Joachim Müncheberg were awarded the Knights Cross in August and September of 1940, the first for JG 26. Schöpfel scored a total of 40 victories by war's end Galland 103, and Müncheberg 135.

When Galland's most important promotions were thrust on him by this complex and difficult man, Goering was old enough to be his father. To the Supreme Commander's high military rank was added his vast life experience, his maturity, and his status in the German state. All these things could overawe almost any young Luftwaffe officer. Against this lumbering bull in a technological china shop, Galland had only his intelligence, ability, experience, and integrity. Clash between them was inevitable, given Galland's resolve never to lick the Reich Marshal's boots, or meet him on any other ground than that of intellectual logic.

NINE

Miscalculation

The young Gruppenkommandeur in the Pas de Calais had no inkling in the summer of 1940 of the pressures building up at high levels in Germany's armed forces. Galland was confident, superbly trained, and determined to do his best against the RAF. His combat experience and demonstrated competence united III/JG 26 behind him as one of the finest operational fighter units in the world. They were ready. That was not true elsewhere.

When Hitler on 16 July 1940 ordered his armed services chiefs to prepare for the invasion of Britain, the three high commands had little of the unity of purpose found in Luftwaffe fighter Gruppen. The Army immediately demanded sufficient shipping space of the Navy to transport troops, weapons, and supplies across the English Channel. The Navy demanded Luftwaffe air cover for the assembly of the invasion fleet in the Channel ports, and an air umbrella for the invasion itself.

The earliest date the Navy could agree to for the invasion, code-named Sealion, was mid-September. That set the time frame for all else. Air superiority was the central hinge upon which Sealion would turn, and air superiority was established by fighter aircraft. The Royal Navy could only be sunk or driven out of the invasion area by air action, since the German Navy was not strong enough on the surface or with U-boats for this task. Such air action required air superiority as basic protection for German bombers. If the Royal Navy could not be driven away from the invasion scene, certain death would await the German Army in transit.

If an invasion force were landed successfully, air superiority would have to be maintained over the beaches. Without this umbrella, German reinforcements and supplies would be halted by British air action. Germany's elite parachute regiments and other airborne forces might well wreak havoc if landed at strategic points in Britain, but they could not be delivered to such points through skies alive with Spitfires and Hurricanes. The air thus emerged as the dominant and decisive element. The Army and Navy found themselves dependent upon the Luftwaffe – the newest and least understood service branch – in forging strategy for a high-risk amphibious operation.

Germany's able planners were sobered by the magnitude and hazards of Sealion. Lack of professional enthusiasm for the operation followed. Hitler had personally ordered that Sealion was to proceed, although his main hope at that time was to force Britain into peace talks. This was not communicated to the planners, of course. Fear of Hitler's wrath drove professional pessimism underground, whence it emerged in the form of inordinate demands made by the services on each other. Resources and capabilities were pushed beyond their limits by these demands.

Three strategic missions for the Luftwaffe came out of Sealion planning. All three missions depended upon the Fighter Arm:

1. Britain had to be air blockaded in cooperation with the Navy, through attacks on shipping and ports. Such attacks required fighter protection.
2. Air superiority had to be won over southeastern England, to secure invasion areas against British air attack. Fighter Command had to be mastered in its own airspace.
3. Aerial bombardment of British targets by the Bomber Arm. Fighter escort and fighter protection were essential to such attacks.

This was a tall order for the Luftwaffe. Primacy had also come to the Fighter Arm, a status unforeseen by the Luftwaffe High Command. Given the strictly tactical structure of the Luftwaffe, enormous luck and substantial enemy errors would be necessary for successful discharge of its threefold Sealion mission.

Apprehensions over Sealion surfaced in high conferences. Well-founded professional misgivings made little impression on Goering. He was out to please his hero. Goering therefore assumed the responsibility for subduing Britain "with my

Luftwaffe." Such total air war had been theorized by Douhet, embraced and touted by air power visionaries, and debated in war colleges. Never yet had it been seen in the real world.

Goering's penchant for exaggeration was a dangerous trait to have running amok in highly technical matters. The Reich Marshal committed the Luftwaffe to a truly immense operational task, motivated by a desire to please Hitler and consolidate his own status. Goering would soon have cause to regret this precipitate offering of his bright weapon.

Only five days after issuing his Directive 16 for Sealion, Hitler told Field Marshal Walther von Brauchitsch, C.-in-C. of the Army, to make immediate plans for invasion of the Soviet Union. This dampened Goering's enthusiasm for Directive 17, issued on 1 August 1940, calling for unrestricted air-sea warfare against Britain. Hitler wanted to see what the Luftwaffe could do to make feasible the tentative mid-September invasion of England – the technical feasibility of which the Fuehrer increasingly doubted.

Hitler's emotional commitment was to the conquest of Bolshevist Russia. England could be dealt with later. Luftwaffe forces required for invasion of the Soviet Union would soon be removed from the West. Goering was meanwhile authorized to try and conquer the RAF. The Fat One was therefore under extreme pressure. Hitler was keeping his options open at Luftwaffe expense.

The largest aerial assault in history up to that time was to go westward, simultaneously with preparations for a land invasion of unprecedented scope – in the opposite direction. Hitler and Goering were involving Germany in a two front war, and Goering was opposed to the attack on Russia. This was all beyond the ken of young Major Galland in August of 1940. Like all other Luftwaffe pilots, he was completely unaware that Goering and Hitler were pointed in opposite directions.

Galland's unit was part of Air Fleet 2, commanded by Field Marshal Albert Kesselring from his HQ in Brussels. Only these fighter aircraft, based in the Pas de Calais, could reach London and operate for 10 minutes before returning to their bases. Fighter units under Air Fleet 3, commanded by Field Marshal Hugo Sperrle in Paris, were on a shorter leash. From bases around Le Havre, they could make it only to the southern outskirts of London.

Jettisonable auxiliary fuel tanks were not available for the Me 109 at this time. They had been proposed to the Technical Office, but not acted upon with sufficient energy or dispatch. Such tanks had been successfully improvised by the Condor legion in Spain, and their feasibility had been firmly established on the Curtiss Hawk fighter in 1933. The Me 109 needed another 100 miles of range. This deficiency would bedevil Galland and the rest of the Fighter Arm in their life-and-death struggle with the RAF.

A third Luftwaffe strike force against England was Colonel-General Stumpff's Air Fleet 5, based in Norway and Denmark. Bombers of this force were to make outflanking attacks on northeastern Britain. Their long approach across the North Sea precluded Me 109 escort. Only the slower and less maneuverable twin-engined Me 110 could cross with Stumpff's bombers. The Luftwaffe High Command intended through such attacks to increase the pressure on RAF Fighter Command. Thanks to Ultra intercepts, Air Chief Marshal Dowding of Fighter Command knew of these German plans. He took steps to counter Stumpff's force.

GALLAND AND VON SCHLEICH
Meeting at Wissant in the Pas de Calais Major Adolf Galland and Major General Eduard Ritter von Schleich discussed serious business over breakfast in 1941. Von Schleich was a World War I ace.

Luftwaffe fighter pilots in 1940 were operating without any fighter control system. German radar lagged technically far behind the British. For the struggle in English skies radar control of Luftwaffe fighters was nonexistent. In the battle's first phase, when the Luftwaffe attacked English Channel shipping, the absence of such control was not felt. German pilots were not accustomed to such aid from the ground. Airborne formation leaders controlled operations. That is the way things were when Luftwaffe fighters began sweeping over the English Channel and the southeastern English coast from 24 July 1940 onward. Nearly sixty years after these events, it is easy to see how lack of adequate fighter control seriously disadvantaged the Luftwaffe fighter pilots.

Leading his Gruppe over English territory, Galland took part in this first effort to get RAF Fighter Command up into mass combat. The RAF rose to the challenge with its Hurricanes and Spitfires, making good interceptions through their fighter control system. Unfortunately for the RAF, their obsolescent three-fighter Vics were tactically eclipsed by the modern, finger-four Luftwaffe formations developed by Moelders in Spain. When the British operated in squadrons in tight formation, they could be spotted at great distances. The advantages of their fighter control system were thereby partially neutralized. Loose and widely strung out, the German formations were harder to see. Their staggered altitudes were a lesson to the RAF in the value of dispersal in sweep operations. British fighters waiting on the perch to bounce their incoming foes would sometimes be taken from behind by Galland's unob-

SPORTSMAN ADOLF GALLAND
Right: One of Galland's favorite pastimes was hunting game birds. This photo taken in France during the late winter of 1940.

1940 - GALLAND SHOOTING SKEET
Far right: During moments of quiet on the Channel Front, Galland spent a lot of time on the skeet range or hunting birds. Note the spent cartridge being ejected from his shotgun.

served formation, because they had been spotted far away. This occurred despite British radar. Galland found the Hurricane well outclassed by his Me 109. Spitfires of that period were marginally slower than the Me 109, but compensated for that with superior maneuverability. The Me 109's fuel injection pumps had an edge over the Merlin-powered RAF fighters, whose carburetors tended to produce engine misfiring during negative-G combat maneuvers. The Luftwaffe had first class armament and ammunition that Galland felt were superior to those then in use by the RAF.

After about three weeks of combat, in which the RAF suffered heavier losses than the Luftwaffe, the British slowly switched to German-style formations. The RAF also rapidly adapted their tactics to the new realities. British fighters made precise interceptions through their early warning and fighter control systems. The integrated chain of radar stations along the southeastern coast of England detected Galland and his Gruppe shortly after their Pas de Calais takeoff. Once the Germans climbed to 2,000 meters, they were on the RAF plot.

Radar sets electronically determined course, altitude, and speed of the raiders. These data were put on the central plot at Fighter Command in Stanmore. Such a comprehensive radar system permitted substantial economies, as well as precision in the commitment of RAF fighters. Radar information was supplemented with the visual reports of the Ground Observer Corps. The existence of such a sophisticated, well-integrated system gave the Luftwaffe High Command a nasty jolt, since it soon became obvious to the Germans that they were making dispositions and decisions based on faulty intelligence.

Major Josef "Beppo" Schmid, the Luftwaffe High Command's Chief Intelligence Officer, had drawn up a study entitled "Comparative Survey of RAF and Luftwaffe Striking Power" on 16 July 1940 – the day Hitler ordered Sealion. This study contained no mention of long distance radio detection and ranging, and what it might mean to diminish Luftwaffe striking power. Schmid made other gross errors that were fed to Luftwaffe commanders via this study.

RAF fighter strength was overestimated by thirty percent. British aircraft production and repair capabilities were seriously underestimated. These erroneous appraisals became a fount of subsequent German miscalculations. The German High Command went through the Battle of Britain without any accurate information about the status of RAF Fighter Command or the true results of their own operations.

Using Ultra decrypts and other intelligence, the British captured more than twenty German agents dispatched to Britain by various means in the summer and autumn of 1940. These spies were either imprisoned, or "bent" into double agents and used to feed disinformation to the Germans. The Luftwaffe thus went through the entire battle minus any worthwhile spies on enemy ground. The Luftwaffe attitude toward intelligence, furthermore, remains one of its more notorious failures.

Goering had a typical politician's talent for ignoring unwelcome or politically distasteful facts. This spirit spread downwards. Notably infected was General Hans Jeschonnek, Chief of the Luftwaffe General Staff, among others. Galland would in due course encounter incredible examples of the way in which crucial information could be ignored, shunted aside, or papered over if it ran counter to Goering's own politically-based ideas. Goering dealt with adverse factual information by ordering that it did not exist.

Air Chief Marshal Sir Hugh Dowding at Stanmore, meanwhile, was receiving priceless information from the Ultra decrypting teams at Bletchley Park. Immense skill and intellect went into the decrypts received by Dowding. The elaborate electromechanical decrypting was in itself a nightmare of complexity, but thereafter, translations, analyses, and assessments had to be made of the decrypts. There was not always a lot of material available, but what reached Dowding had high value because he knew how to use the information.

Almost from day to day Dowding knew Luftwaffe intentions. He knew in advance the changes in strategy that Goering, Kesselring, and Sperrle were about to make. Information on the status of the Air Fleets across the Channel was sufficient to enable Dowding to orchestrate RAF fighter operations with consummate skill and subtlety. He husbanded his precious Spitfires and Hurricanes and his even more precious pilots – the latter his Achilles heel in the battle. Dowding had more factual information about the course of the Battle of Britain than all the German commanders facing him combined. He also had the training, mentality, experience, and judgment to interpret these facts correctly.

Dowding's career had started as a combat pilot with the RFC in World War I. He rose in the service in a varied career always close to fighters. The British were acutely conscious of their need for a strong fighter defense. Zeppelins and the German Gotha bombers of the first war had driven this lesson home. The secondary, limited role assigned to fighters in the Luftwaffe was something that Dowding did not have to struggle against, as Galland would have to do in Germany almost to the end of the war.

Between 1930 and 1936, Dowding was responsible with others for the development and acceptance of all-metal, 8-gun, monoplane fighters in the RAF. When he became A.O.C. Fighter Command in 1936, Dowding was intimately involved in the subsequent development of the British early warning radar system. He had been present at Dr. Robert Watson-Watt's first tests of radiolocation, as radar was initially called. Integration of this revolutionary development with Fighter Command control took place under Dowding.

What came as a shock to Dowding's opponents across the Channel was long since woven into his mental fabric and incorporated into his management of events in 1940. The Germans had nothing to match Dowding's organic understanding of the complex weaponry involved in defending Britain. When the Ultra information was added to this, Dowding became the ultimate air general in 1940. His brave pilots, upon whom all would depend, had the best man in Britain to lead them.

Hermann Goering, by contrast, was probably the most incompetent battle commander the Luftwaffe could have had at the most important moment in its existence. He had been disconnected from aviation technically since World War I. Although he had no background for the exacting responsibilities of high command, that did not stop him from shoving professionals aside and taking over personally.

None of these factors was even remotely in the mind of Adolf Galland during these hectic summer weeks. The battle simply came at him over the cowling of his Me 109 in a blazing maelstrom of kill-or-be-killed aloft. Strategy and military principles weren't considered. Leading III/JG 26 on up to four sweeps a day over southeastern England put him to his limit. The strain was almost as lethal as the RAF, pushing the German pilots and their aircraft to the ragged end of their endurance.

As a Gruppenkommandeur, Galland was haunted by many anxieties other than the taxing presence of imminent combat. Newer and less able pilots had to be watched over, and if possible, guided through to expertise. Always there was the damned "English Channel" chewing up their fuel as they commuted to their few minutes of combat over or near England.

After combat, the leaden waters awaited them if they were shot up or ran out of fuel on the way back to France. Victories over the RAF were soured when they went into the drink themselves, although unwounded and with their fighters fully operational. The RAF sent Spitfires to finish off cripples and stragglers. At Udet's initiative, an air-sea rescue service was set up to save pilots from the sea, and buoys with survival gear were used by both sides. The Germans also set up "reception" operations, in which fresh Me 109s would fly out over the Channel to protect fighters and bombers returning to France.

Galland's own fighting spirit remained undiminished in spite of the cares of a Gruppenkommandeur. His wingmen could hardly stay with him as hurled himself on the RAF. His old and finely honed aerobatic skills and his marksmanship proved invaluable. In the absence of radar, so did his hunter's nose. He found continuous combat success. Field Marshal Kesselring pinned the Knight's Cross to the Iron Cross on him at a field investiture in the Pas de Calais on 1 August 1940.

His fame as a fighter ace and combat leader was spreading. Magazines and newspapers began publishing articles on him and publishing photographs – including a profile that vividly illustrated his bent nose. The Galland legend was taking form. The Germans needed success in the Battle of Britain, and their top-scoring fighter pilots epitomized success. They were the most dazzling feature on the German side, amid the many frustrations inflicted by the RAF. Galland's friend Moelders was still the Luftwaffe's top scorer, but Galland, Helmut Wieck, and Wilhelm Balthasar were likely to overtake him if Moelders had to take a few weeks off for any reason. Rivalry was intense among these friends.

CAPT. HERMANN-FRIEDRICH JOPPIEN
Joppien, flying as Kommandeur of I/JG 51, shot down 25 British airplanes during the Battle of Britain. He was the 5th Luftwaffe ace to score 40 victories. This photo taken 16 September 1940. He was killed in action in Russia on 25 August 1941 after scoring his 70th victory.

Dowding remained undeceived by German efforts to lure his fighters into massive battle with the Luftwaffe. A trait of fighter pilots all over the world is aggressiveness. They want to hurl themselves on an enemy aircraft as though their own lives depend on clawing the enemy machine down immediately. Dowding knew this, as an old fighter pilot himself. Commanders of large fighter forces cannot always afford to indulge this aggressive practice. Dowding had Britain's fate in his hands.

Knowing through Ultra the size and scope of the bombing attacks to be launched by the enemy Air Fleets, Dowding practiced artistic restraint in using his fighters. Fighter sweeps by the Luftwaffe, or small decoy flights of a few bombers on isolated targets, could not seriously injure Britain. If Dowding rose to every challenge, however, his fighters would be frittered away. England would be naked before the Luftwaffe Bomber Arm.

During the weeks of provocative German fighter sweeps over England, Stukas and Ju 88 bombers attacked shipping in the Thames estuary and off the English coast. Fierce fighter battles developed around these operations. Casualties among the Stukas were fearful. Escorting them was a nerve-wracking task, because the loaded dive bombers had a top speed of around 250 mph. With an approach altitude varying between 10,000 and 15,000 feet, down in denser air the Stukas drew the Me 109s out of their best element and into increased vulnerability to the controlled RAF interceptions. Stukas pulling up out of their dives were easy targets for the aggressive RAF fighter pilots.

Pilots of the much-vaunted Stukas had been largely drawn from the Fighter Arm before the war, in one of the numerous raids made by the High Command on fighter pilot personnel. They were among the best-trained flyers in the Luftwaffe. Irreplaceable now, they went down in dozens over England in a futile sacrifice that made Galland blanch. He knew many of them personally. He did not like seeing them massacred.

For the Luftwaffe's numerous dive bomber advocates in high rank, the Stuka slaughter over Britain was a stunning setback. The Stuka survived to serve with distinction in close support of the German Army everywhere, but it did not belong in skies haunted by 8-gun British fighters. Unacceptable losses of Stukas and crews forced their final withdrawal from the Battle of Britain by mid-September.

The RAF continued to come up for battle, never in large wings but always enough to give trouble. They made operations expensive for the Luftwaffe, and held their own casualties within tolerable limits. Flying two, three, and sometimes four sweeps or escorts a day, Galland felt the mounting inroads on his own reserves of energy and morale. Individual successes by his Gruppe against RAF fighters continued as the only ray of light in a darkening situation. By switching stratagems and continually failing to lure the RAF into a fighter battle of annihilation, the Luftwaffe High Command was slowly eroding the confidence of its own pilots. Competent top leadership is essential to fighting spirit. No matter what the Luftwaffe High Command tried, RAF fighters just kept coming up in potent little packets, and they chipped away steadily at both Luftwaffe aircraft and pilot morale.

GALLAND IN CARICATURE
Rudolf Blank of Dinkelsbuhl, Germany furnished us this sketch of Galland in the cockpit by artist Wolfgang Willrich.

Bad weather gave occasional respite from the grind. Relief from battle tension acted on Galland like a tonic. His vitality would rebound. Fortified by extra sleep, he would take his shotgun and go hunting, bringing back pheasants and hares for the pot. Quarters were comfortable, usually in a pleasant country home that had been commandeered. Fresh food was plentiful, and so was good French wine.

He tried during these weather breaks to forget the war. Writing letters to the families of his dead pilots precluded that – and it was a depressing task. An optimistic weather forecast might mean operations on the morrow. That would mean more letters to write and new gaps at the mess table. Galland felt every loss personally.

Galland was strongly critical of himself and his own leadership, taking himself to task and analyzing every operation for mistakes and oversights. The system of escorting and protecting bombers was highly imperfect, and further complicated by the twin-engined Me 110 fighter. Despite its greater range

HUNTERS THREE
Colonel Huth was a fighter pilot in WWI. Lt. Erbo Graf von Kageneck (67 victories) and Captain Joachim Müncheberg enjoy a brief respite from the war by hunting pheasant.

1940 ON THE CHANNEL FRONT
Reich Marshal Hermann Göring, with his private train in the background, listens to Adolf Galland, Kommodore of JG 26, and Werner Mölders, Kommodore of JG 51.

and heavier firepower, the Me 110 needed fighter escort itself. The much-vaunted Destroyer could not fulfill its designed mission of protecting the bombers at longer ranges.

Procedures were set up in Galland's Gruppe under which an element leader who lost a wingman, or vice versa, had to report on why their comrade was lost. The young Gruppenkommandeur made a searching analysis of each such report. He hunted down inadequacies and omissions within his own Gruppe with the same determination as he hunted the RAF.

Goering and other high Luftwaffe personages, accustomed to quick and dazzling success, were upset by the RAF's continuing resilience. Goering for years had demanded prompt compliance with his orders. People jumped to satisfy his every whim. The RAF was frustrating his wishes. Goering's irrational character traits caused him to project on to others his own failures as Luftwaffe Supreme Commander. He reacted to the frustrating situation over England by reproaching his warriors.

When the first recriminatory teletype was put in front of the nearly exhausted Galland, the tension of battle still shaking him, his reaction was incredulous rage. He was doing his utmost. *Gott im Himmel!* The Reich Marshal could not possibly mean what he was saying. Further similar teletypes erased all doubt. Goering was laying blame. After scores of sorties over the damned Channel, one milling air battle after another – with the RAF always in the right attack position – Galland was being reproached. Worse than that, the courage of his pilots was being impugned.

Goering's actions made no sense to the battle-weary young Gruppenkommandeur. Orders then came through to attend a war conference at Karinhall, Goering's country estate northeast of Berlin. Good. Perhaps he would have the opportunity to explain to the Reich Marshal, in person, exactly what the Fighter Arm was up against. Galland knew that somewhere there had been a serious miscalculation.

TEN

Eagle Day – And After

Flying back to Berlin, Galland pondered while airborne the problems of the ongoing battle. He recognized that he could not see the whole picture, commanding less than 40 fighters in daily operations. He nevertheless grasped intuitively that this mighty air battle was pivotal and must not be lost. Everything had come to depend on the Luftwaffe fighter pilots for a German victory. The High Command had not foreseen that development. Nearly two weeks previously, the battle to subdue RAF Fighter Command had been activated on 8 August 1940 as "Eagle Day" (*Adler Tag*). Bad weather forced delays, but by 12 August Kesselring and Sperrle were putting 300 aircraft into the air. RAF forward airfields like Manston, Hawkinge, and Lympne were being hammered in a crescendo of strikes. German operations on 12, 13, and 14 August were not the real Eagle Day. From Ultra decrypts, Air Chief Marshal Dowding knew that 15 August 1940 would be Goering's maximum effort thus far to conquer Fighter Command.

Goering's plans and intentions were completely known to Dowding through Ultra intercepts. The British commander once more was compelled to orchestrate his response carefully, avoiding premature over-commitment. Goering planned staggered strikes against airfields and radar installations in southern England. This ruse would make the attacks seem to come from all directions. Goering intended to hammer at Fighter Command not only in the air, and through its airfields, but also through its morale. Goering's main goal was to goad the RAF fighters up in force so that they could be destroyed by the superior weight and tactics of the Luftwaffe.

Heavy pressure in the south of England would also draw down into the battle fighter units guarding northeastern Britain. Stumpff's bombers from Norway and Denmark, with their Me 110 escort, would come hurtling in to assault an undefended northeast coast. These blows would create additional strain on Fighter Command and help break its spirit. This was the plan for Goering's Eagle Day. Over 1,700 sorties would be flown by the Luftwaffe.

Sound in principle, the plan's defect was that it was known to Dowding. He turned Eagle Day into a Luftwaffe debacle by continuing his masterly handling of his fighters. 75 German aircraft were downed, for the loss of 34 RAF fighters. Goering's losses were neither irreparable, nor out of proportion to his goal. The Luftwaffe reverse was nevertheless unexpected, hurt Goering's pride, and gave the British a propaganda binge with their ecstatic overclaims of downings. British claims went as high as 182 aircraft.

Despite intense pressure on the RAF over southeastern England, Dowding did not strip the northeast coast of fighters. Ultra decrypts gave precise information on General Stumpff's Eagle Day bomber strikes. This advance information, in combination with radar, resulted in RAF fighters meeting their 100 uninvited visitors well out over the open sea. The British claimed 15 aircraft downed from this first formation. A second wave of 50 German aircraft was also roughly handled, with the RAF claiming 8 downings for no losses of their own. Stumpff's Air Fleet contributed only casualties to Eagle Day.

Galland had been flying with his Gruppe in the August battles before, during, and after Eagle Day. He had seen how Goering's fighter escort policy had played into the hands of the RAF. The German fighter pilots in their majority were forbidden to wade into the RAF as they came up, but were required under strict orders to stay close to the bombers.

Galland had found it bitterly frustrating to wait while he could see RAF fighters positioning themselves for attacks on the bombers he was escorting. Experience had already proven repeatedly in this war that attack by a fighter was its best defense. Going at the enemy hard and fast seized the psychological as well as the tactical initiative. *Waiting to be attacked* was the absolute negation of the purpose and mission of a fighter pilot. The strict close escort order led to heavy Luftwaffe losses – both bombers and fighters.

This third phase of the Battle of Britain struck Galland as basically unsound in concept. He had an acumen for what was effective against the enemy. Bombers may have been punching lines of craters in the turf at Manston in the morning, but when the Germans returned in the afternoon, the British had filled the craters. The fighters had been able to take off. The bombers would punch more holes in the turf. The aerodromes and buildings were obviously being battered, but the undeniable reality was that the RAF fighters were still operating.

Amid the hot combat, Galland tried to keep a cool perspective. The airfields were being hit, but most British aircraft on the ground were cunningly parked behind high banks and revetments. Designed to frustrate strafing runs and minimize splinter and blast damage, these shelters protected against anything except a direct hit. There were more airfields farther inland. The RAF could move to those. That would make it harder still for Galland and his pilots, cursed by their short fuel leash, to tangle with their foes.

The Luftwaffe fighters were flying escort missions of four kinds:

1. Direct escort.
2. Indirect or deployed escort.
3. Freelance patrols, coordinated timewise with and ahead of the fighter protected bomber stream.
4. Supplementary escorts, to pick up and cover returning bombers and to protect air-sea rescue.

Direct escort missions involved squadrons split up into flights of two or four aircraft, providing direct cover for the bombers. They used their superior speed to weave in zig-zag fashion around and among the bombers. This purely defensive mission was disliked by the German fighter pilots and was rarely effective against attacking RAF fighters. The Germans were robbed in these missions of the high-speed aggressive role – a serious drawback. Bomber crews favored such direct escort, which was reassuring to them in their near-defenseless state, and insisted that they be maintained.

Indirect or deployed escort missions were carried out in squadron strength at a higher altitude than the direct escort. The deployed escort flew in the general direction of anticipated British attacks. Their task was to jump RAF fighters before the latter could attack the bombers. The deployed escort remained in visual contact with the bomber force it was protecting. This meant that in actual operations, these escorts could only engage in one combat before re-forming and continuing the escort mission. Neutralization of imminent fighter attacks was the main object of this type of escort mission.

Freelance fighter patrols were sent ahead into areas through which the following bomber and escort forces would fly, and also over the target itself. Flying on the approximate course of the bombers, but on that side from which RAF attacks were anticipated, freelance patrols were carried out in squadron or Gruppe strength. Out of visual contact with the bombers, they were to seek out RAF fighters and shoot them down, fighting the way clear for the bombers. German fighter pilots preferred freelance patrols to all other escort work.

SCORING RACE: MÖLDERS vs. GALLAND
Gen. Ernst Udet liked to doodle on scrap paper during meetings with Hitler and Göring. He drew this one showing Mölders and Galland with Spitfires and Hurricanes lined up like Pheasant trophies.

"FOR HE'S A JOLLY GOOD FELLOW..."
Galland, having just scored his 40th victory, is welcomed back to base by members of JG 26 with a victory song and "Hussassa!" It was 25 September 1940.

After a mission, the freelance patrols were the rearguards. Dowding largely frustrated the freelance patrols by not rising to meet every fighter sweep. When RAF fighters were scrambled, they had to gather and climb up, at which time the Me 109s would press their attacks.

The supplementary escort missions were also carried out in squadron or Gruppe strength. Their task was to counter the inevitable dispersal of the original formation of bombers and fighters after reaching their objective and after aerial battles. Supplementary escorts took station on damaged bombers limping home, and usually met the returning main formation over the English coast between Manston and Dungeness. These escorts made it hazardous for British fighters to operate beyond mid-Channel.

Luftwaffe bombers and fighters made their rendezvous near the fighter airfields, usually over a prominent coastal landmark, at predetermined times and altitudes. Galland observed how frequently late-arriving bombers attached themselves to fighter escorts other than their assigned ones. Following bomber formations found themselves often with no escort. They had to face the RAF that way or abort the mission.

Incompatibility between bomber and fighter R/T equipment made it impossible for them to cooperate through air-to-air communication. Relays through ground stations were used between bombers and fighters, but it was a clumsy and inefficient arrangement. RAF communications were markedly superior. Special tactical rules or uniformities in planning were non-existent in the Luftwaffe at this time for the task at hand. Each fighter Geschwader discharged its missions as it thought best. Wide disparities in performance were the result.

Galland chafed under these deficiencies and shortcomings in the escort "system" – if it could be dignified by that word – and especially at the way advantage in attack was usually passed to the RAF. The young Major recalled ruefully that in peacetime they had carried out innumerable exercises and maneuvers, but never had they practiced missions escorting bombers. The High Command had assumed for years that Germany's fast new bombers would not need fighter escort.

The excessively passive escort system that had now spuriously evolved also allowed escaping RAF fighters a head start after their attacks on the bombers. Hindsight decades later makes obvious the critical error of rigorously restricting most German fighters to close bomber escort in this August period. Goering's obstinacy in this respect tipped the battle balance away from the Luftwaffe. Galland had seen the dynamic essentials of the problem from the middle of the maelstrom. He was eager for the chance now imminent to tell Goering personally the facts of the escort situation. The young pilot landed in Berlin with his thoughts well organized, but with his body still tense from the strain of battle.

The civilian scene in Berlin was shockingly unreal. A flying soldier only hours from mortal combat, Galland gaped at carefree crowds splashing money around as though it were carnival time. Movies, nightclubs, and theaters were packed, with long queues of waiting pleasure seekers jostling for sidewalk space. Every bar was jumping with people. Music and laughter rippled everywhere. The deadly struggle he had just left was as remote as the moon to these crowds. The Berlin scene left him depressed.

Whisked by staff car to Karinhall, Goering's estate on the Schorfheide northeast of Berlin, the woodsman lurking inside the young fighter ace reveled in the rural panoramas unfolding beside the speeding Mercedes. This was the Germany he loved. Then it was another dose of unreality – Karinhall.

A feudal monarch could not have dwelled in a more imposing forest stronghold. Reeded buildings surrounded an immense courtyard. Lily ponds, garden beds, and a statue of a nude hunter sighting his bow from horseback dominated the exterior. Inside the main hall, mighty oak beams soared overhead. Pine-lined walls were hung with stagheads, and bearskin rugs lay about the floor. Almost the whole width of the room at one end was filled by a massive stone fireplace. As a hunter Galland could admire Karinhall. As a fighter leader, he could not help reflecting on how far all this was from the English Channel, and the problems there needing urgent solution.

CAPTAIN KIENZLE AND THE BOSS
Visibly tired after a harrowing mission, Galland and Kienzle debrief while toasting their success with a glass of wine.

DEBRIEFING AFTER A BATTLE
Galland, wearing the RAF winter flying suit, talks with Lt. Eberhard Henrici. Looking on at left is Gallands crew chief Gerhard Meyer.

GALLAND, CIGAR AND MICKEY MOUSE.
The personality of the Fighter General is apparent in this photo. He wears an captured wool-lined flying suit found in a one-time RAF Resupply Depot at St. Pol France.

Colonels and generals present for the conference were optimistic and confident. Major Galland felt a certain shrinkage in his own concerns in the presence of such high-level confidence. These officers had unfortunately formed their opinions on the ground. They had not experienced the resilience and skill of the RAF, or the way the British fighters just kept coming up.

Senior officers listened attentively and made suggestions. Their aides made notes. There was soldierly concern, but between the fighting pilots and their higher commanders there was a massive gulf. Galland was concerned that the operational problems of escorting bombers were not comprehended by the higher commanders or by the Luftwaffe General Staff officers present.

Goering was initially at his paternal best. Werner Moelders had also been ordered to attend this conference. Now the two rivals were taken aside by their Supreme Commander, and an animated discussion ensued. Galland and Moelders between them gave Goering an accurate, up-to-the-minute summation of why Eagle Day and the battle to date had not gone well – from their point of view as fighter pilots and combat leaders.

They explained the operational drawbacks of close escort orders. They described first hand the complex problems of rendezvous, station-keeping, communications, fuel limitations, and flak, which made the close escort system the least effective way to damage the RAF. Free chase of RAF fighters, by contrast, had been highly effective. These downed RAF fighters could not come up again to attack German bombers. Goering listened glumly. He had obviously already made up his mind.

Taking two small leather cases out of his pocket, the Reich Marshal presented Galland and Moelders with the Pilot's Badge in massive Gold, with Diamonds. Goering praised their bravery. The shimmering decorations symbolized Germany's gratitude for their accomplishments.

"You two have done splendidly, *as individuals*," said Goering, "but I am not satisfied with the overall performance of my Fighter Arm. There isn't enough aggressive spirit. *That* is the real reason our escorts are letting the RAF through to shoot down our bombers. Our fighters must show more willingness to fling themselves on the enemy, just as we did in the first war."

"WHAT? NO VICTORY?"
Günther Lützow chides Werner Moelders after returning from a fruitless sortie. "Papi" Causin laughs while the armament chief stands on the Me 109 wing.

Practical operational problems of crucial importance were thus avoided. In Goering's eyes, Eagle Day had failed because of the fighter pilots. When Galland and Moelders began responding to this slur, Goering curtly held up his hand.

"I'm going to revive the aggressive spirit of my Fighter Arm, no matter what steps I have to take," he said. "First step is to make both of you a Kommodore – give each of you a full Geschwader to command. I'm getting rid of all the older pilots. You young and successful ones are going up to command. Moelders, you will now command JG 51. Galland, you take over JG 26 right away – as soon as you get back to the coast."

Galland objected immediately to this promotion.

"If I am a Kommodore," he said, ''I will be stuck on the ground. I won't see the action I am seeing now."

"Don't worry about that," said Goering. "My new regulations are that each Geschwader must be led in the air by its Kommodore. He must be the most successful pilot. We've got to get some spirit into these fighter pilots somehow. Putting young men quickly into high rank and full charge hasn't been done before. Some won't be able to handle it. Others will. Now, any request to make before you go back to the front?"

Galland asked to be left in his present Gruppe command. Goering denied this request and stalked out. Galland was going to be a Kommodore, like it or not.

As they sped back to Berlin by car, Galland and Moelders discussed the new arrangements. Moelders disagreed strongly with his friend's wish to remain a Gruppenkommandeur for the sake of more combat action. Moelders sought responsibility, and told Galland that his abilities as a tactician would carry more weight if he were a Kommodore. Moelders met large challenges with ease and confidence. Galland already knew that his rival was an excellent organizer. Moelders would take larger responsibilities in his stride.

Galland by contrast was a hunter and fighter above all else. His hatred of desks and paperwork, and the personal paralysis they induced, was implacable. The hunt, the chase, and victory dominated his existence. Conversation swung back to the First World War, when Oswald Boelcke and Manfred von Richthofen were the luminaries of the German Air Service. Boelcke was the master tactician, acting with development of the service uppermost. Von Richthofen was the supreme aerial hunter.

Moelders at this moment was the leading ace, but his aspirations were directed toward the development of the Fighter Arm. Moelders realized that this meant one day surrendering his top scoring spot to Galland or someone else. Galland always wanted to be the best, and now he wanted to be the best fighter pilot and the best Kommodore. Their conversation ranged over these matters.

"As far as I am concerned," said Moelders, with just a touch of indignation, "you can be the Richthofen of the Luftwaffe. I prefer to be someday its Boelcke."

These words of Moelders kept running through Galland's mind as he flew back to the Pas de Calais and his new command. The right elements were available to make him the new Richthofen. RAF fighters were waiting out there over southeast England, dozens of them. His mission was to find them and shoot them down. "Anything else is nonsense," the Red Baron had once said. Galland believed that.

FRIENDS AND RIVALS
Majors Galland and Mölders meet on the veranda at JG 26 HQ in Audembert. Galland often chided Mölders not to be so rigid in his social life.

The young major knew well the Colonel he was replacing in command of JG 26. Gotthardt Handrick was his old Condor Legion comrade and C.O. of J/88. They had enjoyed the good Spanish wine together too often for there to be any hard feelings over Handrick's relief. He was a sportsman of great merit, the Gold Medal pentathlon winner in the 1936 Olympiad. He took his removal from command in a sporting spirit. Handrick was able and experienced, but had not been sufficiently successful in aerial combat to meet Goering's new standards. He had only 10 aerial victories.

Galland immediately began remaking JG 26, putting his own ideas and experience into effect. He set high performance standards for his own Staff Flight, based upon his own eminence in aerial fighting. Handing over III/JG 26 to Gerhard Schoepfel, he moved himself to JG 26 HQ at Audembert. Schoepfel was an ace and an experienced leader. Galland further improved JG 26 leadership by putting Walter Adolph in command of II/JG 26, and Rolf Pingel in command of I/JG 26. Both officers were Condor Legion veterans, and experienced fighter pilots and leaders. Battles ahead would prove the soundness of these appointments.

Galland made it his policy to command every JG 26 operation in the air, except when he was officially absent or wounded. His expectations of excellence were made known throughout the Geschwader. The highest bravery was expected of every pilot. Their C.O. exemplified what he was asking of them. Galland's Staff Flight became a model of efficiency and effectiveness. Where others might send warriors to war before the lash, Galland applied the spiritual magic of example. JG 26 was extremely popular with the Bomber Arm for escort duty, and under its young Kommodore became the premier German fighter unit of the Battle of Britain.

Other units were revived under new leaders. Moelders took over JG 51 from the gallant Major General Theo Osterkamp. JG 51 became unofficially *JG 51 Mölders*. Galland's comrade of Condor Legion days, Captain Guenther Luetzow, was given command of JG 3. There was no finer leader in the Luftwaffe. JG 54 was blessed at this time by the appointment of big, convincing, and popular Captain Hannes Trautloft as its Kommodore. Other appointments further helped each Geschwader with fresh, new-generation leadership.

Galland was promoted Kommodore of JG 26 on 21 August 1940, after the Karinhall conference of the previous two days. Fighter Command at this time had been more seriously battered than the Germans realized. Had the Germans enjoyed comparable intelligence to that provided Dowding by the Ultra decrypts, they would have been encouraged by the toll they were taking of Fighter Command's precious pilots. In the twelve days between 8 and 20 August, 94 RAF pilots had been killed or were missing. A further 60 were wounded. Pilot losses from drowning after ditching offshore forced the British to revamp and reinforce their scattered air-sea rescue efforts. Air Vice-Marshal Park had to take steps to keep his fighter operations within gliding distance of land.

Galland was still getting his replacement pilots, but they were filling the cockpits of irreplaceable experts. Young pilots fresh from training school were green, and that showed in the air. Watching over them was a distraction for experienced pilots. Soon there were too many greenhorns in JG 26, and in all other units, for every green pilot to be protected. Many of them went down before they had survived their running-in period. Then came more green replacements. Galland was sharply aware that JG 26 pilot quality was declining. His Geschwader almost always took heavier pilot casualties than the bombers they were escorting.

Even amid the havoc of this terrible struggle, the traditional humor of the German fighter pilots broke through often enough to keep them all buoyed up. Taking off one morning with his Staff Flight, all four fighters moving out together, Galland was astonished to see his No.4 pilot execute a wild ground loop. This was not hard to do in the Me 109 with its

GOOD DOGGIE!
Adolf Galland and Joachim Müncheberg plus an unidentified friend take time to give some affection to Dolfo's hunting dog.

A FONDNESS FOR HUNTING DOGS
Galland, while on alert duty, spends a few quality moments with his favorite hunting dog. Note the fur-lined flying suit. The cockpit of the 109 was very cold in winter and at high altitudes.

COCKPIT ALERT
Oberst Adolf Galland sits on the canopy rail of his Me 109, ready to go the instant the scramble alarm sounds. He is sharing a joke with one of the "Black Men", the aircraft mechanics.

narrow undercarriage. In seconds the fighter was transformed into a smoldering pile of scrap, as though it had taken a direct hit from a 500-lb bomb. Over the R/T came the Bavarian voice of his No.4, "Adam 1 from Adam 4 – I believe I have a flat tire."

Notoriously talkative when aloft, Luftwaffe fighter pilots found it hard to maintain radio silence. They were young men of high energy and strong spirit. Many fighter pilots of all nations confess to giving themselves pep talks when setting out on a mission. In a formation of 70 fighters from JG 26 one morning, there was such a pilot present, whose microphone was inadvertently left open. In this mode, he could not hear any commands to shut up or get off the air. Galland listened to the Britain-bound pilot's stream-of-consciousness pep talk. "... everything is fine ... still got plenty of fuel ... no Spitfires in the blue, blue sky ... very soon I will be back home ... and in the evening, ho ho, I will need a girl ..."

Then came dirty songs. Galland's barked orders for silence went unheard. The "entertainment," continued until a wall of flak rose in front of them and a gaggle of Spitfires bounced them from superior altitude. Amid the milling battle, Galland could still hear the offending pilot, cursing now between gun bursts and breathing heavily as he hauled his Me 109 around the sky. In a lull in the battle, the offending microphone suddenly went off. A new and different voice came on the air. "Why don't you sing now, you son of a bitch?"

Humor helped both sides amid the high-altitude holocaust. As August rolled toward its end, Galland knew in his warrior's core that this greatest of all air battles would be decided in the next two to three weeks. Beyond that, the spirit might be willing to take off on more operations, but it was likely that the flesh would not obey, be that flesh British or German. All involved were nearing their absolute limit.

ELEVEN

Climax

On 24 August 1940, Goering shifted the main weight of his bombing attacks on to RAF fighter airfields farther inland. This accorded temporary relief to the badly beaten up airfields near the coast, but at a high price. What Goering did not know, due to the inadequacies of German intelligence, was that he was now assaulting the vital sector aerodromes of the RAF. From these electronic nerve centers, British fighters were vectored into tactically best contact with the Luftwaffe. Knocking out British fighter control would have ended the radar-based interceptions that allowed Dowding crucial economy in committing his fighters.

The sector aerodromes now reeled under the thunder of bombs for two grueling weeks. Fighter Command's life was on the line, but the British were helped in their extremity by having additional time for interceptions before the bombers attacked. Galland and his pilots were again near the end of their fuel endurance with the deeper penetrations. Fuel worries added to the strain of ceaseless escort flying. Galland from the air could have a presentiment of the shambles being created by the bombers. He wondered how he would fare with JG 26 if Audembert and his other airfields were being plastered with bombs day after day. Keeping operational would tax all pilots, crews, and facilities.

This was exactly the situation for the RAF now. Main sector aerodromes like Biggin Hill were often reduced to handling a single fighter squadron. Sometimes they were lucky even to manage a squadron. When Goering took personal command of the assault on 30 August 1940, he immediately laid on a series of even more massive strikes. Ultra decrypts warned the British of these monster operations, but these warnings did not halt the rain of explosives that pushed the RAF to desperation. Another two weeks of such blows, and Goering would have Fighter Command on the very brink of defeat.

Dowding's practice of sending worn out squadrons to the northeast for rest and refit, bringing freshened squadrons back to the south of England to replace them, was only good for a limited time. Worn out pilots were soon being replaced by pilots who were not quite so worn out. Fighter Command had sufficient aircraft, but was approaching its human limits. Any able-bodied man in Britain who had flying experience was likely to be training as a fighter pilot. The Luftwaffe was pressing Britain's back to the wall.

Across the Channel, the Germans had their own acute difficulties. Replacement aircraft were down to a trickle. Supply and repair services could not stay abreast of the losses and damage. Ultra decrypts detailed for Dowding the woes of his opponents. The British leader knew better than anyone how narrow the margin had become. A major mistake by either side would tip the balance of the battle irretrievably. Goering was to make that mistake.

On 3 September 1940, while RAF sector aerodromes and fighter control were again being pounded, Goering summoned Kesselring and Sperrle to the Hague for a council of war. The Reich Marshal wanted to turn his bomber fleets on to London, the political and spiritual center of the British Commonwealth and Empire. Pressing his two Air Fleet chiefs hard, Goering wanted to know if the RAF had been badly enough stricken to permit the bombing of London with bearable losses.

Goering's sudden urge to switch strategy and targets had an overriding political dimension. RAF bombers had attacked Berlin at night on 25 and 29 August 1940. Minimal damage was inflicted, but the raids sent Hitler into a fury. Until these Berlin attacks, Hitler had personally ordered, under pain of court martial, that London was not to be bombed. Approximately 10 off-course German bombers on the night of 24 August 1940 had mistakenly bombed London when haze and fog blanketed southeastern England. Prodded by Churchill, the RAF struck at Berlin in reprisal. A mighty nocturnal holocaust, lasting four and a half years, was thereby ignited.

Hitler canceled his restraining order. London was to be wiped out. Goering got the word from the Fuehrer. Eager to please Hitler, and impatient to smash Britain quickly in view of the planned invasion of Russia, Goering passed all this pressure down on to Kesselring and Sperrle. The Reich Marshal's historic question was, could London be bombed without prohibitive losses, and was the RAF now hurt sufficiently to permit the London assault?

The towering, monocled Hugo Sperrle was among the most experienced leaders in the Luftwaffe. Command of the Condor Legion had taught him plenty about tactical air power. In Spain he had shown himself oblivious to personal risk and shrewd in assessing his enemy. He recommended that Goering continue assaulting the RAF airfields, pressing the attack until the weakening of Fighter Command became a collapse.

Kesselring was not as experienced in war command as Sperrle, but he was a former Chief of the Luftwaffe General Staff and an officer of great prestige in the service. Kesselring told Goering that in his view London could be attacked without excessive losses. In Kesselring's opinion, RAF forward airfields were expendable. Enemy fighters could be moved to bases on the far side of London. He argued that only by going for the heart of Britain could they provoke RAF fighters up in force and thus destroy them. Sperrle strongly disagreed.

Like all men of action, Goering's career abounded with mistakes, but his biggest was deciding to attack London. He sent a teletype to Kesselring on 5 September 1940, ordering a raid on the London docks with full fighter escort. The Ultra decrypting teams delivered this key message to Dowding almost as quickly as it reached its official addressee. The hard-pressed head of Fighter Command saw in it the deliverance of his battered sector aerodromes and their vital fighter control facilities.

Blasted and reeling, they were operating marginally with improvised hookups from emergency quarters. Another dozen big raids would have done them in, and the history of the world altered. Now the fourth phase of the Battle of Britain was beginning, with the removal of this lethal and direct pressure from Fighter Command. The Londoners were going to catch hell, but Fighter Command would be able to come back from the brink.

Across the Channel in the Pas de Calais, the black-maned Galland pondered the problems of escorting bombers over London. His fighters would have no more than ten minutes for combat before turning back to base. This meant that the entire force, bombers and fighters, would have to fly in a straight line from the French coast to London and then straight back. This unvarying approach route made interception even easier for the RAF. The Luftwaffe was also aware that British radar was now picking up German formations as they assembled over France. Bombers and fighters would now have to mass during the climb, en route to the target.

Just before the big bomber assault on London, the strategic error that was to cost him victory, Goering came up to the French coast to put some more fire into his fighter leaders. Galland and Moelders again stood facing an abrasive and reproachful Reich Marshal. "Fighting spirit" was lacking in the Fighter Arm, where it should be greatest, according to Goering. They were supposed to be *fighters*. Railing against his fighter pilots, Goering stalked up and down with his Marshal's baton poking, waving, digging home his vilifications against the brave men Galland and Moelders were leading.

The new Kommodore of JG 26 stood seething with rage. In his soldier's mind, he saw the struggle not only in terms of strategy, tactics, and technical deficiencies, but also in terms of the men he had led and lost. As unjustified allegations of cowardice poured out of Goering, Galland's mind swept over the shoals of letters he had written to the families of his fallen

THE FOCKE-WULF 190
The Fw 190 was, arguably, the best fighter produced in WWII. It outperformed all except the P-51 "Mustang" and, if flown by an experienced pilot, was superior to it, too. Luftwaffe pilots loved this aircraft.

SEPTEMBER 1940
Field Marshal Milch visited JG 26 to discuss fighter operations. Milch, nearest camera on left, talks to Galland. On right is Generalmajor von Döring. Between Milch and Galland in background is Hptm. Adolph.

pilots. He thought about all the letters he had still to write. He saw their faces as surely as he knew their sacrifices. For Goering to accuse such valiant men of cowardice was monstrous.

With the bomber crews claiming that they were not being closely enough escorted, an adversary relationship had developed between fighter pilots and bomber pilots. Goering sided unreservedly with the bomber pilots. He returned now to the necessity for close escort, in view of the imminent use of hundreds of bombers in the London assault. Galland choked down his anger, and tried again to explain to Goering some of the fighters' difficulties.

"Herr Reich Marshal, our Me 109 is superior to the Spitfire in the attack. That is the way we should use our fighters, hunting down the RAF and attacking them. We have a clear advantage in such operations."

"Galland, the size of your personal bag of enemy fighters is unimportant compared with the protection of my bombers. I am telling you what is important."

"Sir, the Spitfire is an excellent defensive fighter because it is more maneuverable than our Me 109, even if a little slower – especially in acceleration. Such a fighter is much better suited to close escort than our Me 109, which is handicapped in that role."

"I reject your arguments categorically, Major Galland. The bombers must be protected at all costs. You've got to get some fighting spirit into these pilots, instead of giving me reasons why you cannot protect my bombers."

Goering followed with more scathing criticisms, but when he glanced at his wrist watch and realized his time was short, his mood changed abruptly. From reproachful abuse, he turned suddenly amiable, like the sun coming from behind a cloud.

"Now then, Moelders" he said, "what can I help you get for your Geschwader?"

Moelders asked for a new series of Me 109's fitted with the more powerful DB 605 N engines. Goering said he would get them, and turned to Galland.

"And you? What do you want?"

"I'd like an outfit of Spitfires for my Geschwader!"

Galland heard his impudent request go blurting out of himself as though coming from a third party. The words rushed out, propelled by his rage over Goering's vilifications of his pilots. Goering's amiable facade disappeared. The second greatest orator in Germany, he stood speechless at the insolence of the young Kommodore he had just promoted. Scowling and growling, he went stomping off to his train.

Galland's request would survive down through the decades as one of his most famous and oft-quoted remarks. In social gatherings and lectures all over the world, his request for Spitfires always surfaced. The full background to the remark is rarely understood, and it should be recorded that Galland definitely preferred the Me 109 to the Spitfire, not only in September 1940, but also later after he had personally flown the British thoroughbred.

GALLAND SAFELY ON THE GROUND AFTER SIXTY.
Number 60 was sort of a benchmark in Galland's career. Here he is shown in full combat equipment as he springs from the cockpit on 15 April 1941.

He was seeking to emphasize with Goering that it was a disadvantage to fly the Me 109 and use the tactics suited to the Spitfire in escort missions. The advantage of the Me 109 became a disadvantage under these conditions. When Galland and Moelders put their heads together and adopted hit-and-run tactics with their speedy Me 109s – avoiding the turning dogfight where the Spitfire was superior – both their units did much better against the RAF fighters.

By 7 September 1940, the "Battle of London" had begun, as 625 bombers escorted by 648 single and twin-engined fighters were dispatched to the attack. Goering and Kesselring watched from Cap Blanc Nez as the armada thundered majestically toward England. With them was General Bruno Loerzer, who had started Goering as an airman in World War I. In the history of the world, no such large force of aircraft had ever been seen. Supreme Commander of all these aircraft, Goering had come a long way since his days as the Flying Trapezist on the Western Front, but he still had a long way to go to win the present battle.

Throughout this fourth phase of the Battle of Britain, Galland found all his operations, plans, and tactical ideas overshadowed by the fuel problem. Everything was affected by the fighters going to the absolute limit of their fuel endurance, not only the operations themselves, but also pilot psychology and morale. The bomber men had no fuel problem, and their importunings for close protection took insufficient account of what this meant to fighter fuel consumption.

When the London flak punished the bombers with its accuracy and volume, the bomber pilots flew at 21,000 to 23,000 feet. This altitude was too great for their power and loading, slowing them down considerably. Escorting fighters had to make huge, wide weaves to maintain station. Weaving chewed up fuel and often carried the fighters out of sight of the bomber crews, who complained once more that the fighters were not protecting them.

Pushing Me 109 fuel endurance to its limits resulted in a large number of Channel swimmers in the Fighter Arm. Galland was mortified on one mission when seven of his JG 26 fighters went into the English Channel after surviving combat over England. He all but joined them. Bringing up the rear after staying too long in battle with the Spitfires, Galland's fuel gauge showed empty as he roared over Manston on the coast. He was about to land and surrender on the ground to the RAF, an ignominious fate for a high-scoring holder of the Knight's Cross.

On the verge of turning, he reconsidered; saying to hell with it, he headed out over the hated grey waters.

Staggering across toward France, his engine began blurting in bursts as his fuel ran out. Then came silence, save for the rush of the wind. The lessons of the Borkenberge came in handy. The former sailplane pilot bellied in with a dead engine on a beach near Cap Gris Nez.

Luftwaffe attacking forces in the Battle of London varied usually between 400 and 500 bombers, plus about 200 Stuka dive bombers. The latter were making a last return to English skies at the time of this supreme German effort. 500 single-engine fighters and 200 Me 110s were the escort. For operational purposes, the attackers proceeded in Geschwader strength, each bomber Geschwader (60-90 aircraft) with a fighter Geschwader as escort. Since not more than ten minutes could be allowed for linking up bomber formations with their assigned fighter escorts, these assemblies proved almost as taxing as the raids. Once the whole mass of 1,000 or more aircraft was airborne, the spectacle was terrifying, but only the pilots knew the nerve-clanking strain that had gone into assembling each armada.

Returning the Stuka to the main battle was a disastrous error, a repetition of their earlier debacle. British fighters pounced on the Stukas just as they began their dives, one after another, in the classic Stuka pattern. Galland and his pilots could not protect the Stukas in their dives, since the latter were fitted with air brakes to help their aim. The Me 109 was far too fast to stay with any such aircraft as the Stuka, even if the latter was without air brakes. The RAF also slaughtered the dive bombers during their milling re-assembly phase. Goering blamed these Stuka losses exclusively on his own fighters.

GALLAND'S 56TH VICTIM
Standing on the wing of his Hurricane at RAF Station North Weald in 1940, is South African pilot P.H.V. "Pat" Wells who was shot down by Galland shortly after this photo was taken. Galland and Wells became friends after war's end.

Galland, the former sailplane pilot, kept a wary eye cocked at the weather. The September evenings were getting a nip of autumn, and the summer skies showed the early fingers of fall. On 10 September 1940, clouds and rain interrupted the daily thunder of bombs into London. The murk hung around for four days, with fighter activity continuing. Galland was well aware that the Luftwaffe had entered a race with the autumn weather of the English Channel, notorious for its inclement character.

Whenever weather curtailed fighter operations as fall advanced, Galland and the pilots of his staff and nearby Gruppen switched to another kind of hunting and shooting. Hares, pheasants, and partridges were abundant. The non-hunters among the pilots participated gladly in the game meat. Evenings of any stand-down days saw the pilots patronizing the bars of Lille. Galland's preference was Paris and the famous Scheherezade nightclub, happily haunted also by U-boat and E-boat commanders. Late nights were incompatible with the possibility of morning operations, but the early evening outings were a priceless, brief respite from battle pressure.

SIXTY DOWN AND COUNTING
On 15 April 1941 Adolf Galland scored his 60th aerial victory. This shows the ground crews reacting to the waggle of his wings signifying the shoot-downs.

15 September 1940 dawned with near-ideal flying weather, cloudy but with sufficient gaps for the Luftwaffe to find London. Goering again took personal command. By noon he was hurling everything into the battle. The invaluable Ultra decrypts kept Dowding aware of his opponent's plans, and also of his plight. German morale was wearing down along with their aircraft strength. German losses had been heavy, and especially in pilots and crews. When they survived from shot-up aircraft they became POWs. RAF pilots who survived forced landings or who parachuted were able to return to battle.

Dowding knew through Ultra that 15 September was Goering's main punch. He also knew that Luftwaffe Intelligence had written down Fighter Command to 200 aircraft. His policy of committing limited numbers of fighters had the additional virtue of misleading his enemy. Dowding had considerably more than 200 fighters available. His pilots were near exhaustion, but Dowding judged that the day and time had come to wade into Goering's bombers with everything Fighter Command had available. Goering's big punch would be met with a counterpunch, packing the great imponderable of war – surprise.

Dowding passed the word to Air Vice Marshal Park at No. 11 Fighter Group, and the able New Zealander alerted his 24 squadrons. Radar was following the assembly of huge enemy gaggles over the Channel and French coast. Park began sending his squadrons in two at a time. They went right into the German bombers in line abreast, dispensing with the usual climb to "the perch" for a diving attack. More and more squadrons kept coming up. This was not the pattern of the past.

Churchill was watching in Park's operations room at Uxbridge, as the last six squadrons of No. 11 Group rose to battle. Five more squadrons from No. 12 Group north of London joined Park's final six. All eleven squadrons together slashed into the German bombers. By 1:30 pm, the RAF had over 300 fighters airborne. The effects were devastating, not only to the bombers, but to the morale of the bomber crews. They had been assured by their higher commanders that the RAF was nearly finished. Their own recent experience at least partially supported this estimate. Now out of the blue came immense, terrifying swarms of Hurricanes and Spitfires.

Every German bomber formation was attacked. Galland and his pilots now had their arch foes up to do massed battle.

READY TO ADD ANOTHER VICTORY MARK
One of the JG 26 "Black Men" poses for the camera just before painting another victory symbol on Galland's Me 109.

Their restrictive close escort orders were a continuing handicap, but both the circumstances and the balance of combat were drastically altered on 15 September 1940. RAF roundels seemed to be everywhere. Aircraft twisted and dove, smoked and exploded, tumbled and rolled in the skies all over southeastern England. Vapor trails laced the heavens, and black smokestreams poured from aircraft screaming down to final impact. Somber palls rose from the funeral pyres of brave pilots and crews on both sides.

German bombers bored through, but not in the numbers sent out from France. RAF fighters and clouds over the target scattered the German bombing attacks, and limited damage. Withdrawal by the German forces turned into a nightmare. Shoals of British fighters chased them out over the Channel, damaging and downing more of them far from the main battle scene. The counterpunch of Dowding had been far more effective than the big punch of Goering.

REICH MARSHAL GOERING AND GALLAND
Galland's Me 109 with 94 victory flashes on the rudder, captures the attention of Göring during a visit to the channel front.

The German High Command immediately denied British press and radio claims of more than 180 Luftwaffe aircraft destroyed. For morale purposes, it was essential to minimize the serious reversal of German fortunes on 15 September 1940. 56 German aircraft did not return to base. Many that staggered back across the Channel did so only by the grace of God and the skill of their pilots and crews. These aircraft were often so badly damaged that they were scrapped. Dozens more were heavily shot up, and buried the already overloaded repair depots under an avalanche of wrecks.

In the final reckoning, about one quarter of the bomber force assigned to the Battle of Britain had been put out of action. Personnel losses had been severe numerically, and the missing pilots and crews were an irreplaceable peacetime-trained elite. The British would ever afterward celebrate 15 September each year as Battle of Britain Day. They would always believe that they won the battle on that climactic September afternoon.

Galland believed for many years that with different tactics and proper exploitation of its resources, the Luftwaffe could have done far better. Certainly Goering's presence and style in command was an encumbrance. His gross tactical and political error in bombing London instead of the RAF sector airfields and radar stations was high command at its worst. Goering's misuse of the Fighter Arm was tantamount to reducing its strength in what was essentially a fighter battle.

The Luftwaffe Fighter Arm was the most successful element on the German side in the entire battle. Despite the crippling effect of rigid close escort orders by their High Command, they pushed the RAF to the brink. Mistakes in the battle itself, and derelictions from the past on the part of the German leadership, had a detrimental effect on the efforts of the Fighter Arm. That they had no other single-engined fighter than the short-winded Me 109 was not the fault of the pilots. That chance was cast away years before. The absence of fighter control integrated with radar on the German side was not the fault of the young fighter pilots, nor were their inadequate communications.

British preparations for air defense paid off handsomely in the battle. The RAF's well-coordinated communications, control, and position-fixing facilities were coupled to the scientific triumph of their radar. British top leadership was of high quality, especially Dowding and Park, who were both privy to the Ultra secret. Crowning the British effort was the skill and devotion of the RAF fighter pilots.

Adolf Galland's respected standing among his former foes allowed him to meet in the postwar decades many of his adversaries in the Battle of Britain. Wing Commander Robert Stanford-Tuck became a close personal friend. Galland and Sir Douglas Bader shared many a distinguished podium in several countries and were mutual admirers. Twenty-seven years after the Battle of Britain, Galland finally met his main foe in that struggle, Sir Keith Park, retired to Auckland, New Zealand. In February of 1967 they had a lively meeting and discussion Down Under. Galland was mightily impressed by Park. In their reminiscences of the 1940 battle, Park did not mention the Ultra secret and its role in his handling of No. 11 Group's fighters. Like all others party to the greatest secret of the war, Park kept the faith.

The Battle of Britain did not terminate on 15 September 1940, but continued into the autumn. After that date, nevertheless, the Luftwaffe made no concerted effort to defeat the RAF. Goering's dream of wiping the British Air Force from the sky – the aerial conquest of Britain – dissipated with the rude awakening of 15 September 1940. Although Goering was himself more to blame than anyone for the trend of events, he began a search for culprits. Galland continued to do his duty like the good soldier he had proved himself to be.

TWELVE

Over to Defense

Worse than the heavy material damage to the Luftwaffe on 15 September 1940 was the blow dealt to morale. Sudden RAF resurgence sent a demoralizing shockwave through the Bomber Arm, which loudly blamed the Fighter Arm for its failure to provide protection. Psychological impacts were felt in the Luftwaffe High Command. The RAF's dramatic rebound was irreconcilable with German intelligence estimates. When Goering suffered a defeat instead of an anticipated and badly-needed victory, he was thunderstruck and angry. He blamed the Fighter Arm.

Hastily convening a meeting at Air Fleet 2 HQ in Brussels the following day, Goering delivered a recriminatory diatribe against the fighter pilots. His abuse went too far. Lt. General Theo Osterkamp sprang to his feet. Jafü 2 at Le Touquet and fully in touch with both the young combat commanders and the Air Fleet hierarchy, Osterkamp could endure Goering's insults no longer.

Osterkamp was well qualified to defend the fighter pilots. He had won the Blue Max in World War I and had downed 32 Allied aircraft. He added 6 more in World War II, while flying as Kommodore of JG 51, which formation he had raised and trained in 1939. He was one of the grand old eagles around whom the new Fighter Arm had been built, and the young pilots nicknamed him "Uncle Theo." He had been in aerial combat as recently as July of 1940. As Jafü 2, he was direct liaison between the combat fighter units and his Fleet HQ. He knew the problems first hand.

The slender Uncle Theo faced the bully Goering unflinchingly. The Reich Marshal was livid with rage, but Osterkamp's bearing and expression made Goering fall silent. Osterkamp vehemently emphasized how the rigid direct escort orders tied his fighter pilots' hands. He stressed how the recommendations of the best combat leaders to improve efficiency and inflict losses on the RAF were consistently ignored. The fixed close escort orders resulted in heavy bomber losses and the High Command blamed the fighter pilots.

Goering reddened at this rebuke, ready to explode. Osterkamp adopted a cooler tone.

"Yesterday the English used new tactics. They started using much larger formations to attack our bombers in force. They took us by surprise with this change in tactics."

Osterkamp's competent summation did not get through to Goering. His reaction was that if the RAF were finally committing fighters in large numbers, Luftwaffe fighters should be downing them in large numbers. He refused to see that he was binding down the majority of his own fighters. Goering saw highly technical and tactical matters in a simplistic way. Professional counsel could not change his mind. The Reich Marshal's need for victory was personally and politically urgent. Technical problems obstructing victory were an irritation.

With air superiority over the invasion beaches now impossible before the onset of adverse weather, Sealion could not go forward. Goering also knew that the planned invasion of Russia would require him to move most of his Air Fleets to the east before the favorable English Channel weather in the summer of 1941. His Douhet-style aerial conquest of England had failed. Goering knew he would have to make a humiliating change, and that his numerous detractors in the Army General Staff and high political spheres would enjoy his discomfort.

Worst of all, he had bungled his grandiose gamble to please Hitler. Although the Fuehrer had no real intention of invading England, Goering had hoped to score a major personal triumph by presenting him with the prize – exclusively by aerial action. Goering took out his frustration on the Fighter Arm. He now insisted that since his fighters could not protect his bombers, the fighters would carry the bombs to England themselves.

As mass daylight raids were phased out in the latter half of September, fighter-bomber attacks were phased in, using both Me 109s and Me 110s. Galland maintained a high level of combat activity. By 25 September 1940 he had confirmed his 40th aerial victory.

His HQ teleprinter at Audembert hammered out a telex from Hitler. Galland's combat achievement of 40 aerial victories was being recognized with the newly created Oak Leaves to the Knight's Cross. This then highest class of the decoration had thus far only been awarded twice. One of the recipients was Werner Moelders. Their rivalry was continuing, as emphasis passed to the fighter-bombers.

Experimental Gruppe 210, in which the first fighter-bomber conversions had been made earlier in 1940, moved into the Pas de Calais. Soon this unit was joined by Galland's old formation from the Polish campaign, II/SLG 2, now equipped with bomb-carrying Me 109s. To the chagrin of the fighter pilots, Willi Messerschmitt's slender, streamlined brainchild was loaded with a 250-Kg bomb that bulged down below its belly. Performance was seriously degraded by this protuberance.

The Me 110 was more suited to the fighter-bomber role, at least as far as bomb load was concerned. The heavy, twin-engined aircraft could carry 1,400 pounds of bombs – two 500-pounders and four 100-pounders. Each Gruppe in every fighter Geschwader assigned to the Channel area was required to convert one squadron to fighter-bombers.

In what Galland regarded as the craziest High Command order yet, the remaining fighters escorted the fighter-bombers until they dropped their loads. They could marginally defend themselves then, because the drag of the bomb rack was still a handicap. More importantly, fighter-bomber operations became far too defensive in character to suit the fighter pilots or to get significant results. Most of the fighter pilots assigned to the new fighter-bombers hated this duty. They got rid of their bombs as soon as was decently possible, in order to join combat with the RAF.

The newly-decorated young Kommodore of JG 26 was not opposed to fighter-bombers as such. He had himself proved in Spain what they could do in suitable situations. The task of suppressing the RAF fighter force was not a rational assignment for the limited numbers of fighter-bombers available. Maintenance of such an ineffective offensive required the Luftwaffe Fighter Arm on the Channel to give up one third of its strength. Each week, meanwhile, RAF Fighter Command grew stronger.

Fighters were the only means of gaining air superiority. Now that the long-coveted drop tanks were available for the Me 109, the same external rack was being used for bombs. The extra range advantage that had come too late for the biggest battles was thereby nullified. Confidence in high leadership cannot develop via such expedient and ineffective tactical shifts.

When the RAF maintained its tactical policy of jumping the bombers and avoiding the fighters, the fighter-bombers were taken out of formation, and distributed among the escort. This made them harder to single out and made their escort to targets reasonably certain, but it slowed down the whole formation. When Galland, from his cockpit, thought about the organization, labor, casualties, and material losses that were required to drop each bomb from an Me 109, he was both disgusted and disquieted. This fifth phase of the Battle of Britain plainly had no more than nuisance value for all involved. The Luftwaffe fighter pilots were still being handicapped by their own High Command in doing what they did best.

Generalleutnant Theo Osterkamp, center, listens to the debate between the new and the older generations. Back to camera is Field Marshal "Smiling Albert" Kesselring (1885-1960) C.O. of Air Fleet 2, and right is Göring's friend General Lörzer (1892-1960) WWI ace and General of Luftwaffe Personnel Office in the Luftwaffe in WWII. Osterkamp, with 32 victories in WWI and winner of the Pour le Merite, was also an ace in WWII with 6 victories. He was born in 1892 and passed away in 1975. Adolf Galland listens intently.

Ordered to Berlin to receive the Oak Leaves to his Knight's Cross from Hitler personally, Galland had some guilt feelings on leaving the combat zone. He hated to leave his pilots fighting while he went off to Berlin. There was nevertheless a feeling of deep bodily relief at the removal of daily combat strain. He was physically and mentally exhausted, He knew it in his bones.

When Galland had been introduced to the Fuehrer for the first time in 1939, he had been just one of the highest decorated pilots officially welcomed home from Spain. This time things were different. After receiving the Oak Leaves and Hitler's congratulations, they sat down facing each other. He was alone with Germany's most powerful man, whose authority was unquestioned within the German state. They were sitting in the Reich Chancellery, center of Hitler's world.

Hitler has been commonly depicted in films as constantly raving like a maniac, but the Hitler now confronting Galland was the able politician, fully in command of himself. A former front line soldier of World War I, Hitler admired the new generation of combat heroes, which Galland exemplified. The Fuehrer quietly questioned the young pilot about the battle over England and the fighting qualities of the Royal Air Force. Galland reported to Hitler the resentment that he and his pilots felt toward the German press and radio, because of their condescending comments on the RAF. The British were the toughest aerial fighters the Luftwaffe had ever faced.

When the young Major further enlarged upon the fighting spirit of the RAF, which persisted despite heavy losses, Hitler continued listening and nodding. The Fuehrer said that Galland's experience in this new war confirmed his own view on the high quality of the Anglo-Saxon race. The war with them now was a world historical tragedy, which Hitler said he had struggled in vain to avert.

Hitler spoke admiringly of Britain's political development, and regretted his inability to bring Britain and Germany together. He showed quick comprehension of Galland's views. The Fuehrer marshaled and presented his own facts with impressive lucidity. His reasonable reactions surprised Galland, who had expected to be interrupted, corrected, or silenced. The Fuehrer actually sided with him over the patronizing treatment of the RAF by Germany's news media. Galland left the Chancellery after this lengthy interview impressed by the Fuehrer and without any of the resentments that Goering always seemed to provoke.

The young ace was scheduled to give an interview to the foreign press corps in Berlin. At the Ministry of Propaganda in the Wilhelmsplatz, he found himself facing a large group of reporters in the Theatersaal. Initially resentful of this limelight, Galland's mood improved when the reporters asked him questions about the RAF. This gave him an opportunity to offset the German propaganda about which he had just complained to Hitler. Years later, Galland would listen to a recording of this interview that was presented to him by the Ministry of Propaganda, and find his opinions unchanged from 1940 on these matters.

Goering now summoned him from Berlin for a congratulatory hunting trip at the legendary Reichsjägerhof, situated on Rominten Heath in East Prussia. Every German hunter dreamed of a sporting visit to the famous lodge, built of mighty tree trunks, with its thatched roof extending far out over the eaves. As Galland reached the gate, out came his rival Werner Moelders, now on his way back to the Channel front. Moelders was in a hurry.

"The Fuehrer and the Fat One have been keeping me on these social visits as though the war is over," said Moelders. "I'm on my way back now, and I just got the Fat One's promise to keep you here for three days. Good luck with the stag. I missed him. *Auf Wiedersehen*"

As Moelders disappeared from view, Goering came in sight from the Reichsjägerhof, traditionally attired. High hunting boots, silk blouse with puffed sleeves, and green suede jacket made him a figure of which his godfather would have been proud. Goering was beaming with pleasure. Galland's request for a Geschwader of Spitfires, and the war itself, had been forgotten amid the joys of the hunt.

Galland had the same feeling of unreality now that had bothered him during the Karinhall conference in August. While he and Goering talked about stags, the Luftwaffe on the coast was attacking the Supermarine works at Southampton, home of the Spitfire. Goering's numerous offices and titles included Master of the Hunt. A privilege of that office was the exclusive right to hunt in the magnificent royal preserve at Rominten.

With his love of animal life, in such contrast to his political ruthlessness, Goering even had pet names for the special strong stags at Rominten. As a congratulatory gesture for his 40 aerial victories, Goering invited Major Galland to shoot one of these strong royal stags.

"You have three days to do it" said Goering. "I promised Moelders to keep you here at least that long."

On the next morning, 27 September 1940, Galland's hunter's nose had led him to one of the superb beasts. By 10.05 AM he had a trophy of unforgettable magnificence. Galland was ecstatic. His early triumph meant that he could now return to the front. The stag was also the one missed by Moelders the

Me 109G IN THE MEDITERRANEAN THEATRE
The Me 109s of JG 27 dlisplay the different types of camouflage used in this war theatre.

previous day. His eagerness to get back to the front was to minimize Moelders' extra scoring days while he was at Rominten. Goering forbade his return to the front. The Reich Marshal was going to keep his promise to Moelders. All this, thought Galland, while the war burns on every day, and my pilots are dying in combat.

Goering's resolution lasted until the evening casualty reports came in from Kesselring and Sperrle on the coast. Initially bad, the news grew steadily worse. By final tally, 55 Luftwaffe aircraft were missing, including 21 bombers and several fighters from Galland's JG 26. Goering took the bad tidings right to heart.

In this essentially social setting, Galland saw how Goering reacted to the deaths of good men under his command. The Reich Marshal was now totally unlike his public image. There was no bluster. Shattered and shaken, Goering was unable to put it all together in his mind. The continuing inability of the fighters to protect his bombers was incomprehensible. With his frame of reference in World War I, Goering simply could not come to grips with the realities of this dynamic modern battle over England. He was nevertheless Supreme Commander of this powerful yet sensitive weapon called the Luftwaffe.

Galland understood the Reich Marshal's distress. The JG 26 pilots who had been posted missing or killed in action this day were men he knew and had led in combat. That hurt. Once more the young Kommodore tried to explain to Goering how the close escort orders were largely responsible for the high casualties. Gently but clearly, he emphasized the price that was being paid for robbing most of the fighters of their offensive and aggressive role.

Little of what he said penetrated even this Goering, grief-stricken and far removed from the forceful public figure. Galland found himself bemused by the inability of this highly intelligent and cultivated man – a trained Army officer and a former ace fighter pilot and leader – to grasp the core of the problem. Galland finally turned this awkward interview to good account.

"Sir, I would like to return to my Geschwader on the Channel immediately."

Goering nodded, his promise to Moelders forgotten. Shortly afterwards, Galland was out of the Reichsjägerhof, stag head and all, and on his way back to JG 26. When he was compelled to make part of his journey by rail, after a forced landing on farmland, his fellow passengers gawked at the stag head. Then they blanched at its odor. Their comments were appropriately pungent. Even the Knight's Cross with Oak Leaves at his throat did not mollify his traveling companions. Heroes were not expected to smell bad.

The Luftwaffe High Command made a brief attempt to improve striking power against London by using small formations of Ju 88s, their fastest bombers. Fighter escort for these missions was in the ratio of seven fighters to each bomber. This proved unsuccessful, and the RAF continued taking a toll of the raiders despite their own severe shortage of pilots. On 30 September 1940, the Bomber Arm lost 47 aircraft, and that was the end of daylight formation bombing. The RAF inflicted this reverse at a cost of 8 pilots and 20 aircraft.

The Bomber Arm now went over to night attacks. Daylight bombing was left to the fighter-bombers. Despite the obvious scaling down of daylight operations, none of the fighter Kommodores on the Channel front could shake the feeling of being hampered. Their fighting power was not being fully utilized. Losses of the Me 110 fighter-bombers and crews were high, but losses remained within reason in the fighter units. Galland, Moelders, Trautloft, von Maltzahn, and the other Kommodores all discussed the problems with Osterkamp, who was their advocate with Kesselring, Sperrle, and Stumpff.

No significant changes were made. Air war against England kept easing down through October, when Luftwaffe losses dropped to 325 machines of all types. In the bloody September clashes German losses had exceeded 500 machines. RAF losses also dropped in September to 251 machines. RAF pilots killed in action totaled 100 for October, against 148 and 159 for August and September, respectively. Already dramatically outproducing the Luftwaffe in fighter aircraft, the RAF got substantial relief in its most critical category: available fighter pilots. By October's end, the worst was over for the RAF.

These are hindsight assessments from nearly sixty years later. To the ardent Major Galland of JG 26, events in October of 1940 did not appear in such a cool perspective. Luftwaffe pilots had no consciousness of having been defeated. As attackers they expected losses. Galland and his pilots recognized in the events crashing around them, only that a peak had occurred in the struggle during September. The Luftwaffe was clearly unable to master Britain exclusively from the air. Cooler and damper autumn weather had come, and soon embraced all the combatants with clammy impartiality. As the weeks wore on, more and longer stand-downs were forced on JG 26 by the weather.

Animated conversations took place around the mess table during these stand-downs and between operations. Galland told his pilots that in the spring they would be forced to hurl themselves again in large numbers at the RAF. Together they had made JG 26 the most celebrated and sought-after German fighter unit of the battle. They had traditions to uphold. Galland

Pages 78-80:
GALLAND COMBAT REPORT
Page 78: The combat reports were generally in three parts. This detailed form claims his 94th victory which was the 91st for the lead unit and the 903rd for JG 26. His Kaczmarek or wingman witness was Lt. Hilgendorf.

COMBAT REPORT - Page 79:
In addition to the claim form, each pilot making the claim was required to provide a written account of the action. This is Galland's account for the action on 18 November 1941, his 94th victory.

COMBAT REPORT - Page 80:
Galland's witness, Lt. Hilgendorff, wrote this account of the action, confirming Galland's 94th victory.

Stab / J.G.26
(Dienstelle)

Einsatzort, den 18.11.1941

Oberstlt. Galland 94. Abschuß
Stab J.G.26 91. "

ABSCHUSSMELDUNG

J. G. 26 903. Abschuß

1. Zeit (Tag, Stunde, Minute) und Gegend des Absturzes : 18.11.41 12.32 Uhr
   Höhe : 4000 Meter : 2o km westl. Boulogne
2. Durch wen ist der Abschuss/Zerstörung erfolgt ? Obstlt. Galland
3. Flugzeugtyp des abgeschossenen Flugzeuges : Spitfire
4. Staatsangehörigkeit des Gegners : engl.
   Werk-Nr. bzw. Kennzeichen : Kokarde
5. Art der Vernichtung :
   a.) Flammen mit dunkler Fahne, Flammen mit heller Fahne,
   b.) Einzelteile weggeflogen, abmontiert (Art der Teile erläutern), auseinandergeplatzt rechtes Querruder abgeschossen
   c.) zur Landung gezwungen (diesseits oder jenseits der Front, glatt bzw. mit Bruch)
   d.) jenseits der Front am Bodem im Brand geschossen
6. Art des Aufschlages (nur wenn dieser beobachtet werden konnte)
   a.) diesseits oder jenseits der Front
   b.) senkrecht, flachen Winkel, Aufschlagbrand, Staubwolke in See abgestürzt
   c.) nicht beobachtet, warum nicht ?
7. Schicksal der Insassen (tot, mit Fallschirm abgesprungen, nicht beobachtet
8. Gefechtsbericht des Schützen ist in der Anlage beigefügt.
9. Zeugen :
   a.) Luft : Lt. Hilgendorff
   b.) Erde ;
10. Anzahl der Angriffe, die auf das feindliche Flugzeug gemacht wurden ; 1
11. Richtung, aus der die einzelnen Angriffe erfolgten ; in scharfer Rechtskurve
12. Entfernung, aus der der Abschuss erfolgte ; 5o m
13. Takt. Position aus der der Abschuss angesetzt wurde ; Kurvenkampf
14. Ist einer der feindl. Bordschützen kampfunfähig gemacht worden ?
15. Verwandte Munitionsart ; S.m.K.v., P.m.K.v., M.H 1, Br.Spr.FF, Panzer Spr.151/2o
16. Munitionsverbrauch ; 62 MG 17/22 MG FF/2 cm, 14 MG 151/2o cm M 151/2o, Br.Spr.151/
17. Art und Anzahl der waffen, die bei dem Abschuss gebraucht wurden ? 1 MG 151/2o, 2 MG FF/2 cm, 2 MG 17
18. Typ der eigene Maschine ; F 6 U .
19. Weiteres taktisch oder technisch Bemerkenswertes ;
20. Treffer in der eigenen Maschine; ./.
21. Beteiligung weiterer Einheiten (auch Flak) ;

(Unterschrift)

Obstlt. Galland ,
Stab J.G.26

Gefechtsstand, 18.11.1941

Gefechtsmeldung.

Ich flog mit meiner Staffel auf Flakfeuer in die Gegend Boulogne.Plötzlich sah ich genau auf Gegenkurs 500 m unter mir 2 Spitfire.Ich setzte mich nach Abschwung sofort dahinter. Inzwischen sah ich 6 Spitfire.Es entwickelte sich ein wilder Kurvenkampf.Die Spitfire zeigten sich sehr angriffslustig und bewiesen ausgezeichnete fliegerische Fähigkeiten. Inzwischen griffen noch 15 Bf 190 in den Luftkampf ein mit dem Erfolg, daß sich die eigenen Jäger äußerst behinderten und gefährdeten.

Nach mehreren Ansätzen kam ich in scharfer Rechtskurve auf nächste Entfernung hinter eine Spitfire und feuerte mit ungeheurem Vorhaltemaß darauf los.

Ein Kanonentreffer riß der Spitfire ein großes Loch aus dem rechten Querruder. Kurz darauf flog etwa die Hälfte des Querruders weg. Die Spitfire ging in Rollen gedrückt auf See zu. Ich blieb hinter ihr. Der Pilot gewann die Gewalt über die Maschine nicht wieder. Ich bekam die Spitfire infolge der wilden Flugfiguren auch nicht wieder ins Revi, verfolgte sie aber bis zum Aufschlag. Kurz vorher versuchte der Pilot auszusteigen. Der halbgeöffnete Schirm war an der Aufschlagstelle noch länger zu sehen.

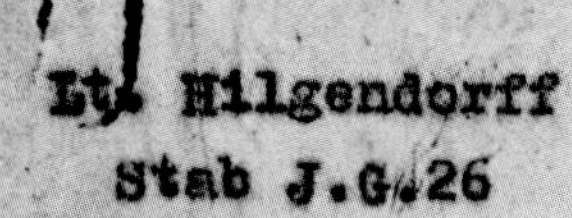

Lt. Hilgendorff
Stab J.G.26

Gefechtsstand, 18.11.1941

Luftkampfzeugenbericht
zu dem Abschuß Obstlt.Galland vom 18.11.41

Am 18.11.41 flog ich als Rottenflieger bei Obstlt.Galland. Um 12.32 Uhr beschoß Obstlt.Galland eine Spitfire aus einer scharfen Rechtskurve. Die Höhe betrug 4000 m . Der Spitfire riß durch den Beschuß das rechte Querruder ab. Der Pilot versuchte die Maschine wiederholt zu fangen,doch schmierte sie ihm flach ab und schlug 20 km westlich Boulogne ins Wasser. Der Pilot stieg nicht aus .

Hilgendorff

promised to do everything in his power to bring about the necessary tactical changes. In JG 26 they saw themselves in a draw rather than as a defeated formation. There was no lack of stomach for further battle amongst any of the fighter pilots in all the Geschwader on the Channel front.

Unfortunately for Germany, not all her leaders were as honest and open as Adolf Galland. He knew absolutely nothing in the autumn of 1940 about the coming attack on Russia. Nor did the young men flying under his command. The observable decline of attacks on England took place against a subtle backdrop not evident to combat pilots. This backdrop was the mental pressure exerted on high Luftwaffe leaders by the demands of the colossal task looming in the East. These leaders had been blocked and frustrated by the RAF. In the presence of this uncompleted venture, the forthcoming plunge into Russia could only have generated anxiety. From this stemmed the steady shift of English Channel operations over to the defensive.

By the end of November 1940, something had to be done to refresh the human element in the fighter units. Galland and his fellow Kommodores on the Channel, petitioned the High Command for a rest. They asked that each Geschwader be taken out of combat for three to four weeks, in rotation. Personnel were to recuperate, and their hard-driven aircraft would be refitted and brought up to full efficiency. This request was granted, though not immediately executed, and the forthcoming vacation became the main subject of pilot conversation.

By 5 December 1940, Galland had raised his victory tally to 58, despite bad weather and reduced opportunities. Christmas rolled around, by which time JG 26 had moved its HQ to Abbeville. In a season of surprise gifts, Galland and JG 26 got one that they had not remotely expected – a personal visit from the Fuehrer.

Hitler spoke to the JG 26 pilots in terms of the renewed assault on England that would take place in the spring of 1941. Operations would then be on a bigger scale. The English would be forced to surrender. The Fighter Arm on the English Channel would be strengthened. Nothing was said about the massive second front that Hitler was planning to open against the Soviet Union in 1941. The Fuehrer wished Galland and his pilots a Happy New Year. For many of these young men at the peak of physical life, it would be their last year.

As Luftwaffe fighter forces on the Channel front passed over to defense, Galland mulled over and over the lessons of the 1940 summer battle. Bad communications had cost them dearly in their operations. Before any new major assault on

Britain, the Luftwaffe needed to acquire an effective fighter control system like the RAF. British fighter control efficiencies had magnified the power of Fighter Command.

There had been no fighter control for the Luftwaffe in the worst of their struggle with the RAF. The only serviceable substitute had been provided by the foresight and remarkable abilities of Specialist (*Sonderführer*) Horst Barth. He was a linguist and radio operator of great skill. Most of the combat leaders, including Galland, were skeptical of any ground-based control system that encroached on their airborne direction of operations. Barth's radio listening unit was doubly difficult to accept, because it did not seem feasible to get timely combat information just by listening to enemy radio traffic.

Barth's elite group of linguist-radio operators was sited at Wissant, near Cap Gris Nez. They had completely mastered the jargon of RAF fighter controllers directing British aircraft on interceptions. All slang, code, and nickname terms were penetrated. Individual RAF controllers became known by their voices just as if they were actors in radio serials.

Using a 1:50,000 scale map of southern England, Barth could listen to this jumble of jargon and put RAF fighters "on the plot" just about as well as it was being done across the Channel at Bentley Priory. As he put RAF operations together from the cacophony of RAF slang and jargon in English, he would pass the distilled data down the telephone line to Osterkamp's HQ in German. This was a stellar feat of high operational value.

When Galland learned of this work he was highly skeptical. He stoutly resisted the idea that perhaps someone as improbable as Horst Barth might tell him where to fly and fight. Uncle Theo Osterkamp was convinced of the value of Barth's unit, which had fed Osterkamp data on RAF operations not otherwise available. Barth also monitored Luftwaffe fighters, thereby earning the sobriquet "Jafü Police," and his operations continued until they were discovered by Goering. Another of the Reich Marshal's extravagant reactions ensued, which blew Barth's unique group to the winds.

Goering immediately enlarged Barth's specialized unit, and in its inflated form placed it under a high-ranking officer. Barth's precious pioneer linguist-operators were promoted and posted away. Barth himself would later become Chief of the Fighter Interrogation Section at Auswertestelle West, where captured Allied pilots were interrogated by the Luftwaffe. Many downed American pilots got to meet Horst Barth.

Galland hoped at New Year of 1941 that the big new attacks on England promised by Hitler would be carried out not just with better-developed fighter control facilities, but also with better-integrated strategy and coherent operational goals. Radar added to his hunter's nose would certainly make finding his opponents easier. In the unfolding of 1941, Galland was to have no difficulty finding the RAF fighters. They came right at him, continuously and in force.

THIRTEEN

Swords, 1941

Promotion to Lt. Colonel on 1 November 1940 was a bright note for Galland amid the autumn drizzle. New Year 1941 brought even better tidings for JG 26. The long awaited vacation granted by Goering was finally being organized. "The Abbeville Boys," as the RAF had come to know JG 26, looked forward to this break as small children long for Christmas. As JG 51 under the command of Werner Moelders moved into Abbeville to replace them, JG 26 personnel spoke and thought of little else but the Austrian Tirol.

Vacation for the technical staff took place in shifts. Pilots were sent for a short home leave, after which they met at St. Anton and Zuers on the Arlberg. Goering, in a generous gesture arranged a pay bonus to cover expenses on an unforgettable skiing vacation. Every pilot present had earned this break, and all of them needed the therapeutic effects of a complete change of venue and action.

Stimulating exercise in mountain sunshine, combined with the exhilaration of the ski slopes, soon turned the pale pilots back into tanned and radiant youngsters. Completely absent from these heights was that characteristic reek of a Me 109 cockpit. Evenings spent around roaring logs crowned each invigorating day. Good drinks, wine, and beer eased nervous tautness. Strain and tremblings from the hard months against the RAF gradually disappeared.

Staying in the best hotels, the Abbeville Boys were surrounded by pretty and friendly girls, some of them famous actresses. All of them knew how to treat tired combat pilots, deflecting their memories from lost comrades and recent battles. Many of these young women were strongly drawn to the dark-haired, mustached Galland. His many nicknames now included Muiti, Red Knight, and Dolfo, added to Capitano of the Condor Legion. He was already famous throughout Germany.

Galland's photographs had appeared in countless magazines and newspapers. Along with Werner Moelders, he was already in the company of von Richthofen, Boelcke and Udet, according to the writers who were publicizing the new generation of air heroes. Dashing in appearance, and especially arresting in uniform with his decorations, Galland certainly was good copy.

Vacationing on the Arlberg, he was not in uniform. To the casual glance he was just another middle-sized guy who looked as though someone had slammed a door on his nose. Still, he drew women to himself as though he were a giant magnet. There was always more to this than his fame, rank, and status.

Call it a powerful aura, a strong bioplasmic field, animal magnetism, or call it star quality, scientists investigating the arcane force that animates living beings are on the trail of what Galland always exuded. He pulled people to him. Women reacted to this magnetism directly, without intellectual notions of how it came about. They simply went for him.

The authors in 1983 attended an aerospace industry barbecue with Galland in Bonn. As he strolled across the grounds, the authors were astonished to see numerous ladies of all ages pivot around on their heels to follow him with fascinated and entranced expressions. Asked about this, Galland merely shrugged. "You get used to it," he said laconically. He was in his 72nd year when this Bonn incident occurred. Back on that 1941 Arlberg ski vacation, when Dolfo had plenty of flux in his magnet, the lovelies reacted by being attracted. Galland got all the attention he could handle.

From among these adoring ladies, the Red Knight selected Monica, a stunning divorcee who was taking the mountain air after shedding her elderly husband. With her was Michael, her four year old son. On the social scene Galland liked things organized. Arrangements were soon made for Monica to help him forget the RAF for a while. They would remain close friends until 1945. Monica would reside near him in Berlin, and she would eventually help save his life. His relationship with her caused him many difficulties, because her friends in the film industry and other circles were anti-Nazi and anti-war.

Galland's attractiveness to women, which many more handsome men could never understand, had already proved to be a little problem in France. Again it was a question of getting organized socially. The dashing young Kommodore could not possibly deal with all the young women who sought him out by various ruses. Galland set up what he called a "filter," in the person of "Papi" Causin, a reserve officer from World War I assigned to JG 26 for administrative tasks.

Genial, tactful, and with plenty of worldly experience, Papi Causin was interposed between Galland and his female admirers. In private life, Papi was director of a brewery. On Galland's staff, he directed the diplomatic defense of his C.O. against excessive romantic entanglement. Papi continued to act as a filter on Galland's staff throughout the war. Galland admitted at age 72 that there were "occasionally some holes in the filter." He punched some of those holes himself, by commissioning Papi to organize dates for him with chosen ladies. This occurred when the circumstances – or the ladies – were exceptional. Papi proved as adroit at inviting the desired ladies in as he was at filtering the others out.

Entertainment troupes visited JG 26 and other service units in France, and were the counterpart of the USO entertainment teams for the American forces. The German groups invariably featured dazzling actresses, dancers, and entertainers from the Berlin scene. Dolfo did not believe that their talent had to be spread around quite so widely, and so Papi arranged for that. An exceptionally gorgeous actress named Joshy shared her talents exclusively with the famous Kommodore of JG 26.

Papi in Paris lined up a beautiful Belgian named Monique. Galland found excuses thereafter to visit Air Fleet 2 HQ from time to time. At the luxury night club Scheherezade in Paris, there was yet another stunning female that Papi dated for his C.O. in advance. All this followed the pattern of Galland's early life, when he discovered his passion for good-looking girls. Unable to conquer this passion, he indulged it instead. There were plenty of women in his life, but Monica of the celebrated 1941 Arlberg vacation was undoubtedly closest to him until he married long after the war.

Just how memorable this particular vacation was for the premier fighter Geschwader of the Luftwaffe can be judged from Galland's 70th birthday party in Cologne. In March of 1982, the heads were grey and bald, but the somewhat aged survivors of JG 26 present were still talking about the Arlberg vacation – 41 years later! While they rebuilt their stamina in the Alps, their aircraft, vehicles, and equipment were overhauled at the home bases of JG 26 at Düsseldorf, Mönchengladbach, and Krefeld. The Gruppen had not seen these places since the beginning of the Battle of France.

Ready for operations again by 1 March 1941, the three Gruppen of JG 26 were ordered to Brest, Morlaix, and Lannion in Britanny. They were assigned to protect the German battleships in Brest and the major new U-boat bases being established there and at Lorient. Galland disliked the posture of defense, and they were too far from action. A fighter pilot becomes like a fire horse. He wants to rush full speed to the action. He is restless pulling a milk cart.

Right at this time, Galland's youngest brother, Paul, finished his training as a fighter pilot. The Kommodore of JG 26 arranged for his brother's assignment to III/JG 26, where he could keep an eye on him. Off duty, they could be Keffer and Paulinchen, sharing memories of Westerholt and home, a human touch amid war's turmoil.

His next youngest brother, Wilhelm-Ferdinand, called Wutz, had met with him often on the Channel coast during the Battle of Britain. Wutz was adjutant of an elite flak training battalion, but wanted to get into the Fighter Arm. He asked for his famous brother's help. In a short time, Wutz was transferred to an accelerated pilot training course. He would soon join the Fighter Arm in JG 26.

Completing the family scene, Keffer even did a favor for his eldest brother, Fritz. Although he still did not care too much for Fritz, always recalling the time in his teens when Fritz tried to steal his girl, Galland made some arrangements. Fritz was duly transferred to a similar course as Wutz. He served out the war as a reconnaissance and fighter pilot.

As Galland took off for transfer to Brittany bases, he realized that it was an incredible three months since he had last downed an enemy aircraft. Morose over his new defensive assignment, Galland decided to take the offensive personally, however briefly. After refueling at Le Touquet, Galland took off with Master Sergeant Menge for a provocative two-plane sweep over southern England.

"Find the enemy and shoot him down" said the Red Baron in 1917. The black-haired Galland, with his big black cigar parked in its special cockpit ashtray, stooged around over England to find the enemy so he could shoot him down. Pilot shortages of the Battle of Britain were long gone. Up came a whole squadron of Spitfires to clean Galland's clock.

Spotting the Spits on their way up, Galland plunged down on the climbing fighters for an unexpected bounce at 3,000 feet. Surprise was decisive. In short order, Galland and Menge each shot down a Spitfire, and were barreling like hell for the Brittany coast. When they touched down at Brest, they had added two aerial victories to the JG 26 tally. Their gaping fellow pilots were astonished. They had not even sighted an enemy aircraft.

There was little action for a fighter Geschwader where they were stationed. Up in the Pas de Calais things were lively. Werner Moelders was piling up more victories. The scoring race was now between Moelders and Galland. The two other leading scorers of the Battle of Britain period were unfortunately out of the running. Major Helmut Wieck of JG 2 had been killed off the south coast of England. Captain Wilhelm Balthasar had been wounded and was now well back behind Galland in the scoring. As Moelders steadily increased his score, Galland's envy grew. He wished he were in Moelders's place, and soon he would be, but not in the way that he wanted.

Galland pulled another unauthorized two-plane sweep over southern England on General Osterkamp's birthday on 15 April 1941. Uncle Theo was Jafü 2 at Le Touquet, and since nobody knew in those days how many more birthdays anyone might have – due to all the lead in the air – he invited Galland over to help him celebrate. The young Kommodore had just turned 29 himself three weeks earlier.

Galland's staff packed a huge basket full of fresh lobsters and champagne, stuffing this cargo into the small space behind the pilot's seat in the Me 109F-2. Taking off from Brest with 1st Lieutenant Westphal as his wingman, Galland's sense of mischief took charge. Despite the insignia of a Lt. Colonel on his uniform, and despite the lobsters and champagne behind him, he led the way to England. They would go again and tweak the British lion's tail.

His luck held. Near the narrowest part of the Channel he spotted a lone Spitfire, probably a returning reconnaissance aircraft. A wild chase immediately ensued. The champagne was subjected to more G-force than its bottler ever intended, but the corks held. Caught with a burst, the Spitfire crashed into a village west of Dover.

Turning for Le Touquet, Galland was astonished to see a squadron of Spitfires climbing ahead of him – probably scrambled on intercept. One British fighter was lagging badly. Galland came up on him unseen and shot him down with a short burst from astern. The high likelihood was that the two German planes had merged on radar with the echoes from their opponents. Keeping his cool, Galland closed in on a third Spitfire, hitting him immediately from short range. Losing speed instantly upon taking the burst, the stricken Spitfire nearly collided with Galland. Westphal was about to nail another Spitfire when his guns jammed. The British pilots now realized that German fighters were in their midst. They turned to wade into the invaders.

Firewalling his throttle, Galland put the nose of his fighter down and went racing across the Channel, tracers criss-crossing around his Me 109F-2. Tearing across the hostile grey sea, engines snarling and with tracers and Spitfires streaming after them, Galland saw Westphal pulling ahead of him. Some part of his plane must have been hit. His mind turned oddly to the champagne behind him. What would an impact do to Uncle Theo's birthday present?

Outrunning the Spitfires by the barest margin, they went roaring in over Le Touquet. Starting to let down, Galland saw red flares arc up in front of him. Ground staff on the field below were giving him a frenzied wave-off. Puzzled and cursing, he went around the field again, wondering what was amiss. Finally, he tumbled to the problem. He had been about to land with his gear up. What a birthday present for Uncle Theo. Lt. Colonel Galland, second-ranking ace of the Luftwaffe, landing gear up on the doorstep of his Jafü. One Me 109F-2 wiped out, plus the lobsters and champagne.

In action with the Spitfires, his knee had probably hit the landing gear button, drooping the gear while he was in combat. He had flown home across the Channel gear down. No wonder he had to re-trim his aircraft, or that Westphal had outstripped him. When he hit the landing gear button on final approach to Le Touquet, his landing gear had retracted. Just in time he had spotted the warning flares. Galland and Uncle Theo Osterkamp had more than one reason to say "Good Luck" when they raised their champagne glasses.

HAPPY BIRTHDAY, ONKEL THEO!
Galland fastens his helmet as he prepares to fly a basket of lobsters and champagne to Gen.Lt. Osterkamp as a birthday present on 15 April 1941. Galland's crew chief thought Dolfo was crazy to put the weight in the airplane, but Galland shot down 3 Spitfires before landing.

In April of 1941, the Luftwaffe Bomber Arm was building up its night attacks on Britain. This effort was to divert attention from the movement of most air units eastward for the assault on Russia. Multiple missions were flown by Bomber Arm units remaining in the west, to maintain an illusion of continuing strength. This was an exhausting ordeal for the bomber crews, but they managed to fly over 5,400 sorties in April 1941, or more than they flew in August 1940. London suffered its two heaviest raids of the war in this period. On the nights of 16 and 19 April 1941, approximately 700 bombers struck each time at the British capital. Despite a diminishing number of available bombers, Goering was keeping alive the idea of another round to the Battle of Britain. German propaganda further emphasized this prospect.

Goering's deception efforts included calling an ostentatious April conference of air commanders and combat leaders in Paris. Galland and Moelders were present. Goering regaled his audience with a list of measures to be taken against the RAF. Galland's spirits rose as orator Goering carried the throng along with his fighting words. Moelders nodded approvingly when Galland shot him a sidelong glance.

The two young combat leaders were afterward ordered to meet privately with the Reich Marshal.

"How did you like my speech?" said Goering. "Was it convincing?"

Their approval caused Goering to rub his nose with glee, a characteristic gesture of the Reich Marshal.

"Good. Very good. You believed it, and that is good. Now I will tell you that there isn't a word of truth in it."

Goering then launched into a description of the new glories his Luftwaffe would win in the *forthcoming invasion of Russia*! Galland was dumbfounded. Moelders's face was a mask as Goering laid out the plan. A short, violent campaign with about six weeks actual fighting. Perhaps two or three months with all the cleaning up. Most of the Fighter Arm was being transferred eastward forthwith, including Moelders and his JG 51. The Channel front would be defended by JG 2 and JG 26 alone.

Other fighter units would return to the west when Russia was conquered. Reinforced by the vast material resources of Russia, Goering's Luftwaffe would then bring Britain to her knees – unless the British came to their senses in the meantime. The Soviet Air Force? Nothing to worry about. "Shoot down the leaders and the illiterates won't even be able to find their way home."

While Goering was dismissing Soviet air power in this irresponsible fashion, Germany's air attaché in Moscow had formed a different impression. Lt. Colonel Aschenbrenner, who later rose to Lt. General, arranged for a German engineering team to tour the Soviet aircraft industry. An immense flood of machines was being produced. Factories were employing 30,000 workers per shift, three shifts a day, seven days a week. Soviet aircraft designer Artemis Mikoyan told Aschenbrenner at the end of the conducted tour that the Soviet Union would destroy any attacker. This full blast activity in the Russian aircraft industry contrasted starkly with the Luftwaffe, where Battle of Britain losses had barely been replaced.

Goering had initially opposed the invasion of Russia, directly to Hitler. The Reich Marshal cited the exhaustion of his Luftwaffe and the need for rest, refit, and expansion. When Hitler remained adamant in his plan to smash the Bolshevist colossus, Goering knuckled under. He fell again to the task of pleasing his hero. Hence his ridiculous minimization of the Soviet Air Force in discussing the invasion of Russia with Galland and Moelders. Goering's relentless overworking of bomber crews to fool the British was a completely wasted effort.

Priceless Ultra decrypts, combined with more orthodox intelligence from Germany, Poland, and the Balkans, clearly foretold Hitler's invasion of Russia. A copy of the actual *Barbarossa* directive of 18 December 1940 was supplied to Moscow by Washington, the USA still being neutral. An anonymous anti-Hitler official in Berlin passed the document to the U.S. commercial attaché in a movie theater. Careful planning and stealth availed the Germans nothing. Through Ultra decrypts, the British gained encyclopedic knowledge of German movements, operational plans, and commanders.

Ultra and RAF intelligence were familiar with personalities like Galland's old boss in Spain and Poland, General Wolfram von Richthofen. When this capable commander and his 8th Air Corps were moved from the Channel coast to Rumania and Bulgaria, as part of an aerial build-up to support twenty Army divisions, the British certainly knew that the Germans were not on maneuvers. Russia's Ambassador in London, Ivan Maisky, was summoned to the Foreign Office. He was given a comprehensive and forceful review of these vast German movements toward Soviet frontiers.

Goering made the invasion of Russia sound easy to his two leading fighter pilots. Galland was not persuaded. The Reich Marshal's Eagle Day telex kept echoing in his mind. "Soon you will wipe the British Air Force from the sky." That was also supposed to be an easy assignment. A desperate, bloody, nerve-draining ordeal had ensued, that had still not been forced to a final decision. In the light of this situation, Galland's shock over the coming invasion of Russia was considerable, and did not readily subside.

His logic, common sense, and acumen for aerial warfare saw attacking Russia as an immense gamble. Even blacker were the prospects on the Channel front. Just two Geschwader were to face the mounting power of the RAF, a skeleton defense by any measure. Galland's apprehensions are justified by the now known historical facts. By 1 April 1941, RAF Fighter Command had over 1,200 aircraft in strength and 1,700 available pilots. The massive Empire Air Training Scheme was beginning its large scale production of pilots, while training remained the Luftwaffe's ragged stepchild.

RAF Bomber Command was also rapidly expanding. An alarming production of 4-engined strategic bombers was scheduled. Against this uncoiling strike power, the Luftwaffe was setting JG 2 and JG 26 – one fifth of the fighter strength deployed for the Battle of Britain. Kesselring was posted to the eastern theater, Air Fleet 2 and all. Hugo Sperrle was left in solitary splendor on the Channel with his rump command, JG 2 plus JG 26, and four bomber Gruppen where once there had been forty-four.

Besiegers in 1940, the Luftwaffe on the Channel became the besieged of 1941. Numerical ascendancy by the British was backed with an aggressive spirit. They were out to even the score for 1940. Now it was the Luftwaffe's turn to wait for raiders from across the Channel. Blenheims, Bostons, and Stirlings started crossing the Channel in gaggles of about two dozen, with about three times their own number in fighter escort. The Spitfires were new marques, better armed and well flown.

Railroad terminals, airfields, and strategic industrial targets in France as far as Paris and Lille were now subjected to steady RAF attack. Appearance of the British in a daylight attacking role caused a sensation at Luftwaffe HQ in Paris and Berlin. The tables had been turned, and again the Luftwaffe became dependent upon its Fighter Arm.

Colonel Joachim Huth, as Osterkamp's successor as Jafü 2 at Le Touquet, now had radar. This was a large benefit to the defenders. Luftwaffe fighters on the Channel began operating on the alarm-start system, scrambling against British raids as warning, weather, and time permitted. The numerical odds were against the Luftwaffe and continued to lengthen.

When Germany invaded Russia in June of 1941, the RAF bombing operations against targets in northern France were intensified. From operations in Gruppe strength, Galland was forced to begin leading his entire Geschwader against British incursions, as the RAF increased the number of escorting fighters. The British took their losses and made them up. Galland took his losses and felt them steadily. Sufficient replacement pilots and planes were simply not available. JG 2 and JG 26 both markedly declined in strength. Instead of the normal 80 fighters apiece, the two Geschwader defending the Channel coast were lucky to have 50 aircraft each in a serviceable state.

Part of Adolf Galland's lifelong respect for the RAF stems from this period, when he was living the life of a defending fighter pilot. RAF raids coming in daily, often twice daily and sometimes thrice daily, created a siege existence for JG 26. British bombers and fighters were being shot down, but their raiding strength never diminished. Losses were obviously made up immediately. For Galland and his pilots, the strain was again intense on bodies, minds, and machines, just as it had been in the Battle of Britain.

Attrition of the defenders was exemplified by a couple of successive orders from the High Command. First the German pilots were forbidden to fly over England. Then they were forbidden to pursue the enemy beyond mid-Channel. There would be no more "champagne flights" for Lt. Colonel Galland under these restrictions. Things had changed radically since August of 1940.

21 June 1941 saw Galland in a noontime battle with a formation of Blenheim bombers near St. Omer. Leaving his formation to the task of tackling the escort fighters, Galland led his wingman, Sergeant Hegenauer, into an attack on the bombers. Two firing passes resulted in two Blenheims downed, victories 68 and 69, but the Spitfires quickly intervened. Galland felt hits slamming into his fighter, and he went plunging for some low haze. Tracer laced around him, and black smoke trailed behind his aircraft.

Whizzing into the haze, he was grateful for the white veil between him and his pursuers. His Me 109 still flew, but his temperature gauge was up in the red. His engine soon seized. Again he was drawing on knowledge gained in his soaring days at the Borkenberge. Emerging into clear air as he descended, he was over the Dalais-Marck airfield – luck indeed. Bellying in and climbing out of the fighter safely, he was picked up within the hour by an Me 108 Taifun and flown back to his HQ at Audembert.

ARTIST'S SKETCH OF GALLAND'S BAILOUT
George Lucas of Nunda New York made this drawing showing Galland barely escaping from his plunging Me 109.

Over in England, he thought to himself, some RAF pilots would be carving up the credit for his downing. Hegenauer had also been shot down, but his trusty wingman from Battle of Britain days was unwounded. The ever-aggressive RAF were soon back. More bombers droned over, with another horde of escort fighters.

Taking off alone, Galland went climbing up on intercept. He intended to rendezvous with I/JG 26 during the climb. Southeast of Boulougne he could see the German fighters and a Spitfire formation to their left. There were British stragglers. Hunter Galland forgot the axiom that "a fighter pilot without a wingman has less than half his strength." He went racing for his quarry.

Hitting what he thought was the tail-end Spitfire straggler, he suddenly realized that he had no wingman to confirm this victory. The British machine was spinning downward. This was his 70th victory. Important to get confirmation of this one.

BANG!

A merged chain of rapid explosions ended in a big blast, right in his Me 109. Heavy blows to his head and arm brought rushes of pain. Holes appeared in his wings, jagged and gaping. Cannon fire ripped away part of the fuselage, leaving the wounded Kommodore sitting half in the open at 18,000 feet. The stench of gasoline rose through the cockpit, and coolant went streaming away from the now engineless fighter.

He had learned a new the lesson he impressed continually on the young pilots he commanded: never seek combat without your wingman. That 70th victory he had just shot down was not the last Spitfire straggler. He had been blasted by another unseen Spit approaching from the distant rear.

His soaring skills came in handy for the second time that day, as he banked around to the north and found his shattered Me 109 still under control in the gliding mode. Blood was running down from his head. More blood was dripping from his torn sleeve. He could glide to a friendly field, maybe even get back to Audembert, if he could stay conscious. Without an engine, the aircraft seemed strangely quiet, despite the wind whining through the many holes in its fuselage and wings ... he could make it, he could make it. BOOM!

Igniting gasoline fumes sent a muffled explosion woofing through the fuselage like a fiery wraith. Blazing gasoline came running into the cockpit. Flames leaped around him. Frantically he tore at the cockpit roof release. Stuck. Stuck. Stuck. More flames now, clawing, searing, scorching. Tearing open his safety belt, he thrust upwards at the hinged canopy. Air pressure was pinning it shut.

Terrified, choking, and verging on panic, he thrust upwards at the canopy with his back, putting all his strength into a do-or-die upward shove. Bursting off its mounting, the canopy went flashing away in the slipstream. Momentum from his upward thrust carried Galland halfway out of the cockpit, but again he was stuck. His parachute was jammed in the cockpit canopy support. Roaring earthward, his fighter was an inferno, dragging him to his doom.

Wrapping one arm around the aerial mast, he shoved and pushed with his booted feet against anything that would give traction. Pull, haul, twist, turn, pull more, twist again, and all the while the infernal earth was coming up at him like thunder. Miraculously he burst free, tumbling like an acrobat. In his shaken state, he went to pull his ripcord, noticing just in time that he was fumbling inadvertently with his parachute harness quick-release – a passport to the next world. Making very sure he had the ripcord, he pulled. A plumping noise and a bone-straining jerk told him he would survive.

Squelching down in a boggy meadow, he now paid the price for the surge of adrenaline that had powered him through his ordeal. He went instantly to the fringe of complete collapse. Pain pulsed from his gunshot wounds and burns. Blood was all over him. A wrenched ankle sustained in his final landing ballooned up inside his boot. He could not even stand.

French farmers who had seen him descend nervously carried him into a nearby farmhouse. A Todt organization car soon afterwards whisked him back to Audembert. His fate was unknown at his own HQ. Fears had been expressed of his death. Papi Causin was again the sterling aide, providing a hefty jolt of cognac and a big, black cigar to the wounded Kommodore.

At Hardinghem hospital, Dr. Heim of the German Navy sewed up his wounds. Heim was a good friend that Galland appreciated even more in his present extremity. Not every doctor could be responsible surgeon and friend simultaneously. Fighter pilot survival from such a brink was known as a "birthday." Luftwaffe pilots held that the fortunate flyer had been "born again" after a brush with death.

Galland staged the required birthday party at Audembert, celebrating his 70th victory at the same time. Congratulations came from Hitler via telex. The Fuehrer also announced the award to Galland, as the first officer of the Wehrmacht so honored, of a newly instituted order of the Knight's Cross.

To his Oak Leaves were now added the Swords (*Schwerter*). The Swords were celebrated with high consumption of champagne. The bubbly wine helped drown for a while the pains of his wounds, but it could not wash away a Hitler order contained in the same telex: Lt. Colonel Galland was to cease operational flying on the express orders of the Fuehrer.

The grounding order was initially unnecessary. Galland wasn't fit to fly. He needed two weeks even to begin walking properly again. The RAF, meanwhile, just kept coming in day after day. Galland nearly died of frustration. He began edging his way back into the air with "test flights" and similar ruses.

Galland was unable to restrain himself from going back to regular missions. On the first such operation, he sprang into the cockpit of the new Me 109 prepared for his exclusive use by his crew chief, Sergeant Meyer. Upset by his Kommodore's near-fatal head wound, Meyer had thoughtfully fitted an extra piece of armor plate on top of the canopy, but neglected to inform Galland. The Kommodore got a thump on his already tender head from the changed geometry of the cockpit roof. He bawled something like "Dummkopf" as he roared away, leaving Meyer aghast.

In the ensuing wild battle with Blenheim bombers and their Spitfire escort, Galland sustained further head damage. A Spitfire shot his cockpit to bits and got him in the head. Blood running down his face, he landed at Audembert and got out of the aircraft before the horrified gaze of Meyer. Galland was lucky. Meyer's custom-fitted armor plate had absorbed a cannon hit, which would have ended Galland's life and terminated the worries he was now having over violating Hitler's personal grounding order.

Meyer got 100 marks and special leave as a token of his Kommodore's gratitude. The tolerant Dr. Heim again sewed up Galland's head, while shaking his own with incredulity. Ordered to the Wolf's Redoubt to receive his Swords award, Galland arrived in East Prussia highly apprehensive over his violation of Hitler's order grounding him.

The Fuehrer showed appreciation of JG 26 and JG 2 in defending the Channel coast. He recognized the higher burden they were carrying. Hitler promised that he would soon relieve

50 Army divisions in the east, and more fighter Geschwader would be available to fight the RAF. Hitler made no reference to his grounding order. Galland had the eerie feeling, nevertheless, that Hitler knew he was worried about the Fuehrer's adverse reaction.

As he dismissed the young ace, Hitler descended for a fleeting moment from his Fuehrer's pedestal.

"We like your bravery," he said, "but please look after yourself."

On the Channel coast in 1941, any Luftwaffe fighter pilot who didn't look after himself had a short life expectancy. Galland loved life too much to throw his away.

FOURTEEN

"Now It's Your Turn"

Constant operational activity in 1941, with numerous targets provided by the RAF on every day suitable for flying, made this the most successful period in Galland's career as a fighter pilot. His expertise and acumen continued to increase, despite fatigue. His victory tally rose steadily. His boyhood dream of excellence was being lived out daily in this world at war.

Warriors have always followed the exemplar-leader, and the pilots of JG 26 would have followed Adolf Galland anywhere. Among them in 1941 were his brothers Paul and Wutz. Hardly an operational day passed that did not involve one of the three brothers in action, and often all three were in combat simultaneously. Paul required a lengthy running-in period, during which success in aerial combat eluded him. For the 21 year-old youngster this time was especially frustrating. His brother was not only the famous ace-leader, but also the Kommodore.

Paul therefore felt obliged to do well. Pressure on him became even greater when Wutz joined JG 26 as a fledgling fighter pilot and was quickly successful. Wutz had a marked talent for air-to-air shooting. Paul in the beginning thus had his moments of envy and regret. In due course, the youngster's patient persistence was rewarded, and he became an ace along with his brothers Wutz and Keffer.

Galland's leadership style as Kommodore was to be always first into the air. Any pilot quick enough to get airborne ahead of him would find his Kommodore hard behind. Tactics had to be devised to inflict maximum casualties on the RAF, with minimum attrition on his own numerically inferior forces. Aggressive defense keynoted his tactics, which always sought to keep the battle initiative for JG 26.

With sardonic joy he noticed how the British fighters were tied to the bombers, just as most of his fighters had been in the Battle of Britain. He could readily imagine the frustrations of the British fighter pilots. They would be cursing their damned orders, just as he had done when tied down to close escort flying. They would be longing to lunge after JG 26 in the free chase.

Galland's usual tactic was to lead his fighters above and behind the bomber formation, up in the sun if possible. Diving down through the escorting fighters, they would attack the bombers and then dive away at full throttle. Initially ordered to attack the bombers only, Galland was able to get this restriction modified. This prevented his needless loss of part of the initiative.

After these diving attacks, the Spitfires would go after the JG 26 fighters furiously, chasing them right down to the deck. Quickly the Germans learned respect for the cannon fire from these new Spitfire variants. German numerical inferiority at this time foreshadowed the coming years, in which Allied numerical ascendancy would be extended into Germany's own airspace.

Galland developed tactics with his own staff flight that demanded the top performance in his entire Geschwader. Later on, the same excellence would be demanded from the squadron that was ordered to fly with him. His tactics were dangerous, but effective. When cloudy conditions prevailed, he would cunningly inch his formation right in among the Spitfire escort.

Unless the enemy were super sharp and perceptive, the similarity between Spitfire and Me 109 silhouettes made this tactic feasible. Colors and markings were also difficult to distinguish at this speed amid the diffuse glare of cloudy conditions. Easing along amid the escort, Galland would reach a position of advantage for readily attacking a bomber. Diving down suddenly, the German formation would clobber the bombers and be away into the distance, sometimes before the Spitfires knew what had happened. These tactics called for a cool head and nerves of steel. Pilot quality in Galland's formations was excellent, and they pulled off this ploy repeatedly.

Another Galland attack stratagem exposed him to the danger of flying alone, but it was also repeatedly successful. Directing the other JG 26 fighters to position themselves "on the perch" above and behind the bombers, Galland would make his stealthy solo approach from below. Cloud was also needed for this tactic, but it depended mainly upon the ostentatious assembly of the other German aircraft capturing the attention of the escorting Spitfires.

If he were able to climb up to the bombers unseen, he would fire a lethal burst into one of the lower British aircraft, then whip away into the clouds before the escort reacted. Risk was high with this tactic. He was vulnerable to diving Spitfires after his attack, and also during the approach. Galland never allowed his tactics to settle into a routine. Variations and innovations kept the enemy fighter escorts off balance.

The strain of leadership in an overworked fighter Geschwader was intensified by the daily combats of his brothers. No one has ever said of Galland that he was inhuman, but the presence of his beloved brothers exposed him to inhuman pressure. One or the other of them was always bailing out, bellying in, or being reported going down somewhere trailing smoke. The nervous strain of having his own blood in jeopardy under his own orders led him to suggest that transfers to other units or fronts were desirable. Wutz and Paul both adamantly declined. They were under no illusions about the risks. None of them expected to be an old, gray-haired fighter pilot describing the war to his grandchildren.

Their evenings and leisure times together became the most precious interludes. The large and comfortable house at Audembert where Galland and the other pilots were quartered became their second home. Over the good French wine they would recapture their loving yesteryears in Westerholt. Boyhood came even closer in the luxury bunker with its open fire. Galland had laid out a huge electric train set for relaxation and diversion, and they played with it for hours. Shut out briefly was the harsh reality that on the morrow one of them – or perhaps all three – might be meeting other fallen pilots in the airmen's heaven.

Not every evening brought relaxation and joy. One such evening was 10 May 1941, when Galland's telephone rang during the last minutes of daylight. An agitated Reich Marshal Goering was calling, his voice a near babble.

"Galland, you are to take off immediately with your whole Geschwader. *With your whole Geschwader, understand*?"

"Herr Reich Marshal, we have no reports of any aircraft flying in."

"Flying in? Flying in?" Goering's voice was near hysterical. "What do you mean, flying in? An aircraft is flying *out*! The Deputy of the Fuehrer has gone mad and is flying to England in a Me 110. He must be shot down. And Galland, call me personally when you get back."

Getting the anticipated course and approximate 6 pm departure time of Hess from Augsburg-Haunstetten, Galland put down the telephone with some of Goering's agitation roiling in his own mind. Ordered to shoot down the Deputy Fuehrer on the personal orders of the Reich Marshal? Galland was accustomed to occasional crazy orders, but this was absolutely cuckoo.

Night was falling fast. About ten minutes flying time remained. If he took off now with his whole Geschwader and went hunting for the Me 110 that Hess was supposed to be flying, how could it be distinguished from other Me 110s of the night fighter force. They would already be up on test flights and other missions around dusk. Even if they found and shot down Hess – a million-to-one chance – how would they get down themselves without wrecking half of JG 26's fighters? In unaccustomed night landings with no guidance, the carnage would be terrible. The whole thing was insane.

Galland accordingly ordered each Gruppe to scramble one or two planes. The aircraft were to make a couple of circuits and then land again. He gave no reason for this strange order. His subordinates would already regard him as slightly crazy for ordering such dusk hops. He felt it wise not to add orders to shoot down the Deputy Fuehrer.

After a suitable interval Galland reported back to Goering. JG 26 had failed to find the missing Me 110. Goering remained distraught. Galland emphasized the slight chance Hess had of making it to Scotland, or of avoiding the Spitfires if he got that far. The Reich Marshal was not placated.

Hess successfully crossed the North Sea as he had long planned. After evading a Spitfire, he parachuted near the estate of the Duke of Hamilton. According to British historian David Irving, a British secret service party awaited Hess that night. Officialdom brought down a security curtain on Hess's lone effort to stop the war, and kept it down by incarcerating Hess in Spandau prison until his mysterious death there.

Official deceit, evasion, and obscurantism provoked much speculation about the Hess affair. Writers have asserted that Galland knew more than he told. All questions posed by various writers about Galland's alleged role in the affair have been asked him by the authors, personally and bluntly. The truth of Galland's involvement is that Goering gave him crazy orders in a bizarre situation. These orders could not be carried out literally, without high hazard to the pilots and fighters of his command. They were therefore obeyed only in token fashion.

After the invasion of Russia, conversations among the three Galland brothers and their comrades centered on news from the Eastern front. The Luftwaffe had covered itself with new glories, as Goering had predicted. In the history of aerial warfare, the greatest one-day victory is the Luftwaffe triumph over the Soviet Air Force on 22 June 1941. Over 2,000 Russian machines were destroyed in the "surprise" assault. Warnings to the Soviet government through diplomatic channels of the imminent blow, as well as Churchill's direct personal warning to Stalin, had resulted in no special vigilance.

Dr. Goebbels knew what to do with such victory tidings. Splashed through the German media with spreads of photographs, and with newsreels graphically depicting the shambles, Luftwaffe triumphs in Russia were difficult for Galland and his pilots to comprehend. Pinned down and outnumbered on the Channel coast, battling a foe who was capable, aggressive, and growing in strength, they were fighting a totally different war.

Soon came the reports of Eastern front fighter pilot victories, many dozens of victories. In the big HQ house at Audembert, they would wonder about the incredible strings of downings in Russia. Moelders quickly reached 100 victories, unprecedented in the history of aerial warfare. Hitler awarded him the Diamonds to his Knight's Cross, the highest order of the decoration.

Other pilots were downing 4 and 5 Soviet planes a day. 20 victories in a month contrasted sharply with the creeping pace of their own victories against the RAF. In May of 1941, Field Marshal Sperrle had congratulated Galland and JG 26 for reaching the all-time Geschwader total of 500 victories. That had seemed like a major achievement then. At the Eastern front scoring rate, a Geschwader there would register 500 victories in a couple of months. Were the pilots in Russia shooting down aircraft or ducks?

Galland and JG 26 had a chance to see at first hand the quality of their own opposition on 9 August 1941. Wing Commander Douglas Bader of the RAF literally "dropped in" on them, by parachute, after combat over the Pas de Calais. First to know of Bader's imminent arrival was the wily specialist and master linguist, Horst Barth, at his listening post in an old farmhouse. He had followed Bader's unit in action, knowing well Bader's voice and nickname – the "Stationmaster" of Tangmere RAF Station. As soon as he heard that Bader was bailing out, Barth contacted HQ immediately, urging them to search for the famous RAF ace. Barth was unaware at this time that Bader had lost both his legs in a 1931 crash.

Bader believed he had collided in mid-air with a Me 109, or even perhaps with one of his own squadron's Spitfires, when he suddenly lost the empennage of his fighter. Many years after the war, he was told that a Luftwaffe fighter pilot had caught him unawares at close range. He bailed out. The Germans were astonished when they located Bader and found that he only had one leg, and that this one leg was artificial. His other leg was jammed in his stricken Spitfire. Impacting on the one artificial leg, Bader was painfully injured when it was rammed up into his chest. He was taken to hospital in St. Omer.

Galland's mechanics retrieved Bader's other leg from his crashed Spitfire, made it serviceable again, and returned the leg to Bader in the hospital. The British ace was gratified. Horst Barth had meanwhile been assigned to watch over Bader until he was taken to formal POW internment. Bravery and courage are much admired by German soldiers, and the pilots of JG 26 were intrigued to learn that the English ace was legless. That won respect.

Once Bader was able to move about a little, Galland invited him to Audembert to see their base and meet his staff and some of the JG 26 pilots. A magnificent Horch sedan was provided by the Luftwaffe to Galland as the normal privilege of a Kommodore. Too grand and conspicuous for Galland's pleasure excursions, the Horch was seldom used. Here was a chance to employ the big car appropriately. Bader was collected at the hospital by an escort officer, a sergeant-major, and a driver from JG 26 HQ. The Stationmaster arrived at Audembert in style.

Squeaking along on his damaged tin legs as though needing oil, Bader stumped into a lavish reception that would have held its own with anything thrown at the London Dorchester. Colonel Joachim Huth had come over from Le Touquet where he was Jafü, and with Barth as a rapid fire interpreter, Bader's initial suspicions quickly disappeared. He realized that Galland was extending a soldierly courtesy and not trying to trap him into giving information. One of Galland's big cigars further helped.

Bader was shown the base facilities. He talked fighter planes and piloting with Galland in detail. Galland even allowed his English visitor to sit in the Kommodore's personal Me 109. Bader was photographed in the cockpit, with the Abbeville Boys' C.O. explaining the layout. Bader's renowned gumption had not been affected by his injuries, or by his POW status. He actually asked Galland if he could take off in the Me 109 and "make a couple of circuits of the field."

Part of Galland wanted to let this admirable foe fly the Me 109, but of course such a request had to be denied. Galland did ask Goering, in Bader's behalf, if arrangements could be made to have his spare legs, his pipe, and his favorite tobacco sent over from England. Full of Old World chivalry, Goering agreed to safe conduct for an aircraft carrying this special cargo. The RAF was notified on a special rescue frequency, but didn't emulate Goering's chivalrous spirit.

The legs duly came in a specially labeled crate during an air raid targeted on JG 26 airfields. The British did not want any local armistices or social matters to slow down their Non Stop Offensive – Bader got his legs and his pipe, but in the interim had tried to escape on his old legs. The dauntless Briton lowered himself on knotted sheets from the top floor of the St. Omer hospital. Free for one night, he was recaptured by Horst Barth, who found him under a haystack.

Galland took considerable flak from the High Command over the escape incident. His reception for Bader was investigated and regarded stonily. The Luftwaffe High Command was as unbending as the RAF. The two great fighter aces both eventually became legends in their own time. They did not regret the humanity of their first wartime encounter, which launched an enduring friendship. Bader enters our story again later, but it was a saddened Galland in California in September of 1982 who learned of Bader's passing. Enemies for a short time because of the decisions and actions of others, they were of their own volition friends for the rest of their lives.

Four months prior to the Bader incident, an aircraft took off from the Heinkel factory that demonstrated Germany's vast technical lead in fighter development. The He 280 was a sleek twin-jet with tricycle landing gear, capable of over 500 mph even on primitive turbojets. Intended armament was initially three 20mm cannons. A proposed variant, the He 280B, was to carry six 20mm cannons and over 1,000 pounds of bombs. This aircraft had stubborn tail flutter problems, and the Air Ministry lost interest in developing the revolutionary machine.

The Heinkel twin-jet was flying and available for development to production when Bader dropped in on Galland. Early in 1942, mock combat with the redoubtable Fw 190 showed the clear superiority of the jet. This digression is made here in the proper time context, because much has to be related shortly about the Messerschmitt jet, the Me 262. Galland became intimately concerned with making the Me 262 operational.

The He 280 flew as a pure twin-jet aircraft more than fifteen months prior to the Me 262. Eight of these aircraft were actually built. Within the time context of the 1939-45 war, this was a very substantial lead for Heinkel. The Germans thus had within their technical grasp, during the RAF's first Non Stop Offensive, the weapon needed to abort the ruin that would later cascade from daylight skies.

As 1941 wore on, the grinding struggle on the Channel coast never diminished. Amid the strain and stress, Galland never lost his ability to find humor even in irritating things. Witness this report to HQ from the Kommodore of JG 26, concerning certain Luftwaffe personnel who were seemingly unaware that Germany was at war.

To Jafü 2 From Kommodore, JG 26:

During several duty flights to the home territory of Germany, conditions were encountered at air bases, not to mention any names, which should be brought to the attention of higher authority. For reasons of military discipline, correction of these conditions seems urgently necessary. The following observations have been made:

1. In general, every landing of an outside aircraft for refueling is perceived as a disturbance of the peace, and as a burden to base personnel.

2. Personnel for start support and especially the refueling personnel are surpassed for their laziness and unmilitary slackness only by the air control personnel.

3. Oil is basically never available at the fuel pump, but in the most remote hangar, which is closed after 5pm.

4. Air control personnel give a most unmilitary impression. Saluting and other military customs are considered completely out of fashion. They also work as slowly as possible and invariably with cigarettes sticking out of their mouths.

5. Weather service stations are occupied almost entirely by officials on crutches, "for war period only," who have to be supported by many girls. The impression is like entering a Strength Through Joy tourist office. Weather for the route is exclusively couched in pessimistic terms, with much fussing and indecision. In the meantime, when the ladies present ask for autographs, the assistant meteorologists not involved loudly crumple sandwich paper wrapping.

6. At some bases, flight orders are controlled by civilian refueling personnel. They say: "I have to see your flight order, or I cannot give you any fuel."

7. When landing after 5 pm, the impression given is that the base has been evacuated for several days. The possibilities for sabotage at the fuel pump, or at the hangars, are wide open for action.

Because of these circumstances, pilots at the front have an antipathy towards flights into the home territory. The difficulties are not the lack of manpower, but the attitude and appearance of the soldiers and the posts themselves that are causing the trouble.

Signed:
Galland
Lt. Col. and Kommodore

RAF ACE DOUGLAS BADER AT AUDEMBERT
Galland was informed "we've caught a Big eagle!" Members of JG 26 crowd around to meet the famous legless ace. Adolph (profile left), Schöpfel, Galland, Causin, Bader, Barth, Huth and Eschwege are present. British newspapers reported Huth had a pistol in his hand but it was gloves, as can be seen here.

AUGUST 1941
Famed RAF ace Douglas Bader was shot down and brought to Galland's airbase. Horst Barth (gesturing) interprets the meeting. Left to right: Seifert, Schmitt, Galland, Meinardus, Causin, Bader and Barth.

On a flight to the home territory about the time he wrote the foregoing complaint, Galland had gone hunting at Elchwald in East Prussia, another of the lodges Goering had assigned to himself as Germany's Master of the Hunt. Galland's companion had been Ernst Udet, Chief of Luftwaffe Procurement and Supply, with whom he enjoyed a warm personal friendship. They had first become friends when Galland was a successful new member of the Luftwaffe trap shooting team, founded by Udet in early Luftwaffe days.

Udet was idolized by the young fighter pilots. He exemplified those qualities that were expected of dashing, early aviators. A humorous, charming, and carefree man who loved aeroplanes, women, champagne, and fun, Udet's checkered interwar career included barnstorming, stunt piloting, test flying, and movie making. He even had a brief fling as an aircraft manufacturer as *Udet Flugzeugbau* in Munich. He was the top scoring living ace of the German Air Corps, with 62 victories, and the most famous active pilot in Germany. His personality and happy temperament made him a charming companion.

As the young aces of the new generation pressed up toward his tally of 62 victories, Udet would chide and josh them that they were under no circumstances to pass his score. In his bachelor pad in Berlin, he would host the young aces with champagne and challenge them to target pistol shooting matches on his indoor range. Udet would ply them with cognac until their aim deteriorated and then outscore them. His legendary cartooning skill is illustrated in this book, with the victory "bags" of aerial hunters Galland and Moelders the subject of his art.

A man of his sunny temperament did not belong in the intrigue-ridden maelstrom of Luftwaffe production. He was unfitted to be either an executive or a high military officer. He was incapable of the ruthlessness essential to any military procurement program, German or otherwise. Goering, as his old C.O. from the Richthofen Circus, nevertheless insisted that Udet join the Luftwaffe for public relations and political reasons. Udet's peace of mind essentially ceased as he sought to discharge duties for which he was not fitted.

As *Generalluftzeugmeister* he was out of his element. He had subordinates who were deceitful and disloyal. Goering's counterproductive organizational arrangements, involving State Secretary Milch, the Luftwaffe General Staff, and Udet have already been recounted. Udet got all the blame for the material consequences of the Luftwaffe's divided hierarchy. Adolf Galland would shortly have to deal with many of those consequences in a position of high responsibility.

The Stuka disaster in the Battle of Britain had hit Udet hard. He was blamed for the Stuka and criticized for failing to expand aircraft production during and following the Battle of Britain. He caught hell for not bringing improved aircraft types quickly into service. By October of 1941, with the German Army in a critical race with the Russian winter, Udet was under heavy pressure from Goering and other high officials. Most of them were responsible in some degree for the things now going awry. Udet was essentially being blamed for being Ernst Udet and for not magically transforming himself into a production wizard. He got all the blame.

When Galland met the normally genial little dynamo at Elchwald, Udet was plunged in gloom. Gone were the smiling charm and warm humor. Depression and guilt were in their place. Over and over, he told Galland that Germany needed many thousands of fighters. He blamed himself for not even being able to make up the battle losses of existing units. Galland left Elchwald with his own spirits markedly lowered by Udet's despondency.

When a radio broadcast on 17 November 1941 announced Udet's death, "while testing a new type of weapon," Galland felt sharp pangs of grief. Such a friend, a historical personality to boot, could never be replaced. Shortly afterward, he was ordered to Berlin for Udet's state funeral on 21 November 1941.

Six of Germany's leading fighter pilots, all holders of the Knight's Cross or its higher orders, formed Udet's honor guard. They wore steel helmets and carried the massive Luftwaffe swords. Word was now out that Udet was a suicide. Galland found himself recalling Udet's recent litany of failure, desperation, and guilt. Goering walked all the way to the cemetery behind the coffin, in a phony show of respect for his old comrade. Udet knew better. On the head of his bed before taking his life he had scrawled, "Iron Man, why have you forsaken me?" Udet was right. Goering started a posthumous investigation to support a court martial of the dead Udet. Political dynamite turned up, and Goering dropped the idea.

Werner Moelders should have been present at the funeral. He had looked up to Udet. Promoted to Colonel and appointed General of the Fighter Arm by Goering, Moelders had recently flown to the Crimea for first hand evaluation of urgent fighter and Luftwaffe problems in that sector. Despite a strict grounding order, he had shot down some more aircraft. He missed Udet's funeral because vile Crimean weather prevented his takeoff that day. The day after Udet's funeral, Moelders insisted on returning to Berlin to report on conditions in the Crimea. Loss of one engine in atrocious weather resulted in the mortal crash of his He 111 at Breslau-Schoengarten. Moelders had been about to achieve his ambition to be the Luftwaffe's Boelcke. He had risen to General of the Fighter Arm, only to be lost in a flying accident.

Galland was returning by train to the Channel coast with Walter Oesau, Kommodore of JG 2, who had also been in the honor guard for Udet. The train suddenly stopped at a small station in the Lippe district, and the local stationmaster ran the length of the train calling Galland's name. There was a telephone call awaiting him from Berlin. General Karl Bodenschatz, Goering's adjutant, gave him the ghastly news that Moelders was dead. Goering's orders were for Galland to return to Berlin immediately. A train passing the opposite way would pick him up in less than an hour.

In a depressing replay of the Udet funeral, Galland was again in the honor guard. This time he was saying his final farewell to his rival and friend, the man who had first shown him how to shoot down aircraft. Now Moelders was being buried in Invaliden cemetery, not far from Udet and von

Richthofen. When the salvoes and tributes ended, Galland stood with five other aces at graveside, in steel helmets and with drawn swords, their heads bowed.

Memories of the departed comrade poured through Galland's mind: his great skill as a teacher; his leadership qualities; his incomparable combat gifts; and his moral stature. From classification as medically unfit for pilot training, Moelders had risen in the short years since the Condor Legion to the highest post in the Fighter Arm. He had not had time to fill the office fully with his talents.

"*Galland! Galland!*"

Goering was calling, interrupting his sad reverie. Galland looked up, and there was the Reich Marshal, urgently beckoning with his gold marshal's baton. Embarrassed at leaving the honor guard, and feeling clumsy and awkward with the unaccustomed sword, Galland made his way to Goering.

"Now it's your turn" said the Reich Marshal. "I name you herewith as Moelders' successor, to be General of the Fighter Arm."

In the most terrible fashion imaginable, Galland had finally caught up to his rival. Destiny had thrust upon him the Boelckean challenge.

FIFTEEN

General of the Fighter Arm

Conflicting thoughts whirled through Galland's head as the significance of his new appointment dawned on him. Reluctance to leave his beloved JG 26 was his main reaction. Commanding his elite Geschwader had been the pride and joy of his life. General of the Fighter Arm? That meant desks, paper work, telephones, staff officers, and no combat action.

When he mentioned this to Goering, the Reich Marshal brushed it all aside. The Fuehrer had approved his appointment. A man of his ability had to be given wider scope. The death of Moelders was a tragedy for the Fighter Arm, but Galland had to carry on. Already the post had been given new and more comprehensive responsibilities, according to Goering.

The Reich Marshal mollified Galland's pangs at leaving JG 26 by promising to convey the ex-Kommodore's farewell wishes to his men personally. Goering was to visit his dead nephew's grave in Abbeville in a few days, and JG 26 HQ at Audembert was nearby. Peter Goering had died in combat under Galland's command and flying as his wingman.

Goering duly delivered Galland's farewell, his last Special Geschwader Report:

> "For 15 months I led JG 26 during the hardest combats as your Kommodore. The Commander-in-Chief of the Luftwaffe has appointed me as General of the Fighter Arm, to his HQ, which became effective immediately. The death of Colonel Moelders has hit us all very hard.
>
> "With a broken heart, I leave this Geschwader. The proud memory of having mastered every mission with you great fighter pilots, and the obligation we have towards the war heroes killed in action, give me the strength for a new and great task.
>
> "You will fight on with your new Kommodore, and you will be victorious. My thoughts will always be with you. The name of our wing must be covered with glory to enter the history of war."

Galland's promotion to Colonel was also celebrated at the farewell gathering. Amid the toasting and reminiscing, the departing Kommodore realized how well he had been served by his able Gruppenkommandeure in JG 26. Pingel had been downed pursuing Stirlings over England and was now a POW. Adolph had been killed in action. Muencheberg had been transferred to the Mediterranean. Here in the room now were Seifert and the diminutive "Pips" Priller. The swarthy, dark-haired, and dependable Gerhard Schoepfel had been named as his successor in command of JG 26. No Kommodore had ever been better served than by men like these.

Galland smiled and smoked his endless cigars, and downed his share of the champagne, but inwardly he was in turmoil. The honor of commanding JG 26 had been torn from him, when he was at his peak as a combat leader and ace pilot. In exchange, what was he getting? A brass hat, a desk in Berlin, and mountains of paperwork. General of the Fighter Arm was the highest post a fighter pilot could reach and still be wholly involved with fighters. The magnitude of the responsibility still had him stunned.

A quantum jump upwards, the new job exacted a high price: relinquishment of the Kommodore's tasks that he had tackled with passionate interest.

Through the haze of cigar smoke, and over the top of the ambient chatter in the room, several times Galland heard what others were thinking. "Mufti will know how to get things done in Berlin, and he will help us here," and, "If Mufti has to leave us, thank God it is for a job where he can really help the fighters." He wondered how he would fare, the hunter and fighter, in that Berlin anthill. His memory of its oppressive atmosphere when he had returned from Spain was still clear.

Galland's apprehensions about his new job were enhanced by his hazy ideas relative to its scope and nature. Goering had not discussed this with him. The Reich Marshal had been more concerned with crushing Galland's objections to leaving the front. The office assigned to the General of the Fighters on the

Lindenstrasse in Berlin caused Galland to groan inwardly. A typical Air Ministry paper mill, it was manned by lethargic, old-fashioned bureaucrats in the classic governmental pattern.

When Moelders had been appointed General of the Fighters on 7 July 1941, he spent little time in the office before going out on a full-scale inspection of fighter units. He wanted an accurate perspective of front line conditions. That was typical of the analytical Moelders. Galland knew his late rival well enough to know that there would have been sweeping changes in this part of the Air Ministry once Moelders settled into his job. Now Galland would have to build up the modern, forward-looking staff essential to his needs.

The Luftwaffe from its inception had always had an Inspector of the Fighters, the department being originally known as the Office for the Inspection of Fighter and Bomber Aircraft. Udet was the first Inspector, followed by Robert Ritter Von Greim and Bruno Loerzer, both of whom had been fighter aces in World War I. Raithel, Werner Junck, and von Massow – all belonging to the infant days of fighter aviation – were next in succession. Major General Kurt von Doering had immediately preceded Moelders. At the time of von Doering's appointment early in 1941, Goering re-titled the office as *General der Jagdflieger*, meaning literally, General of the Fighter Pilots. Loosely and usually, the appointment was referred to as General of the Fighter Arm, or simply General of the Fighters.

Functions of inspection which had previously occupied the office were now augmented with new powers of command, advice, and consultation in technical development, operations, personnel selection, and planning. These were steps that should have been taken before the war. The scope of the office was thus made nominally extensive, as a new assignment within the Luftwaffe hierarchy. The post of General of the Fighters would be essentially shaped by the personality discharging its responsibilities.

Moelders had vision, but had been killed before he could set his stamp on the office. All Galland's other predecessors were not men of either vision or strong inspiration. This fitted in well with the secondary and limited role originally assigned to fighters in the Luftwaffe. Goering's flair for administration may be seen in the way he extended the responsibilities of the General of the Fighter Arm, as compared with the largely ceremonial Inspector's post. He was late in making the changes, which had been largely forced by the march of events.

Goering did not shrink from the ultimate application of his 1940 policy of promoting successful young fighter leaders to significant commands. Moelders and Galland were both on the sunny side of 30 when named General of the Fighter Arm. Such promotions were unimaginable in the pre-war Luftwaffe. Goering added another touch. Galland was made responsible to the Chief of the Luftwaffe General Staff in operational matters, and to the Commander-in-Chief of the Luftwaffe in disciplinary matters. This meant, in effect, that Adolf Galland, not yet 30 years of age, had only two superiors – Goering and Hitler.

GALLAND NOW GENERAL OF THE FIGHTERS
On the last day of Galland's reign as Kommodore of JG 26, Goering visited the Geschwader to decorate other officers. Second from right is Oberleutnant Schneider.

Such arrangements raised eyebrows and temperatures among Air Ministry bureaucrats and high Luftwaffe personages. The currents of distrust and suspicion that run through all governmental organizations when innovations are proposed were now strongly stimulated. Everyone was mindful that this young Colonel had Hitler's support, as well as being Goering's choice. An officer of such tender years with enormous responsibilities, *and minus any staff training whatsoever*, was looked upon as a phenomenon. His direct access to the two most powerful men in Germany excited considerable high-level disquiet.

These reactions of distrust communicated themselves to Galland as he began phasing himself into the Berlin scene. He made courtesy visits to the various bureaus and inspectorates. Although he had the advantages of his fame, outstanding combat record, and the Swords to his Knight's Cross, he had also been preceded by his reputation for outspoken frankness. A few high officials found it memorable to meet Germany's most successful fighter ace. Coolness elsewhere was marked, and he was greeted with bland, official correctitude.

His charisma with the ladies was still in full function and reached with its usual power into the Air Ministry secretarial pools. His appearance in offices with female secretaries and clerks generated the same excitement as a visit from a movie star. This made the bureaucrats all the more suspicious, and envious, of the black-haired, mustached General of the Fighter Arm.

His black cigars had acquired similar symbolic status for his image as those of Winston Churchill's across the Channel. Galland's promotion to General of the Fighter Arm was a golden business opportunity for Germany's cigar makers. Here was a charismatic cigar smoker who was being prodigiously publicized throughout Germany. His picture was everywhere. Five companies wrote Galland, begging for the honor of being his exclusive cigar supplier for the duration. His personal cigars would be free. Galland magnanimously accepted all five offers, "so nobody would feel slighted." At the surrender in 1945, he still had a stock of sixty boxes.

Cigars remained a bone of contention with Hitler. Galland was never permitted to smoke them in the Fuehrer's presence. Hitler declared pointedly time and again how undesirable the cigar habit was for both health and educational reasons. Seeing a hero of Galland's stature with a cigar in his hand, or sticking out of his mouth, was a bad example to German youth, according to the Fuehrer. Despite these admonishments, Galland could not bring himself to throw away good cigars every time a photographer approached, even if they were free cigars. He was inevitably caught in photographs with the cigars. Hitler eventually forbade him to have his photograph taken smoking, holding, or flourishing a cigar.

As soon as he had made his Berlin rounds in December 1941, Galland flew to Goldap in East Prussia. Luftwaffe HQ was set up here in a specially-equipped train, carrying the good old English name of "Robinson." A suitably furnished additional car was coupled on to "Robinson" for the exclusive use of the General of the Fighters. He would thenceforth always have accommodation, communications, and a staff available at Goldap, immediately adjacent to the Chief of the Luftwaffe General Staff. He was also handy to Goering at Rominten Heath, and to Hitler at the Wolf's Lair east of nearby Rastenburg.

His first official call at Goldap was on General der Flieger Hans Jeschonnek, Chief of the Luftwaffe General Staff. One of the architects of the Luftwaffe, Jeschonnek was occupying his high post at the age of only 42. His brilliant career was emblematic of both the strengths and weaknesses of the Luftwaffe. While Galland had no conception of it at the time he met with Jeschonnek, he had inherited a complex legacy as General of the Fighter Arm that was due in many ways to Jeschonnek's past actions.

The Chief of the Luftwaffe General Staff had devoted his entire life to military service. He was commissioned out of the Prussian Cadet Corps into the infantry in 1915, not yet aged 16. Like Goering and many others, he volunteered for the German Flying Corps, became a pilot at age 17, and was able to shoot down two Allied aircraft before the 1918 armistice. He was selected for permanent duty with the 100,000-man Reichswehr permitted Germany after World War I. Assignment as adjutant to State Secretary of Aviation Erhard Milch was an important career step. He helped organize the Air Ministry and participated in the secret preparations for the new Luftwaffe.

Jeschonnek's intellectual capacity and energy marked him early for a significant career in the Luftwaffe. Appointed Kommodore of the Training Geschwader after the Luftwaffe's official birth, he was frequently consulted on operational, technical, and training requirements. Air power conceptions at this time were largely theoretical, and mistakes were easy to make. Operational requirements and goals for the massive air fleets that were planned were ill-defined. In this developmental period, Jeschonnek's abilities became widely respected, and on 1 October 1937 he was made chief of Branch I, the Operational Branch of the Luftwaffe General Staff.

As a rising star with access to the brilliant General Walter Wever – historically considered the first Chief of the Luftwaffe General Staff – Jeschonnek was regarded as a potential successor to Wever despite his youth. Rapid promotions through significant posts saw Jeschonnek reach colonel at age 38, at a time when virtually all other colonels were past 50. On 1 February 1939, Colonel Hans Jeschonnek was appointed Chief of the Luftwaffe General Staff. He held this post when World War II broke out.

The string of early Luftwaffe victories in which Galland had participated as a combat pilot further boosted Jeschonneks's prestige. He was promoted up to Colonel General at the early age of 42, the youngest officer in that rank in the Wehrmacht. Like Galland, his rise had been meteoric. Jeschonnek had risen as rapidly as the Luftwaffe itself. He had been close to, or directly involved in, all major decisions since the termination of Wever's strategic bomber program.

After Wever's death, Jeschonnek had advocated a strictly tactical air force. He backed the dive bomber concept with missionary zeal. Jeschonnek poured his energies into giving Germany the most effective striking air force in the shortest possible time. He translated Hitler's wishes into hardware. The efficient tactical Luftwaffe of 1939 owed much to Jeschonnek's dedication and ability.

Where all this impinged on the career of Galland was in Jeschonnek's indifference to anything that did not serve the goal of the largest possible force in being. Only the immediately foreseeable tomorrows of the Luftwaffe counted. Training programs were not set up comprehensively as Hitler had demanded in October of 1938. Incredibly enough, there was no reserve of pilots at all when the Luftwaffe went to war in 1939. Jeschonnek had made neither provision nor effort to expand training. There was only one fighter pilot school when war broke out in 1939, epitomizing this cardinal pre-war failure.

Organization of training in the Luftwaffe, furthermore, put pilot training commanders under the authority of the Air Fleets. The consequences were disastrous. Training units were relentlessly raided by Air Fleet commanders for both pilots and aircraft. Ju 52s widely used for training were snapped up by Air Fleet orders for transport duty. Air transport had similarly been neglected, in the single-minded drive to maximize the striking force in being. Germany therefore never ceased being short of air transport. Skilled flying instructors were used as replacements for the Bomber Arm in the Battle of Britain, and were drained away into such ventures as the airlift supporting the Battle for Crete.

Jeschonnek's achievements were thus offset by many errors and deficiencies, concealed initially by the great opening victories of the Luftwaffe. Disaster, nevertheless, resided in Jeschonnek's mistakes in key areas, as Galland would progressively discover. Although a man of integrity, Jeschonnek was a loner, minus close personal friends. He was not spiritually strong enough to deal with a juggernaut C.-in-C. like Goering. Hitler left Jeschonnek awe-struck.

Jeschonnek's vantage point near the heart of the Luftwaffe made him aware that Hitler's pre-war triumphs had been accomplished with the Luftwaffe as his trump card. He saw Hitler as Germany's savior, and regarded him as a genius of infallible insight. Despite this infatuation with the Fuehrer, the intelligent Jeschonnek was professionally realistic. *He knew that Germany had to win quickly.* The substance of the Luftwaffe was being consumed from the war's first day. His professional life thus became one gigantic roll of the dice. Jeschonnek was gambling on the Fuehrer – all or nothing.

As Adolf Galland sat across from this ill-fated man in the HQ train at Goldap, Jeschonnek's world was beginning to disintegrate. America had come into the war. The conflict was now a full-scale world struggle. Even without American participation, the Luftwaffe was already pinned down on the Channel and battling a determined RAF in the Mediterranean. Operations in Russia were chewing up the Luftwaffe in ceaseless close-support operations. A fierce winter was proving itself a savage ally of the Soviet Union.

Galland was received courteously by Jeschonnek, whose attitude was helpful. Unfortunately, the Chief of the Luftwaffe General Staff had no guidance whatever to offer the distinguished newcomer from the air war. Jeschonnek was obviously under heavy pressure. His worst fears were beginning to be realized. Although nothing to this effect emerged in their correct and professional conversation, a certain disquiet communicated itself to Galland from within Jeschonnek. The man obviously had bigger things to worry about than the Fighter Arm.

Feeling again completely out of place, just as he had in his Berlin HQ office, Galland left Goldap sick at heart. His soul cried out for the upright comradeship of JG 26. Using his new independence as General of the Fighter Arm, he flew straight to Audembert. He wanted to spend Christmas 1941 with the men he knew. In the atmosphere of his beloved JG 26 he renewed his perspective. His new job gave him the chance to help such men as these, with whom he had so often flown into battle. His New Year resolution was to press forward into his new job and give it his best.

The Byzantine world of the Air Ministry, with its intrigues, bureaucracies, politics, and ambitious climbers of all kinds, was a world totally alien to Colonel Galland. Often he wondered in his first weeks if he had been teleported to some bizarre, hidden world, so radically different was his new role from that of a fighter Kommodore. He had no staff training. According to the whispered judgments of the bureaucracy, that would result in his failure. Those whispers duly reached him and hardened his resolve. He had more experience of modern fighter aviation than anyone else in the Luftwaffe. His intellectual logic and common sense, combined with his experience, would compensate for his lack of staff training. His old drive to excel was taking a new direction.

Certain inspection functions in the Fighter Arm, had to be promptly delegated to lighten his own load. He brought in Lt. Colonel Guenther Luetzow, his comrade from the Condor Legion, as Inspector of the Fighter Units. Since the Ground Attack Arm (*Schlachtflieger*) also came under his office, Galland appointed Lt. Colonel Weiss, a Battle of Britain veteran, as their Inspector. From this beginning came the staff that would develop deep loyalty to him and to the Fighter Arm that was his passion.

Galland was often criticized for some of the men he appointed to his staff. Not all the officers he chose worked out in their jobs. Those that did became an elite group, and those who survived the war would cherish into their evening the memory of having served on Galland's staff. This elite included Luetzow, Trautloft, Brustellin, Seitz, Schmoller-Haldy, von Maltzahn, and Andres, the latter doing a giant's work in training. Contributing mightily to the good spirit at Fighter Arm HQ was the tireless Chief Secretary, Anneliese Stiller. She had served in the office since 1936. After the war, she became a secretary in the office of economics minister Ludwig Erhard.

Galland was now moving in high councils where three or four fighter Geschwader were moved about as flags on a map. Until now, he had understood moving a Geschwader only in

GENERAL GALLAND AT HIS DESK
Though he hated administrative paper work, he got it done. Edu Neumann comments that Galland was twice as good as anyone else no matter what he was doing.

terms of the turmoil involved in shifting 80-odd fighters in three Gruppen from one set of bases to another. A big undertaking when you were supervising it as a Kommodore, it was easy when you pulled some pins out of a map and pressed them back in somewhere else.

The decisive spring push against the Soviet Union involved a heavy demand for combat fighters. Another raid was staged on the training schools. Conferences with Jeschonnek, in which Galland objected to these actions, gave the General of the Fighters insight into the High Command concept of the war.

Jeschonnek was sympathetic to Galland's desire to protect the Fighter Arm's future, since the young Colonel's viewpoint was rooted in facts and logic. Jeschonnek nevertheless gave primary to the Fuehrer's view, which was that the war against Russia was almost won. A massive spring push would favorably decide the campaign. Victory over Russia would secure the east, make Russia's resources available to Germany, and allow the war in the west to be similarly fought through to victory.

Jeschonnek was accordingly pouring all available Luftwaffe resources into winning the spring victory. Quick defeat of Russia was vital. Galland readily comprehended the consequences of a protracted struggle against the Soviets. Jeschonnek spoke of it all in laconic, professional terms and heard Galland's views with attention and courtesy.

The General of the Fighter Arm had no option but to acquiesce in the training school raids and other emergency measures to reinforce the east. Goering backed Jeschonnek, closing any appeal in that direction. Galland's growing grasp of the true state of the Fighter Arm began to illuminate the errors, oversights, and omissions he had inherited from the past.

Recognizing the urgent situation in the east did not blind Galland to the threat from the west. As a Channel front combat commander, he had seen and felt the mounting power of the RAF. American airpower would inevitably flow into the fight, increasing the weight from the west. East and west, prospects were gloomy. One fundamental towered above all murky imponderables. Fighters would be needed on a scale never previously envisioned. No matter what direction the war might take, the Luftwaffe needed thousands upon thousands of fighters.

Galland went to see the man most concerned with fighter production, Field Marshal Milch. Germany's aircraft production czar at that time, Milch had taken over Udet's functions as *Generalluftzeugmeister*. Cordial relations were immediately established between Galland and Milch. Although highly egocentric, when it came to the war Milch was a total realist. He had been to America and seen their mass production feats. He had also visited England before the war, and talked at length with Churchill, Viscount Swinton, and the RAF's great progenitor, "Boom" Trenchard. Milch was sharply aware of the aerial threat from the west – and knew that fighters were needed in hordes. He also knew Jeschonnek well, having been his squadron commander in World War I, and his chief in Black Luftwaffe days. Milch now regarded Jeschonnek with contempt.

STAFF VISIT
The General of the Fighters, Galland, tried to visit every Luftwaffe fighter unit. Russia, Africa, France, Italy, you name it! Some of the units moved around so fast that it was impossible to get to all of them. This shows Galland on a visit to JG 5 "Eismeer" in Finland.

Galland and Milch planned a fighter production increase from the current 250 per month to more than 1,000 per month by mid-1943. Milch had the know-how and drive to achieve this goal. He arranged for Galland to attend the *Generalluftzeugmeister* conferences and provide direct input from the Fighter Arm. These regular conferences were to bring Milch and his staff together with manufacturers, engineers, and designers. Galland was amazed in some of these meetings at the way Professors Heinkel and Messerschmitt went at each other like a couple of strange bulldogs. Milch's realism was refreshing to Galland, and Milch had trust and confidence in the young fighter general. Their relationship aided the Fighter Arm.

Galland was now able to see how Goering operated in high Luftwaffe circles. Previous contacts with the Reich Marshal in brief meetings at the front, at HQ, or in the social setting of hunting, did not provide such insight. Goering's lack of technical knowledge was appalling. This lack of technical expertise was shamelessly exploited by a circle of sycophants around him. Galland experienced a certain disgust at the way these officers fawned over and toadied to the Reich Marnhal. They brought him gifts. They filled his insatiable ego with ceaseless flattery.

Galland had to make an early decision about Goering and his personal weaknesses. If he flattered Goering a little, the Fighter Arm might benefit. Strictly as a means to an end, it might be worthwhile. Galland's own character structure would not allow him to take this approach. He therefore decided to deal with Goering entirely on a factual and logical basis in any given situation. Galland never departed from this resolution. In the twilight of his own life, he was without regrets over taking this stand.

Weeks passed quickly after his appointment, and as the scope and dimensions of his responsibilities became clearer, he was awed by what was expected of him as an officer not yet

IM NAMEN
DES DEUTSCHEN VOLKES
VERLEIHE ICH
DEM OBERST
ADOLF GALLAND
DAS EICHENLAUB MIT
SCHWERTERN UND BRILLANTEN
ZUM RITTERKREUZ
DES EISERNEN KREUZES

FÜHRERHAUPTQUARTIER
DEN 28. JANUAR 1942

DER FÜHRER
UND OBERSTE BEFEHLSHABER
DER WEHRMACHT

GALLAND'S DIAMONDS AWARD CERTIFICATE
Hitler's signature can be seen at the bottom. Gilt in gold, Hitler soon complained the certificates cost too much. Galland's certificate was stolen by the Russians when they occupied Berlin.

30 years of age. The various powers and functions of the General of the Fighter Arm were as follows:

1. Inspection of operational units, training units, and schools, especially the Operational Training Units.
2. Direct liaison between operational units and Goering, Hitler, Jeschonnek, and other figures, avoiding all ordinary channels.
3. Evaluation of tactical and technical experience of operational units and dissemination of results.
4. Preparation of Tactical Regulations for all phases of fighter operations.
5. Continuous evaluation of all material and armament under development.
6. Provision for combat testing of all equipment, either in regular fighter units or in special Test Commandos.
7. Technical recommendations to industry for improvement of equipment based on combat experience.
8. Expediting of equipment not forthcoming through normal supply channels, or otherwise held up.
9. Proposals for new organization or reorganization of fighter control systems and operational administration.
10. Proposals for setting up of operational units.
11. Recommendations for personnel in operational fighter posts from squadron commander upwards. The Personnel Branch, in practice, always accepted Galland's recommendations.
12. Maintenance of a card index of all aircrews under Fighter Arm jurisdiction.
13. Recommendations for the award of the Knight's Cross and its higher orders for Fighter Arm personnel.
14. Supply of the Fighter Arm with all new regulations and instructional material. Galland disseminated this material direct to operational units.
15. Control of training in Operational Training Units. Advisory supervision of other flying training as related to the supply of fighter pilots.
16. Absolute control over personnel assignment from Operational Training Units to operational units.
17. Suggestions, recommendations, and demands for development of organization and equipment for the reporting services, radar service, and other signals units.
18. Evaluation of operational experience with signals equipment, in cooperation with the Chief of Luftwaffe Signals, General Wolfgang Martini.
19. Advising the Luftwaffe Operations Staff, the Luftwaffe High Command, and Goering on Fighter Arm matters.
20. Cooperation and liaison with other offices, such as those of Milch, Speer, and, later, Saur.
21. Special duties assigned from time to time, such as preparations for the Channel dash by the battleships *Scharnhorst* and *Gneisenau*, and control of fighters in Sicily.

A fair assessment of these responsibilities fifty years later is that no other officer aged 30, in either the Wehrmacht or the Allied forces, was charged with such burdens. The certainty of the old bureaucrats in the Air Ministry that he would fail is easy to understand. A successful fighter Kommodore had little of the background necessary to get things done in Berlin, where the inept and the inexperienced were "shot down" in an altogether different way.

Galland was awarded the Diamonds to his Knight's Cross on 28 January 1942. He was the second member of the Wehrmacht to receive the decoration, being preceded only by Moelders. Earlier on the Channel front, Galland noted that when Moelders was awarded the Diamonds, the Fuehrer also prohibited him from further combat flying. Moelders had reached 100 victories. Since Galland had 94 victories at the time of Moelders's award, he discreetly ceased counting his victories to avoid being taken off operations. In this way he was able to fly combat until his promotion to Colonel and General of the Fighter Arm.

Through his many informants, Hitler nevertheless knew what was happening. The Fuehrer appreciated that a grounding order that went with Galland's appointment as General of the Fighters would prevent his reaching 100 victories.

Hitler also rated victories in the west more highly than those won in Russia. Therefore, he bestowed Germany's highest decoration on his new General of the Fighter Arm. The Diamonds would become the subject of an inimitable Galland after-dinner story, which he would tell into his eighth decade in many different countries. At the end of January 1942, he was Germany's most highly decorated living ace. An appropriately important assignment was given him at this time: twisting the British lion's tail in a way that had not been equaled in two centuries.

SIXTEEN

Thunderbolt

Operational authority was denied to the General of the Fighter Arm under Goering's arrangements. Galland disliked intensely this particular limitation. The appointment to his high post had been thrust upon him because of his success as an operational fighter pilot and Kommodore, and yet in the Fighter Arm's highest appointment he was unable to order even a single squadron into the air. Exceptions to this were made only in specific assignments given to Galland by the Reich Marshal, whose personal intoxication with command has already been described. An important exception was made early in Galland's high command career. Goering assigned him to command Luftwaffe forces giving air cover to the planned breakout of the heavy ships *Gneisenau*, *Scharnhorst*, and *Prinz Eugen* from Brest.

British Intelligence had subtly continued with strategic deception over British intentions toward Norway. A Scandinavian invasion actually presented insuperable logistical problems, and the British had no operational plan for such an undertaking. They nevertheless kept this pot quietly boiling with a multitude of deceptive stratagems, drawing off substantial German forces that would otherwise face them on active fronts. Hitler was the main dupe of this intelligence ploy. He was the one who counted. The Fuehrer wanted the big ships to return to Norway, where they would discourage an invasion and intercept Allied convoys to Russia from secure bases.

The German heavy ships were a constant threat to Britain's Atlantic lifeline as long as they were in Brest. They drew off the Royal Navy's Force H from vital duty in the Mediterranean, and thus weakened Britain's ability to reinforce the Middle East. *Scharnhorst* and *Gneisenau* therefore had high naval value even if they never left port. Alongside the dock in Brest, they were nevertheless a routine Bomber Command target and were subject to continual damage. These damage reports and Hitler's fears of an invasion of Norway prompted his decision at the end of 1941 to move the ships out of Brest as soon as possible.

Galland was summoned to the Wolf's Lair with Jeschonnek on 12 January 1942. Hitler had called a conference of naval and air leaders to plan the breakout. Goering shunted responsibility for Luftwaffe participation on to Jeschonnek. This put some distance between the Reich Marshal and any potential disaster that might arise. Goering instructed Jeschonnek to propose Galland as commander of the Operational Fighter Protection. The famous young fighter general's popularity would thus provide additional insulation for Goering in the event of a catastrophic outcome. Goering's view that the Luftwaffe would be blamed by the Navy in the event of failure was substantiated by the tenor of the conference.

Goering was able to stay away from these proceedings, but Grand Admiral Erich Raeder, commander-in-chief of the Navy, did not have Goering's political influence and had to attend. Loss of the *Bismarck* had placed Raeder low in Hitler's esteem, and he shared Goering's wish to be remote from a risky venture. Raeder emphasized to the conference that he was not proposing or recommending the breakout. Vice Admiral Otto Ciliax, O.C. battleships, and Commodore Ruge, O.C. minesweepers, were delegated to outline operational plans. In Raeder's words, this was "to make your decision easier, *mein Fuehrer*"

In just such ways did Germany's highest commanders facilitate Hitler's meddling in their affairs. If they took a polite "hands off" attitude toward important operations, Hitler would take over. He had taken over Germany politically. Any high officer leaving a void in operational planning would soon find Hitler filling that void. What began as meddling by Hitler developed eventually into control of the entire war effort by one man. Galland saw this baleful trend at an early stage in the Channel dash conference.

Air cover for the ships passing through the English Channel in daylight was tactically essential. The Navy's main fear was that a sufficiently strong fighter screen could not be provided. General Jeschonnek stated that the 250 fighters available on the Channel front were barely adequate for dawn-to-dusk air cover – considering the manifold problems of range, refueling, rearmament, and potential losses. Eastern Front demands made reinforcement impossible. Night fighters could give supplementary protection around dawn and dusk, but that was the extent of the forces available. Numerical inferiority of the German fighters to their RAF foes could not be redressed. Continuous protection of the ships could not be guaranteed.

Hitler decided to proceed with the operation. Breakout from Brest would be in darkness. Transit of Dover Strait would occur in daylight. The best possible fighter cover was to be given with the available forces. The Fuehrer decreed absolute secrecy from that moment. Hitler circulated a secrecy pledge, and all present were required to sign this document. Galland listened closely to the give-and-take of the conference, conducted by high-ranking officers many years his senior. He gave opinions at appropriate points. His knowledge of fighter operations and flying conditions on the Channel was unrivaled and current. This more than compensated for his lack of seniority, and quickly communicated itself to Hitler. The Fuehrer took his young general aside afterwards, and asked him what the chances of success were, given the dependency of the operation on the air umbrella. Galland had already weighed the involved factors in his own mind.

"Everything depends on how much time the English have to mobilize the RAF against the ships" he told Hitler.

"We need complete surprise and a bit of luck into the bargain. My fighter pilots will give their very best when they know what is at stake."

This was to prove a prescient estimate.

Galland chose the code name Thunderbolt for the operation, while Navy planning went forward as Cerberus. The secrecy ordered by Hitler was strictly observed. The fighter pilots were told that Thunderbolt was a new bomber offensive against Britain. Spies in the Brest docks reported to the British as activity began intensifying. The long electronic ears of Ultra overheard the German radioteletype traffic and left no doubt as to German intentions.

Ronald Lewin describes the unfolding situation of the British cryptanalysts in his *Ultra Goes to War*:

> "Ultra converted speculation into reality. All those small preliminaries necessary for the secret move of a considerable naval force were identified by Denning and his colleagues in the Operational Intelligence Center – the particular arrangements for U-boats and the Luftwaffe's fighters, the increased and clandestine activity of minesweepers along significant channels, the assembly of extra destroyers as escorts in the dash. A full appreciation was laid before Admiral Pound, and as early as 2 February the Admiralty issued its detailed conclusions which ended: 'Taking all factors into consideration, it appears that the Germans can pass east up the Channel with much less risk than they will incur if they attempt an ocean passage.' Coastal Command (of the RAF) took the same view."

The British Admiralty thus unwittingly endorsed the Channel dash that Hitler had thrust on his reluctant naval chiefs. The British cryptanalysts at Bletchley Park continued to break the insecure Luftwaffe ciphers and the Hydra ciphers of the German Navy. The Admiralty's Operational Intelligence Center distilled all this into coherent, hard information upon which commanders based their plans for turning the breakout into a German disaster.

Codebreakers provide information. How that information is used in making dispositions and conducting operations is the province of those in command of the forces involved. The information is thus mute and impotent until translated into action and orders. The battle is the payoff; and in dealing with the breakout, the British command made poor use of the superior cryptanalytic intelligence that was abundantly available.

The British already had their Channel Stop Force in operation. Consisting of a squadron of Blenheim bombers based at Manston in Kent, and torpedo boats operating out of Dover, the Stop Force was charged with interdicting German surface traffic in the Dover Strait. Stop Force operations were eventually extended to include daily air reconnaissance of Brest by RAF Bomber Command, and nightly reconnaissance flights over the German heavy ships by Coastal Command.

Bomber Command was to make daylight attacks only, because at full speed the German ships could only make half the distance from Brest to a German port by night. Departure from Brest had to be by 1300 in order to transit the Dover Strait before daylight the following morning. RAF bombers would thus have about three hours to attack the ships after their escape from Brest was discovered. This entire operation was code-named Fuller. Preparations were code-named Executive Fuller. Many important officers involved in the coming action did not know this code-name.

Arrangements were in place for eight months prior to the accelerated naval activity around Brest in January of 1942. Short trial runs by the German heavy ships in the Gulf of Brest foretold the approaching breakout. RAF and Luftwaffe fighters clashed above these trials. Weather and tides were in favorable combination. A new moon was due 15 February. The British were able to calculate all these key elements as easily as the Germans. Knowing that a breakout was imminent, the Admiralty put Executive Fuller on alert on 4 February 1942. While unwilling to bring Home Fleet heavy ships within reach of German bombers, the Admiralty ordered six additional old destroyers into Harwich, and six additional torpedo boats into Ramsgate.

Six Swordfish torpedo planes of No.825 Squadron of the Fleet Air Arm were based at Manston. The S-Class submarine *Sealion* was sent to reinforce two older submarines already patrolling outside Brest. The Royal Navy was ready for the Germans, whether they took the Channel or the ocean route for their breakout.

Even more massive British forces were poised at the same time, in addition to the naval units. RAF Coastal Command had No.86 Squadron right opposite Brest at St. Eval in

Cornwall. Twelve Beaufort torpedo carriers were there, reinforced by three additional aircraft from No. 217 Squadron, the latter being stationed with its other seven torpedo carriers on Torney Island near Portsmouth. Coastal Command also transferred No.14 Squadron from Scotland to Manston in Kent, to operate with fourteen more Beauforts.

These three Beaufort squadrons were therefore spread out over the entire length of the breakout route. A joint attack could be mounted by all three in combination if the situation so dictated. Normal vigilance would see them sweeping hundreds of square miles of the English Channel and adjacent waters.

The RAF assigned 300 bombers to Fuller. Only daylight attacks were possible, but mass strikes on the German ships in the crucial waters between Brest and Dover could easily seal their doom. On 6 February 1942 the RAF reduced its commitment to 100 bombers, despite the high likelihood that the breakout would come between 10 and 15 February. This was a clear failure to use correctly the available intelligence on enemy intentions, even if 100 bombers was still an adequate force to sink the ships.

RAF Fighter Command had available at this time approximately 600 fighters. The well-tested No.11 Fighter Group, Galland's adversaries in the Battle of Britain, would protect RAF bombers against the anticipated Luftwaffe fighter umbrella. From bases at Kenley, Hornchurch, Debden, Biggin Hill, and Tangmere, No. 11 Fighter Group would deploy its squadrons against its old foes across the Channel.

German preparations for the breakout went forward in January with all speed. Secrecy and security seemed irrelevant, as the ships and docks, the Brest approaches, and the adjacent Channel waters swarmed with activity. Camouflaging such massive preparations was impossible. The Germans attempted deception by circulating rumors of a breakout to the Pacific and loading slings of tropical uniforms and pith helmets aboard the ships in full view of Brest's dockside spies.

Installation of additional 20mm quad mounts, jury structures that obviously would not survive a high seas voyage, virtually nullified the Pacific yarn. Rumors were deliberately circulated in the dockyard and conflicted with other rumors passed to the crews. Sea lawyers and hammock strategists were thoroughly confused as to the intentions of their own side. A dash through the Channel ranked as the least likely possibility among the battleship crews.

Eighty minesweepers toiled through each icy night to clear three minefields astride the best escape route. The heavy ships required a minimum water depth of 80 feet for safety. A channel was laid out and marked. The Vice Admiral had as ship commanders reporting to him, Captain Kurt Hoffman in *Scharnhorst*, Captain Otto Fein in *Gneisenau*, and Captain Helmuth Brinkmann in *Prinz Eugen*.

Complex planning for the fighter umbrella went forward under Galland. Thunderbolt was made to order for a general in search of a challenging operational command. Control of fighter units, communications, and ground operations for both Air Fleet 3 and Air Fleet Reich was centralized under Galland's personal command. These were considerable encroachments on the domains of Field Marshal Sperrle and General Weise, the two Air Fleet commanders, but neither of them seemed to mind. Probably sharing Goering's apprehension and seeing failure inherent in the Channel dash, they watched Galland pile into his task with enthusiasm and energy. Galland would say whimsically, in later years, that Sperrle and Weise took "malicious pleasure" in seeing him stick his neck out.

Three fighter command centers were organized to cover the escape route progressively. The sector Abbeville-Lille-Calais had its HQ at Le Touquet in France. The Schelde-Rhine-Zuider Zee sector had its command center at Schiphol in the Netherlands. For the final stretch between Jever and Wilhelmshaven in Germany, HQ was set up at Jever. Good planning allows for contingencies. Galland held that a delay early in the breakout was the most likely modification of the plan. He prepared for this by setting up an emergency sector of bases in the area Le Havre-Caen-Cherbourg, with HQ at Caen.

Since success depended upon communications, an elaborate series of radio links was established. VHF radiotelephone communication, with its line-of-sight range limitation, was supplemented by lower frequency contact direct to the flotilla commander. Differences between Navy and Luftwaffe radio procedure, practices, and jargon had to be reconciled. Galland considered a fighter controller aboard the ships to be essential. He put his old C.O. from the French campaign, Colonel Max Ibel, aboard *Scharnhorst* with a small staff. Ibel had direct radio contact with the fighters overhead, as well as with Galland ashore. Ibel was designated Fighter Controller on Board. Luftwaffe liaison officers who were qualified pilots, with assisting Luftwaffe radio operators, were placed aboard both *Gneisenau* and *Prinz Eugen*.

A continuous fighter umbrella over the ships involved complex planning. Galland and his staff calculated that no more than 16 fighters could be maintained in the air cover. Each wave of 16 fighters would have 35 minutes on station. Time over the ships could be extended to 45 minutes if there was no combat. Each relief flight would have a 10-minute overlap with the fighters it was replacing. For 20 minutes of each hour, there would therefore be 32 fighters in the umbrella.

All this called for top leadership, good navigation, tremendous pilot endurance, and a maximum effort from the ground crews. Galland was forced to limit turnaround times on the ground. Refueling, rearming, and minor servicing were held to a scant 30 minutes. Even with everything going to plan, there still were not enough fighters available to give the Navy all the cover the admirals would have liked.

Galland's limited resources consisted mainly of JG 2 and JG 26, veteran formations on the Channel front, each with 90 fighters. An additional 60 fighters could be allotted from JG 1 for the morning of the breakout day. These aircraft would not be available for breakout afternoon operations, since they were responsible for protecting the ships the following morning as they crossed the German Bight.

Galland scraped up an additional dozen Me 109s from an Operational Training Unit at Paris, posting them to Le Havre. From the Night Fighter Arm he assigned 30 twin-engined Me 110s to the half-light periods at dawn and sunset. They were too vulnerable to Spitfires by day, but they bridged the dawn and dusk gaps. Galland's grand aircraft total was 252 fighters maximum, with less than 200 available for the afternoon following the breakout.

Galland ordered total radio silence. German fighter pilots were notoriously talkative aloft. Their flow of chatter, slang, warnings, and commands was almost continuous on normal operations. Absolute radio silence was essential until Galland was certain that the British had discovered the breakout. The order "Open Visor" would cancel radio silence. Pilots were ordered to fly low, for a minimal return on British radar, upon which some electronic deception was being practiced.

General Martini as Head of the Luftwaffe Signal Corps, possessed jamming devices and other electronic counter measures (ECM) to disturb British radar. These technical advances had been kept under security ready for just such an introduction to operations. At dawn each day in January of 1942 British radars were subtly exposed to Martini's ECM for just a few minutes.

British radar displays appeared to lose considerable returns. Gradually lengthening the duration of the ECM, the Germans accustomed the British radar operators to its presence. Since these effects were not continuous, the British attributed it to atmospheric conditions or enemy action, and the interference gradually seemed to become unimportant. The British had a few E-radars operating on 7-8 centimeters that Martini could not corrupt, but most of their radar stations on the south coast were set up by the Germans for jamming on breakout day.

Galland issued operational orders to Geschwader, Gruppe, and Staffel commanders in sealed envelopes, to be opened only upon receipt of the code word Thunderbolt. The fighter pilots had been told that another big bombing offensive was about to open against England. Ranging them along the French coast in full available strength was consistent with another Blitz.

Despite a bleak weather forecast, Admiral Alfreid Saalwaechter of High Command West ordered the operation to commence at 2000 on 11 February 1942. Cerberus/Thunderbolt was on. Galland flew directly from Paris to the Pas de

LeBOURGET AIRDROME IN PARIS - 1942
At the time II Group of JG 26 was transitioning to Fw 190's, Galland visited to try the new bird. Left to right: Heinrich Brustellin, Galland and an aide.

Calais, to confer with command personnel of the flying units – all men who knew, trusted, and respected him.

Opening and studying their orders, these veteran fighter leaders found their warrior hearts quickening. Immediate attacks on hostile aircraft from any position were demanded, the "aggressive defense" credo of Galland. *Attack* was the keynote. Any British machine penetrating the fighter screen was to be destroyed at all costs, even by ramming. Enemy aircraft leaving the combat area with no further offensive power were to be ignored. Downed enemy aircraft would not measure the success of Thunderbolt. Their objective was the safety and protection of the heavy ships.

The fighter officers who would lead Thunderbolt in the air were elated by their clear, aggressive orders from a trusted commander. An historic task awaited with the dawn. In high anticipation, they sprawled on their beds for a restless night. Galland went sleepless, his being boiling with excitement. His whole life had been a preparation for this moment. All his experience, skill, and acumen had been poured into planning Thunderbolt, the biggest operation of his career thus far, and the most important. His mettle in handling operational high command was about to be tested.

SEVENTEEN

Breakout and Battle

By midnight on 12 February 1942, the German heavy ships were rounding Ushant with their escort and heading into the English Channel. Despite a two-hour delay in their Brest departure due to an RAF raid, they were in luck. The submarine *Sealion*, guardian of the Brest approaches, was 30 miles away on the surface, charging its batteries. The German force went racing up into the Channel at nearly 30 knots, with Admiral Ciliax and all hands alert for British warships and aircraft.

Along and over the Channel, an incredible chain of British misadventures and mismanagement was beginning. In all three zones into which RAF Coastal Command had divided the Channel for interlocking radar search patterns, British aircraft had difficulties. Mechanical, electronic, and meteorological problems disrupted normal patrol schedules. The German heavy ships slipped through the resultant gaps. By 0730 they were off Cherbourg, making rendezvous with an escorting E-boat flotilla, and the British were unaware that they had left Brest.

Radar deception measures by General Martini's experts, meanwhile, had begun with the dispatch of two He 111 radar decoy aircraft from a base north of Paris well before dawn. Each aircraft electronically simulated 25 circling aircraft. They flew parallel with the English coast, diverting the electronic attention of British radar operators from the Brest force. The German heavy ships thus reached the mouth of the Seine without any major reaction from the British. Royal Navy channel forces went through a routine alert in routine fashion at 0500, from which they were stood down at 0835 – unaware that the German Navy was steaming up the Channel.

At 0750 the first Me 110 night fighters arrived over the German ships in the first hint of dawn, thundering under a 1,500-foot ceiling. These aircraft were flying higher than required by their orders. Across the Channel at Beachy Head, they were detected by one of the 7-cm wavelength radars that the Germans were unable to jam. Beachy Head radar reported aircraft circling over ships moving on the surface at 25 knots. Both the Royal Navy and the RAF were advised, but neither acted.

A second British E radar at Swingate also detected the circling fighters at 0824, and evaluated the radar information similarly to Beachy Bead. Repeated plots were made. Other radars reported interference, as the decoy He 111s moved down the Channel. Fighter Command at Stanmore received all this crucial radar data. In consultation with No.11 Fighter Group's Duty Controller at Hornchurch, it was decided that a German air-sea rescue operation was in progress. The German battleships kept forging unmolested through hostile waters.

Galland had watched the progress of the German battleships up the Channel during the night, as German coastal radars periodically reported their position. His excitement mounted as by 0900 the big ships had almost made up the time lost in their late breakout from Brest. Daylight had now eliminated the hazard of British night attack. The young Colonel was further encouraged as the timing of the day's dismal weather forecast proved wrong. His fighter bases along the east side of the Channel continued to have good weather, while the English coast had low cloud and poor visibility.

Squadron Leader William Igoe was the senior RAF fighter controller at Biggin Hill, the most important fighter station in southern England. Radar blips and their evaluation were important parts of his job. Igoe tracked a string of aircraft returns from Cotentin to the Channel, and calculated a speed of advance of 25 knots – consistent with a fighter escort for battleships. At 0905, Igoe telephoned No. 11 Fighter Group HQ at Uxbridge and said: "I believe it is *Fuller*!"' The crucial codeword seemed to make no impression on personnel at Uxbridge, where Fuller orders were locked in a safe for security. RAF secrecy on Fuller was so tight that many people about to be critically involved were not even apprised of the codeword.

Igoe's counterpart at Stanmore, Wing Commander Davies, became convinced also by 1000 that the German heavy ships were out of Brest and coming up the Channel. Like Igoe, he was unable to get his signal conclusion across to No. 11 Fighter Group HQ. By this time, Galland's first relay of Me 109s arrived over the battleships, and British radar detected their entry into the drama. Each day at dawn and dusk, No. 91 Squadron based at Hawkinge, under Squadron Leader Robert Oxspring, sent out two "Jim Crow" patrol Spitfires. Reconnaissance of French offport and offshore areas was their assignment. On 13 February 1942, the Spitfire covering the Gris Nez to Le Havre sector spotted an E-boat flotilla moving out of Boulogne. These German units were assigned as part of the Dover Strait escort for the heavy ships. Their presence and movement was duly reported and added to the mosaic.

When Squadron Leader Igoe at Biggin Hill found that comprehension of Fuller was lacking at No. 11 Fighter Group HQ at Uxbridge, he telephoned Oxspring at Hawkinge and asked him to make a special second sweep. Oxspring agreed to go personally. Warned by Igoe of the intense German air activity, Oxspring took along a wingman. Sergeant Beaumont had formerly been with the RAF Marine Section in high speed launches and knew his ships. They took off shortly after 1000, heading out into the Channel murk.

A few minutes later, another and entirely unofficial Spitfire element took off from Kenley. Group Captain Victor Beamish and Wing Commander Finlay Boyd were two of Fighter Command's bright lights. As Operations Officer of No. 11 Fighter Group, Beamish seized any excuse to get back into a fighter cockpit. With the weather too unfavorable for less experienced pilots, this was a Special Beamish Mission, and the Battle of Britain ace headed his Spitfire into the mist. Strict radio silence was required over the Channel, so Beamish and Boyd vanished from human ken, unaware that Oxspring and Beaumont were buzzing around in the same soup as themselves.

By 1020, the German heavy ships had been at sea undetected for almost eleven hours. They were bearing down rapidly on Dover Strait. In his control center at Le Touquet, Galland tensely followed the unfolding drama. The radio loudspeaker for communication with the aircraft carried the only sound, and for now it was still silent. Weather information, radar data, and monitoring of British communications were registered via switching lights. Galland did not speak aloud, but wrote down his orders on paper and passed them to a staff officer for broadcast as appropriate.

Both of the two Spitfire elements discovered the German heavy ships within a few minutes of each other fifteen miles west of Le Touquet. Both pairs of Spitfires were bounced by German fighters and taken under fire by the shipboard flak. In the getaway, Oxspring and Beaumont almost pressed an attack on Beamish and Boyd, mistaking them for Me 109s in the poor visibility.

Despite the vital significance of the sighting, Group Captain Victor Beamish followed orders to maintain radio silence and flew back to Kenley with Boyd. Squadron Leader Oxspring had initiative enough to know when to disobey orders. At 1035, Oxspring broke radio silence. He reported battle cruisers and escort off Le Touquet heading for Dover.

The German listening service intercepted his report, and it was almost instantly in front of Adolf Galland. The battleships had been discovered and identified. Galland had now to decide whether to continue radio silence and low-level flying, or cancel these orders. Maintaining radio silence cut him off from direct contact with Ibel aboard *Scharnhorst* for a situation report. Luftwaffe fighters would be vulnerable to Spitfires bouncing the battleships from out of the clouds. Every man in high command eventually reaches such a juncture, where men's lives hang in the balance along with the outcome of great events. Galland decided to keep the lid on.

The British did not act on Squadron Leader Oxspring's dramatic sighting report, but waited instead for him to land. After he repeated his sighting report in person, buttressed by Beaumont who had seen the Scharnhorst close-up in peacetime, he was still not fully believed. A book of warship silhouettes was sent for, and after an additional delay while its bearer stopped for tea, Oxspring and Beaumont made a firm identification of the big ships. All this went on as Galland, on the other side of the Channel, won more miles of safety for the German battleships. He kept both his nerve and radio silence.

Squadron Leader Oxspring tried personally to contact Air Vice-Marshal Leigh-Mallory, AOC No. 11 Fighter Group, and was rebuffed. Leigh-Mallory's staff refused to interrupt his inspection of Belgian RAF units at Northolt. Operations officers simply did not get excited over Oxspring's report. They promised only to enlarge an attack on the E-boats exiting Boulogne, which was already in preparation.

Oxspring telephoned back to fighter controller Igoe at Biggin Hill. He confirmed for him that the German heavy ships were moving up the Channel. Group Captain Victor Beamish landed at Fenley at 1110, and confirmed Oxpring's sighting. Both Beamish and Oxspring now continued independently to try and contact Leigh-Mallory, without whose orders No. 11 Fighter Group continued to decline decisive action.

While the Spitfire sightings were in progress, RAF radar at Swingate had picked up the large blips of the heavy ships at 1016. Range was 56 miles. Galland's circling fighter escort was detected by other coastal radars and interpreted as E-boat activity. When the C.O. of Swingate radar tried to notify Royal Navy HQ at Dover Castle, defective communications blocked him for nearly half an hour.

The Swingate report and other radar information convinced Admiral Ramsey's Air Liaison Officer at Dover that Scharnhorst and Gneisenau were forcing the Channel. Wing-Commander Constable-Roberts was responsible for liaison with No. 11 Fighter Group, but he fared no better than Oxspring, Beamish, and Igoe in convincing the staff at Uxbridge that the battleships were out. Alarmed and determined to act to the limit of his authority, Constable-Roberts telephoned Manston and requested Lt.-Commander Esmonde to put his six Fairey Swordfish torpedo bombers in ready condition. He requested similar status for the Beauforts at St. Eval and for the Beauforts of No. 42 Squadron, then belatedly en route from Scotland to Coltishall in Norwich.

28 JANUARY 1942
Hitler, diamonds award in hand, prepares to award the decoration to then-Colonel Adolf Galland, who had 94 victories at the time. Galland was the second soldier to receive the decoration. Moelders preceded him.

BRILLANTS (DIAMONDS) TO ADOLF GALLAND
On 28 January 1942, Hitler awarded the Diamonds to Galland. Hitler, (back to camera) Galland, and looking on are Peltz, Lützow and Wilcke.

These actions by Constable-Roberts were the first decisive steps taken against *Scharnhorst* and *Gneisenau* by the British armed forces. Constable-Roberts initiated action without even being aware that Oxspring, Beaumont, Beamish, and Boyd had all physically sighted the battleships. Galland's maintenance of radio silence continued to prolong British uncertainty during the most critical time of the Channel dash for the Germans.

By 1130 Group Captain Beamish had forced reluctant aides and adjutants to bring Air Vice-Marshal Leigh-Mallory to the telephone, interrupting his inspection of the Belgians. Leigh-Mallory quickly grasped the importance of what his own No. 11 Fighter Group operations officer was reporting. The British now began to move, both RAF and Royal Navy. Operation Fuller was on. More than three hours had uselessly drained away since Squadron Leader Igoe had first called Fuller to No. 11 Fighter Group's duty officer. Those three hours translated into at least 75 nautical miles of unhampered steaming for the German battleships. Near noon, the German force was already in the narrowest part of the Channel.

British countermeasures were mainly planned against a night passage through the narrows by any major German force. Conceived to meet the highest probabilities, British plans envisaged the brilliantly illuminated German ships being attacked by coastal artillery, torpedo and bomber aircraft, motor torpedo-boats, and destroyers. Remnants of this nocturnal assault would be finished off at first light by Bomber Command. As the Germans now began forcing the narrows at high noon, surprise, confusion, and operational clumsiness hampered British reaction.

At 1225 the six Fairey Swordfish biplanes lumbered across the snow-covered Manston airfield and into the air. They were the only striking force available and ready to tackle the battleships. Five fighter squadrons were assigned as their escort, but only one squadron made the rendezvous over Manston with the old torpedo planes. Diving down to 50 feet, his attack altitude, Esmonde led his six wood and canvas relics out over the Channel to certain death.

Torpedo boats were already lancing towards the Germans. Coastal Command Beauforts that were supposed to attack with the Swordfish were not in position for a combined strike. British shelling by coastal guns was ineffective, and thus the obsolescent Swordfish were the first main British attack. The storm of fire from the German ships would inevitably bring them down, even though their fabric wings and fuselages might allow the harmless passage of many bullets and cannon shells. At 90 knots, they would be little more than target drogues for Galland's fighters, who would not be deterred by a fighter escort of only ten Spitfires.

At Le Touquet in his Fighter Control Center, Galland received word of shelling shortly after noon by British coastal guns around Dover. The battleships were not hit, but it meant that the British knew about the escaping heavy ships and were going into action. He wrote down the order "Open Visor" on his message pad, and it was immediately transmitted to Colonel Ibel on *Scharnhorst*, to all fighter units, and to other fighter control centers. Galland and the Luftwaffe officers around him were elated by the inertia of the British.

The entire German fighter force was still in readiness without losses. Fighter escort for the convoy's passage through the narrows could therefore be doubled. As the weather deteriorated, the cloud base hung at about 1,000 feet, and vertical separation of the fighters reduced the danger of a surprise British bounce out of the clouds.

The circling German fighters over the ships began seriously their task of beating off attackers. Five motor torpedo boats made the first thrust. German E-boats went into counter attack, and fighters swooped down, strafing the British small craft. The British MTBs nevertheless launched their torpedoes, forcing *Scharnhorst* and *Prinz Eugen* into evasive maneuvers. More MTBs broke through astern, but were unable to close the racing German fleet due to engine malfunctions.

No sooner had the MTBs receded into the murk than the ghostly forms of the Swordfish materialized to the astonished gaze of the Germans. Galland's pilots seemed as though they had flown into a time warp, as they fell upon the gaunt old canvas phantoms pressing their torpedo attack a few feet above the sea. The Swordfish flew into a fiery hell.

All six Swordfish were consumed by the hail of fire from the ships and escort fighters. They scored no hits on the German ships, and Esmonde's aircraft was blown to pieces in midair by a direct flak hit. 18 British crew members had flown the Swordfish out of Manston, and only 5 survived. This extraordinary bravery deeply impressed the German officers who witnessed it, and left Galland in awe even forty years later.

In Le Touquet, Galland could now hear the progress of the constantly moving air-sea battle on his loudspeaker. Shouts and barked commands, fighter pilot jargon, cursing and slang, the lingo and tumult he knew so well, told of aerial battle joined. He yearned to be aloft amid the fray. His wings clipped, he lit cigar after cigar and listened intently.

By 1400 the battleships were through Dover Strait, but an RAF bombing onslaught was continuously expected. All eyes scanned the sky in search of hostile silhouettes amid the mist, cloud, and rain. From the ships, little of the aerial combat could actually be observed, but occasionally dogfights took place close aboard and aircraft were seen plummeting into the sea in flames.

Scharnhorst hit a mine at 1432, losing all electric power as her boiler room was flooded. Belching black smoke and oozing oil behind her, she wallowed to a halt. Without waiting for full assessment of the damage, Admiral Ciliax transferred himself, Ibel, and some of their staffs to destroyer Z-29. In accordance with operational orders, *Scharnhorst* was hit and therefore was to be left behind. Two destroyers and two E-boats were left as protection, but most of Galland's fighters continued to follow and protect the main convoy.

The RAF made only one ineffective attack on *Scharnhorst*, but by 1500 had the main force under heavy aerial pressure. Waves of Whirlwinds, Blenheims, Beauforts, Hudsons, Wellingtons, and Hampdens successively pressed through the mist with bombing strikes. Under a 1,000-foot ceiling in low visibility, the convoy made an elusive target. Each RAF strike was greeted with a hail of retaliatory flak and was bounced by German fighters.

By 1540 the ceiling was down to 450 feet, rain lashed the scene, and visibility was no more than a mile and a half. Galland listened in his Fighter Control Center to his fighter pilots seeking the British bombers in the murk. Time after time they overshot in low visibility. Near-collisions abounded, between friend and foe and between friend and friend on both sides. British bombers shot often at their own Spitfire escort. About 100 aircraft were milling in the mist, while the ships sped toward Germany under the grey veil below.

The desperate maelstrom in the sky, where almost any moving form was fair game, had its counterpart down on the surface. *Gneisenau* and *Prinz Eugen* both took British destroyers under fire. When they sent *HMS Worcester* reeling out of the battle ablaze, two other British destroyers sped to her aid. British bombers hammered this trio of British ships, and the

CHANNEL DASH
Adolf Galland planned and executed the air umbrella over the German fleet as it made its way north from Brest. Galland considered it the highlight of his entire career during WWII. This shows Me 110s patrolling over some of the ships.

Luftwaffe joined in with strafing. The German destroyer *Hermann Schömann* was also strafed by Luftwaffe fighters. Far back in the gloom, engine room personnel had miraculously breathed life back into *Scharnhorst*. She began steaming hard after the main fleet.

Command decision was again thrust on Galland, as operational difficulties for his fighters increased. Diminishing daylight after 1500, plus the 450-foot ceiling, rain, and visibility sometimes less than a mile, all united to reduce the effectiveness of the fighter escort. Takeoff and landing from French airfields remained undisturbed, but the distance between these bases and the ships was continually increasing.

Galland had to land his fighters in Holland, where low cloud was beginning to sock in large tracts of countryside. To keep sending in waves of fighters without being able to assign safe landing areas put plenty of pressure on Galland. Continuous British air attacks on-the ships left him no choice. He kept his fighters in action, wave after wave, determined not to squander the success already won.

Galland knew his pilots well. He had personally led many of the pilots now over the battleships and whose voices he recognized. Despite this familiarity with their capabilities, they still surprised him with their skill and ingenuity in making emergency landings. When they ran out of fuel or failed to find assigned landing grounds, they landed wherever they could. losses remained far below Galland's estimates when he planned the operation.

Final British bombing attacks went in around 1800 in near darkness, a tenacious strike by Wellingtons that cost them several aircraft. Fifteen minutes later, the last RAF aircraft had departed and German day fighters were groping their way down on to Dutch landing grounds in dim twilight. Night fighters took over the protective vigil. Galland transferred himself to his Fighter Control Center in Jever. His first high command task had been successful. The air umbrella had protected the Navy.

Later that night, while steaming in relative safety down the Dutch coast, both *Scharnhorst* and *Gneisenau* struck mines off Terschelling. They both made port under their own power despite this final ill fortune. The British knew that both ships had hit these mines, through Ultra decrypts, but the angry Churchill, humiliated by the Channel Dash, could not release the information publicly. The greatest secret of the war had to be protected even when the British were smarting from a comprehensive tactical defeat.

Both sides in their official communiqués played down Thunderbolt. The Germans did not want to emphasize that it was an *escape* from Brest, which would automatically infer that Germany did not control the air and sea off the French Atlantic coast. The British had suffered a colossal shock and a national humiliation. No such naval force had been allowed to pass through the English Channel in two and a half centuries.

Officially Britain handled Thunderbolt by casting the German feat in a specious strategic light, barely comprehensible

GERMAN NAVY ESCAPING FROM BREST
At flank speed these naval vessels churn through the English Channel. The British were unable to stop the action.

to the outraged British public. Getting the ships out of Brest was depicted as being of "extreme advantage" to Britain. The British public stoically choked down the humiliation, and went on with the war while an official British inquiry was launched.

Seen with nearly sixty years of perspective, the air operation Thunderbolt was a masterpiece of operational planning and execution by Adolf Galland. Major Hans-Heinrich Brustellin, who helped him plan Thunderbolt and served on his staff right through the war, described Thunderbolt to the authors as Galland's best moment in high command. In his own evening, Galland himself numbered Thunderbolt among the greatest moments of his life, ranking it equally with the births of his son and daughter.

Exemplary cooperation between the German Navy and Luftwaffe can also be largely attributed to Galland's qualities as a leader and planner. Everything was subordinated to operational success. Galland's professional skill and his long experience of modern combat guided the operational planning unerringly. His background allowed him to foresee and plan for virtually every eventuality. Thunderbolt was essentially flawless.

Galland won his Thunderbolt victory with a total of 252 fighters of all types. This inferiority of force compared with the RAF was overcome by excellent planning and a stellar performance by the German fighter pilots. Galland's decisions from inception to end showed a cool command brain and the firmness of mind essential to high command. The Luftwaffe lost 17 aircraft and 11 pilots in Thunderbolt, and the British lost more than 60 aircraft of all types.

Gneisenau never went to sea again. RAF Bomber Command blasted her in the Kiel drydock within two weeks. She was eventually filled with concrete and used as a flak fort at Gdynia in the bay of Danzig. *Scharnhorst* underwent extensive repairs for months, and duly reached Altenfjord in Norway early in 1943. When she was ordered to sea by Admiral Doenitz on Christmas Day 1943, to attack convoy JW55B, Ultra overheard all the preparatory phases and final orders. Admiral Fraser in HMS *Duke of York* was promptly informed, and *Scharnhorst* went down under Royal Navy guns on 26 December 1943.

Although the Channel Dash was a tactical triumph and a strategic defeat, the operation strengthened Hitler's status with his admirals. The Fuehrer had correctly assessed British inertia and inability to improvise in the face of surprise. Galland's personal estimate of Thunderbolt's likelihood of success, given to Hitler at the initial conference, had proved remarkably accurate. Galland's stock rose with Hitler, and for a relatively short time thereafter he was one of the Fuehrer's military favorites. With Thunderbolt successfully concluded, Colonel Galland turned his attention to pressing problems afflicting the far-flung Fighter Arm.

EIGHTEEN

The Elastic Umbrella

Hitler vowed during his drive to power, and later, that Germany would never again be exposed to the fatal strain of war on two fronts. Galland's new vantage point in early 1942 let him see how comprehensively Hitler had violated his vow – as far as the Fighter Arm was concerned. German fighters were in combat on six distinct fronts.

JG 5 operated over Scandinavia and the Arctic, mainly from Norwegian bases. Fighter cover for the Navy and assisting in attacks on Allied convoys to Russia were JG 5's main missions. Four more Geschwader were strung out thinly from the Baltic to the Caucasus. They were providing local air superiority and close support for a battlefront of unprecedented length.

JG 2 and JG 26 struggled far below full strength on the Channel, battling the RAF's Non-Stop Offensive. JG 27 and JG 53, the latter with one Gruppe from JG 3 *Udet* added, fought on yet another two front war. In the central Mediterranean against Malta, and over the deserts of North Africa, they had been successful – for the moment.

The sixth fighter front was over the homeland itself at night. The RAF had bombed Germany at night from the time of the Battle of Britain onward, stepping up this effort in 1942. The Luftwaffe High Command had been forced to set up a completely new organization of fighters and ground control facilities. Night fighting required specially-developed tactics and new electronic techniques for detection and control. Night fighting had not been taken seriously in the short peacetime life of the Luftwaffe. This sixth fighter front was now consuming immense resources in dealing with British night attacks.

Each of these six fronts had its own special needs, but they were commonly dominated by four problems: numerical inferiority, replacement aircraft, pilots to fly them, and the manifold needs of service and supply. The night fighters were not under Galland at this time, but the rest of his fighter empire sprawled from the Arctic to the Middle East, and from the English Channel to the Caucasus. The responsibility was sobering to a man just turned 30. War dynamics had proved decisively that *no major military operation could be sustained without fighter aircraft.*

The successful umbrella provided by the Fighter Arm for the geographically compact and brief Polish, Norwegian, French, and Balkan campaigns had now been stretched out in all directions like elastic. JG 5 and JG 27 were thousands of miles apart. The protective capabilities of this umbrella were thus sharply reduced. This stretched umbrella was also relatively delicate and fragile. Heavy and concentrated blows against it at any point could bring about its local collapse, from which disaster could be transmitted to the whole military structure. The most important single action in Galland's effort to keep the umbrella intact, was somehow to increase the number of fighters and pilots available for combat.

Galland had already taken action through Milch to substantially increase fighter production. To obtain more pilots, Galland surveyed and then radically reorganized his own creation – the Operational Training Units (*Ergänzungsgruppen*). The system he initiated as Kommodore of JG 26, where freshly trained pilots were taken under the care of active fighter units and familiarized with current experience, had spread through the Fighter Arm. The merits of these OTUs were well-established.

In JG 26 Galland had kept his pioneer OTU administratively lean. His resources there were limited and he did not want the OTU to generate paper work. Analyzing the OTUs now in early 1942, he could see that a large, cumbersome bureaucracy had developed around the units. Vast resources were being absorbed. Efficiency was low. Standards and methods of OTU training differed widely.

Galland consolidated the OTUs into three OTU Gruppen, assigned to the East, West, and South. Five full Gruppen of fighters were made available for the front by this reorganization. Part of this newfound power was used to form JG 1, which was assigned to Holland and the German Bight, easing the strain on JG 2 and JG 26. Other personnel and aircraft "wrung out" of the reorganization helped to form two new twin-engined fighter units and a fighter-bomber unit for the Eastern Front. Galland had begun his struggle to increase the size of the Fighter Arm.

In the forefront of his mind even at this time was the production power of the Allies. Interested in aircraft since boyhood, he had a profound respect for the American aircraft industry. Americans had invented the airplane.

They were a competitive people who liked to be the world's best at everything. In the light of his own desire always to be the best, Galland knew what might be expected from this facet of American national character.

His recent experience combating the rising power of the RAF on the Channel, made him apprehensive about the aerial threat from the West. Intelligence reports he was now routinely receiving as General of the Fighter Arm dealt frequently with American aircraft production goals. With their superior resources, the Americans would soon eclipse British aircraft production. The combined production of these two powerful Allies would then come winging across the Channel. This specter of enemy air power never left him, because experience had proved that only a large fighter force could stop such an assault.

Japan had inflicted a series of defeats on the USA at this time, but they had failed to deliver a finishing blow. In Galland's military estimation, Japan's lack of a final victory could only mean that the Americans would recover and strike back. The continental USA was untouched and contained colossal human and material resources. Parts of Roosevelt's "fireside chats" that appeared in German newspapers promised massive bombing fleets. The 4-engined B-17 Fortress and the B-24 Liberator were already in production, tested and ready for combat. British 4-engined production was also going full blast.

These were the strategic bombers, the master offensive air weapon advocated by Douhet. The German media ridiculed the American production figures, but the intelligence reports crossing Galland's desk told a sobering, factual story, divested of all political rhetoric and wishful thinking. With his own logic and professional experience Galland could readily draw the outline of tomorrow in the air: a veritable blizzard of aircraft, attacking Germany from British bases. The storm would probably come before he could build up air defense with the Fighter Arm sufficiently to protect his homeland.

German fighters were holding their own in Russia and had temporary ascendancy in the central Mediterranean, but on the Channel they were already beleaguered. A potential catastrophe loomed. Galland was appalled to find that even some responsible, high-ranking members of the High Command looked on the American threat as a bluff.

The more he learned of the true state of the Fighter Arm, the more Galland was convinced that only a Herculean effort would suffice. That effort would also have to be timely. He was confident that current marques of the Me 109 with the new DB 605 engine, and the Fw 190, would be able to handle the daylight threat in the West – if there were enough of them available with well-trained replacement pilots. The measures he was now taking would have to be greatly magnified to meet the USAAF-RAF threat. Maintenance of the elastic fighter umbrella was meanwhile devouring everything that he could find.

When Galland took up with Goering the impact that USAAF reinforcement of the RAF offensive would have on the Fighter Arm in the West, the Reich Marshal waved it all aside with his gold baton.

"The Americans?" said Goering blandly, "they are being badly beaten by the Japanese. Besides, Galland, you should remember that the Americans are good at making fancy cars and refrigerators, but that doesn't mean that they are any good at making aircraft. They are bluffing. They are excellent at bluffing."

This interview was in March or April. As late as Harvest Thanksgiving, in October of 1942, Goering repeated these trite notions in a public speech. This was three months after the USAAF had dropped its first bombs on continental targets. With juvenile words did the Luftwaffe's Supreme Commander thus dispose of both the U.S. aviation industry and the USAAF. Galland was shocked by this irresponsibility toward an urgent national danger.

After several months as General of the Fighters, Galland had seen plenty of Goering's reactions to weighty technical matters. They did not inspire confidence. USAAF daylight bombing of Germany could be foreseen – technically, tactically, and strategically – but Goering could not accept such a development politically. When Goering made a fatuous response to such serious questions, often a member of his sycophantic personal circle would chime in with supportive comments.

Anything the Reich Marshal said that was derogatory to the Fighter Arm was endorsed within his circle. Galland found this highly irritating. Young Bomber Arm personalities around Goering used his favor to produce a destructive polarization of the Luftwaffe. Bomber Arm was pitted against Fighter Arm in an internecine contest for Goering's approval. Galland's basic emotional cleanliness put Germany first, although he unfailingly defended the Fighter Arm. He saw Bomber Arm and Fighter Arm as sword and flail, commonly fighting a powerful alliance in mortal combat. Goering's sycophants preferred divisive, counter-productive rivalry.

Goering's personal idleness, egotism, vanity, and incompetence promoted this internal schism and all its destructive consequences. His own best leaders were induced to struggle with each other. As these crazy rivalries began spoiling the best impulses and ideas, Galland's mind went back to the smooth-working Condor Legion. All then worked as one. Those were becoming the "good old days" for him as 1942 wore on.

Galland had problems now that he had never encountered or contemplated as a combat Kommodore. How was he to get

HANS-JOACHIM MARSEILLE - 158 VICTORIES
JG 27s top ace, Marseille shot down 17 aircraft in one day over the sands of Africa. Twenty-nine days later, on 30 September 1942, Marseille lost his life when the engine of his Me 109 caught fire and he hit the horizontal stabilizer when he baled out.

MARSEILLE IN THE COCKPIT
As his crew chief watches, Marseille runs up the engine on his Me 109. The rpm drop when the magneto was checked was found to be within the limits.

HANS-JOACHIM MARSEILLE
Formal portrait of "The Star of Africa." Marseille was the top ace of JG 27. Flying three sorties in one day, he shot down 17 opponents.

his ideas through to such a man as Goering? The Reich Marshal was an overpowering personality oblivious to his own command shortcomings, and supported always by his brain trust of "yes men," not one of whom was a fighter pilot. The employment, technical performance, and training of the Fighter Arm required practical, realistic, wide-ranging knowledge that could give due weight to the crucial human element.

Goering liked to preface his views by emphasizing that he was himself "a former successful fighter ace." By this device he assumed contemporary expertise. The Western Front of World War I was light-years behind this present aerial struggle. Goering's fawning circle of advisers had no fighter expertise. They gave the Reich Marshal no useful technical help, and played instead upon his rampant vanity. These officers were interested solely in expanding their personal influence and in having a good life – to which Goering held their passports.

The smallness of these officers was galling to Galland. Their influence was one more deplorable and needless problem that he had to contend with in running the Fighter Arm. What hit him hardest as the weeks passed was the substantial number of high-level Luftwaffe people who were opposing any strong enlargement of the Fighter Arm. Goering's circle, and many others, as well, were restraining the Fighter Arm expansion that Galland regarded as vital for Germany's survival. He had his own personal two-front war as a result.

While the highly secret Thunderbolt preparations had been in progress, Galland had been occupied as well with the Malta situation. After Thunderbolt, the island came to the center of his attention, reaching out to dominate his thoughts, even as it dominated the Axis supply lines to Rommel. Many echoes of the Battle of Britain appeared in the new air assault on Malta. Among them was the presence of Galland's Battle of Britain Air Fleet Commander, Field Marshal Kesselring. He was to orchestrate the aerial campaign.

Kesselring had urged Goering and Hitler to seize Malta from 1941 onward. Capturing the island was essential to a successful Axis North African campaign. Only 153 square miles in area, Malta lies 56 miles south of Sicily, a distance not significantly greater than France to Britain in terms of air assault. Malta is also 225 miles from the African coast at Tunis. This unique and isolated position allowed British aircraft and submarines to control the shipping of Axis logistics from Italy and Sicily to North Africa.

By cutting off Rommel's vital supplies, Malta was more effective against the Afrika Korps than many divisions in the field. Interdiction operations from Malta in October of 1941 sank over 60 percent of the supplies shipped to Rommel. The tally rose by more than 15 percent in November. Field Marshal Kesselring was thereupon sent to Sicily from Russia, with part of his Air Fleet 2, to mount countermeasures.

German intelligence did not report large air, naval, or army forces on Malta. Galland wondered at the time how such modest forces were able to inflict such heavy losses on Axis convoys. He therefore tended to discount the intelligence reports. Ultra decrypts were again responsible for Malta's efficiency. Kesselring's detailed reports to Berlin and to Rommel on convoy loadings, routes, and estimated arrival times were decoded promptly, and were probably read in London before Rommel received his copy.

In possession of comprehensive information on convoy composition, routes, and departure times, the RAF readily intercepted and sank Rommel's supplies. To protect Ultra, RAF reconnaissance pilots were instructed to deliberately allow themselves to be sighted by the convoys. British pilots were mystified by these orders, but must have guessed that British intelligence was good when they were repeatedly vectored to areas where the convoys appeared.

Substantial economy of effort was thereby made possible out of Malta. The small, Malta-based RAF contingent was concentrated on its targets through Ultra. Within individual convoys, specific ships were singled out for concentrated attacks if they carried critical cargoes such as gasoline, tanks, or spare parts. Kesselring had unwittingly supplied such detail. The Germans wrongly blamed Italian Navy Intelligence and British spies for the security leaks.

The fighter component of Air Fleet 2 withdrawn from Russia was commanded by the tireless Major Guenther von Maltzahn of JG 53. Galland knew him well from Battle of Britain days. "Henri" von Maltzahn's leadership had made JG 53 the Luftwaffe's top-scoring Geschwader. He now had available four under-strength Me 109F Gruppen, plus one Gruppe of Me 110s. This day fighter force consisted of no more than 80 serviceable fighters. Von Maltzahn was to escort and protect the bombers that would blast Malta into impotence.

The main bombing force was five Gruppen of the fast Ju 88A-4s, with one Gruppe of Stukas in support. Early in 1942, the Malta attacks did not go well, despite many downings credited to JG 53. Dive bombing was still being employed, in accordance with High Command obsessions and directives. The proficient Malta flak and British fighters were chewing up too many German aircraft. Goering blamed Galland and the fighters for these losses.

Kesselring and his chief of staff, Colonel Paul Deichmann, were able to convince the High Command by March of 1942 of the costly ineffectiveness of dive bombing at Malta. Successive concentrated attacks were approved on the RAF fighter base at Ta Kali, the torpedo-plane and bomber bases at Hal Far, and the docks at Valetta harbor. Level bombardment was authorized instead of dive bombing. Galland followed reports from this theater with limited satisfaction.

The combination of concentrated carpet bombing and aggressive action by JG 53 virtually suppressed British fighter activity. By the end of March 1942, the Luftwaffe held air superiority over Malta, and by mid-April had virtually driven out the Royal Navy. British bomber and torpedo-bomber action was also suppressed. British supply convoys to Malta were now heavily attacked from the air, and thousands of tons of food, ammunition, and fuel were sunk by the Luftwaffe.

By the end of April, von Maltzahn's fighters had flown well over 5,000 sorties. German bombers had been successfully escorted and dropped almost as much explosive on Malta as the entire Bomber Arm dropped on England in September of 1940. Malta was toothless. Rommel again received his supplies. The Fighter Arm had won a hard victory over their old RAF adversaries.

NORTH AFRICA
Left: Hans-Joachim Marseille, the top ace of JG 27 in Africa, listens intently to his mentor and boss, Kommodore Edu Neumann.

MARSEILLE IS DECORATED
Right: Kommodore Eduard Neumann of JG 27 awards a medal to his star fighter pilot Hans-Joachim Marseille. Observing the ceremony is General Geisler.

Both Hitler and Mussolini had been dithering over a Malta invasion for months. Now the Luftwaffe had provided air superiority over the island and its lengthy coastline. Germany's elite XI Air Corps was ready with its experienced paratroops and was waiting to drop on the island. In support were German-trained Italian paratroops, who outnumbered Malta's defenders. 70,000 more Italian troops were earmarked for the invasion force.

Hitler was suspicious of Italian ability to carry out their end of the proposed Operation "Hercules" for Malta's capture. Shadows of the Pyrrhic paratroop victory in Crete the previous year still loomed in the Fuehrer's mind. A prize had been won then that events had since proved was not worth its high cost. Goering fanned Hitler's fears, being himself opposed to the Malta invasion.

After two days of conferences with their military chiefs at the Obersalzberg, Hitler and Mussolini decided on 30 April 1942 to postpone the Malta assault for three months. This was to prove a fateful decision for Axis fortunes in the Mediterranean. Rommel wanted to strike at the British immediately, before they could mount a desert offensive to take pressure off Malta. The Axis leaders let Rommel have his way. After his successful attack on Tobruk, Rommel would wait at Halfaya Pass on the Egyptian border while Operation Hercules seized Malta. Supplies then secure, the Desert Fox would immediately press on to take Alexandria and topple Allied power in the Middle East.

Postponement of Hercules lost the Germans their golden chalice. The dynamic Mediterranean war once again showed its sensitivity to air superiority, the pivot upon which everything turned. On 9 May 1942 on a second attempt, 61 RAF Spitfires were flown off the U.S. aircraft carrier *Wasp* to provide mass fighter reinforcement to Malta. A finely orchestrated reception had them refueled and back in the air in a few minutes. They waded into an incoming Luftwaffe force that had expected them to be on the ground when they struck. Fighters again demonstrated their ability to reverse a military situation.

When the Luftwaffe renewed its bombing offensive on 10 May 1942, the new Spitfires began hacking German formations to pieces. At their best defending close to their bases, the Spitfires inflicted more losses in the ensuing three days than Kesselring had suffered in his entire five-week offensive. Having advised his superiors that Malta had been eliminated, Kesselring suddenly found his fighter force halved as three Gruppen were ordered away from his Malta operations – two to Russia and one to North Africa. The elastic umbrella was under too much strain to provide fighters for the continuing operations against targets that the C.-in-C. South had reported as "eliminated." Bombers were similarly taken from Kesselring and re-assigned to Russia, Greece, and Africa.

Drastic reversal of Luftwaffe fortunes over Malta had its impact at Luftwaffe HQ in Goldap, East Prussia. From triumph and victory, with air superiority hard won over the troublesome island, the Luftwaffe descended again into grinding weeks of struggle and losses. Galland was dismayed by the increasing fighter attrition, but did not regard this as disproportionate to the task of neutralizing Malta, the key to North African success.

Amid the decline of Luftwaffe fortunes over Malta, the first great hammer blows against German cities and the civil population were being driven home at night by RAF Bomber Command. Air Marshal A.T. "Bomber" Harris launched a series of area attacks, culminating with history's first thousand-bomber raid at Cologne on the night of 30/31 May 1942. The center of the city was burned out, and the swamped German night fighters were only able to claw down 41 of the 1,046 raiding bombers.

The night fighters were obviously facing serious difficulties. Massed formations of bombers called for new tactics and control techniques. Here was the very situation against which Galland had already warned Goering – the blizzard from the West. Holes were appearing in the umbrella.

Dismayed by the sarcastic, unforgiving comments of Hitler after Cologne, and incensed by bomber losses over Malta, Goering ordered a conference in Naples. The Reich Marshal was visiting there with his wife, Emmy. Every Kommodore and Gruppenkommandeur from every fighter unit on the southern front was summoned. Galland flew down in his personal He 111. Here, in another way and place, the phantoms of the Battle of Britain rose again.

In the warm Italian weather, Goering turned the heat on the Fighter Arm. He launched an abusive tirade that had Galland seething. Galland could see von Maltzahn, Neumann, Luetzow,

KOMMODORE OF JG 27 IN AFRICA
Oberst Eduard Neumann was considered one of the finest of the fighter leaders in the Luftwaffe, and was Galland's lifelong confidant.

and others sitting white-faced with anger as Goering lashed at them with allegations of cowardice. Galland contained himself until it was his turn to speak. He sprang to his feet. Countering every Goering charge with logic, facts, and the competence born of leading fighter formations personally, the young General of the Fighters spoke for all the leaders in the room. A noisy and bitter argument with Goering ensued. The Reich Marshal ended proceedings by ordering Galland to fly over to Sicily, inspect the fighter units and "put some spine into them."

Taking "Franzl" Luetzow with him, Galland went over to the dusty and scorching airstrips on Sicily to investigate the fighter situation. Hard flying on escort missions had taken some toll of the pilots and aircraft, and so had the unaccustomed heat. Morale was good. A negative factor was open resentment of Goering's telexed allegations of cowardice.

At Taormina, Galland found Kesselring to be his usual optimistic self. He had been the first high Luftwaffe officer to urge on Hitler the invasion of Malta. He had in recent days laid the groundwork in vain for Malta's capture. Yet here at this time he knew that it could not be done with air power alone, and certainly not with the reduced Luftwaffe forces he now commanded.

Galland was concerned by a practical gulf that existed between Kesselring and current realities of fighter operations on this front. Optimist Kesselring was expecting too much of his fighters. Kesselring overestimated the possibilities of fighter units that were geographically scattered and below strength. His part of the umbrella was too thin. Instead of concentrating his fighter forces on reduced main operations, Kesselring split them up and still wanted to fulfill all requirements, despite their weakness.

Kesselring touched on some of his differences with Rommel. From JG 27 leaders at Naples, Galland already knew that Rommel was asking more of the fighters than they could possibly deliver. Rommel's genius sense of mobility did not extend to appreciating the limits of fighter power. He saw fighters in World War I terms – as boys playing in the air. These reports, and Kesselring's seeming inability to find a center of gravity for his operations, boded ill for the Luftwaffe on the southern front.

Galland flew back to Berlin to write new Tactical Regulations for escorting bomber missions and to other pressing tasks. The consequences of unleashing Rommel and postponing the Malta invasion were soon apparent. Seizing a vast hoard of supplies in Tobruk on 21 June 1942, Rommel had sufficient logistics, in his own opinion, to reach Alexandria. On 26 June 1942, the now famous "Field Marshals' Conference" took place at Sidi Barrani. Against Kesselring's strongest opposition, Rommel persuaded the two Italian marshals, Bastico and Cavallero, that he could be in Cairo in ten days.

Although Kesselring was a hard driver, ready to push his Luftwaffe units to their absolute limits, he balked at the Alexandria thrust. Supply problems were basically unsolved. The fighter umbrella was stretched to its breaking point. Enemy power was not only growing, but also being compressed by the Axis advance closer and closer to its main base. Kesselring called Rommel's plans to advance "madness," but the Italians were convinced by Rommel. Hitler ordered Kesselring to cease his objections.

Rommel was subsequently blocked at Alam El Halfa and at El Alamein, with Ultra decrypts playing a major role in frustrating his thrust. Rommel's dream of the Nile was replaced by an imminent nightmare. When Galland flew down to Africa to evaluate the situation, Colonel Hoffman von Waldau was awaiting him at Fuka. As *Fliegerführer Afrika*, von Waldau had wrung the last ounce out of the Luftwaffe in aiding Rommel. One of the most capable officers in the Luftwaffe, von Waldau was under no illusions about the current predicament of the German forces. Galland's old Condor Legion friend, Major Eduard Neumann, was Kommodore of JG 27, and added further detail to von Waldau's grim summary.

The greatest German ace of the North African campaign, Captain Hans-Joachim Marseille, had died in a crash on 30 September 1942. He was credited with 158 victories and had been awarded the Diamonds to his Knight's Cross. His death had shocked and saddened the JG 27 fighter pilots. Marseille's loss was highly symbolic.

Worn out men and materiel were only one aspect of the desert crisis. Aerial reconnaissance and photographs showed massive enemy air fleets deployed close to the front. Studying the aerial photographs, Galland's apprehensions turned to alarm. Unleashing this armada of nearly 800 aircraft would rapidly obliterate Rommel's exhausted air power.

Impelled by the need for urgent action, Galland wrote a realistic and bitterly pessimistic report to Goering and the High Command. He warned of the debacle that total Allied air supremacy would inflict. With thousands of German and Italian soldiers about to feel this aerial lash, Goering and the High Command directed their concern to the tone in which Galland's report had been couched.

ADOLF GALLAND AND GÜNTHER LÜTZOW
On 1 April 1943, they met again where Lützow was Inspektor of Southern Forces. Galland did not like the name "Adolf" and was called Dolfo, Mufti, Gallani, Capitano, Red Knight, and others. Lützow was called "Franzl." Lützow, who had 110 aerial victories, was called "the finest leader in the Luftwaffe" by Galland. Flying an Me 262 jet from Galland's JV 44 squadron, Lützow was shot down and killed on 24 April 1945. USAAF records credit 9th Air Force pilots led by Major James E. Hill with the victory.

Kesselring was also resentful of Galland's "unwarranted intrusion" on his sphere of authority. When Galland flew back to Germany and showed Goering the aerial reconnaissance photos, the Reich Marshal demonstrated how to handle such problems. Riffling the photographs in his pudgy hands, Goering smiled triumphantly. "Dummies," he said. "Dummy aircraft. Nothing but dummy aircraft."

Without operational power of command, Galland could not change any disposition in Africa. Other events pressed in on him. He had to begin organizing the Fighter Divisions (*Jagdivisionen*), a step he had recommended and which the High Command had approved. The Fighter Divisions consolidated Day Fighter, Night Fighter, Signals and Observer Corps control into one organization for each region. Substantial manpower economies, greater efficiency, and improved control were thereby achieved. These consolidations continued into 1943.

Considerable staff work was required for this reorganization, and the lack of Fighter Arm officers with General Staff training was severely felt. Due to the primacy given to the Bomber Arm in the Luftwaffe's in infancy, Fighter Arm officers had in general not done well at the War Academy, nor been there in appropriate numbers.

Galland's reaction to this had been similar to that of most Fighter Arm officers – hurt pride. In his new post with its heavy responsibilities, he could see the need for General Staff training. Organic, systematic, detailed military management would have facilitated the formation of the Fighter Divisions. He was nevertheless convinced that an experienced combat leader's eye could see many things to which the General Staff types seemed oblivious. Both were clearly needed for a successful Fighter Arm. *Rapprochement* with the War Academy was indicated, but he procrastinated over its initiation.

USAAF bombers were meanwhile being flown across the Atlantic to England by their own combat crews. Thousands of USAAF personnel were arriving in England by air and sea. On 18 June 1942, the British published a list of 87 British airfields being made available to the USAAF. By the end of August, the USAAF had put in a bombing strike against the Potez aircraft works at Meaulte, which were being used as a repair depot for Luftwaffe aircraft. This was closer than it seemed. Fighters of Galland's own former JG 26 were repaired at Meaulte.

The Battle of El Alamein on 2 October 1942 launched the end of the Afrika Korps, and the disaster that Galland had warned against was soon in horrifying progress. JG 27 was overwhelmed, and hounded relentlessly by Allied fighters that swarmed in the desert air like locusts. They ate up every German aircraft in sight. Roaring down to strafe everything that moved on the single coast road, or across the desert floor, they drove home the true meaning of air supremacy.

On 8 November 1942, as Rommel's remnants retreated across Egypt and into Libya, the Americans struck with Operation Torch at the western end of the Mediterranean. A fresh horde of aircraft entered the fray there. Another front to fight on while JG 27 struggled for its existence, struck at Luftwaffe morale. The elastic umbrella began its collapse in North Africa.

As Galland had feared, and as he had forecast, too much had been asked, expected, and demanded of a Fighter Arm stretched beyond its capacities. Neither verbal nor military abuse of the fighter units had served the German cause. The gloomy tidings from Africa brought Galland no joy in having been proved right. He knew personally far too many of the brave pilots who were now statistics.

Another brave fighter pilot close to Galland's heart had fallen on 31 October 1942. His youngest brother Paul, a developing ace with 17 victories, was shot down and killed over the Channel front. Pangs in the heart came with that particular telex. The beloved Paulinchen and Wutz had often joked with him in JG 26 that "there'll be no 'after the war' for us." Nothing dulled the pain of such a deep personal blow.

On 19 November 1942, a telephone call from the Reich Marshal advised him of his promotion to Major General (*Generalmajor*). Goering proudly pointed out that the youngest general in the German Armed Forces was in "his" Luftwaffe. November was otherwise noteworthy as USAAF heavy bombers began battering U-boat pens on the French coast and struck at airfields and repair depots.

Africa provided an unbroken chain of disasters. The elastic umbrella had given way at its southern extremity. Galland hated to contemplate the further consequences. Massive and diverse problems pressed in on him from all quarters. By Christmas of 1942 he was ready again to seek brief sanctuary with JG 26 on the Channel, his second home.

CAPITANO AND THE SIEBEL 104
General Galland used this small twin-engined airplane for some staff visits. It met a calamitous end when Edu Neumann was flying it and says, "I crash landed it beside a canal near Leipzig and it burned after the right engine caught fire in the air." Galland adds: "because Edu switched to the wrong fuel tank!"

Christmas 1942 was much more serious than the previous Yule season. Nobody was as light-hearted as they were a year ago. Galland was also now a general officer. That changed slightly the relationship he had previously enjoyed with the pilots and leaders he knew well. This change had nothing to do with standing on ceremony, and they drank wine together as always.

The change was most evident when they told him of their difficulties and problems. These ranged from the number and quality of the enemy to materiel and supply difficulties, by way of tactics, weapons, and training. This was the terminal point for all the mistakes that were made higher up. This was where the suffering and bleeding were done.

Subtly, respectfully and sincerely, these brave men were expecting that Galland would help them – that he had the power now to do so. He had left them and gone to dwell among the great gods of the Luftwaffe. Ethics and good discipline precluded his telling these warriors how things really were in the pantheon. He made a New Year resolution to himself instead. He would throw himself into his tasks with all his strength in 1943. The fighting pilots deserved no less.

NINETEEN

Crisis

Galland carried his New Year resolution into effect in January 1943 by summoning every Kommodore in the Fighter Arm to a Berlin conference. These men were the cream of Fighter Arm leadership, and all of them were also successful aces. They carried within themselves a vast store of current knowledge about fighter operations. The conference was to pool this knowledge and experience, with cross-fertilization of ideas. New tactical insights and initiatives were expected to result.

For eight days the cadre of top-flight pilot-leaders conferred on weapons and tactics, further developments, results from test units, logistics, training, personnel, and the enemy. Each Kommodore gave a one-hour speech on the experiences and most important requirements of his Geschwader. With solidified morale, each left the gathering understanding his task anew, and with a grasp of the challenges faced by the Fighter Arm as a whole. Shorthand transcripts were made, and Galland had these typed and distributed to each Geschwader at the front.

On 21 January 1943, Allied leaders at the Casablanca Conference set up round-the-clock bombing of Germany. The Casablanca Directive issued by the Allied Combined Chiefs of Staff was to have a profound influence on the life and career of Adolf Galland. The objectives of British and American airpowers based in Britain were broadly defined as:

1. Destruction of the German military, economic, and industrial systems.
2. Undermining the morale of the German people.

Primary target priorities were listed as U-boat building yards, aircraft plants, transportation, petroleum facilities, and other war industries. General Ira Eaker, the able commander of the 8th USAAF, made the main case for daylight bombing at the Conference. Eaker converted Churchill to his views. RAF Bomber Command would henceforth raze German cities by night. Eaker's daylight heavies would wage the strategic bombing offensive. Galland's fighters were the main opposition.

German fighter wastage on the Southern Front by early 1943 far exceeded losses on the Channel or on the huge Eastern Front. In North Africa, Tunis, and Sicily, JG 27, JG 53, and JG 77 struggled not only against overwhelming Allied air power, but against the disintegration of the Axis African effort. Allied airpower grew continually in weight and expertise. Luftwaffe casualties rose proportionately. Galland regarded this wastage as futile. He favored saving irreplaceable pilots and crews for battles looming ahead.

Hitler persisted with his "victory-or-death" edicts. Every position was either lost or abandoned only at the last possible moment. Ground support equipment, spare parts, fuel, and other stores, as well as unserviceable aircraft, had to be blown up as the Germans fell back before Allied power. Their formations were therefore equipped over and over with new aircraft from Germany. The pilots fought to exhaustion. This high wastage gave no useful return.

On the Eastern Front, five Geschwader were strung out thinly from Norway and Finland to the Caucasus. With unimpaired morale and excellent leadership, they were able to provide local and temporary air superiority for the Army, like a fire brigade. They were less worrisome to Galland than the other fronts. Mediterranean demands had slowed the development of Eaker's 8th USAAF, but their experimentation with escorted daylight raids over France continued. Similar daylight raids on Germany were an inevitable extension of this beginning, unless it could be stopped. Galland's concerns grew as the American effort developed.

68 American heavy bombers struck at the St. Nazaire U-boat pens on 3 January 1943. German fighters met them in force. 7 bombers were downed and 47 damaged. The Americans returned to their British bases with 70 men missing and killed. The Luftwaffe had inflicted 10 percent losses.

American leaders were bedeviled at this time by complex operational problems and decisions. General Eaker remained certain that B-17 Fortresses could fly unescorted in daylight in

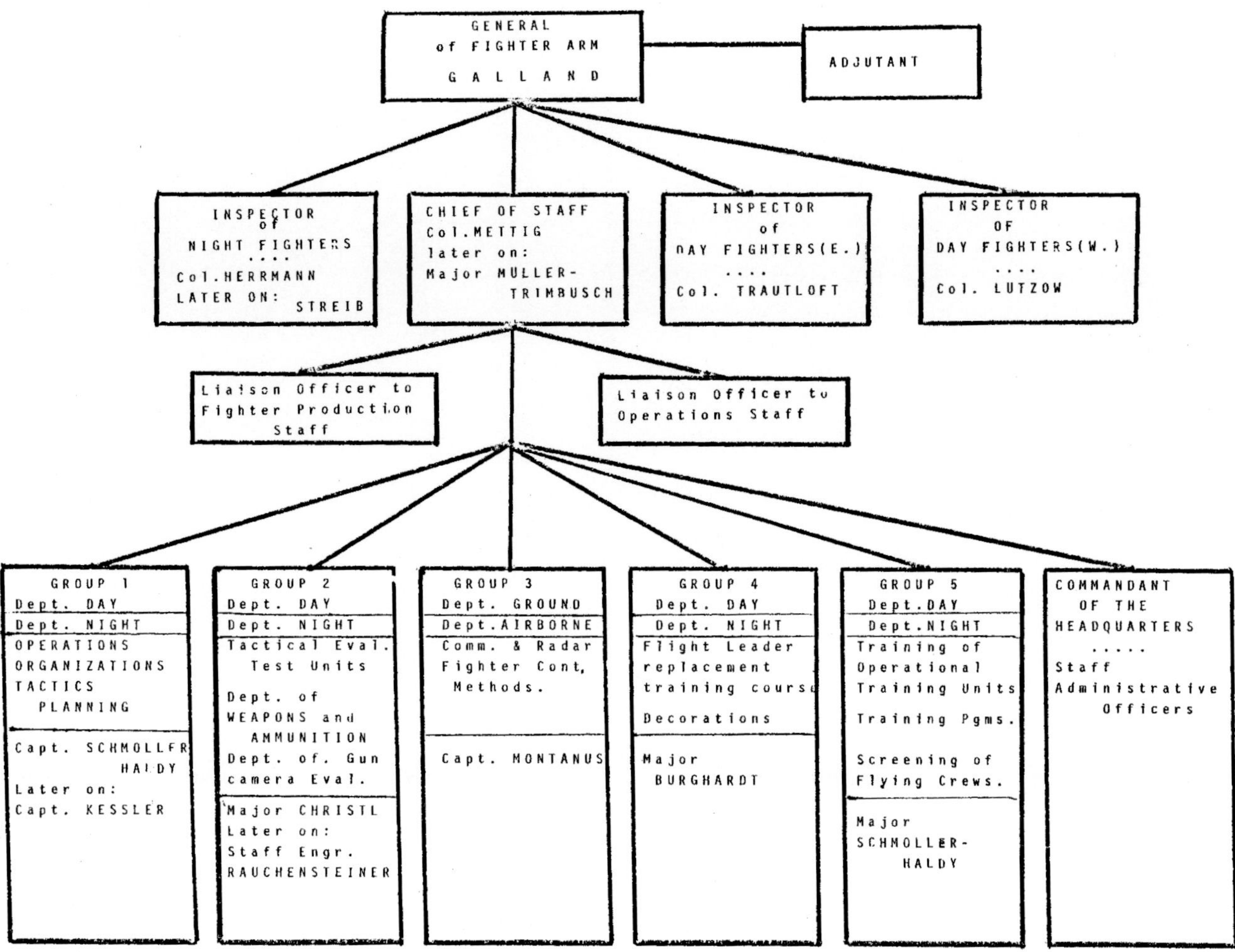

large formations. Eaker's boss and personal friend, General Carl "Tooey" Spaatz, was not so sure, but remained optimistic that American heavies could repel German fighter attack without relying on a fighter escort. The Battle of Britain had written the lesson in blood: *Daylight bombing operations require a fighter escort in the presence of an enemy fighter force*. General Jimmy Doolittle in North Africa had abundantly proved the value of his P-38 escort fighters in daylight bombing missions. Insufficient attention was paid to this experience as ETO commanders grappled with their problems. In January of 1943, the undetermined factor in the B-17 escort question was the self-defensive power of these aircraft. Never before had there been such strongly-armed bombers. Operational experience gained with lightly-armed British and German bombers in prior battles might not be valid for American B-17 formations carrying many hundreds of guns. War's crucible would soon boil away any theoretical falsehoods. Galland's brother Wutz was among the German pilots notably successful in downing the B-17 with a head-on attack. The forward-firing hemisphere of the B-17 was a relatively weak spot, but attacking fighters had to face a daunting hail of tracer on every pass. Skill, daring, and success in such attacks won Wutz Galland command of II/JG 26. His famous brother sent him written counsel on 17 January 1943, along with his congratulations.

"Dear Wutz,

I was very pleased with your letter and your attitude towards your new task. My congratulations on your promotion and appointment.

"... here are a few more hints. At the beginning, everybody will now look more or less critically at your efficiency as a Gruppenkommandeur. I urge you to work like a lion for your Gruppe. The last man must feel that there is a leader in charge, and then they will go through the fire for you.

Regard nothing as self-evident or as running by itself. Everything has to be checked and re-checked. You must work for every success. How much a man can endure you cannot foresee, but let there not be a failure that could have been prevented by better planning, clearer orders, or by more accurate execution.

It is not advisable to be on intimate terms with your

squadron commanders or other officers. By avoiding such intimacy you can be their best comrade. This does not mean you cease caring. The NCOs and ground crews show full gratitude for the presence of a gulf. The highest principle to seek is for them to say among themselves, 'Our C.O. knows the worries and needs of the last man. He is accessible to everybody. What he demands is necessary, and he never demands more than he is willing to do himself at any time,'

Now one more word about your new Kommodore. There is only one acceptable attitude, and that is to be a faithful and sincere follower of your Kommodore, as nothing will work without this. He is responsible for everything. He can lead efficiently only when he can count on every Gruppenkommandeur. The alternative is that the whole Geschwader will fail.

The parliamentary system of leadership, with its free and wild criticism, is a thing of the past. There is only one conception – that of the Kommodore. Then the entire Geschwader acts in unity. JG 26 fought for its reputation under my leadership, and my wish is that its reputation would continue to grow.

Now you know clearly what I expect from you. Any time, you can count on my advice and help. I wish you complete success in your new military position, and I know that you will make it. Good luck.

A.G."

The USAAF took its losses in the feeling out period of 1942 and early 1943. Faith in their heavy bombers was resolute. On 27 January 1943 they finally struck at Germany by day. 53 USAAF heavies raided U-boat facilities at Wilhelmshaven in an unescorted raid, and lost only 3 aircraft. This opened a new phase of the air war.

Hitler promptly summoned Galland to the Wolf's lair. Heavy pressure was on the Fuehrer at this time. A near-rout in North Africa and a national tragedy at Stalingrad were happening simultaneously. American unescorted bombers over the Reich in daylight made everything even worse. Galland was asked what it would take to stop these raids completely. He replied that the Luftwaffe Day Fighter Force would have to be substantially enlarged.

"Enlarged how much?" the Fuehrer demanded. "How many? Must you outnumber the enemy?"

Galland had already studied the problem, convinced that the Western air offensive was the major threat to Germany's war potential.

"For each unescorted enemy bomber, sir, I will need three or four single-engined fighters airborne."

"And if you had such a number of machines available, what results can I expect?"

"The daylight raids will be stopped, based upon losses unbearable to the enemy."

ADOLF GALLAND'S BROTHERS.
Wilhelm-Ferdinand Galland and Paul Galland. "Wutz" and Paul flew with JG 26 and both were killed in combat, Paul on 31 October 1942 after 17 victories, and Wilhelm on 17 August 1943 after 55 victories.

Galland threw another factor into the equation without being invited.

"When the American bombers come escorted by fighters, sir, I will need in addition one single-engined fighter airborne for each enemy fighter."

Hitler's face darkened.

"The question of enemy fighter escort over the Reich does not arise" said the Fuehrer harshly.

"Reich Marshal Goering has assured me that it is not technically possible to build such fighter planes."

Galland was thereupon dismissed. Events in the next two years would verify the general validity of Galland's estimates in this conversation with Hitler. Galland's evaluations took no account of the later advent of radar bombing, which he did not foresee. He did not allow, furthermore, for the significant deterioration of Luftwaffe pilot training or the fuel shortage that was later consequent to U.S. strategic bombing.

Had such forces as Galland specified to Hitler in February of 1943 been available to him even by mid-year, there is the highest probability that daylight bombing of Germany would have been made too expensive for the Americans to sustain. The 8th U.S. command was deeply concerned about casualties and aircraft losses in what was a highly uncertain time for them. In the spring of 1943, proper defensive and escort tactics had not yet been developed by 8th USAAF Fighter Command. Large-scale Luftwaffe fighter defense of the Reich might well have changed Allied minds about daylight strategic bombing.

Goering's assurance to Hitler that no long range fighter could be built to penetrate German airspace was a serious error. The Reich Marshal made many other mistakes in this period through incompetence. As Milch boosted fighter production, Goering dispersed hundreds of these vital new aircraft to units outside the Fighter Arm. Fighters were issued to *Jabo* units for long-range, but inconsequential operations against shipping on the Channel front, and into the Bay of Biscay. More

A SERIOUS FIGHTER PILOT GALLAND
This photo, taken in 1944, shows a more serious, contemplative Adolf Galland. One did not take things lightly when in the presence of Goering or Hitler.

A GENERAL WITH ELAN
Visibly oozing the panache and dash for which he became noted before, during and after the war, Galland dismounts from an He 111 and returns a salute to a friend on the Eastern front. Galland says "I never flew a He 111 on the channel front, respecting the Spits and Mustangs!"

fighters went to reconnaissance units in Russia. Still more were issued to the Ground Attack Arm. All these operations were essential in their own way, but they consumed Fw 190s and Me 109s crucially required for the air superiority task over Germany.

Despite Milch's feat of 7,600 fighters produced in the first eight months of 1943, Galland therefore found himself minus the forces necessary to counter the daylight threat at its inception. Goering had created these numerical deficiencies through his own misassignment of aircraft. He tried now to compensate through greater utilization of existing fighter aircraft in Germany.

Drop tanks for Me 109s and Fw 190s on the Channel Front increased their flying time to two hours. They still had difficulty climbing to combat altitude, after scrambling, in time to intercept the enemy. Goering devised a way of further increasing endurance, against Galland's strongest opposition.

The Reich Marshal ordered that no fighter was to jettison its drop tanks until actually hit by enemy fire. Goering's anxieties over the political consequences for him of daylight raids over Germany were considerable. This induced him to issue such an inhuman and stupid order. Mistrust between the fighting pilots and their Supreme Commander resulted from this and other erroneous decisions. When reports came in that fine young pilots had been blown to bits or incinerated in mid-air when their drop tanks exploded, a shaken Goering withdrew his order.

Galland discharged fully his responsibility to warn about the daylight aerial menace from the West, with Goering and others in high posts. When Armaments and War Production Minister Albert Speer asked him about possible daylight bombing of the Ruhr, Galland told him the truth. Such strikes could be expected, and soon. When Speer later voiced his concern about such attacks on war production, Goering was furious. Sending for Galland, he ordered him not to further discuss the matter with Speer or anyone else. Daylight bombing was a political nightmare for Goering. He tried to order this nightmare to vanish.

In a further effort to increase the fighters available in daytime, German night fighters were pressed into daylight service. Equipped mostly with heavier armament, and with longer endurance, these night fighters provided a supplement for the single-engined day fighters – in theory. Normal night fighter operations saw them working singly, directed by their radar controller on the ground. Assignment of these crews to the daytime melees proved disastrous.

Night fighter crews were not used to operating in formation, or to launching concentrated attacks. Out of their element, they suffered heavy losses from the American defensive fire. They were no match for the nimbler U.S. fighter escorts, wherever such fighters appeared. This abortive effort by the High Command to boost Germany's day fighter defense destroyed many well-trained and successful night fighter crews. Each such crew had required many hours on night operations together to become effective.

The night fighter force viewed daytime operations with disfavor. Although such operations were an official order, night fighter units were instructed by their own command not to send top-flight crews to day operations. The High Command began backing down by ordering day-employed night fighters to attack only those bombers that were separated from their formations. The costly misuse of the night fighters in daytime was eventually halted.

March of 1943 saw the enactment of the final scenes in the Stalingrad disaster. Despite the pressure of events in his own sphere, Galland experienced personal depression at the catastrophic loss of the German Sixth Army. Goering's precipitate undertaking to supply the Sixth Army by air had been a key factor in the disaster. Hard on the heels of Stalingrad came the moment of truth in Tunisia. Again Galland went winging southward for a personal evaluation of the growing shambles.

JG 27 and JG 53 had been ground down in Tunisia to impotency. They were hard pressed just to stay alive. Even local and temporary air superiority for Axis rearguard actions was beyond their power. Like any army without air cover, the Afrika Korps was doomed – pushed, rolled, and bludgeoned back by swarms of Allied aircraft and the armies they protected.

Right before Galland's eyes now was the disaster scenario he had drawn for Goering and the High Command from Fuka, a bare six months previously. Skinny, half-starved, nervous pilots tried to recount their haunted existence aloft, their words drowned out by the roar of Allied bombers overhead. Worried, driven fighter leaders with worn out and battered aircraft, harassed by lack of fuel and supplies, told him of air superiority gone with the wind and enemy air supremacy in its place. For his prediction of these conditions, Galland had been castigated for the sharp and pessimistic tone of his report.

Galland was pained and embarrassed, as a general standing before old comrades, not to have the power to order them out of Africa immediately. Sicily would provide at least temporary sanctuary. Orders had to come from Berlin to save these men. No retreats were permitted.

Evacuation orders finally came at the absolute end in Tunisia. Surviving German pilots ferried out their own ground crews, somehow stuffing two men into the slender tail sections of their Me 109s and three men into the Fw 190s. Pilots made repeated ferry flights to get the ground crews out, exemplifying the bond between pilots and crews in the Fighter Arm. Taking off in the face of such enemy air supremacy was in itself a gamble.

THE SOVIET STORMOVIK - THE IL-2
Armor plate made these dive bombers extremely hard to shoot down.

AMERICAN AIRCRAFT FLOWN BY RUSSIANS
The Lend-lease Program furnished hundreds of aircraft to our communist friends the Soviets. This included the Bell P-39 and Bell P-63 which were able to garner a modicum of success in Russia.

General von Arnim surrendered what was left of the Afrika Korps on 7 May 1943, after Hitler had again tried to supply a beleaguered army by air. Allied aircraft shot down scores of German transports like ducks in a gallery. Through Ultra decrypts, Allied air forces were supplied with the German air transport operating schedules, with fearful subsequent carnage.

After the Tunisian surrender, Galland was given his second operational command as a General. Goering put him in personal charge of the remaining German fighters based in Sicily. This proved to be a hectic, high-pressure assignment, as Allied aircraft bombed and strafed German airfields in Sicily relentlessly.

With their best ground equipment lost in Africa and not replaced, the Luftwaffe fighters in Sicily had their backs to the wall. Commanding successively from Trapani, Comiso, and Catania, Galland used every ounce of his experience to keep his small force operating and inflicting losses on the Allies. More aircraft might well have been available to him, had Hitler not been hoaxed by British deception teams into reinforcing Sardinia and Greece at the expense of Sicily.

The story of "Major Martin," the celebrated "Man Who Never Was" has become well-known since the war. The British planted fake high-level dispatches on a corpse dressed as a Royal Marine major. They dropped the body in known ocean currents so that it would wash ashore near Huelva in Spain. Fake dispatches to General Alexander and Admiral Cunningham identified Sardinia and Greece as Allied invasion sites.

When this was buttressed by other deception stratagems, Hitler was convinced. His directive of 12 May 1943 de-emphasized Sicily and ordered that measures for Sardinia and the Peloponnese Islands take top priority. Panzer divisions were switched from France to Greece, and even from Russia to Greece. Sardinia was reinforced. The 400-odd Luftwaffe aircraft in Sicily after the African surrender were in the right strategic and tactical place. Only 125 Luftwaffe aircraft were in Greece and Crete. When Hitler finished his changes, there were fewer than 300 aircraft in Sicily, and more than 300 in Greece and Crete. That is one reason why Galland found himself with such slender resources in Sicily.

A graphic account of Luftwaffe fighter travails in Sicily appears in Johannes Steinhoff's *Straits of Messina*, published by Andre Deutsch of London in 1971. Steinhoff gives sensitive insight into the pressures on Galland at this time. Steinhoff recounts how the young general's burdens are increased by an irrational telex from Goering. Referring to a recent unsuccessful fighter attack on bombers in the Straits of Messina, Goering orders that one pilot from each participating Gruppe is to be tried by court martial for cowardice in the face of the enemy.

This notorious order was never carried out, but it was devastating to the morale of the spent young pilots who had just escaped the African collapse. Galland had to maintain the appearance of loyalty to his Commander-in-Chief, despite deep personal revulsion at the order. He sought to mollify the angry young Steinhoff by assuring him that the Reich Marshal "didn't really mean" the order. While Galland's personal sympathies were with the pilots, he made it clear to Steinhoff that he was first of all a General with a job to do. He laid down the law to Steinhoff about the need to tackle the B-17s head on, and to get in close before firing.

"As he spoke" says Steinhoff, "he transferred his black cigar from one corner of his mouth to the other, and looked at me in an unfriendly manner."

No generalship on the spot, or spiteful reprisals from Berlin could change the facts in Sicily. Overwhelming Allied air power was concentrated on the island with the inevitable result. Once more the remnants of the Fighter Arm crammed their ground crews into the tail sections of their fighters. Leaving everything behind, they withdrew to Viterbo, in Italy. Permission to leave came only at the last hour.

Within 24 hours of this desperate withdrawal, the German command was ordering the exhausted fighters from Sicily back into the air from their new Italian base. The USAAF intervened. A massive American bombing strike targeted on the fugitive Luftwaffe units sent their aircraft up in smoke at Viterbo. The Mediterranean thereafter declined steadily in importance as a sphere of Fighter Arm engagement.

COLONEL HERBERT IHLEFELD
Left: In Spain, Ihlefeld scored 9 victories flying with Mölders. In WWII he added 123 making it a total of 132. He flew with JG 77, JG 52, JG 11 and JG 1. Galland considered him one of the top Kommodores of the Luftwaffe Fighter arm.

MAJOR HEINZ-WOLFGANG SCHNAUFER
Right: The top night fighter of the world with 121 victories in just 164 sorties, Schnaufer was awarded the Diamonds on 16 Oct. 1944. He survived the war but died two days after an automobile accident in France on 13 July 1952. The rudder from his fighter has been displayed in London and in Australia.

As Goering in 1943 began taking more and more pressure from Hitler, he steadily sought to shift the blame for Luftwaffe failures on to ordinary combat fighter pilots. The court martial order to Sicily is a case in point. Goering's response to Hitler's increasingly bitter reproaches about the Luftwaffe was essentially, "I am not responsible. Failures are due to the pussyfoot fighter pilots."

At a 1943 conference of Fighter Division and Air District (*Luftgau*) leaders in Schleissheim, the Reich Marshal decided

"WOLFS SCHANZE", LOTZEN, EAST PRUSSIA
At this investiture by Hitler were Lt.Col. Dietrich Hrabak (Oakleaves), Col. Hans-Ulrich Rudel (Noted Stuka pilot, Swords) and Sgt. Erwin Hentschel (Rudels backseat gunner. He was awarded the Knights Cross a month later.)

to pass on some of the heat that Hitler had been turning on him. Galland was present. Goering's opening speech referred to the Battle of Britain, but he did not deal with the consequences of his own command meddling. He warmed to the theme of fighter pilots' failings – and their frauds.

"Then there are those Battle of Britain heroes, in the Fighter Arm" said Goering, "who lied in mutual support of each other's victories – false victories so that they could get the Knight's Cross."

Galland saw red. He wanted to hurl himself at Goering, to grab him by the throat, but instead his hands went to his own. Tearing off his Knight's Cross with its Oak Leaves, Swords, and Diamonds – Germany's highest award for valor – he slammed it down resoundingly on the table in front of Goering. Galland said nothing. His action said everything. His hunter's eyes bored into Goering's soul. Total silence reigned in the room.

Rarely at a loss for words, the Reich Marshal was clearly flustered by Galland's action. He resumed haltingly, his criticisms markedly toned down. Many other fighter pilots present wanted to take off their decorations in protest and in solidarity with Galland. He would not allow this. More fighter pilots volunteered this same protest when word of the incident spread to the combat units. Galland denied them permission.

He made his own removal of the Knight's Cross an enduring symbol. Even though Goering later apologized for his remarks, the General of the Fighter Arm did not wear his Knight's Cross again for at least six months. Photographs in this book taken during this period show that the decoration is missing from his throat. Hitler eventually noticed its absence and inquired through his Luftwaffe aide why General Galland was not wearing his decorations. Galland was not known as the *enfant terrible* of the Luftwaffe for nothing.

His presence as an operational commander in Sicily could not make a difference to the outcome. No commander with a gross inferiority of force ever prevailed in a battle of attrition. As crisis piled upon crisis in the air war, still the young General of the Fighter Arm felt that he knew what must be done to protect his country. His homeland and his people had to be shielded somehow from the kind of aerial flail he had seen wielded in Africa and Sicily. Everything possible had to be done to diminish their coming ordeal by fire. He returned to Germany with hardened resolve. A bloody summer lay ahead.

TWENTY

Bloody Summer

Galland kept pressing in 1943 for timely and vigorous fighter action against the American daylight bombing menace. Goering and the Luftwaffe High Command, including Jeschonnek, continued to discount the danger. High officers cited the Luftwaffe's daylight bombing failure over Britain and asserted that the Americans would fare no better attacking Germany. Galland, by contrast, saw the center of gravity of the entire air war inexorably moving towards German skies. If this process were not checked, measureless ruin lay ahead for Germany.

Galland's untiring theme in 1943 was strong and rapid reinforcement of the Western Front fighter forces. Only by this means could unacceptable losses be inflicted on the Americans at the outset of their strategic offensive. Aborting the U.S. effort was preferable to tackling it when fully developed. Such a Frankenstein should be strangled at birth.

Galland's analysis appears strikingly prescient from the perspective of more than five decades, especially considering that the travails of his American foes in the spring of 1943 were unknown to him. Nobody in the USAAF then knew with certainty the practical methods of operating strategic bombers in daylight successfully. War games and doctrine were one thing. Real war was something else. Massive and immediate fighter opposition by the Luftwaffe could well have decided the issue against daylight bombing.

Pressure remained strong at the highest Allied political and command levels against the strategic daylight bombing program. Skepticism and resistance continued despite the temporary agreements reached at Casablanca in January of 1943. Breaking-in was therefore not confined to bomber crews gaining combat experience, but extended to the highest levels of leadership. At stake was a doctrinal principle dear to the hearts of American high commanders: B-17s and B-24s could penetrate German skies in daylight unescorted.

Study of correspondence and official reports of this period, containing the contemporary thinking of such famous generals as Eaker, Spaatz, Arnold, Stratemeyer, Anderson, and Hunter, conveys dramatically the numerous imponderables that haunted the American command. Chief among these unknowns, and the factor involving the greatest apprehension, was the potential power of Luftwaffe fighters to make daylight bombing too expensive. Galland was thus right at the heart of the problem with his recommendations for urgent Western Front fighter reinforcement.

Had the early operations of USAAF heavies encountered opposition from four or five Geschwader of Galland's fighters, instead of half that number, there can be little doubt that their losses would have been severe. This was the program being urged on his superiors by Galland. Given the circumstances and the psychological climate, a fair supposition is that the Allied air offensive would have become exclusively a night operation. Fortunately for the Allies, Galland's recommendations were not followed. Hundreds of German fighters were instead hurled into the consuming maw of the Mediterranean war, where overwhelming Allied air power was already decisive. Only after the Hamburg fire raids in late July did Goering and the High Command recognize fully the aerial threat from the west.

American air leaders clung strongly to the hope that their heavy bombers could fly missions into Germany minus escort, and with bearable losses. These hopes still were held as late as May of 1943. No official requirement or specifications for a long range escort fighter had yet been developed by the USAAF. The confrontation between Luftwaffe fighters and U.S. heavy bombers on their first unescorted strikes into Germany became known in the 8th USAAF as The Bloody Summer.

The shape of things to come was emergent in the first week of May. On 4 May 1943, a force of 65 American heavies attacked Antwerp in Belgium, with Ford and General Motors plants as their targets. P-47 Thunderbolt fighters, minus belly tanks, could accompany the bombers for only 175 miles. Aided by a diversionary USAAF thrust at the French coast, which

THUNDERBOLTS OVER EUROPE
American fighters began to appear over Europe in 1944 in very large numbers, with plenty of pilots and an abundance of fuel, something lacking now in the Luftwaffe. This one was flown by Major Eugene Roberts of the 76th Fighter Group, 8th Air Force. His logo was "Spokane Chief."

THE LOCKHEED P-38 "LIGHTNING"
The Me 109 and Fw 190 pilots found the P-38 "easy pickins" until Lockheed came up with the hydraulic-assist ailerons which made its roll rate equal the German fighters.

drew more than 100 German fighters onto itself, the Antwerp mission was a success. Fighter escort and diversionary tactics resulted in a mission without a single aircraft missing. The Americans were elated.

Three days later the battle pendulum swung to the Luftwaffe. German fighters shot down 7 of a force of 31 U.S. heavies raiding St. Nazaire. Unescorted Fortresses and Liberators began more frequent sallies into Germany itself. Raids on Kiel by 126 heavies on 14 May and by 102 heavies on 14 May saw the USAAF lose a total of only 14 bombers in both operations. Yet when the Americans returned to Kiel on 13 June with an even heavier force of 182 bombers, the Luftwaffe clawed down 26 American aircraft – a loss rate that could not be consistently borne.

On 18 May 1943, the Allied Combined Bomber Offensive plan for round-the-clock bombing of Germany was approved by the Combined Chiefs of Staff. Eaker's 8th USAAF was now formally authorized to proceed with the strategic offensive against key targets. Galland may well have gained some grim satisfaction from the projected program had he been able to study its detail. Listed as the top priority objective: destruction of the Luftwaffe Fighter Arm.

On 29 May 1943 the Americans put their first YB-40s into battle, in an interim effort to solve the escort problem. Heavily armored B-17s with increased firepower, loaded with additional ammunition instead of bombs, the YB-40s were an operational failure. Too heavy and too slow to keep up with a B-17 formation, their local increase in firepower did not compensate for their drawbacks. B-17s in formation did better without them. At about the time of the YB-40 experiments, some of the intercepting Fw 190 fighters began mounting 30mm cannons. Their attacks were devastating.

By mid-June the Allies were convinced that the Luftwaffe Fighter Arm had to be conquered, or the strategic bombing program would not succeed. Since most major strategic targets lay beyond the reach of fighter escort, even with belly tanks, past mistakes and oversights caught up with the American High Command. A long range escort fighter became absolutely essential. A technical miracle was needed.

General "Hap" Arnold had initiated an all-out program by 28 June 1943 to produce escort fighters for all U.S. bombers operating from England over Germany, and later from Italy. Industry was to "start from scratch" if need be. Arnold cared not how the job was done, as long as he got the aircraft. President Roosevelt backed him. The evidence is historically clear that the Luftwaffe fighter defense forced a massive technical development program on the USAAF. This requirement had not been foreseen, and this was understandable. Most aeronautical engineers regarded such a long-range fighter as beyond existing technical capabilities. Goering had reported in this vein to Hitler. The superb P-51 Mustang resulted from this crash development program.

Germany was still technologically ahead of the USA in mid-1943. Amid the intensifying battles with the American heavy bombers, Galland got a clear look at what the Luftwaffe Fighter Arm's future might hold. On 22 May 1943, he was invited to fly a prototype of Willy Messerschmitt's Me 262 twin-jet fighter. This was an unforgettable moment for the General of the Fighter Arm, militarily, technically, and emotionally.

Galland had advocated jet fighter development from the time he was first apprised of this new propulsion method in December of 1941. A jet-propelled "speed bomber" was discussed at the first procurement and supply conference he had attended, at the invitation of Erhard Milch, early in 1942. The young leader immediately recommended that fighter aircraft should be included in jet development. Emphasizing the vast resources of the Americans, he pointed out the existing urgent need for a superior fighter to offset expected Allied progress in both performance and numbers.

Messerschmitt agreed with these views. He sought permission to build some jet fighters as well as speed bombers. Galland henceforth hung on to his vision of operational jet fighters like a bulldog. He was willing to risk his career for the sake of getting his pilots a superior weapon. Hard-driving Karl-Otto Saur, Albert Speer's deputy, would later call Galland "the father of the Me 262." There may well never have been an Me 262 jet fighter in combat had it not been for Galland's relentless determination.

At Lechfeld on 22 May 1943, Galland lowered himself into the unfamiliar cockpit of the sleek, propellerless aircraft. He watched with intense interest as the ground crew started one turbine. When they tried the other turbine, it burst into flames, a typical reaction with the immature Jumo 004 jet engine. Like any good combat pilot, Galland was out of the aircraft instantly, and heading for the second prototype. This machine was being held in readiness against technical failure in the first aircraft.

Taking off in the prototype Me 262 was a hair-raising experience. With no tricycle landing gear, Galland found himself tilted back at a fairly alarming angle, almost like a man awaiting a shave in a barber's chair. He had no forward vision. Whizzing down the 150-foot wide Lechfeld runway, he kept the strange aircraft on the concrete with feather-touches on the brakes, all the while turning his head from side to side. As he came up to 80 mph, the tail of the jet had not lifted. How much more runway was left? Touching the brakes with hardly enough pressure to break an egg, he brought the tail up. Forty years later he would tell lecture audiences in America, "I think it is a good thing that we don't have to do this with our commercial airliners today."

Once the tail came up, the speed of the jet rose rapidly. At 120 mph the former Gelsenkirchen Soaring Club pilot was not only airborne, but entering a new epoch. Thrust from the jet engines gave the sensation of being pushed, with a smoothness and quiet that were incredible after the racket, vibration, and torque of a piston-engined fighter. The Me 262 whistled through the air. "It felt as though angels were pushing" was how he later described the sensation of his first jet flight.

Since the flight was not a joyride but an evaluation of a prototype by the General of the Fighters, Galland probed the Me 262's flying characteristics with his veteran's skill. With a level-flight speed of 520 mph, the aircraft handled smoothly and the controls were well-harmonized. Professor Messerschmitt had also come a long way since sailplane days on the Wasserkuppe. His design skills had been carried into a new era. The Me 262 was sensational.

22 MAY 1943
Adolf Galland taxis out for his first flight in the Me 262 jet. Upon landing he gushed with enthusiasm: "It was as if an angel was pushing me!"

GALLAND WITH HIS TROPHY
Right: In 1943 at Schorfheide, Dolfo shot this huge Wisant. In the USA the Wisant is called a Buffalo!

DECORATIONS BY HITLER - 12 SEPTEMBER 1943
Below: Major Prince Sayn zu Wittgenstein (night fighter with 84 victories), Major Hartmann Grasser (131 day), Capt. Walter Nowotny (258 day), and Major Günther Rall (275 victories) stood before Hitler on 12 September 1943. They were somewhat amused by a comment from Hitler's Luftwaffe aide.

During this test flight with the Me 262 V4, the Me 264 *Amerika-Bomber* ultra-long range prototype happened to pass over Lechfeld. Mentally substituting a B-17 for the friendly four-engined bomber, Galland made a mock attack. The speed and flying qualities of the Me 262, combined with the heavy armament that it had the power to carry, clearly would make it a formidable opponent for four-engined bomber and piston-powered fighter alike. Knowing how the Fighter Arm was having its back pressed to the wall, Galland rejoiced at the new tactical possibilities opened by the jet. Here in his hands was the sorely-needed technical quantum jump.

When the sounds of the turbines died away back on the apron at Lechfeld, Galland hoisted himself out of the Me 262 in a state of high excitement. Enthusiasm largely purged out of him by the Fighter Arm's many reverses and his own battles with Goering, had returned with a rush. The Me 262 could give back air superiority to his pilots, if it were mass produced without delay.

Three days later, Galland reported on the Me 262 to Field Marshal Milch, Head of development and procurement:

> "1. This model is a tremendous stroke of luck for us; it puts us way out in front, provided the enemy continues to use piston engines.

2. As far as I could tell, the fuselage appears to be entirely satisfactory.
3. The engines are everything that has been claimed for them, except for their performance during take-off and landing.
4. The aircraft opens up entirely new possibilities as far as tactics are concerned. "

Galland further recommended that production of the Me 209, a projected successor to the Me 109, be dropped. Professor Messerschmitt was nevertheless determined to make his Me 209 a success, despite predicted inferior performance to Allied fighters, and since he had not yet been ordered to give the Me 262 priority. The jet had long languished in the background. Galland recommended limiting single-engined fighter production to the Fw 190D and turning the productive capacity thereby released to mass production of the Me 262. Galland also insisted on some important design changes, including a tricycle landing-gear for the Me 262.

A proposal was developed to reduce drastically the time needed to get the Me 262 into mass production. 100 Me 262s would be put into series production immediately. These aircraft would be put through both tactical and technical tests simultaneously. This unorthodox approach would allow test results to be incorporated into the aircraft as Engineering Change Proposals, before mass production. Goering and Milch both approved, carried along by Galland's enthusiasm, and prodded as well by the American daylight offensive.

Galland's enthusiasm increased. Suddenly all significant persons were for once in accord. Goering had only to get Hitler's approval, and the two sleek silver arrows at Lechfeld would soon be joined by 100 more. Hitler crushed this bold idea immediately.

GALLAND FLEW THE ME 262 AT LECHFELD
On 22 May 1943, General of the Fighters Galland made his first flight in the jet. At left is Capt. Wolfgang Späte and on the right is Prof. Messerschmitt. Späte passed away in May 1997.

Claiming numerous disappointments at the hands of the Luftwaffe, Hitler cited the still unavailable He 177 four-engined bomber as an example of Goering's unfulfilled promises. Due to the He 177 and other Luftwaffe derelictions, Hitler was adamant that the Me 262 was not going to be rushed. Calling a conference with Messerschmitt and the responsible officials who had assembled the all-out Me 262 proposal, Hitler overruled everyone. Talking them all down, Hitler climaxed the conference with an order expressly forbidding mass production. Only tests with a few prototypes were permitted.

Galland was not invited to this conference. The only Luftwaffe officer present was Goering. Hitler's mistrust of the Reich Marshal was now well-known to all who moved in high

THE MESSERSCHMITT ME 262 JET
Propelled by two Jumo 004 turbo-jet engines the Me 262 was about 100mph faster than any of the Allied propeller driven fighters. They were vulnerable only during landing and takeoff phases of flight. Fuel shortages kept most of them on the ground.

circles. All this transpired just as the Americans were driven by events and experience to develop their long range escort fighter. They had made their mistakes and errors just like the Germans. The Americans recognized their mistakes in timely fashion and took action. What a contrast appears between the reactions to crisis by the German and American leaderships. Hitler's exaggerated caution again wasted six crucial months in the final development of the Me 262. During those same months, the P-51 learned to fly all the way into German skies. The Me 262 was not aloft to deny air superiority to the Anglo-American fighter. This was a bitter cup for Galland and the Fighter Arm to drain.

Milch agreed personally with Galland's urgent desire to mass produce the Me 262 as rapidly as possible. Milch's position unfortunately was deteriorating. He was often another Goering scapegoat. Milch could not afford a major rift with the Fuehrer. He therefore followed Hitler's orders for limited Me 262 development. Milch's 17 August 1943 announcement of 4,000 fighters per month as the new production target accordingly specified only existing, piston-powered types.

Galland demanded that 1,000 of these fighters be Me 262s. Milch turned him down, emphasizing that other developments could not be halted or postponed for the sake of the Me 262. Milch also said that he was obeying Hitler's orders for caution on the Me 262 as a soldier should obey. Galland could not influence Milch's stance, but hoped that the *Generalluftzeugmeister* might throw his weight behind the Me 262 later on.

The young general felt the wonder weapon slipping from his grasp, even as airborne terror and torment of the civil population increased. Many weeks had passed since his first jet flight, and the project was virtually paralyzed. Galland found himself thinking that refusal to force through the Me 262 bordered on criminal negligence by Germany's leaders.

Galland's forecast of daylight bombing strikes against Ruhr industry came true on 22 June 1943. 182 USAAF heavies ran the Luftwaffe fighter gauntlet to bomb chemical and synthetic rubber plants at Hüls. By early July, the Americans were able to launch over 200 four-engined bombers in daylight operations, despite significant losses to German fighter action.

Galland foresaw that shortly 300, 500, and 700 heavies would be launched on daylight strikes against Germany. He pressed for strong and centralized fighter defense, for concentration as opposed to the dispersal of fighter units ordered by Goering and the Operations Staff. Centralized defense meant maximized attacking power for the Fighter Arm, with superior ground control and improved logistics. Goering clung to the politically desirable idea of stopping bombers before they reached German territory. Such peripheral defense could not be other than weak, since available fighters were geographically dispersed.

The first three weeks of July 1943 were marked by only a few daylight strikes by the USAAF into northwestern Germany. This lull portended a storm, the fiercest in military history up to that time. On the night of 24/25 July 1943, Air Marshal Arthur Harris of Bomber Command launched Operation "Gomorrah" against Hamburg. Four tremendous RAF blows were struck at night, ending on 4 August 1943, which destroyed half the city and killed more than 50,000 civilians. Over 9,000 tons of bombs were dropped. USAAF heavies provided daylight counterpoint with raids on 25 and 26 July as part of the operation.

OBSERVERS AT LECHFELD
On the day Adolf Galland, General der Jagdfliegers, made his first flight in the Me 262, a crowd of engineers, scientists, aides, adjutants and executive officers were on hand.

On the night of 24/25 July, 728 RAF bombers reached Hamburg, after blinding both ground and airborne German radar by dropping "chaff" at intervals during their approach. "Chaff" was the British counterpart of German *Düppel*, strips of tinfoil cut to the wavelengths of enemy radar. These foil strips returned radar echoes out of all proportion to their physical size. Fighter control data were totally corrupted. Since the same data were used by the German flak, Hamburg's hundreds of anti-aircraft guns lost their electronic guidance.

As a consequence, the first raid on Hamburg resulted in heavy destruction and minimal losses for the RAF. The second raid two nights later ignited a firestorm in the city that was to eclipse every prior entry in the index of man's inhumanity to man. Scores of adjacent fires united into a mighty, roaring holocaust that became self-sustaining. Rising superheated air triggered volcanic updrafts, and as surrounding ground-level air rushed into the void, the flames were stoked to blowtorch intensity – and beyond.

Thousands of human beings were instantaneously incinerated in the firestorm, many of them sucked bodily into the fire's maw. Everything combustible in the firestorm area was ashed, and everything non-combustible melted. Entire blocks of houses and apartments were swallowed into the inferno, which seemed to take on a hideous life of its own. Temperatures far exceeding a thousand degrees Fahrenheit literally snuffed out the living. Hundreds of unfortunates who had sought sanctuary in Hamburg's underground air raid shelters were

OBERST JOSEF "PIPS" PRILLER
Kommodore of JG 26 from 11 January 1943 until 27 January 1945, he then became inspektor of the Fighters-West. He had 101 victories and survived the war. His family owned the Riegele Brewery in Augsburg and "Pips" gave jobs to many of the JG 26 troops after the war. He passed away 20 May 1961.

KOMMODORE OF JG 54 "GRÜNHERZ"
Colonel Hannes Trautloft scored 4 victories in Spain, added 45 in Russia and ended the war with a total of 57. Trautloft, about 6'3" tall fit very snugly in the cockpit of the Me 109. A trusted confidant of Galland, he survived the war, and passed away 11 January 1995.

OBERSTLEUTNANT HANS-JOACHIM JABS
A dive-bomber pilot against England early in the war, Jabs transferred to night fighters in 1942. Kommodore of NJG 1 until the end of the war. He scored 22 day and 28 night victories. A good friend of Galland's.

roasted to ash in these chambers. No such devastation, misery, and disaster had ever been inflicted on a city in the history of the world.

Hamburg's soul-searing horror spread to every corner of Germany, as refugees streamed out of the shambles. Books have already been written detailing this nightmare catastrophe, and there is no place for that here. Suffice it to say that Hamburg was a national tragedy for Germany, but it had as an immediate consequence a galvanizing, unifying effect on the entire Luftwaffe.

The fires of Hamburg melted the differences large and small between Luftwaffe leaders high and low. Borne in upon all of them, from Goering downward, was the *unthinkable yet undeniable probability of more such blows*. Action had to be taken, lest every large city in Germany be similarly laid in smoldering ruins.

Aside from surrender, only one rational response was possible: an aggressive defense of the Reich by a much more powerful Fighter Arm. Events had placed Galland at center stage in the Luftwaffe hierarchy. Dreams of vengeance raids on Britain, hopes for super-weapons, ambitions for a massive Bomber Arm, all seemed to evaporate in the heat of the Hamburg holocaust. Goering called a conference of Luftwaffe leaders in his office at Hitler's HQ at Rastenburg.

Almost the entire Luftwaffe pantheon was assembled. A chastened Jeschonnek was present with his many staff officers, convinced finally of the four-engined bombing threat from the west. Erhard Milch had been summoned. He and Galland had agreed all along for a strong homeland fighter defense. Colonel Dietrich Peltz, General of the Bomber Arm and a Goering favorite, sat with others of the Reich Marshal's "brain trust," all of them now serious and silent. Generals Weise, von Axthelm, Kammhuber, and Martini, and numerous other important commanders attended this post-Hamburg conference.

Turning the Luftwaffe to the defense of the German homeland became the unanimous spirit of the conference. Goering summarized by stressing that there must never be another Hamburg in the life of the German people. A defensive role for the Luftwaffe was now essential to maintain the national war potential. Goering for once had united the entire Luftwaffe hierarchy, aided by the Hamburg holocaust. Galland's hopes soared as Goering strode buoyantly away to the nearby *Führerbunker* for Hitler's approval of the new priorities. Top priority was regaining air superiority over the Reich.

When Goering returned from the Fuehrer, he walked wordlessly right through the room, staring straight ahead like a zombie. Entering an adjacent room, Goering closed the door, symbolizing what had happened. Hitler had closed the door on any new priorities.

Summoned to Goering soon afterwards, Galland and Peltz found the Reich Marshal sobbing uncontrollably. Head down on his arms on the desk top, Goering was an embarrassing and pitiful figure. Hitler had reacted with rage to his proposal to switch the Luftwaffe to a defensive role. The Fuehrer would allow no defense except attack. British terror would be met by Luftwaffe terror. A new bombing force was to be assembled and sent against England in retaliation – a deterrent to future Hamburgs. Emerging from his tears, Goering appointed Peltz "Assault Leader Against England" and terminated the interview.

Galland's brain reeled. His personal options swam through his head amid the bizarre unreality of it all. Should he quit? He told himself he ought to get out. Nothing useful could be accomplished without air superiority. That was the only sane strategy. The Fighter Arm had become the key to survival. He decided to keep his job, believing that Hitler could not make such a decision irrevocably. His duty in the meantime was to give his all to the defense of Germany.

A timely counter-blow against the night bombing was struck by Major Hajo Herrmann, who had advocated for some time the use of single-engined fighters at night in flak-free zones over German cities. These aircraft could be guided to their targets visually, since RAF bombers could be held in searchlight crossbeams for long periods. Herrmann's "Wild Boar" night fighter tactics bridged a serious gap in Germany's night defenses, until German radar experts could counter Allied use of "chaff." Favorable weather conditions were necessary for the Wild Boar, but it was summer and many nights were clear enough for Herrmann's operations.

Bomber expert Colonel Viktor von Lossberg also convinced the High Command at this time that night fighters could infiltrate British bomber streams both coming and going, and inflict serious losses. Like the Wild Boar tactics over lighted cities, von Lossberg's infiltration attacks would depend upon direct visual sightings by night fighter crews. Wild Boar and infiltration tactics permitted partial recovery of the night defenses, pending development of radar countermeasures.

General Kammhuber's night fighter empire was centered on the so-called "Himmelbett" tactic, in which a night fighter was directed by an individual radar controller in a given area. British bomber stream tactics and "chaff" had overrun Kammhuber's facilities. The night fighter boss nevertheless disagreed with both the Wild Boar and the infiltration tactics. Galland was grateful that he had not yet been charged with responsibility for the night fighters. He and Kammhuber did not get along.

German civilians by the 1943 summer had become resigned to night bombing attacks. They showed resilience similar to the Londoners of 1940. The sight of American bombers overhead in daylight exceeded civilian tolerance. This was an important morale factor added to the strategic impact of daylight pinpoint bombing.

Combating the USAAF in daylight remained Galland's major concern. The Americans kept pressing unescorted attacks into Germany. Goering's constant importunings to have German fighter pilots fly three missions a day bore fruit on 17 August 1943. A two-pronged assault was made by 315 Fortresses deep into the Reich. Schweinfurt's ball-bearing factories and the Messerschmitt factories at Regensburg were the targets. Schweinfurt was about to enter the war's history as the scene of one of its most bloody and significant battles.

NIGHT FIGHTER ACES AT EASE
On 26 July 1943, the two leaders of Germanys night fighters stood parade at Spieth, Germany. Major Werner Streib had 65 night and 1 day victory, survived the war and retired as a Lt. General. Major Helmut Lent had 102 night and 8 day victories, was awarded the Brillants. Died 7 October 1944 after a crash landing on the 5th.

The Messerschmitt complex was heavily hit. More than 400 aircraft workers perished. Aerial photographs showed more than 80 hits on the Schweinfurt targets, but the Fighter Arm subjected the U.S. bombers to heavy punishment. 60 American bombers went down, with the loss of most of the 600 men in their crews. Over 100 other bombers suffered extensive battle damage and crew casualties. 17 Fortresses that made it back to England were damaged to the point of salvage.

Galland's reaction to Schweinfurt had both personal and professional aspects. Downing 60 heavies in one day proved that strong, persistent attacks by large fighter forces could inflict unbearable losses on the Americans. The numerical increase in fighters had been achieved at Schweinfurt by multiple missions, with fighter pilots operating to the limits of their

DIETRICH PELTZ -
GENERAL OF THE BOMBERS
Peltz played a very big role in Galland's life, particularly at the time the Me 262 jets were being phased into the Luftwaffe inventory.

endurance. Equivalent steady strength would require the provision of many more aircraft and pilots.

Across the Channel the Americans were licking their wounds. General Eaker was already hard pressed for trained crews. Schweinfurt put a large crimp in the expansion of 8th USAAF Bomber Command. The record of these times in Eaker's correspondence and elsewhere testifies to the adverse effect of Schweinfurt on American commanders. 60 heavies down in one day certainly impressed the surviving American crews. Galland's early advocacy of such heavy fighter attacks on the Americans stands historically vindicated.

On a personal basis, Schweinfurt I on 17 August 1943 was to inject into Galland's life one of the worst personal tragedies he would ever suffer. His brother Wutz led II/JG 26 against the bombers on their way back from Schweinfurt. Having downed a B-17, Wutz was shot down by P-47s near St. Trond. The death of young Paul had been a bitter blow, but to lose Wutz as well was a tremendous hammer blow in the heart. Smiling, charming, happy Wutz would grace this world no more. Thunder in the air drowned out the agony in Adolf Galland's heart. He had to go on.

After the Regensburg strike, the 4th Bombardment Wing did not return to England, but flew on in diminished strength to North Africa. This was another baleful development of the bloody summer – shuttle bombing. On 13 August 1943, four days prior to Schweinfurt I, the 9th USAAF in the Mediterranean sent 61 Liberators against the Messerschmitt factory at Wiener-Neustadt, attacking the Reich from the southeast. Surviving bombers from the Regensburg strike later flew from Italy back to their British bases, attacking U-boat facilities at Bordeaux en route. The Fighter Arm had now to contend with another extension of home defense.

Schweinfurt became the *bête noir* of the 8th USAAF. Even after the heavy crew and aircraft losses of the bloody summer, which sorely taxed Eaker's resources, the idea of unescorted deep penetrations into Germany did not die. On into the fall, the Americans clung to an idea whose time had gone. After further heavy losses in the first half of October, in attacking Bremen, Marienburg, Danzig, and Munster, Schweinfurt II taught the Americans their final bloody lesson.

On 14 October 1943, 229 heavies with nearly 200 escort fighters winged out of England for Schweinfurt. The fighters took the big bombers 240 miles and then turned back to the fuel pump. Shadowing the formation, the Luftwaffe had waited for this moment.

Before the target was reached, the Luftwaffe was driving home fighter attacks, initially in javelin formation, from both front and rear. Gaggles of 7 to 15 German fighters hacked away at the heavy bombers with rockets, cannons, and machine guns. Plunging down from near-vertical angles, other German fighters sought to eliminate the forward turrets of the Fortresses.

The Americans pressed on through the fighters and flak to their targets at Schweinfurt, before heading back through more fiery harassment on the return route. As with Schweinfurt I, this raid saw 60 Fortresses downed, with the loss of 600 trained airmen. In American war lore, the day would live forever as Black Thursday.

Black was appropriate, for it was also the death of unescorted daylight bombing over Germany. Galland's fighters had won that particular round, but on the Allied side there were positive effects. More energy than ever went into increasing the range of P-47 and P-38 fighters. Even more vigor was put behind the P-51 project. By December of 1943, P-51s were flying all the way to German targets with the American heavies.

From May of 1943 when he first flew the Me 262 jet, until Schweinfurt II in October, Galland had seen Germany's aerial fortunes drastically decline. The Me 262 had meanwhile languished – the proper technical counter to daylight bombing. Even while living through these events, the whole scenario had seemed to Galland like a nightmare from which he could not awaken. Forty years later, when all the involved and hidden aspects of Me 262 development could be examined in the cool of his evening, it would still seem no less of a nightmare. The real world had been more incredible than any dream.

TWENTY-ONE

Steps and Measures

While the Me 262 was by far the most promising fighter under development, there were other machines in the official program as improvements on the Me 109 and Fw 190. These aircraft should have approached production about the time that the USAAF strategic bombing offensive gained momentum. A prime objective of the USAAF was to stop all German fighter production. Galland had these new fighters dangled in front of him for his hard-pressed pilots. Always they stayed just out of reach.

Dornier's Do 335 Arrow (*Pfeil*) was scheduled for production in the 1943 autumn. Galland intended to re-equip the badly outclassed heavy fighter units with this promising, 413 mph aircraft. Equipped with twin engines in "push-pull," one driving a tractor propeller in the nose and the other a pusher propeller in the tail, the Do 335 ran into delays. Complex technical problems arose from mutual interference between the propellers. All hope of prompt deliveries soon faded.

Similarly planned for assignment to the heavy fighter units was Professor Kurt Tank's twin-engined Focke-Wulf Ta 154 *Moskito*, a fast, heavily-armed response to the RAF Mosquito. Like the Mosquito, Tank's machine made extensive use of wood construction. Based on a German Air Ministry specification issued in September of 1942, the prototype was flying by July of 1943, but without likelihood of production before mid-1944. 30mm MK 103 cannons were planned as armament, weapons with long range and flat trajectory, for downing American heavies from greater distances.

Development problems with engines and aircraft were endless. Deprived of performance improvements that could underpin new tactics, Galland had to soldier on with existing aircraft. The technical race with the Allies was lost before his eyes. The Me 262 jet therefore became a tantalizing vision of re-asserted Luftwaffe air superiority. Failures, deficiencies, intrigue, and boondoggles abounded in the German aircraft industry. All this was made worse by round-the-clock bombing.

Professor Tank's Ta-152, the long-nosed variant of the Fw 190, was another eagerly awaited fighter subject to frequent postponement. Professor Messerschmitt kept struggling to make his Me 209 into a worthwhile successor to the Me 109. He was unsuccessful, despite the commitment of huge resources. Messerschmitt's twin-engined Me 210 and Me 410 were descendants of the Me 110 heavy fighter concept. They were not successful combat aircraft. In daylight attacks against U.S. bomber formations, they had to be provided with a single-engined fighter escort.

Numerous variants of the main fighter types in service created problems operationally that arrived frequently in Galland's office. During one period, the Me 109 was in squadron service with four variants and the Fw 190 with five. Significant performance differences were thereby injected into each Geschwader nominally operating the same type of fighter. Combat regulations issued by Galland required that the fighters stay together. Performance gains in the superior fighter variants were thus virtually nullified, speed being held down to that of the poorest performing aircraft. Logistical requirements increased with each fighter variant that entered operations.

When new fighter types failed to get into production, Galland began expediting armament improvements for increasing combat performance. Downing bombers was the main task. Armament experts and innovators in the fighter units concentrated on improving firing power. Centrally-mounted, heavy caliber weapons were favored. Wing-mounted heavy weapons degraded maneuverability. As U.S. fighters began penetrating deeper into Germany, maneuverability was vital in coping with the American escort. Fuseless incendiary ammunition was copied by the Germans from captured American .50 caliber shells. Installation of the MG 151 20mm cannon on the Me 109 and. Fw 190, as standard armament from 1942 onward, had proved itself a sound step. The MG 151 was dependable, with higher muzzle velocity and rate of fire than the Oerlikon MG-FF 20mm cannon it replaced.

Neglect of airfield development in Germany in 1940-42 had serious consequences in 1943 as daylight bombing of the homeland intensified. Two operational missions a day, and pursuit of U.S. heavies, were scattering fighters far and wide. They were often landing far from their home base, and frequently came down on remote airstrips and improvised fields.

Fighters landing on isolated and unequipped airfields were completely out of the fight. When landing on the last of their fuel, such fighters were immobilized, unable to take off to the nearest fueling point. Galland tackled this problem with Air Fleet Reich and Fighter Corps I.

Concentrating on western Germany, Holland, Belgium, and northern France, the critical areas for fighters pursuing homebound U.S. heavies, Galland organized mini-bases. Facilities for rearming and refueling were established, along with an aerial situation room, refreshments, medical, and meteorological facilities. A telephone to the nearest Fighter Division HQ completed the arrangements. Galland issued regulations for the use of these mini-bases. Slowly the chaos and uncertainty that had surrounded these semi-emergency landings were overcome.

Pilots from different units landing on the same field were placed under the command of the senior pilot present. This officer or NCO was required to lead his conglomerate formation back into the air against the bombers. Once aloft, their instructions were to tune in the Reich Fighter Frequency (*Reichsjägerwelle*), which broadcast a running commentary on aerial action over Germany.

OBERST HAJO HERRMANN
Progenitor of the "Wild Boar" JG 300 idea using single-engine fighters as night fighters. British bombers had dropped "chaff" during the 1943 raids against Hamburg, thereby blinding the radar-equipped night fighters. Hermann's idea was to illuminate the RAF bombers with search lights and the Wild Boars would attack the bombers visually.

The conglomerate formation would direct itself back into combat with the invaders by following the reported position, course, speed, and altitude of enemy formations. Second missions like this were successful as long as the pick-up formations did not encounter strong American fighter opposition. In the ensuing battles, the unfamiliarity of the German pilots with their pick-up leaders and wingmen was a handicap against the ordered opposition of the Americans. Cohesion and operating efficiency in a fighter unit stem from joint experience, mutual knowledge, and mutual confidence of the pilots.

As soon as the strength and range of the U.S. fighter escort increased, high losses resulted from second missions by conglomerate units. Galland knew why. He had personally built up efficiency as a leader from squadron to Geschwader level.

A LITTLE DYNAMO
Left: Hans "Assi" Hahn scored 108 victories before he was forced to land in Russian territory on 21 Feb. 1943. The Soviets found him a tough nut to crack and held him prisoner until 1950. He died 18 December 1982. He was one of Galland's closest friends right up to the date he passed away.

He was not surprised when the Fighter Divisions began rebelling against High Command insistence on second missions in all circumstances. The Fighter Divisions ordered that second missions were only to be mounted when a worthwhile force of at least 20 fighters could be assembled.

Tactical development in 1943 required a lively mobility of mind, as well as experience, for the proper deployment of such tactics. Although forbidden to fly on operations, Galland had the trust and confidence of every significant combat leader in the Fighter Arm. They became his hands, feet, and eyes in the air, as various stratagems were devised and tested. They all knew as well that their boss was making occasional clandestine missions to test his own regulations for attacking heavy bomber formations. Galland maintained touch with battle conditions by downing 3 Fortresses in 1943.

Shadowing aircraft were recommended by the young General for assignment to each incoming U.S. raid. The High Command approved. Twin-engined fighters with good fuel endurance were used. Reporting on the status of each bomber box, the shadowing aircraft detailed bombers shot down or separated from the box. Running commentaries were provided by these *Fühlungshalter* on the effects of German fighter attacks, actions of the U.S. fighter escorts, and also on the state of the weather. Shadowing aircraft were effective until larger U.S. fighter formations started sweeps far ahead of and around the bombers. Heavy losses reduced the shadowing aircraft to a weather observation role by mid-1944.

This typified the tactical ebb-and-flow of the air war. A stratagem that worked well in the spring could be useless by mid-summer. An open mind was essential. Tactical rigidity quickly produced casualties and operational failures. In this spirit, Galland opposed High Command orders that German fighters were to attack bombers only. American fighters were to be ignored, unless the German fighters were themselves jumped by the escort.

German pilots were initially wary of the P-47s. When the Thunderbolts did not attack and clung close to the bombers, German fighters became more aggressive. Galland stated that attacks exclusively on the bombers would inevitably draw the P-47s out of their passive defense of the heavies. He emphasized that once the Thunderbolts broke out of their defensive posture, they would develop a highly aggressive defense. As

IN THE FROZEN NORTH
JG 5 held forth in northern Norway and Finland, with plenty of targets as the Russians tried to keep Murmansk open. This is OFW Rudolf Müller's Me 109 with 66 victory flashes on the rudder. After he scored his 94th victory he force-landed on a frozen lake and disappeared in Russian captivity.

the high priest of aggressive defense himself, Galland implored the High Command not to provoke this change in American escort tactics. The High Command was not persuaded. The "bombers only" order stood.

As Galland had forecast, the American fighter pilots soon tumbled to the significance of their situation when they found themselves ignored by the attackers. They began breaking out of their defensive posture and discarding their defensive frame of mind – the latter having been imposed on them by their orders. Protection of the bombers was paramount. In the USAAF in 1943, as in the Luftwaffe in 1940, bomber crews were reassured to see a "little friend" off their wingtip.

American fighters began tearing into the attacking Germans, who were hell-bent for the bombers in obedience to *their* orders. The Americans began taking the battle initiative away from the Luftwaffe. As Galland's warnings to the High Command had predicted, U.S. fighters were soon departing from close escort to hunt and pursue their foes. These actions frequently took German formations by surprise. Luftwaffe fighters often resorted to bolting when jumped.

Psychological ascendancy rapidly passed to the Americans, fresh and well-trained. To Galland's mortification, German fighters went into the era of "Split-S and Dive Away," as it was called. Friendly terrain was below. Many German pilots began diving for it as though it truly were Mother Earth, warm and safe. American fighters made it the reverse. All American fighters dived faster than German types, especially the Me 109, which was red-lined at about 375 mph in the dive for structural reasons. The Americans overhauled their diving opponents from astern and shot them to pieces.

This psychological malady among some German fighter pilots was called *Jägerschreck*, fear of fighters. Battle-hardened formations like JG 26 and JG 2 were not afflicted. Other units with large complements of young and inexperienced pilots did become infected with this combat malady. In such formations, even some veteran leaders were temporary victims. Until the Fighter Arm snapped out of this embarrassing lapse, Goering had some justification for his vilification of the fighter pilots as cowards.

Jägerschreck was rooted in wrong tactics and showed how dangerous it was to have operational orders issued by officers who had never flown modern fighter combat. A crisis of morale and severe losses resulted. Although the entire train of events was due to ignoring the tactical advice of the General of the Fighter Arm, he was blamed by Goering for the debacle. The Reich Marshal acted as though Galland had issued the orders instead of the Operations Staff.

Galland never relinquished his basic conviction that only an aggressive defense could succeed. He again implored Goering and the High Command to assign part of each Geschwader to attack U.S. fighter escorts. Goering stuck stubbornly to the "bombers only" edict. Most of the battle initiative was thereby handed to the Americans.

Failing in this corrective action, Galland then proposed that JG 26 and JG 2 on the Channel coast attack the fighter escorts as the U.S. bombers passed over their territory. Galland held that such attacks would force the American fighters to drop their belly tanks in order to join combat. They could then not fly into German territory with the bombers, which would then be much more vulnerable to German fighter attacks.

This stratagem was approved by the High Command on a one-time basis. The plan was successful. The USAAF bombers arrived over Germany without most of their fighter escort. Refusing nevertheless to persist with this effective stratagem, the High Command claimed that its steady employment would expose France and the Low Countries to bombing and strafing in the absence of JG 2 and JG 26. The High Command would not allow this. Galland's credulity was strained by this response. The RAF had been attacking these targets steadily since 1941. He had shot down dozens of them himself.

Galland went ahead and issued tactical regulations designed to foster aggressive defense. These regulations conflicted with High Command operational orders for "bombers only" attacks. Other conflicting orders emanated from Fighter Division HQ and Fighter Corps HQ. Combat leaders clearly perceived the high-level policy quarrels reflected in these conflicting orders. High-level disunity disturbed men who were daily dodging lead and tracer aloft. Morale was damaged by the obvious schism between Galland and the High Command. Each Kommodore therefore chose the course that he felt to be most effective. Many ignored all orders from higher up and simply did what they wanted with the Geschwader they commanded.

Galland's tactical expertise was thus largely ignored by the Luftwaffe High Command. Officers without any experience of modern fighter combat had the authority to issue operational orders. Galland would have preferred to demonstrate personally, from a fighter cockpit, the value of his tactical recommendations. Since this was prohibited, he had to live with his frustrations. He felt deeply his responsibility to make tactical knowledge won with blood – paid for with the lives of many pilots – serve other comrades facing the challenges aloft.

He sought a change in arrangements from Goering. He asked specifically for more operational authority over the Fighter Arm. He particularly wanted this authority for dealing with the American heavy bombers.

Goering's gold baton immediately rose, just as though Galland had actuated a mechanism. The baton waved from side to side, denoting negation.

"That is absolutely unnecessary" said Goering emphatically. "If a paper clip falls to the floor anywhere in the Fighter Arm, you know about it immediately. All your excellent advice is taken into account. Therefore, there is *no need* for you to have increased operational authority."

The bizarre and unrealistic command arrangements of the Fighter Arm were thus allowed to continue contributing to its destruction. Goering would never budge on this issue.

LT. COL. HANS PHILIPP
Philipp was shot down and killed by Thunderbolts near Nordhorn on 8 October 1943 after scoring his 206th victory. He was Kommodore of JG 1 at the time of his death. He had been the second pilot to reach the 200 victory mark. His happy smile and demeanor endeared him to everyone who knew him, including Adolf Galland.

MAJOR HEINRICH EHRLER
Another luminary of the frozen north and JG 5, Major Ehrler was Kommodore of "Eismeer." Blamed by Göring for the loss of the battleship Tirpitz, he was saved by Galland who transferred him to jets in JG 7. Died in a mid-air collision 4 April 1945.

13TH RANKING ACE OF THE WORLD
Lt. Walter Schuck scored 198 victories with JG 5 in Finland and Norway and transferred to JG 7 and flew the Me 262 for another 8, making the total 206. Survived the war. His jet was shot down by F/O Eugene W. Andermatt of the USAF 56th FG. on 10 April 1945 although Andermatt received only a "damaged" credit.

Galland knew the Fighter Arm's technical limitations. He therefore declined to try and combat incursions by RAF Mosquito aircraft, which were faster than any German fighter then operating. Goering became incensed by these nuisance-strikes into Germany, by day and by night, especially when Mosquitos arrived over Berlin during one of his fighting speeches. The Reich Marshal became the butt of many jokes and jibes circulating among the German public.

The Germans had been astounded to learn that the wooden Mosquito could carry a larger bomb load than the B-17, carry it faster, and with a crew of only two. The Mosquito could fly at 38,000 feet, but was equally at home roaming Germany at treetop height, harassing Luftwaffe bases and making precision bombing attacks on small, important targets. The Mosquito to Goering was both a technical riddle and a political embarrassment.

Goering was not content with Galland's explanation that the intruders' high speed would prevent interceptions. The wooden Mosquito returned a small radar echo, or none at all if it came in low. This meant insufficient radar warning to scramble German fighters. Fuel shortages precluded standing patrols to await the next Mosquito raid. At high altitude, the Mosquito outpaced existing German fighters.

The angry Goering set up JGr 25 and JGr 50 as special anti-Mosquito units. Two prominent fighter aces, Major Herbert Ihlefeld and Major Hermann Graf, were chosen as commanders of these units, which were based at Neubiberg and Wiesbaden. For five months the two highly decorated leaders struggled with the Mosquito problem. Engine-boosting experiments with their Me 109G-6 fighters and other stratagems ended in failure. Amid pressing demands for fighter aircraft and leaders, JGr 25 and JGr 50 were disbanded without downing a single Mosquito.

Technical difficulties had proved to be exactly as Galland had described. Goering was not satisfied until inordinate manpower, materiel, technical effort, and fuel had been dissipated in the useless project. A more graphic example of the consequences of technical illiteracy in high command would be hard to find.

Galland set up Experimental Unit 25 (*Erprobungskommando 25*) as a special technical tactical force operating directly under his own staff. Experimental and inventive activity flourished in the fighter units as combat pilots devised new and additional weapon mounts, modified gunsights, and fabricated what they wanted within their own units. Experimental Unit 25 with its two combat squadrons winnowed out useful innovations. Initially under Me 110 ace Captain Eduard Tratt, and shortly afterwards under Captain Horst Geyer, Experimental Unit 25 took inventions and innovations into combat, attacking bombers just like other Luftwaffe fighters. Air-to-air bombing, cable bombing, and photocell detonators were just a few of the proposed weapons tested.

Development of wing mountings for the 21-cm Army rocket was successfully carried out and tested in combat by the Kommando. The same large rocket, to be fired backwards and downwards from the Fw 190 fuselage and timed to burst amid the B-17s, was called "Krebs." The Kommando developed and tested this weapon. The R4M rocket finally used in salvoes from the Me 262 was also put through its trials by the Experimental Unit. All results of tests were funneled directly into Galland's office, and thence made available to appropriate Fighter Arm formations.

Galland could not divorce himself from a principle he had helped establish in the Fighter Arm: a fighter leader must be a successful ace pilot, and he must fly with those he leads and orders into combat. Galland therefore continued to sneak off on combat missions, swearing his staff to secrecy when it was necessary for any of them to know his whereabouts. He flew about 10 missions in 1943, taking off with different pilots from Berlin-Staaken. Galland set up a traveling circus (*Wanderzirkus*) of Allied aircraft in flying condition. He remembered how helpful it had been when he had patched up one of the first downed B-17s so that fighter pilots could board and fly in the American bombers, simulating U.S. gunners as Luftwaffe fighters made mock firing passes. That helped morale. The traveling circus expanded this idea.

Commanded by Captain Rosarius, the strange circus of patched up Allied aircraft of all types toured fighter training schools, operational training units, and active fighter bases. German pilots flew in these aircraft. In the bombers, they were placed in different crew stations and got first-hand experience of the aircraft they were trying to down. Rosarius' Traveling Circus broadened their experience and lessened their apprehensions about the enemy.

For years Galland had been aware that gunnery instruction for fighter pilots was inadequate. Hunting parties in France during 1940-41, furthermore, had clearly demonstrated that far too many otherwise good fighter pilots were poor marksmen, and Galland's predecessors had not addressed this problem. Available fuel did not now permit aerial gunnery practice with drogues or mock combat with Robot cameras actuated by gun buttons.

Six instructional firing staffs were organized. These *Schiesslehrstäbe* toured fighter facilities similarly to the Traveling Circus. Weapons experts demonstrated new armament, taught weapons maintenance, and with special sights, aids, and instructional tools hammered home the principles of air-to-air shooting. An improvement in marksmanship resulted.

The human element for the Fighter Arm was a continuing Galland concern. Getting the right kind of men to be pilots and securing them in sufficient numbers was the essence of the problem. Experience had shown a significant temperamental difference between the successful fighter pilot and the ordinary fighter pilot. Those who became aces were tremendously effective. Perhaps 45 percent of all aerial victories were scored by 5 percent of the pilots. Galland reasoned that there must be a way to increase the percentage of successful pilots by preselective analyses of some kind.

He proposed psychological tests in 1943 for all pilot trainees, whether officers or NCOs. Prior to any flight training, these tests would determine a recruit's assignment to bombers, fighters, reconnaissance, or other duties. Flying training for fighter pilots would be specialized from the first flight. Galland backed his proposal with an offer to supply expert instructional personnel. Twelve general flying training schools would be converted to preliminary fighter schools. Three new fighter air war schools would be organized for officers.

Galland's proposal simply died in the Luftwaffe's higher echelons. Worth recording here is that a study of pilot selection was made 34 years later by the U.S. Defense Advanced Research Projects Agency. The American research team, in their 1977 report, concluded that ineffective fighter pilots could be eliminated early by psychological testing and other techniques. Combat effectiveness and ace potential could in some degree be predicted. That was the essence of Galland's proposals to his superiors in the war year 1943.

Fuel shortages seriously curtailed training. As a counter, Galland proposed the transfer of surplus pilots from other branches to the Fighter Arm. He organized a conversion facility at his HQ, where the conversion needs of such pilots could be assessed. Suitable pilots were retrained. Experienced officers were acquired in this way. Even if they were not capable of becoming successful fighter pilots, they could help lead fighter units.

The piloting reactions of these otherwise able officers were, in most cases, not fast enough for the flashing speed of fighter combat. By the end of 1943, Galland was glad to have leaders of any kind for his embattled formations. By the end of 1944, some 12,000 pilots had been through the program. 8,000 were accepted for conversion training as day fighter, night fighter, or ground attack pilots. The program provided pilots and leaders and saved training fuel.

Tardy in taking measures to ensure a supply of formation leaders, Galland found this a particularly awkward problem. His own combat experience led him to expect that leaders would arise through merit and experience, directly from the ranks of active fighter pilots. Losses of experienced formation leaders in 1942-43 were severe, and outran this process of natural selection for replacements.

Galland failed to perceive the problem early enough to prevent its becoming critical. He met the crisis by establishing a formation leaders' course (*Verbandsführer-Lehrgang*) at Koenigsberg-Neumark, in the 1943 autumn. His experience in setting up the first OTUs in JG 26 gave valuable guidance. Three courses were established. One was designed for the future Kommodores and Gruppenkommandeure. A second course was tailored to the aspiring Staffelkapitäne – the squadron commanders. The third course was given to all officers leaving the operational training Gruppen, so that all new officer pilots joining units would have basic training in leading formations. They

KOMMODORES MEETING IN BERLIN
Goring called a meeting of the Wing Commanders. Left center facing camera is Gunther Lützow (5 victories in Spain and 108 in WWII, Hermann Graf (Roman nose; 212) Werner Baumbach (bomber leader), Gordon Gollob (150), Walter Oesau (trimming his fingernails – 8 Spain and 125 WWII), and Adolf Galland (General of the Fighters).

formed a sort of ready-reserve of squadron commanders in each fighter Geschwader.

The shortage of leaders was further countered by increasing the establishment of each Geschwader. Normal strength of 124 aircraft, around which the pre-war fighter Geschwader had been built, was boosted to 160 by adding four aircraft to each squadron. At the end of 1943, a fourth squadron was added to every Gruppe. By November of 1944, Geschwader establishment had risen to 288 aircraft. These increases accommodated the mixed formations of light and heavy fighters set up to combat the American heavies and their escort fighters. Surviving top leaders therefore commanded ever-growing formations – a dilution that was the only way to meet the emergency.

Systematic pilot recruitment for the Fighter Arm was nonexistent, another legacy of Galland's unenterprising predecessors. He sought to organize direct recruitment of air-minded youths as soon as they were of age. The Navy and the Waffen-SS both had such programs. Their expert recruiters haunted the paramilitary Labor Service (*Arbeitsdienst*) camps, which were compulsory for all German boys.

As a famous figure in Germany, Galland was deluged with enthusiastic letters from boys wanting to become fighter pilots. Upon investigating the situation, he was appalled by the divided and self-defeating arrangements that stood between such boys and the Fighter Arm – where their spirit and enthusiasm were sorely needed. The Hitler Flying Youth and the National Socialist Flying Corps (NSFK) were ostensible links between the Luftwaffe and aspiring youths, but they competed with each other. Both of them feuded in turn with the Luftwaffe bureaucracy, The NSFK did not follow up and ensure that their boys got into the Luftwaffe. Petty vanities and squabbles over fiefdoms diminished to a trickle the flow of premium youth to the Fighter Arm.

Luftwaffe recruiting was itself a shambles. All recruiting was lumped under the General for Luftwaffe Personnel Recruitment (*General der Nachwuchs Luftwaffe*). There was no recruiting agency exclusively for aircrew. Camps were organized to provide boys with physical and pre-flight training, in the expectation that this would be an acceptable substitute for Labor Service duty. Hitler killed this idea. The Luftwaffe youth camps faded out. Galland was left with a pilot recruiting problem he could not solve.

After seeing the political mess associated with youthful aspiration to the air, Galland shirked the problem. Goering could have done more to get the best boys for the Fighter Arm, but he stonewalled the issue to avoid Hitler's wrath. The Reich Marshal's extensive wiretapping system kept him abreast of all machinations. He was thereby able to block many stratagems of the SS that aimed at promoting Himmler's status at the expense of his own.

Himmler wanted to breed supermen, with cradle-to-grave saturation in SS dogmas. This came back to Galland by a strange avenue. He strongly disapproved of fighter pilot marriages and made this known throughout the Fighter Arm. He contended that fighter pilots had to be single-minded in their lethal work, with minimum distractions. His opposition to marriage for his fighter pilots was also born of the high probability that widows and fatherless children would be the outcome.

Human concern of this kind never complicated Himmler's views. Goering broached the whole matter to Galland on a hunting trip at Karinhall. Sitting in a horse-drawn landau in the woods, Goering was at his paternal best. Goering the man had appeared from inside the image of the Reich Marshal. He wondered out loud if Galland's anti-marriage policies were not unwise in a broader context.

Goering dwelt with disdain and contempt on Himmler's stud-farm ideas for breeding the new Germans.

"We must not surrender the German youth of tomorrow to the likes of Himmler" said Goering. "We have to perpetuate our own kind in traditional ways."

The astonished Galland did think about Goering's counsel. He saw its merits. He nevertheless maintained his opposition to fighter pilot marriages as the best policy for both the Fighter Arm and the individual pilots. While preference was given to unmarried officers for nomination to such posts as Geschwader Kommodore – when married and unmarried pilots of equal merit were eligible – war needs were more important than Galland's policy. He knew this. No capable leader was ever held back in the Fighter Arm because he was married.

Steps and measures taken by others impacted on Galland's responsibilities in 1943. The ground attack units (*Schlachtflieger*) were anomalously under his office. Ground attack units in direct support of the Army were a tactical world apart from regular fighter missions. As the war advanced, each phase become more demanding and more highly specialized. Galland was therefore gratified when a General of Close Support (*General Der Schlachtflieger*) was appointed in October of 1943.

Under Colonel Dr. Kupfer, their entire activity was removed from his responsibility. His relief at being divested of the ground attack arm was short-lived. The night fighters were placed under his authority in November of 1943, a vast and sophisticated defense empire created by General Josef Kammhuber. General Kammhuber controlled his night fighters through Air Corps XII.

Kammhuber was known for his organizational talents, his inflexible thinking, and his high demands for equipment. Goering described him to Galland as the most expensive general in the Luftwaffe. Kammhuber's *Himmelbett* system of guiding one night fighter within the radius of one radar was doomed when the British began employing bomber stream tactics. After the night fighters were blinded and swamped in the Hamburg disaster, Kammhuber was on his way out.

DORNIER'S LAST WWII FIGHTER, THE Do 335. "PHIEL"
This twin engined fighter was the fastest propeller-driven fighter produced in WWII. It never got into combat. It was reported to have exceeded 500 mph in level flight but this was never documented.

Galland's relations with Kammhuber had always been difficult and barely satisfactory. Goering made Kammhuber Inspector of the Night Fighter Arm in an empty gesture, just prior to banishing him to command Air Fleet 5 in Norway. Galland's responsibilities now became round-the-clock, just like Allied bombing. Heavily overburdened despite his devoted staff, Galland did not want the night fighters. Like the ground attack arm, it was another world, technically and operationally. He nevertheless had to obey orders.

Adding a night fighter staff to his existing staff, Galland brought in Major Hajo Herrmann, originator of Wild Boar night fighting, as Inspector of the Night Fighters. Herrmann handled his responsibilities with capable skill. Later he was succeeded in the Inspector's post by Lt. Colonel Werner Streib, the legendary "Father of Night Fighting." Appalling weather, serious electronic problems, and the RAF night offensive against Berlin taxed the night fighters in the fall and winter of 1943. The center of gravity in the air war had arrived over the Reich as Galland had earlier foreseen. German skies were a round-the-clock battleground.

This chapter has provided a sketched overview of the main responsibilities that devolved on Galland as he grew into his job in 1943. Complete books could be written detailing and documenting each phase of Galland's inhumanly busy life at this time. The former sailplane pilot from Westerholt took every possible step and measure against the coming avalanche from aloft.

TWENTY-TWO

Avalanche

Bad weather hampered full implementation of the U.S. strategic bombing offensive from November 1943 and restricted daylight bombing on into early 1944. While this gave some daytime relief to the German civil populace, Galland watched fighter casualties mount. Goering's policy of meeting every Allied thrust with all available fighters caused the Fighter Arm serious bad weather losses. No comparable losses were inflicted on the Americans. Galland was opposed to this steady wastage of pilots and aircraft.

The ordinary Luftwaffe fighter pilot of 1943-44 had no instrument flying skills or training. They had to learn "on the job." Neglect of training and time pressure in the Luftwaffe's earlier days precluded the establishment of blind flying schools for fighters. When Galland organized some facilities, fuel shortages nullified his efforts. Numerous German fighters crashed in bad weather, untouched by Allied bullets. Fatal crashes into mountains and crackups due to icing and forced landings were numerous. Pilots in extreme situations, often disoriented, bailed out and left their aircraft to crash. Galland saw no return for this attrition. His proposals for husbanding, concentrating, and increasing effective fighter strength went unheeded.

Appalling weather in the 1943-44 winter was too much for all save the best and luckiest German fighter pilots. Even the talented pilots of the single-engined Wild Boar night fighters, some of them with commercial piloting experience and instrument flight capability, suffered in the winter attrition. The night fighters were locked in bitter combat with RAF Bomber Command, as Air Chief Marshal Harris sought to wreck Berlin with area raids, guided by the RAF's Oboe device.

Luftwaffe night fighters met every thrust. They made the RAF pay dearly in the night war, but themselves suffered heavy losses. That Harris did not win the Battle of Berlin was due to the sacrifices of the defenders. Wild Boar losses led eventually to the abandonment of single-engined night fighter operations. In the spring of 1944, Galland was able to have the Wild Boar transferred to the day fighter forces as bad weather units. From inception to end, Galland estimated that the Wild Boar had cost the Luftwaffe over 1,000 aircraft and hundreds of skilled pilots.

By early December 1943, the combined bombing offensive against the German aircraft industry – an operation codenamed "Pointblank" – was three months behind schedule. Pointblank's strategic purpose was the elimination of Galland's fighters prior to the invasion, which was then scheduled for 1 May 1944. General Eaker was under heavy pressure to smash the German aircraft industry. Only the weather and the Luftwaffe Fighter Arm stood in the way. With radar bombing to become available in the spring, even weather hazards would be reduced, but at Christmas of 1943 the Allied timetable was far behind.

The Eighth Air Force by then had 26 groups of heavy bombers, each group consisting of 4 squadrons with 16 aircraft each. 11 Groups of fighters were under Eighth Air Force Fighter Command. The Americans could now put up 600-700 bombers for a massive and escorted attack on German targets. Galland was aware, from the intelligence reports he studied, that this daylight strength would be doubled and tripled in the next year. Emblematic of growing American strength was the 13,142 tons of bombs dropped by U.S. aircraft on European targets in December of 1943. The USAAF had exceeded the RAF's monthly load for the first time.

The winter months of 1943-44 were a brief breathing space for a Germany about to go under the flail. This pause was a last opportunity and a lost opportunity all in one. During these critical winter weeks, gross high-level mistakes by the Germans crucially delayed the Me 262 jet fighter.

Galland was pressing for action on the Me 262 far beyond the theoretical limits of his responsibilities. No opportunity to advocate top priority for the jet fighter was overlooked by the young general. This aircraft was, in his view, the last chance for the Fighter Arm against the impending avalanche. Only a technical quantum jump could change the balance of power in German skies.

Hitler actually saw the Me 262 for the first time on 26 November 1943, as part of a Luftwaffe weapons demonstration at Insterburg airbase in East Prussia, near his HQ. The Fuehrer was well aware of the jet fighter's existence. His overcautious reaction to Galland's bold May proposal for accelerated Me 262 development and production has already been described. The dictator's later insistence that the revolutionary aircraft be produced as a Blitz Bomber is generally accepted as the ruination of Germany's last aerial chance.

Less well known historically is the manner in which the Blitz Bomber entered the Fuehrer's mind, there to become an obsession. Although ignorant of aeronautical engineering, he had long advocated a "speed bomber" for the Luftwaffe. Without comprehending the technical problems involved, Hitler's speed bomber was to be faster than intercepting fighters. The RAF Mosquito bomber actually proved this Hitler concept feasible, through the anachronistic use of wooden construction. German engineers never came up with a comparable speed bomber, but such an aircraft was among Hitler's military visions.

The specific bomber idea for the Me 262 came directly from the fighter's own creator – Professor Messerschmitt. He planted this idea in a personal conference with Hitler on 7 September 1943. The Professor was probably attempting by devious means to keep alive his Me 209 piston-engined fighter, which both Galland and Milch had rejected as insufficient in performance. Messerschmitt's draft for this fateful discussion with the Fuehrer survives as pages 102 and 103 among two bulging files of the Professor's personal papers at the Imperial War Museum in London.

Under heading 5 in this draft, Messerschmitt notes for presentation to the Fuehrer that Colonel Peltz of the Bomber Arm, in a report from Rechlin, had "urgently demanded" the jet bomber for missions against England. "The quickest possibility for the job is the 262" says Messerschmitt's draft. Further searching for the origin of Hitler's "crazy" idea of converting jet fighters into bombers is superfluous. Messerschmitt himself initiated the debacle.

Messerschmitt always had the Fuehrer's ear. Hitler trusted the Professor. What Messerschmitt put into that trusting ear on 7 September 1943, kindled Hitler's fecund imagination. Already present therein was the Fuehrer's unfulfilled speed bomber concept. With this phantom, the Me 262 of the real world was immediately synthesized, complete with Messerschmitt's own seal of feasibility. Thus arose Hitler's Blitz Bomber fantasies, with all their measureless impact on the air defense of Germany and on the hopes of General Galland to counter daylight bombing.

By 28 October 1943, Hitler was describing to Goering his vision of jet fighter bombers. Each carrying a pair of small bombs, these revolutionary machines would streak over the invasion beaches, strafing the landing enemy. Demoralization, death, and panic would ensue. Hitler never relinquished this odd and limited vision of jet operations until it was too late.

ERICH HARTMANN - TOP ACE OF THE WORLD
Hartmann, with 352 aerial victories led all other pilots in the race for top scores. 254 of his opponents were single-engined fighters and 98 were twin-engined. He survived the war, spent 10 years as a Soviet POW, and served in the new Luftwaffe, and passed away 19 September 1993.

On 2 November 1943, less than two months after Messerschmitt had touted the Me 262 to him as a fast bomber, Hitler sent Goering to the Messerschmitt plant at Augsburg. The Reich Marshal was charged with discussing the bomber version of the Me 262 with the Professor. The question of bomb racks was broached. Messerschmitt falsely assured Goering that bomb release devices were incorporated in the original design. The jet fighter could carry either two 550-lb bombs, or a single 1,100-lb bomb.

Hitler's requirement for a couple of small bombs was modest, in view of the bomb-carrying capabilities of every other fighter aircraft in the Luftwaffe. When Goering asked Messerschmitt when the first bomb rack models would be ready, the Professor was forced to admit that they had not yet been designed. When pressed further by Goering – who expected to be grilled later about the whole matter by Hitler – Messerschmitt recklessly asserted that the bomb racks could be made ready in about two weeks. These were deceptive assurances.

On this same day, 2 November 1943, a special commission was established to oversee development of the Me 262.

Colonel Edgar Petersen, Chief of the Research Establishment, headed this evaluation panel. As Kommodore of KG 40 he had flown long range Atlantic reconnaissance missions in the 4-engined Fw 200, and later had evaluated captured Allied aircraft at Rechlin. Other commission members included engine-builder Franz von Jumo, engine designer Dr. Anselm Franz of Junkers Motorenbau, Messerschmitt himself, Chief of Technical Development Lt. Colonel Knemeyer, and a group of top engineers and industrialists. Galland was not appointed to the panel, even though his troops would be receiving the new aircraft. *The Fighter Arm was unrepresented on the evaluation panel.*

The stage was thus set for the Insterburg demonstration. Most of the high-level attendees were ignorant of what had been planted in Hitler's mind by Messerschmitt in September. Galland had no inkling of what was brewing. Famous faces at Insterburg that day included Galland, Goering, Bodenschatz, Milch, Speer, Himmler, Peltz, Kurt Tank, Claudius Dornier, and Chief of the Luftwaffe General Staff, Guenther Korten. Messerschmitt himself stood with Hitler, Goering, and Galland as the Me 262 stole the weapons show.

As the jet went whistling past, Galland heard Hitler ask Goering if this aircraft could carry bombs. Before Goering could reply, Messerschmitt interjected immediately that the aircraft had enough power to carry 1,000 pounds of bombs and "perhaps 2,000 pounds." This latter figure was more than twelve times the bomb weight the Fuehrer originally envisioned for his jet fighter bombers. Hitler nodded knowingly, and turned on the assembled Luftwaffe gods.

"For years I have demanded from the Luftwaffe a speed bomber that can reach its target in spite of enemy fighter defense. In the aircraft you present to me as a fighter plane, I see the *Blitz Bomber*, with which I will repel the invasion in its first and weakest phase ... it will strike the recently landed mass of material and troops, creating panic, death, and destruction."

There was a loaded pause while Hitler glared around at his shocked air chiefs.

GERHARD BARKHORN - NUMBER TWO ACE
"Gerd" with 301 aerial victories ranks number two in the worlds ace list. He flew 1104 combat sorties (including Galland's JV 44), survived the war, served in the new Luftwaffe as a Major General and, along with his wife, was killed in an auto accident on the autobahn on 8 January 1983.

GUNTHER RALL - NUMBER THREE ACE
Left: Rall had 275 victories, survived the war, served as the Commander-in-Chief of the new Luftwaffe from Dec. 1970 until June 1974 and retired as a Lt.General. Considered perhaps the best in the Luftwaffe at shooting at a moving target from a moving platform, there is little doubt he would have been number one ace except for injuries which grounded him many times.

"Of course, none of you thought of that!"

Galland's heart sank. An incredibly bizarre development was beginning before his eyes. Anything that now delayed the combat advent of the Me 262 fighter served the enemy. Only this weapon could deter the masses of daylight bombers. Galland knew all too well how making fighters into bombers degraded performance. The complex factors additionally involved with the revolutionary Me 262 boggled the mind. There was no proper bomb sight. High fuel consumption at low altitude imposed severe range limits. Above 600 mph, the Me 262 became uncontrollable, which precluded dive bombing. Center of gravity problems in a bomber version were likely to be complicated.

Galland foresaw complex training problems with a bomber version. The defensive attitude of bomber pilots toward enemy fighters could not be eradicated. Only the best fighter pilots could be successful with the Me 262. All these thorny technical and human problems militated against an Me 262 Blitz Bomber, but unfortunately that mutant craft was already flying around in Hitler's imagination.

On 5 December 1943, Hitler had Colonel Nicolaus von Below, his Luftwaffe aide, send Goering a telegram in which he stressed the importance attached by the Fuehrer to jet fighter bombers. The language was plain:

> "IT IS IMPERATIVE THAT THE LUFTWAFFE HAVE A NUMBER OF JET FIGHTER BOMBERS READY FOR FRONT COMMITMENT BY THE SPRING OF 1944" telegraphed von Below. He added that "THE FUEHRER FEELS THAT DELAY IN OUR JET FIGHTER PROGRAM WOULD BE TANTAMOUNT TO IRRESPONSIBLE NEGLIGENCE."

Goering was directed to submit bi-monthly reports on the Me 262 directly to Hitler, plus reports on the Arado 234 reconnaissance jet bomber – a parallel project. Hitler thus clearly envisioned the fighter bomber role for the Me 262. Work at the Messerschmitt factory nevertheless remained concentrated on the fighter version, as the company struggled to complete the first series of prototypes. Only prototype V-10, scheduled for completion in May 1944, had experimental bomb racks.

The Germans were thus already losing the race between jet fighter production and the Eighth Air Force. The Allied strategic bombing program had the Messerschmitt factories targeted for obliteration. By early 1944, P-51 groups were going into action with the Eighth Air Force, and production of P-51s in the U.S. was soaring under top priorities. Deep penetrations of German airspace would in 1944 be covered all the way by high performance fighters that outnumbered the German defenders. Only the jet fighter could at this stage deter daylight bombing.

On 6 January 1944, the Eighth Air Force got a new commander, an aviator destined to enjoy a long relationship in peace and war with Adolf Galland. He was Major General James H. Doolittle, whose 1942 Tokyo raid had lifted American spirits. Doolittle had then made an outstanding record commanding the Twelfth Air Force in North Africa. His career as an aviation pioneer, Schneider Cup racing pilot, and businessman had endowed him with acumen, wide vision, and the ability to get things done. Doolittle had moral as well as physical courage, and he was to be the most sagacious Allied air leader in Galland's estimation.

ERICH HARTMANN AND GERHARD BARKHORN
Both aces saw most of their combat flying with JG 52 on the Soviet Front. Both survived the war. A total of 653 opponents fell to their guns. Hartmann died in 1993 and Barkhorn was killed in a road accident.

Eighth Air Force Intelligence presented Doolittle with a report when he took command that defined the essentials of the January 1944 air situation. The strategic bombing program and its critical role in a successful Allied invasion, was threatened unless the German Fighter Arm could be suppressed. Increased fighter production, more fighter pilot trainees, improved German weaponry, and transfer of additional fighters to the defense of Germany from other fronts were all cited as adding to Luftwaffe strength. Issued on 5 January 1944, the report's message was driven home by the downing of 25 American heavy bombers.

Destroying the Luftwaffe Fighter Arm and its industrial infrastructure was code-named "Argument." There was disagreement in high Allied councils about the employment of the Eighth Air Force, for the overall goal was Allied air supremacy over the invasion beaches and immediate hinterland. Pressure was exerted to draw the Eighth into more direct support of tactical operations against French targets. Such a course would have helped Galland build up his fighter reserve for the defense of Germany.

Doolittle saw the war on a broad canvas, as a mighty production struggle. The road to air supremacy in Normandy, in Doolittle's eyes, lay in the destruction of German fighter production centers and the synthetic fuel industry, and to attack aggressively the existing German fighters. Had their positions been reversed, it is fair to say that Galland would have followed the same course.

HUNGARIAN AND GERMAN FIGHTER PILOTS
Some Hungarian units flew with JG 52. This photo made at Spatherbst (Csor) in 1944 show (l to r): Capt. Pottjondy (102 Brigade, Hungary, Lt. Erich Hartmann (JG 52), Capt. Gerhard Barkhorn (JG 52), Major Kovacs (Hungary), Capt. Helmut Lipfert (JG 52), and Capt. Heinz Sturm (JG 52).

Echoes of the Battle of Britain and Galland's hard experiences in that encounter appeared in the way that Doolittle tackled the challenge. General Eaker in building the Eighth into a massive war machine had defined the role of U.S. fighters: escort the heavies and protect them from fighter attack. In practical application, this led to the same close escort orders under which Galland had chafed in the Battle of Britain and which aided the British defenders.

Doolittle analyzed the essentials in the same way as Galland had in 1940. Doolittle's position differed radically, however, inasmuch as he had the authority to make far-reaching operational changes. Doolittle ordered his fighter groups to destroy the Luftwaffe fighters, to find them and shoot them down or strafe them on the ground. German fighters were to be intercepted and downed before they could find the heavies. Eighth Fighter Command leaders greeted these orders with enthusiasm, just as Galland and his pilots would have in the Battle of Britain had they been similarly unleashed.

The U.S. bomber leaders did not like this reversal of established operational procedures. They were comforted by close escort fighters. Setting his fighters free to hunt and destroy Galland's fighters earned the new Eighth Air Force boss the epithet "Killer Doolittle" – used directly to his face. Doolittle stood by his decision despite criticism, some of it from high-ranking officers. In the flaming crucible above Germany, his fighters proved that he was right. The classic success Doolittle enjoyed also proved that in 1940 Galland had urged the correct tactical employment of German fighters on Goering and the High Command – in vain.

Sweeping far ahead of the bomber boxes, usually out of their sight, searching around far to each side of the majestic formations, American fighters carried the battle to the Luftwaffe. Galland's fighter leaders were soon reporting grave difficulties in making proper assemblies as hunting U.S. fighters slashed among them. Galland had long dreaded this unleashment of the U.S. fighter escort.

German fighter formations were scattered and thrown into confusion before they could assemble. When they were able to form up, and lurked awaiting their chance to attack the heavies, the Mustangs jumped them. The inherent defensive power of the bomber box and escort had been projected by these tactics miles out from the bomber formation itself. Well-trained American pilots flying excellent aircraft struck at German morale as surely as they struck at the Messerschmitts and Focke-

END OF WWII COMBAT CAREER
Major Günther Rall's combat in WWII ended when an American P-47 "Thunderbolt" pilot shot Rall's thumb off over Berlin on 12 May 1944. Rall is convinced the incident saved his life, because there was no chance to survive on the Western Front for another year.

LIKEABLE KOMMODORE OF JG 52
Dietrich Hrabak was one of the best and most popular Kommodores. He scored 125 victories, survived the war, became a Lt.General in the new Luftwaffe. He passed away 15 September 1995.

MAJOR WALTER KRUPINSKI - 197 VICTORIES
Nicknamed "Graf Punski" he was another of Galland's stalwart fighter pilots. He survived the war, joined the new Luftwaffe and retired as a Lt. General. Today he lives Neunkirchen, Germany, and although badly treated by his captors at the end of WWII he has retained a fine sense of humor.

Wulfs. Another Luftwaffe era of "split-S and dive away" ensued. The American fighters were relentless, following their opponents down to the deck. If the Americans could not find the Germans aloft, they strafed Luftwaffe airfields.

In later years, General Doolittle would regard unleashing the American fighters as his best decision of the war. Adolf Galland agreed. The two generals often discussed Doolittle's masterstroke in their peacetime meetings. The American's classic employment of fighters on their classic mission was tactically excellent. More than anything else, this decisive change by Doolittle began the twilight of the Fighter Arm.

After a long spell of bad weather, Doolittle got 857 heavies airborne to attack the Frankfurt area on 27 January 1944. Poor visibility over their English bases hampered their assembly, and only about 450 bombers were actually dispatched. In bad weather over Germany fewer than 60 attacked their targets. The weather was blocking the strategic bombing offensive, and there was high-level chagrin and impatience.

On 8 February 1944, General Spaatz ordered that Argument – the destruction of every factory producing fighters and fighter components – would have to be completed no later than 1 March. "Big Week" was accordingly organized to seal the doom of Galland's fighters, by obliterating the German aircraft industry. The weather was the controlling factor. As soon as the weather was good enough, a mighty maximum effort would roar into the sky. Thousands of Allied aircraft stood poised and wet in England.

Galland anticipated Big Week. He had marshaled his resources and overseen the formation of mixed Geschwaders of light and heavy fighters. These units consisted of one Gruppe of heavily armored Fw 190s, strongly armed and somewhat slower than regular single-engined fighters. Two Gruppen of the latter flew escort with the heavily armed fighters to make up the mixed Geschwader. Galland hoped that such composite formations might be more effective if the greater hitting power of the special Fw 190s could be used in close.

These units were moderately successful, but Goering and the High Command continued their "bombers only" attack orders. The single-engined fighters were thus bound down again to an escort role while the heavy fighters were attacking, so that their aggressive potential was negated. Hordes of American fighters made assembly of the mixed German formations extremely difficult. The heavy fighters could not defend themselves against the much nimbler Mustangs. Galland reflected often and bitterly that the "bombers only" attack regulations issued to the Fighter Arm were a certain way to give the American fighters a free hand.

Big Week actually began on the night of 19/20 February 1944. Over 700 RAF Lancasters and Halifaxes struck at Leipzig. These aircraft carried considerably more explosives than the B-17s, and the ancient city took a terrible beating. German night fighters fell on the RAF fiercely. They attacked the British over Leipzig and in pursuit across Germany after the raid, while a sleepless Galland followed the action. 78 British bombers were shot down during the night.

Doolittle opened Big Week by dispatching more than 1,000 American heavies, for the first time in history, on 20 February. 940 of these aircraft reached their German targets, escorted by an incredible 700 fighters. The vast aerial armada, with its fighter escort hunting, sweeping, and hounding, plastered its targets and lost only 21 aircraft.

The RAF hit Stuttgart that same night with another force of 600 bombers, in an area raid intended to help stifle ball-bearing production. On 21 February, the Eighth Air Force put 764 B-17s and B-24s over Germany in daylight. General Twining's Fifteenth Air Force heavies winged in from Italy the next day, blasting the Messerschmitt plant at Regensburg, while more than 100 U.S. bombers from England struck at other aircraft industry targets. Galland's fighters contended hotly with the American bombing pincer. In combination with German flak, they shot down 54 American aircraft.

On 24 February the Eighth returned to its nemesis target – Schweinfurt. 231 bombers attacked the ball-bearing plants. A further 238 Liberators hammered Gotha. Galland's fighters and the flak clawed down another 44 American bombers, but it was not enough. 700 Lancasters droned over Schweinfurt that same night and cast their awesome loads into the flames left by the Americans.

On 25 February 1944, as Allied weather experts were predicting further deterioration, 680 of Doolittle's bombers concentrated on the Me 109 centers at Augsburg and Regensburg, with blows also at Fürth. Fifteenth Air Force bombers from Italy joined in again at Regensburg, at a cost of 30 aircraft shot down. Total U.S. losses for the day were 64 bombers destroyed, with many others damaged. Major General Joachim Huth, Galland's old Jafü from JG 26 days, did an outstanding job in directing fighter operations from Schleissheim, as C.O. of the 7th Fighter Division. The Luftwaffe's best was again insufficient. The numerical odds were against the Germans in their own skies.

As Big Week ended on the night of 25 February 1944, the RAF struck a final blow. They attacked the Messerschmitt factory at Augsburg, once again aiming into the fires started by the Americans during the day. Bad weather then terminated Big Week, but it looked as though Big Week had terminated the German aircraft industry.

The Allies lost nearly 300 aircraft. They could make up such losses rapidly. They dropped over 19,000 tons of bombs on the German aircraft industry, blasting or burying over 700 Me 109s that were either complete or in final production. More than a thousand German aircraft, mostly Me 109s and Fw 190s, were lost in the factory attacks. Galland's own heavy losses in combat with the raiders had to be added to the tally, as well as numerous losses from flying accidents.

Here was the avalanche of aircraft and explosives that Galland had dreaded, endlessly warned against, and sought by every means in his power to abort. Usually imperturbable in his outward bearing, his inner turmoil was intense. The shambles, ruin, and suffering were indescribable in themselves, but were doubly painful because it was a body blow at the Fighter Arm. There were private, quiet moments when he put his head in his hands, but they were brief. He was always wanted or needed somewhere, so he put on his imperturbable expression and his cigar and went to work.

WOLFGANG FALCK AND WERNER STREIB
Streib (right) helps Falck get into his combination flying suit which was worn over the Luftwaffe uniform. Both pilots survived the war and were long-time loyal friends of Galland. Streib passed away 15 June 1986.

Hundreds of trained aircraft workers were among the civilians who perished in the Big Week raids. They were irreplaceable. Hundreds of others were injured. Many more bolted their jobs and homes in terror, disappearing in the confusion to seek refuge away from the targeted cities. Messerschmitt's factory at Regensburg had been leveled. Four months would be needed to make it operational again – Allied bombers permitting.

Other critical aircraft and component factories had been reduced to rubble. Allied commanders studying aerial reconnaissance photographs could hardly believe the extent of the destruction. They were justified in believing that Big Week had smashed German aircraft production.

Alarming reports of aircraft industry devastation and production losses came quickly to Galland's staff. The Luftwaffe High Command functioned now in a fever of consternation. These were the same officers, pale and confused, who had refused to believe intelligence reports from America about the fleets of bombers and fighters being produced. Goering had called these reports "bluff." The Reich Marshal was now appropriately on leave, insulated against bad tidings by the medieval splendor of Castle Veldenstein. When Galland had warned that this terrible scenario was coming, Goering and others on the High Command had told him he was a defeatist. Events had proved Galland's realism. Defeat came from unrealistic policies followed by his superiors.

Pulling the aircraft industry back into function was a Herculean task. Field Marshal Milch worked wonders in reestablishing the supply of fighters, despite his waning status with Hitler and Goering's now open and abusive animosity. Due largely to Milch's energy, ideas, and optimism, blue sky was somehow found amid the gloom.

Large numbers of aircraft bombed and buried proved to be repairable. Precious machine tools exhumed from under rubble required only to be cleaned up and checked before going back into use. All kinds of equipment proved salvageable, except where fires had raged. Industry labored feverishly. Messerschmitt at Augsburg was back in production a month later.

Armaments Minister Speer, with whom Galland had always enjoyed frank and cordial relations, decreed industrial dispersal as state policy. Aircraft production began rising again from new and dispersed facilities. Galland took grim satisfaction at the way fighters had finally come to center stage. He still found it incredible, nevertheless, that such enemy blows were necessary to drive home the importance of fighter production. Everyone now finally agreed, amid the ruin and wreckage, that only fighters could protect German war potential. Galland had urged top priority for fighter production virtually from the time he became General of the Fighter Arm.

The Fighter Staff was organized, a new bureau within the Ministry of Armaments, charged with dispersing, expediting, and expanding fighter production. Milch was inspired with the Fighter Staff idea during Big Week: top priority for fighters, the best talent from his own and Speer's ministries, and authority to boost fighter production to record levels. Milch recommended Karl-Otto Saur, Speer's deputy, as head of the Fighter Staff. Milch's own star was setting. Saur in the past had frustrated many Luftwaffe requirements in favor of the Army, but now he was fighter production czar of Germany. Hitler promptly approved the Fighter Staff.

Galland had only the slightest inkling of the complex power, personality, and political plays behind these events. He had no taste for any kind of machinations. His straightforward fighter pilot's approach to life was that merit ought to rule everything. Only the air defense of Germany and the welfare of the Fighter Arm mattered in his eyes. On this account, he rejoiced that finally his beloved fighters were to have first priority.

Despite the bombing, Big Week, and all the ruin, there would henceforth be plenty of fighters, once Saur dragged production out of the February-March abyss. Rough, brutal, and relentless, Saur raised fighter production by June of 1944 to unprecedented levels. Fuel was by then an irremovable bottleneck, and fuel was the problem rather than aircraft. Saur's fighter production feats did not include the Me 262, which Galland desperately needed – all the more so because jet fuel was relatively abundant. The Me 262 drama continued unfolding against the backdrop of imminent Allied invasion.

TWENTY-THREE

Dissolution

Miraculously, the series of Me 262 prototypes escaped the avalanche of Allied bombs targeted on Messerschmitt factories. So vast was the destruction at Augsburg that Galland could hardly believe that the precious jets had survived virtually unscathed. Even at the eleventh hour, as he saw things, there remained a chance. His optimism grew as he saw the aircraft industry being rapidly resurrected, but fuel was already a limiting factor. Fighter pilot flying training was hamstrung by fuel shortages.

Plans were made by Saur to produce 1,000 Me 262 jet fighters per month, together with their engines, in a vast underground complex at Nordhausen. By April of 1944, Hitler was giving top priority to a fighter umbrella over the Fatherland. Accepting at last that he needed at least 2,000 fighters to defend the Reich, Hitler ordered the construction of new bombproof factories. These immense facilities were to be established under mushroom canopies of reinforced concrete.

Galland learned with relief of the Fuehrer's new priorities. The General of the Fighters reflected wryly on the recommendations he had made to Hitler when U.S. heavies first bombed German targets. Galland had waited vainly for appropriate action to be taken, while misery and death cascaded from the skies upon the civil population. The USAAF kept the problem in the forefront of Hitler's mind by bombing German industry one day out of two in April, despite adverse weather.

Galland's most urgent task early in 1944 was the refreshment, reinforcement, and rebuilding of existing fighter formations. Round-the-clock defense of Germany worked a heavy attrition on both pilots and units. The continuing High Command policy of sending all available fighters against every raid, regardless of weather, lowered combat effectiveness and undermined morale. Pilots and aircraft were scattered far and wide by this policy, posing a virtually insuperable problem.

Too many pilots were operating too often in pick-up formations from strange airfields. Using the same aircraft for day and night operations intensified mechanical attrition. Fighter Arm battle losses were nominally less most of the time than the casualties inflicted on the raiders, but overall Fighter Arm losses were amounting to about 50 pilots and aircraft for each incursion by the American heavies. As the Fighter Arm declined in combat effectiveness and efficiency, the Americans kept improving.

General Doolittle concluded that a standard operational tour of 25 missions for his bomber crews was too short. He reasoned that they were being taken out of combat just as they reached peak team efficiency manning a bomber. Doolittle increased their duty tour to 30 missions and raised efficiency by more than 30 percent. Later tours were extended to 35 missions. Doolittle made his bombers fly at the speed of the slowest aircraft, thereby using the firepower of the bomber box to protect the cripples. U.S. efficiency thus rose as that of the Fighter Arm declined, a tipping of the combat balance of which Galland was well aware.

The narrow pre-war training base of the Luftwaffe, and its subsequent neglect and ruin after the war began, now seriously bedeviled Galland. Pilots simply could not be produced fast enough in Germany. Capable instructors were woefully rare. Fuel allocations for training were progressively curtailed, necessitating constant reductions in flying training. Young boys were sent to the fighter squadrons with 65 hours total flying time, and sometimes less. The Allies, meanwhile, were producing thousands of pilots at modern facilities far from the war zone. Dissolution of the Fighter Arm was immanent in this single fact.

Galland was finally able to persuade Goering to create a reserve of fighters, instead of hurling every plane and pilot piecemeal into the shambles. In his recommendations and proposals, as well as in his personal encounters with Goering, Galland kept stressing the need for such a reserve. His conviction was that only a Big Blow – a strike with perhaps 2,000 fighters in the fighter daytime – could saturate the American defense and inflict unacceptable losses on the bombers.

Galland also emphasized the coming invasion of Europe, a military certainty as soon as the weather permitted. Field Marshal Sperrle on the Channel coast had less than 200 fighters to face the combined might of the Ninth Tactical Air Force, the Second Tactical Air Force, and RAF Fighter Command. A Luftwaffe fighter reserve was essential, unless air superiority were to be simply surrendered to the powerful Allied air fleets, especially the Eighth and Fifteenth Air Forces that were now hammering the homeland.

In finally assenting to Galland's program for building a fighter reserve in the Reich, Goering added a proviso: in addition to the reserve held ready for the Big Blow, the Reich fighter defense was to be built up to 2,000 fighters. Hitler was to cite this same figure in April. Galland considered such a force unattainable, since Hitler had earlier forbidden the withdrawal of any more Geschwader from other fronts for the defense of Germany.

Galland accordingly proposed, and Goering agreed, that they transfer one squadron from each Gruppe in the north and east, to add a fourth squadron to each Gruppe defending the Reich. Each Geschwader would also receive an additional Gruppe. Galland had already used this stratagem in 1943 to increase the establishment of each home defense Geschwader. An additional operational squadron was to be formed with each fighter pilot school, and also with each Operational Training Unit. Full implementation of these measures could give Galland a reserve of 1,800 fighters. Their necessity was driven home by the Ninth Air Force on 23 April 1944. More than 1,000 American fighters and fighter bombers were sent to beat up French, Belgian, and Dutch targets. As Galland had emphasized in his proposals for the fighter reserve, such Allied air supremacy would make operations almost impossible for the German Army in France.

The invasion aborted Galland's goal of 1,800 fighters for Reich defense by mid-June 1944, exclusive of JG 2 and JG 26 on the Channel coast. Galland had intended to stretch the limited supply of experienced combat leaders over the larger establishments. The number of officers able to lead effectively a Gruppe or Geschwader was now dwindling dangerously. The 7 to 1 numerical edge in fighters held by the Allies proved lethal even to Germany's most capable aces and leaders. Dissolution of leadership in this way haunted the General of the Fighters.

Highly-decorated, high-scoring ace-leaders lost in the spring of 1944 included the redoubtable Lt. Colonel Egon Mayer, Kommodore of JG 2. He was shot down over Montmedy on 2 March by pilots of the U.S. 365th Fighter Group. Colonel Wolf-Dietrich "Fürst" Wilcke died over Schoppenstadt on 23 March. The irreplaceable Colonel Walter "Gulle" Oesau was shot down over St. Vith in the Ardennes. Oesau was Kommodore of JG 1, with a splendid combat career extending back to the Condor Legion in Spain. All these Kommodores were personally well-known by Galland. "They belonged to the inestimable elite of our fighter leaders" said Galland. "They were irreplaceable, and their deaths shook me."

Such crippling losses went far beyond the three lives. Galland well understood the damage done to operational effectiveness when great fighter leaders were killed. Their presence leading in the air was enormously reassuring to raw young pilots and essential to keeping the youngsters alive long enough to gain experience and become effective. Their combat deaths struck hammer blows at morale.

Only the night fighters against the RAF provided encouragement in the winter and spring of 1944. "Bomber" Harris of the RAF had launched his Berlin wrecking program back in November of 1943. He kept the pressure on despite heavy losses inflicted by the Luftwaffe night fighters. On 24 March 1944, Harris sent 811 heavies to Berlin, and 72 of them were downed before dawn. The German night fighters were proving incredibly resilient and capable.

Deep penetration night raids climaxed on 30 March 1944, when Harris sent nearly 800 bombers to Nuremberg. Due to British meteorological miscalculation, the raiders found themselves over the Continent in unrestricted visibility and all-revealing moonlight. Their contrails etched their tracks across the frosty sky. German night fighters began attacking near Aachen. Repeated attacks were driven home under conditions requiring no radar or groping in the clouds.

The greatest fighter victory of all time, day or night, resulted from the German attacks. 94 RAF heavies were downed. After hours of wild pursuit across Germany, and savage hunting amid thunderheads over the North Sea, another 20 RAF heavies landed in England ready for the scrapheap. Losses had exceeded 11 percent. This severe defeat was the culmination of earlier losses and led to curtailment of RAF deep penetration night raids. "Bomber" Harris had not won his greatest battle, despite a swathe of destruction inflicted on Berlin.

Galland was gratified by this significant night fighter victory. A string of similar but even more effective triumphs by day was what he now planned against the Eighth Air Force. Swarming and aggressive U.S. fighters made daylight victories extremely difficult. Even days like 6 March 1944, when 69 American heavies went down in Berlin raids, exacted an insupportable price in life, aircraft, and leaders from the Fighter Arm. only a Big Blow, with a blizzard of fighters, could bring down 200 or more heavy bombers in one big daylight attack. For this Galland continued his planning.

Many German minds focused on how to down more bombers in daylight. Proposals for ramming attacks were inevitable under the circumstances. Fighters would ram heavy bombers for a sure downing and wherever possible German pilots would bail out after the impact. Ramming suggestions came from combat units, from individual combat pilots, and from leaders like the redoubtable Colonel Hajo Herrmann. The latter's "Wild Boar" night fighters had frustrated "Bomber" Harris in 1943. Herrmann came to Galland now to advocate the immediate use of ram-and-bail-out tactics. Galland heard him out but turned him down. The young general was opposed to any suicidal approach to combat. He believed that a fighter pilot was owed the chance to survive his victory over a foe. Ramming at 700 mph in a head-on attack made survival improbable.

Herrmann was a superb pilot who became an ace at night. He later briefly led Rammkommando Elbe, but had the misfortune to fall into Soviet hands at war's end. Ten years in Russian POW jails ensued. Herrmann proved to be one of the strong men during this ordeal, which was an unrelenting test of character for every German POW.

Upon his release in 1955 aged 43, he rebuilt his life. Hajo Herrmann became a lawyer. In this role he remained a fighter probably longer than any other pilot of the World War II Luftwaffe. He fought in court for truth and justice, right through to the time of this book's writing in 1997, defending many causes as unpopular as ramming was with General Galland in World War II.

Desperation was inherent in such tactics, and to Galland they were further signals of the proximity of dissolution. The ramming idea was nevertheless translated into the Assault Squadrons (*Sturmgruppen*). These elite units were to press home their attacks to the fullest extent short of ramming. Going straight to the bombers on the shortest distance, they were to open fire with all armament at the last possible moment. The blast of close-range fire, with almost no projectiles missing the target, was expected to bring down the heavies. Nerves of steel and a dauntless heart were essential.

Pilots for the assault fighters were all volunteers, and they came forward in droves. The best of these brave men were given special training. Here was the answer of the fighting pilots to Goering's carping allegations of cowardice in the Fighter Arm. *These men willingly sought the highest risk assignment aloft for a chance to bring down more bombers.*

Assault units were equipped with a specially armored marque of the Fw 190 (Fw 190A-8/R7) carrying four 20mm cannons, and later, two 20mm and two 30mm cannons MK-108. These aircraft had cockpit armor and carried a 66-gallon additional external fuel tank to increase their endurance and range. Under Major von Kornatzki, a leading advocate of these tactics, the first units did well. Kornatzki's force was enlarged to a Gruppe. Major Wilhelm Moritz and others distinguished themselves with the assault squadrons.

Galland proposed setting up one Sturmgruppe in each Geschwader for Reich defense. Special assault fighter training was organized with the OTU Gruppen, all this being put in hand in the 1944 spring. The Normandy invasion then upset these preparations. Assault fighter successes were usually achieved by line abreast attacks on the bombers from astern. The fighters went sweeping through the bomber boxes in three or more waves.

Encouraging successes were achieved initially. Early triumphs were soon nullified by the increasing vulnerability of the heavier assault fighters to the nimbler Mustangs. Keeping the assault fighters competitive necessitated in due course the removal of their armorplate and long range tanks. Loss of the armor was a physical and psychological drawback in point-blank attacks. The assault fighter pilots had to compensate with their fighting hearts for the lack of armor. Outstanding gun camera films of attacks by these fighters on B-17s and B-24s are still in existence today.

Early in May of 1944, General Doolittle's bombers were being diverted increasingly from strategic targets to support of invasion preparations. V-weapon sites in France received special attention. By 12 May, nevertheless, Doolittle was able to launch a strategic attack that he had long advocated – a major blow against the German synthetic fuel industry. Bad weather and invasion support demands had held him up for three weeks after he received approval for these attacks.

Galland, meanwhile, had been anticipating precision daylight bombing of the synthetic fuel industry with trepidation. The Fighter Arm already had serious fuel difficulties, most keenly felt in the training schools, but slowly extending to operational units. Luftwaffe fighter units defending Rumanian oil installations had for weeks reported consistent attacks by Fifteenth Air Force bombers. As Rumanian oil production fell, German synthetic fuel facilities became an especially critical target.

Gratified and amazed as Galland was by Saur's fighter production miracle, he had a grim intuition about fuel. Saur had produced 2,000 fighters in April and was improving on that tally for May. Galland was haunted by the strategic realities. Fighters without fuel did not need to be shot down by the enemy. They would already be useless, whatever their numbers.

On 12 May 1944, 800 American heavies struck at synthetic oil plants and the Leuna facilities at Merseburg, Böhlau, Zwickau, Lutzendorf, Brux, and Troglitz. All targets were heavily hit. Over 400 Luftwaffe fighters milled in combat with the bombers and their escort, clawing down 46 heavies. Galland took only slight comfort from these downings. He knew that Doolittle had gone for the Fighter Arm's jugular vein.

Production of synthetic fuel dropped sharply. Consternation and alarm swept through the oil industry, the Ministry of Armaments, and Galland's office. Persistent similar strikes against synthetic fuels would clearly cause Germany's war potential to wither. This stunning blow by Doolittle on 12 May was fortunately not immediately repeated. The Eighth Air Force was again mainly engaged in invasion area attacks. Synthetic fuel facilities were not battered again until 28 May 1944. During the intervening 16 days, the most fateful decisions of all were taken on the Me 262 – Galland's last hope for a fighting chance against the Eighth Air Force.

Immense increases in fighter production had been achieved by Saur partly via diversions of manpower, materials, and manufacturing space from bomber construction. Less than 700 bombers were produced in April of 1944, as fighter production soared to more than 2,000 aircraft. Aiming at production of 1,000 fighters per week, an incredible figure by all prior Luftwaffe standards, Saur's projections showed an eventual drop in bomber production to around 300 machines a month. This was the price for a vast fleet of fighters.

This feat of deliverance, giving Germany the fighter umbrella that Hitler himself had latterly demanded, was evaluated negatively and narrowly by the Luftwaffe High Command. Chief of the Luftwaffe General Staff Guenther Korten regarded the drop in bomber production, and Saur's goals for the coming months, as the death of the Bomber Arm. General Karl Koller, Korten's deputy and later his successor, held a similar view. Failing to grasp fully that strategic bombing had to be stopped if Germany were to have any war potential at all, the High Command indulged in fantasies about the role of bombers in the year 1944.

The High Command failed to see that in an improved aerial situation, where such steps made military sense, Saur would be able to deliver a flood of bombers comparable to the current fighter production miracle. Regardless of the aerial situation over the Reich, the top Luftwaffe leaders wanted more bombers immediately. Goering agreed.

General Koller prepared a memorandum on the need for increased bomber production and sent it to Hitler. Amid the relative respite provided by diminished bombing of Germany by day and night in May, Hitler's April resolve for a massive fighter umbrella began evaporating. Intoxicated by the opportunity for attack, Hitler developed fantastic notions about a revitalized Bomber Arm. Goering further stoked the Fuehrer's imagination with visions of more than 10,000 bombers on first line strength, in a phantasmagoric future Luftwaffe.

The real-world ruin at the synthetic fuel facilities, and its crippling consequences, failed to disperse these aggressive fantasies. Hitler accordingly decided on 23 May 1944 that Saur's skeleton bomber production was unacceptable. With this in view, and under the impression that the Me 262 was coming shortly as a Blitz Bomber, Hitler met with his Luftwaffe chiefs on 23 May 1944 at the Berghof at Obersalzberg.

Galland was not asked to be present at this meeting. He was at his HQ in Berlin-Kladow. The consequences of the discussions were nevertheless to affect him intimately. Goering was present with his entourage. Speer, Milch, Saur, Colonel Petersen, and several members of the Me 262 commission also participated. As discussion moved to Saur's large production program for the Me 262 jet fighter, Hitler sat bolt upright and interrupted.

"Jet *fighter*?" he said. "I thought the Me 262 was coming out as a speed bomber."

Obviously agitated, the Fuehrer then asked the question that would wreck Galland's chances for a reversal of the aerial situation.

"*How many of the Me 262s already produced can carry bombs?*"

Field Marshal Milch replied that none could carry bombs. The aircraft was being manufactured exclusively as a fighter. He emphasized the design revisions that would be required to convert the Me 262 into a fighter bomber. Hitler was turning purple. This was an almost poetic situation, for Milch had deliberately circumvented Hitler's orders to produce the Me 262 as a Blitz Bomber.

Milch had gambled. Basing his actions largely on Galland's evaluation of the Me 262 fighter, Milch believed that only this machine could salvage the situation. Now he had been compelled to personally drop this bomb of bad news on the Fuehrer.

Hitler passed into a violent rage. Since long before the Insterburg demonstration the previous November, he had nurtured his vision of Blitz Bombers, immune to interception, racing over the invasion beaches and terrorizing Allied troops. The Allies would land any day. Now, at the last minute, he was being informed by his highest and most trusted officials that his orders on the Blitz Bomber had been disobeyed. Hitler raked the men before him unsparingly.

With maniacal determination, the Fuehrer began on the spot the conversion of the Me 262s to Blitz Bombers. With armament and load statistics produced by the stunned Saur, Hitler stripped the aircraft of guns, ammunition, and armorplate. In a few minutes he had shown them all how to modify a jet fighter plane. His rage was such that the gathering of high officials stood mute before it, except Milch, who urged Hitler to think over the matter. Having already completed the re-design of the Me 262 on the Berghof table top, the Fuehrer poured out on Milch a torrent of vituperation and abuse.

Stung by Hitler's invective, Milch shouted that "the smallest child" could see that the Me 262 was a fighter aircraft. The Field Marshal thereby essentially ended his career. Hitler refused to address him again. The Me 262 was ordered into service exclusively as a high speed bomber. Reference to the aircraft as a fighter was forbidden.

When word of these new edicts reached Galland from Milch and Colonel Petersen, he found them almost impossible to comprehend. Germany was being battered to pieces from the air. He felt rebellion rise inside himself. Even though he had heard Hitler regale the Luftwaffe chiefs at Insterburg with his vision of the Blitz Bomber, Galland never believed that such a technical travesty could be forced on the Luftwaffe. The small Me 262 commando operating at Lechfeld under his supervision had been proceeding well. Their work had received his special attention and interest. Saur's plans for 1,000 Me 262 fighters per month had given everyone hope. All this was now to be swept away by the Fuehrer's pique and Goering's supine acquiescence.

On 29 May 1944, as though nailing the coffin shut, Goering issued orders transferring the Me 262 from Galland's office to that of Colonel Dieter Peltz, General of the Bomber Arm. This stroke was intended to silence all talk of a Me 262 fighter. Relations with the Bomber Arm thereafter became increasingly strained, as Peltz took steps to prepare bomber Geschwader for Me 262 operations. There would be no more prototypes officially supplied to Galland's test commando at Lechfeld. The young general therefore began organizing additional aircraft via various *sub rosa* routes. The two major arms of the Luftwaffe struggled with each other while the Allies blasted them both. Goering's appalling leadership had brought them to this.

The disheartening diversion of the Me 262 to the Bomber Arm came as Galland and his staff were already under multiple pressures. The master plan for countering the invasion had proceeded since February of 1944, while the defense of the homeland had to be simultaneously sustained. The central fighter reserve was being built up after Goering's belated approval. Galland's intention was to keep these new units in Germany while they acquired strength, experience, and coordination.

The main Reich defense after the invasion would be carried out by JG 300 and JG 301, backed up by the twin-engined fighters of ZG 26 and ZG 76. All other Geschwader were to be transferred under the master plan to France, as soon as the Allies were committed to their main landings. Luftwaffe airfields were being prepared and provisioned in France, in the face of constant Allied bombing and strafing.

Once again the Allied deception experts, basing their actions largely on Ultra intelligence intercepts, set about misleading the Germans. These experts created a phantom army in Kent. Purportedly commanded by General George S. Patton, this non-existent army generated vast radio traffic, studded with clues that Patton would land in the Pas de Calais. These deception stratagems were designed to reinforce the personal conviction of Field Marshal von Rundstedt that the Pas de Calais would be the main Allied invasion area. German Panzer dispositions were made accordingly. Other deception tactics prepared the Germans for a feint landing.

All the careful planning done in Galland's office for rapid transfer of the Fighter Arm to France was virtually nullified by these successful Allied deceptions. Germany's High Command West initially evaluated the Normandy landing as a feint, predisposed as they were by Allied deception to focus on the Pas de Calais. Movement of Fighter Arm units was therefore not ordered for more than 24 hours. Transfer of fighters to invasion area airfields became a wild scramble, as the Luftwaffe finally issued its own orders for the move.

Galland's pilots flew barely 300 sorties on the invasion day, against more than 10,000 sorties by the Allies. Only a handful of fighter bombers took off on missions against the beachheads. All save a few were forced to jettison their bombs to survive, as Allied fighters in swarms attacked relentlessly. Hardly a single Geschwader or Gruppe reached its French bases with its own squadrons attached. Every Gruppe became a mix of squadrons from other Gruppen.

Invasion zone airfields on which such effort had been expended were mostly bombed out, and the installations wrecked by strafing. Other landing grounds were now chosen and prepared in feverish haste, with all the mistakes that stem from action under pressure. Fighter Arm signals broke down. Coordination became virtually non-existent. Pilots accustomed to the sophisticated fighter control of Reich defense proved to be sadly deficient in navigation when divested of such aids. They came down in dozens on the wrong airfields, miles from those to which they were assigned.

MAJOR WOLFGANG SPÄTE
This 99-victory ace actually scored over 100 because confirmations in the final days of the war were never processed. A brilliant engineer and test pilot, Späte took part in the development of the new jets and rocket-powered aircraft.

Missions degenerated into miserable hedge-hopping sorties around the beachhead areas. The small Luftwaffe pick-up formations were hounded relentlessly by Allied aircraft in hordes. When the Germans were lucky enough to get back down on a Luftwaffe-controlled airfield, they would find only skeleton ground crews present, flown in by Ju 52s that had braved the Allied air armadas. The full ground crew complement would be days or even weeks away, advancing over battered railways that were dominated by Allied fighter bombers. Supply problems became acute for fields that were too few and too poorly camouflaged to sustain successful fighter operations. Disorganization and disaster engulfed the Luftwaffe effort.

Galland set up a new supply system a week after the invasion. Ferry pilots minus combat or navigational skills were incapable of delivering new fighters to France. Galland organized a central supply base in Wiesbaden, with sub-depots at Cologne and Mannheim, from which combat pilots could take aircraft on into France. Fighter Corps II, with General Werner Junck in command, allocated replacement fighters. Allied air dominance forced these German fighters to fly to their French fields late in the evening, when Allied air activity diminished.

MESSERSCHMITT ME 262A-2a
Termed a "Blitzbomber" by Hitler, the Luftwaffe fighter arm had to fight politics strenuously in order to get a share of the jets as interceptors. When Galland was fired as General of the Fighters he was assigned a squadron of Me 262s and told to prove they should be interceptors.

MESSERSCHMITT ME 163B-1
This "power egg" was the first in a series of rocket-powered interceptors. Wolfgang Späte was one of the test pilots. The landing wheels were dropped on takeoff and landing was accomplished on the skid seen below the fuselage. Many pilots injured their spine on landing.

Galland dispatched Colonel Hannes Trautloft, the Inspector of Day Fighters, to evaluate the situation in France and pull the Fighter Arm together. Although he was one of the most capable officers in the Fighter Arm, Trautloft's best efforts were needed just to keep the German fighters functioning at a minimum. He sought to keep his formations as large as possible, for mutual protection and increased striking power, and did everything possible to effect rapid assemblies. This was a tall order in the shooting gallery of French airspace. Just getting back down safely after operations was in itself a small victory.

In the lull before the Allied breakout from Avranches, Galland flew out for a personal tour of the invasion area airfields. His report to Goering was a catalog of deficiencies and errors, crowned by the technical performance inferiority of German fighters to the best Allied machines. Pilot skill and morale were at an all-time low. German fighter pilots soon had to keep their heads down even walking on their own airfields, since everything that moved on the ground was hosed with Allied fire from the air. In Galland's words, "It was like a Wild West show."

Touring Fighter Arm units in this cauldron was a grim experience. Getting from airfield to airfield in one piece was a major feat. Galland's feelings of dismay and sadness, as once-proud Gruppen were reduced to sending up a handful of fighters each day, were intense. He had to conceal these feelings. Giving in to any kind of negative emotion was unthinkable. These embattled pilots and their commanders still looked on him with the greatest respect and trust. This touched him amid the shambles, and made the dissolution all the harder to bear.

Across the Channel, the enciphered radio traffic of Speer's repair organization had been monitored and broken by the Ultra decrypters. This significant information, combined with other intelligence, made clear how drastically the German war effort had been hampered by the May attacks on synthetic fuel targets. On 8 June 1944, strategic bombing chief General Spaatz assigned top priority to further attacks on the German oil industry. Misburg was struck on 15 June, and on 20 June more than 1,200 heavy bombers drove home devastating attacks on synthetic fuel facilities. These blows and those that followed aimed at the complete paralysis of German war potential.

Fighter Arm fortunes in Galland's eyes at this time held only one positive aspect – the Reich central fighter reserve. Events were proving the wisdom of organizing this force. Allied air power was grinding away at the ragged Luftwaffe formations in France. The first four post-invasion weeks had cost the Fighter Arm more than 1,000 aircraft. Approximately 800 fighters were now in the central reserve. Straitened fuel supplies were making it difficult for them to become battle-worthy, but their efficiency was slowly rising. The Fighter Staff had provided these 800 planes. Even if the pilots were inexperienced, Germany was not naked before the storm of renewed strategic bombing.

Resumption of massive daylight attacks on Germany, with fleets of more than 1,000 heavy bombers, compelled Hitler to forsake his fantasies of a renewed Luftwaffe Bomber Arm. The Fuehrer became disillusioned with the bombers. Renewed attacks on synthetic fuel facilities prompted Hitler to insist on 29 June 1944 that only fighter aircraft were henceforth to be built. The Me 262 was to come as a Blitz Bomber. Anyone disobeying these orders was to be shot. The Fuehrer was dissuaded from these extreme measures, and limited bomber production continued while the Fighter Arm fought for its existence in France.

Galland was able to extricate fighter units from the French maelstrom for rebuilding, but getting them back to Germany was hazardous and costly. He continued wangling Me 262s for his test commando. Sympathetic officers in high posts smuggled sufficient jets to the test commando to keep it functioning. Experience with these bootlegged jet fighters in test operations provided exciting evidence of their decisive performance edge. The Me 262 was an interceptor *par excellence*.

The attempt on Hitler's life on 20 July 1944 added to the atmosphere of dissolution. Details were lacking and rumors were rife, but when the dust settled, Hitler was still in charge. Heinrich Himmler rose in authority and status. Himmler's SS hunted down and executed the plotters. Galland would shortly find out that Himmler and the SS had a strong interest in the Me 262.

Early in August the Allied breakout from Avranches sent armored spearheads racing across France. Rout threatened the German Army, battered at every turn by overwhelming Allied air power. Galland and Speer were summoned to a conference with Hitler. Present also were Saur and General Kreipe, the new Chief of the Luftwaffe General Staff. Kreipe had replaced Guenther Korten, who had died of wounds sustained in the Hitler assassination attempt.

Hitler demanded immediate commitment of the central fighter reserve against the Allied breakout from Avranches. Galland was not permitted to voice his objections, which were based on the chastening experience of the post-invasion disaster. Inexperienced reserve pilots could accomplish something in air defense under homeland conditions. Under current conditions in France, where the Allies enjoyed a numerical superiority of 20 to 1, the raw pilots would be rapidly devoured.

The "conference" continued as a Hitler monologue. Even Speer was not permitted to speak. He also objected to the wasting of the central fighter reserve, which would leave German industry naked. Factories, synthetic fuel plants, and railways had to be protected or the war effort would collapse. Speer had to remain silent about these crucial matters, as Hitler held the floor.

The Fuehrer's commitment of the fighter reserve began turning into a diatribe against the Fighter Arm. Standing with cotton wool in his damaged ears, trembling and shaking, the Fuehrer was becoming irritated by his own oratory. He was considering doing away with the Fighter Arm, or reducing it to a few Geschwader equipped with new-type aircraft – but not the Me 262. Hitler glared at Galland.

"The rest of these," he said harshly, "I am going to *scrap*, in favor of a tremendous production increase in flak."

The word "scrap" hit Galland like a whiplash. He hardly heard Speer's desperate attempt to explain to Hitler that reducing fighter production did not mean that flak production could be automatically increased. Available explosives imposed a limit. General Kreipe cut the ground from under Galland and Speer by taking Hitler's side. Kreipe asserted that the 800 fighters of the reserve could easily fly 1,000 missions a day in the West. The Chief of the Luftwaffe General Staff had not recently been in France. Galland and Speer were not permitted to respond.

"I have no more time for you," said the Fuehrer, turning to his maps. The General of the Fighter Arm and the Minister of Armaments were thus thrown out.

The central fighter reserve was hurled in. Conditions in France were now far worse than in the first invasion days. Paris had fallen. The situation was irretrievably lost, with a highly fluid ground war complicating the transfer of a large fighter force to France. Pilots in unfamiliar terrain, minus cross-country flight experience, landed on airfields that were deserted, wrecked, or behind the rapidly advancing Allied armor. Communications were a shambles. Many aircraft had to be destroyed by their own pilots for lack of fuel upon landing in France.

Fighter units already caught up in the general retreat had to give up part of their invaluable ground crews to the paratroops. Many were left behind to fight as infantry. The pilots who got out, ferrying ground crews in their fighters where possible, were lucky to survive. German Army and SS units seized Luftwaffe transports at gunpoint and drove off, leaving the Luftwaffe men to destroy their own installations and await capture.

These days of dissolution would be burned into Galland's soul forever. Behind his imperturbable expression and manner, and the jaunty cigar, there churned a corrosive inner turmoil. His beloved Fighter Arm, the pride of his life, was being smashed before his eyes. This was happening less by the hands of the enemy than by the Fuehrer's crazy order to throw in everything. Telephone, radio, and teletype poured out a ceaseless litany of disaster.

The immense and dedicated labors of his staff in creating the reserve, all his hopes for the Big Blow and the production miracles of the workers who built the 800 fighters were simply being flushed down the drain. The fate of the inexperienced young pilots did not bear thinking about. Most of them were killed, wounded, or captured without having the slightest effect on the Allied breakthrough.

Galland searched desperately for some redeeming element in all this mindless ruin. All he could find was that the 800 fighters of the reserve had shot down 12 Allied aircraft in France before disappearing into the void. *A fighter force as large as that used in the Battle of Britain had vanished from the earth.* Galland told himself that he should quit. He'd had more than enough of Hitler and Goering. He would be better off fighting to the death in the air, finding an honest soldier's end. Then he thought about the peerless leaders, pilots, and crews in the Fighter Arm who trusted him. They were men whose advocate he had always been in high councils. He could not put from his mind the people in the cities. Fighters were still being built in droves.

He decided that he would stay until sacked. The Fighter Arm had to be rebuilt.

TWENTY-FOUR

Toward Dismissal

The Big Blow remained Galland's prime objective as he drove forward with another rebuilding of the Fighter Arm. Only the downing of 300-400 American heavy bombers in a day could possibly halt strategic bombing, through which Germany's war potential was now being systematically smashed. This final rebuilding of the Fighter Arm was a taxing and complex task.

Fighter units struggling back to Germany from their French ordeal had lost pilots, aircraft, unit cohesion, and much of their morale. Weeks of desperate operations, while they were hunted relentlessly in the air and on the ground, had taken a psychological toll to match the physical damage. Confusion reigned as every Gruppe operated with at least one squadron mixed into it from a different Gruppe. Operational efficiency was at an all-time low, despite the leadership of outstanding Kommodores in most Geschwader.

Returning to Germany also were the battered remnants of the once-vaunted IX *Fliegerkorps*, with which Hitler, Goering, and Peltz had intended to terrorize Britain. The brave crews in this formation would be remembered mainly for their heavy losses. Barely able even to find London, the vengeance mission of IX.*Fliegerkorps* turned out to be futile and wasteful, as Galland had predicted. Reduced now to fewer than 200 aircraft, IX. *Fliegerkorps* was virtually finished as a striking force, and its remnants were immobilized by the fuel shortage. Peltz himself nevertheless remained active, under the patronage of the Reich Marshal. The unsuccessful Assault Leader Against England was casting an ambitious eye on the Fighter Arm.

Galland persuaded Goering and the High Command to allow the Fighter Arm a brief respite, before again committing it in strength. Lowered morale was seriously reducing combat efficiency. The only remedy was a combination of rest, re-equipment, reorganization, and improvement of pilot quality, the latter within the strict limits imposed by available fuel. Galland faced a monumental task in rebuilding the Fighter Arm's striking power.

Fighter aircraft were now abundant. Saur had pushed fighter production to record heights in June and July. More than 1,000 pilots came out of the training schools in August. They were not the pilots of 1940 in terms of skill, but they were able to bring down bombers if properly employed and rightly led. Galland shaped everything toward his goal of mighty, concentrated blows against the daylight raids. All pilots and units were trained, prepared, and directed toward this end. Goering put his full authority behind the effort to refurbish the Fighter Arm and plan its tactical employment.

Galland stripped Austria and the southern front of fighters. The Italian front henceforth would be weakly guarded by two Gruppen of Me 109s, manned by Italian pilots and commanded by his trusted friend and old comrade, Colonel Eduard Neumann. For additional protection of key Italian targets, Galland planned to set up an Me 163 rocket fighter unit in Italy. 20 Italian pilots were actually brought to Germany for Me 163 training. Fuel shortages brought this idea to nothing.

By early fall of 1944, the Luftwaffe had in the West JG 2, JG 26, JG 27, and JG 53. For the defense of the Reich, JG 3, JG 300, and JG 301 were assigned. In the South were the two Italian Gruppen already mentioned. Resting and refitting in Germany were JG 1, JG 6, JG 11, and JG 77. JG 4, JG 7, and JG 76 were newly-formed Geschwader. The Eastern Front was left intact.

Once more Galland raised Gruppe strength to stretch out the thinning supply of experienced leaders, whose numbers had been further reduced in France. Gruppe strength now became 68 aircraft, including reserves. In each Gruppe, pilots were given 15 hours of additional training, specialized to Reich defense operations. JG 27 was duly moved from the West to central Germany for rest and refurbishment.

The assault fighters (*Sturmgruppen*) were exchanged with those in stronger Geschwader to increase overall efficiency. Squadrons mixed into strange Gruppen during the French debacle were left where they were to save fuel, which was now almost as precious as blood. The various Geschwader were simply re-constituted with their adopted squadrons. Graduates were now being turned out rapidly from the formation leaders' courses. Officers were in short supply. Galland broke this bottleneck by promoting 350 NCO pilots to war commissions, simultaneously and without ceremony.

By early November of 1944, the Fighter Arm had reached a strength of 3,000 aircraft, with about 2,500 operational. Creating this force out of the post-invasion chaos was probably Galland's major organizational achievement. Even his development of the central fighter reserve prior to D-day had been surpassed. This incredible resurrection brought into being a Fighter Arm nearly double the size of that available in 1943. The feat was accomplished despite U.S. strategic bombing attacks.

Correct tactical employment of this potential blizzard of fighters was absolutely vital. Tactical operations of this reborn force were accordingly well-rehearsed. Preparations were made to meet several different types of American raids, with all unit officers participating in the drills and exercises. In overseeing all this planning and training for the Big Blow, Galland continuously marveled at the sterling efforts of his staff. Without their dedication, this eleventh hour rebirth of the Fighter Arm would not have been possible.

The Assault Fighters (*Sturmgruppen)* again came to the fore, charged with carrying out massed attacks from the rear at close range. Development of these units had been largely aborted by the invasion and its aftermath. The fighter Kommodores had called for them again in the new build-up, with Goering's support. Galland was compelled to fall in with these developments, although personally opposed to the way in which the Assault Fighters were to be used.

Galland objected to the proposed repetition of a past costly mistake – fighters flying defensively. The combination of Assault Fighters (mostly heavily-armed Fw 190s) with a lighter escort of Me 109s and regular Fw 190s, was called a *Gefechtsverband.* Consisting of up to 300 aircraft in three or four Gruppen, these formations flew defensively, with the fighter escort to the sides and above the Assault Fighters.

Strict High Command orders required the Assault Fighters to attack straight to the bombers. Numerous and nimble American fighters were able to sweep in behind these Assault Fighter vees and shoot them down readily, since the German pilots refused to engage. They also would not flee. This brave adherence to orders was costly in German lives.

Galland's unimplemented recommendation to the High Command was to assign only half the light fighters as escorts, leaving the remainder free to tackle the American fighters. Such aggressive action would force the American fighters into defending themselves, instead of leaving them free to intercept and engage the German Assault Fighters. Despite the inherent drawbacks of the High Command's close-escort orders, considerable successes were scored by the Assault Fighters in September, October, and November. Success was dependent upon

MAJOR WALTER NOWOTNY (1920-1944)
"Nowi" was one of the finest of the fighter pilots in the Luftwaffe. The first to score 250 aerial victories, he was shot down while flying a Me 262 jet on 8 November 1944 after his 258th victory. He was one of Galland's favorites.

getting behind the American formations and making close-range firing sweeps through the bombers. Assembling these large Luftwaffe fighter formations nevertheless proved increasingly difficult. American fighter opposition continually grew stronger.

When Luftwaffe fighters became fewer after the withdrawal from France, the Americans went hunting for them. Strafing of Luftwaffe bases became commonplace. Any attempt to assemble a formation the size of a *Gefechtsverband* received immediate and aggressive attention from U.S. fighters. Since the majority of German pilots were not only inexperienced but also outnumbered in their own airspace, Fighter Arm morale continued to decline.

Galland analyzed the entire aerial situation as being determined by the impact of fighter on fighter. The Big Blow would be the Luftwaffe's last chance. Beyond that, only the massive employment of Me 262 interceptors, with the most experienced and successful pilots, could possibly affect Allied ascendancy.

When Doolittle sent a mighty bombing force of more than 1,100 heavies to Germany on 2 November 1944, most of them were assigned to synthetic fuel targets. Most important of these were the Leuna plants. Seventeen groups of American fighters escorted the bombers. A force of about 500 German fighters bitterly contested the skies over the Merseburg area. Assault

Fighters from JG 300 and JG 3 claimed 30 U.S. bombers downed, and 28 American fighters were shot down that same day. There were still too many American fighters in the sky for a Luftwaffe force of up to 500 fighters to handle.

Galland's forces suffered the loss of 70 pilots killed and 28 wounded. The newly refreshed JG 27 was heavily stricken with 25 pilots killed. The Leuna Company's synthetic fuel facilities around Merseburg were seriously damaged. As a large-scale interception, the Merseburg battle was not successful, but Galland's thinking was still directed toward a much larger scale of operations. He planned the mass commitment of 2,500 fighters, saturating the American defense and allowing the Assault Fighters through to the bombers. The essence of the Big Blow was tilting the all-important numerical advantage over to the Fighter Arm, suddenly and decisively, in a determined area and time.

Galland continued flying occasional combat missions against the strictest orders. This experience confirmed how vital it was to get Me 262 fighters for attacking the American heavies. None of the elaborate ploys and stratagems the Fighter Arm was now using to get Assault Fighters into contact with the bombers would be needed. The Me 262's great speed would allow it to simply break through the escort, and with its heavy armament, the Me 262 was an assault fighter par excellence. Fire from four 30 mm cannons could literally saw the wing off a B-17. The jet could outdistance its pursuers.

Reports from Test Commando 262 at Lechfeld, equipped with its own fighter control station and radar, continued to confirm the high promise of the Me 262 as an interceptor. Many Mosquito reconnaissance aircraft were downed. On the basis of these reports and results, and out of his own professional convictions, Galland continued his struggle for the Me 262 fighter. Not even the ruin raining down on Germany from the air prevented the irrational misuse of the world's fastest fighter.

While Galland pressed for the establishment of jet fighter units manned by the most capable aces in the Luftwaffe, the limited Me 262 production was scandalously misassigned. From Galland's viewpoint, there was something almost diabolical in supplying Me 262s to ground attack units, the Bomber Arm, and to research and testing stations unconnected with the Fighter Arm. Even Mistel composite pick-a-back experiments were authorized. All this went on while American bombers droned over Germany in their thousands.

Galland tackled Goering repeatedly about the Me 262. These interviews left Galland convinced that Goering knew deep inside that the Me 262 was a superlative interceptor. The Reich Marshal's personal political policy nevertheless remained firm. He would do nothing that would increase Hitler's disapproval or provoke his wrath. Goering had lost Hitler's confidence long ago. The Reich Marshal therefore deflected all Galland's urgent requests to get the Me 262 into squadron service without delay.

Even Germany's foes knew what a threat the Me 262 fighter posed. Allied air intelligence had comprehensive knowledge of all Germany's jet and rocket developments, information largely provided through the Ultra decrypting teams. As Germany's internal communications were disrupted, radioteletype was used increasingly as a replacement for landline. This fed the data directly to the Allies. Far remote from this high secrecy level, American fighter pilots formed their own opinions of the Test Commando Me 262s that occasionally slashed among them. They were in awe of the German jet.

One American fighter pilot, interrogated by the masterful Hans Scharff at Auswertestelle West, ridiculed the misuse of the Me 262 as a bomber. He further asserted that the USAAF was living in fear of the day when the Me 262 would fly against them in the hands of top German aces. Galland fell on this report like a gold nugget and showed it to Goering. The Reich Marshal was impressed, but politics came first. He remained loyal to Hitler's edicts. The report was widely circulated. Eventually, the American pilot's views were read by the only other man in Germany besides Hitler who could make Goering shake in his boots – Heinrich Himmler.

The gimlet-eyed SS Chief nurtured the idea that the SS should take over the Fighter Arm. He welcomed any evidence of Goering's incompetence. Himmler's standing with Hitler was high, while Goering was barely hanging on. Through the SS and Gestapo, Himmler controlled the internal security of Germany, so he held all the cards in any poker game with Goering. When Himmler put pressure on Goering to set up Me 262 fighter units, the Reich Marshal had to comply. Himmler would henceforth meddle continually in Luftwaffe business.

Galland's surprise was total when ordered early in October by Goering to set up an operational jet fighter unit. The Lechfeld Test Commando was to serve as a nucleus. Galland's joy was lessened when Goering insisted that the new unit be set up in western Germany, so that it could operate early against the Allied bomber streams and their escort. Galland recommended basing the jets in central Germany, where operations and tactics could be developed with less harassment from Allied air power. Goering rejected this recommendation. The new unit was based accordingly northwest of Osnabruck, at Achmer and Hesepe, with a nominal establishment of 40 aircraft, 12 officers, and 315 other ranks. Major Walter Nowotny, an Austrian and former Gruppenkommandeur of I/JG 54, was put in command.

Nowotny was only 24 years old, but had already won the Diamonds, and was credited with over 250 aerial victories. Galland considered him the best young ace in the Luftwaffe. He was entrusted now with a considerable and historic responsibility. The first operational jet fighter unit in the world was named Kommando Nowotny in his honor. Everything about the new unit was known instantly to the Allies through Ultra decrypts. Allied air intelligence ensured that Achmer and Hesepe were made hot.

Two squadrons of JG 54 were assigned to the specific operational task of protecting the jet airfields. They were kept busy. Allied fighters haunted the area, awaiting the golden chance to catch an Me 262 landing or taking off – their most vulnerable moments. These harassments added a nasty aspect to technical problems in preparing, servicing, and maintaining the Me 262s that were especially complex. At peak initial strength, *Kommando Nowotny* had about 30 jets, but technical difficulties lowered this number rapidly, despite excellent combat successes. Galland followed Nowotny's activities with passionate interest. The tally of jet downings kept rising despite the unit's low serviceability.

Combat successes with *Kommando Nowotny* crowned the efforts of Galland, Saur, Speer, Milch, and many others to get Hitler's approval for series production of the Me 262 fighter. The Fuehrer liked to hear of raiding aircraft being shot out of the sky by Nowotny's jets. On 4 November 1944, Hitler finally gave in. Even if he required that each fighter aircraft must be able to carry a 550-lb bomb in an emergency, his approval for jet fighter production was a landmark.

On 7 November 1944, as the refurbished Fighter Reserve approached final readiness, Goering summoned a conference at Air Fleet Reich HQ at Berlin-Wanssee. All high officers of the Fighter Arm and all combat formation commanders down to squadron level were ordered to attend. The Reich Marshal delivered yet another abusive diatribe against the Fighter Arm that was monstrous both in content and in length. For an incredible three and a half hours, Goering laid all the blame for Germany's woes on the "pussy foot fighter pilots.'" There were aces in the room who had flown over 1,000 combat missions. Others had been shot down five and more times, returning always to the shambles aloft. Many had bodies under their uniforms that were laced with wound scars. The burned faces of others were special combat badges that they would wear for the rest of their lives.

This was Goering's way of inspiring the most important officers in the Fighter Arm: his top leadership who would direct operations and the officers who would lead the formations into battle. All of them were too war-weary to be uplifted by abuse from a superior, and least of all from one who had concentrated with such visible effects upon the joys of the table. The consequences were unpleasant and destructive.

Galland heard and saw the open grumbling, protests, and disillusionment. Goering had cast an appalling spell of negativity over the assembly. Even that was not enough for the Reich Marshal. Recorded excerpts from his speech were distributed by his orders to all fighter units, with instructions that all pilots were to hear his speech. The incensed Galland left Berlin immediately. He flew to Achmer, where Nowotny and his commando were casting positive light, despite comprehensive technical difficulties.

Nowotny was full of enthusiasm for the Me 262. He described to Galland his tactical experience in closing with American bomber formations. Totally absorbed in the conversation, Galland did not notice how the hours flew. Hardly anything in life meant more to him now than proving this aircraft, and here was a top quality fighter pilot who was doing the job. They retired late, fired with hope.

On the morning of the next day, 8 November 1944, air raid sirens and barking flak signaled American bombers approaching. Nowotny took off with other commando pilots. Galland prayed for him to get airborne before American fighters found the airfield. Nowotny disappeared safely into the overcast. Radio chatter soon reported that he had downed a bomber, but had lost one engine to hits. He was trying to make it back, but was jumped by fighters. Close to the airfield, but out of sight above the overcast, Galland heard the firing. Then Nowotny's Me 262 came straight down to impact with a thunderous explosion.

Galland had seen many fighter pilots die, but this scenario shook him. Nowotny was not only a splendid young man, but in the vanguard of a new epoch. Standing beside Galland throughout the tragedy was his old boss from the commercial pilots' school at Braunschweig, Colonel-General Alfred Keller – veteran of an earlier epoch. Galland telephoned immediately for permission to move the remaining jet fighters to Brandenburg.

As Nowotny had made clear in their discussions, more pilot and crew training and experience in the ground handling of the Me 262 were all needed. Too much radically new technology had come too quickly for instant absorption. Kommando Nowotny was disbanded and became a cadre around which III/JG 7 was formed as the first successful jet fighter unit. Nowotny's few hectic weeks had been invaluable. Theoretical objections to the Me 262 fighter had been overcome. The allegedly poor maneuverability of the jet, the purportedly intolerable strain on the pilot, anticipated difficulties in accurate shooting, and the claimed inability of the Me 262 to fly in formations had been proved nonsensical. Jet fighter operations had been moved forward – at last.

Immediately after Nowotny's death, Goering called yet another meeting, this time in Berlin-Gatow. Goering's abusive 7 November speech had meanwhile been distributed on recordings to the fighter squadrons. Near-rebellion ensued as pilots reacted with rage to the Reich Marshal berating them as cowards. Not content with this morale-eroding mischief, Goering now brought together 30 leading Luftwaffe figures in a symposium. They were to develop proposals for rapid renewal of Luftwaffe striking power. In all of the Luftwaffe's colorful and sometimes bizarre history, there had been nothing quite like this event.

Goering opened the symposium, calling for proposals to refurbish the whole functioning of the Luftwaffe. Recommendations were to be made for the transfer or retention of various officers in highly responsible posts. Everything was up for wide-open discussion.

"Permission is hereby granted" said Goering, "for criticism of anything in the Luftwaffe, or anybody ... except me. Since I have been appointed by the Fuehrer, there is no need to discuss or criticize me or my office.'"

Goering appointed Peltz as symposium leader. Despite the scope of the proposals being demanded, effectively a top-to-bottom revision of Luftwaffe organization and appointments, Goering had not invited the Chief of the Luftwaffe General Staff. Similarly omitted was the Chief of the Operations Staff. Goering's revision of the Luftwaffe was being undertaken mainly by a parliament of high-ranking young officers, who were mostly combat veterans. The majority were unballasted by either maturity or long military experience. Rivalry between Fighter Arm and Bomber Arm officers ran strongly.

Studying the assembly while Goering detailed its alleged purposes, Galland could not believe that anything constructive could develop from such a symposium. There would be friction and acrimony. Goering's kindergarten was there in force, including Peltz, Kraft von Delmensingen, the young von Brauchitsch, Diesing, Storp, and Knemeyer. The Fighter Arm's mainstream thinking was represented by Galland, Trautloft, Luetzow, von Maltzahn, Roedel, and Streib – all high-quality fighter leaders.

A third group represented the Bomber Arm, with Baumbach, Harlinghausen, Schubert, and Mueller in attendance. The fourth group of fighter officers, mostly of lesser stature than those backing Galland, gave proceedings a somewhat awkward political dimension. While they were brave and decorated fighter aces, they tended to believe that more political indoctrination of the troops would improve Fighter Arm morale and efficiency. That set this small group of officers aside from those who stood with Galland.

Bomber Arm officers immediately proposed a scheme of strategic bombing, so unrealistic as to be absurd. Galland faced each day the tactical and strategic crux of the air war: Allied air supremacy in German skies. Such air supremacy precluded any strategic bombing by the Luftwaffe. Fighter Arm officers advocated what seemed to them a realistic program. They wanted a greatly enlarged fighter force to regain air superiority over Germany, as a fundamental first step. All other Luftwaffe activity was to be subordinated to this goal.

The second group of fighter officers proposed to redeem the situation by a massive infusion of Nazism into the Luftwaffe. All formation leaders should attend immediately a four-week indoctrination course. This group did not address problems of personnel, armament, or operations.

While stenographers frantically wrote down the proceedings in shorthand, for Goering's study and historical purposes, chits were passed out for recommendation or dismissals, transfers, and appointments. Tempers boiled and nerves frayed as old grievances erupted. Galland perceived that Goering's minions were determined to have him removed. Not one of the purposes for which the meeting was allegedly convened was ever achieved. Discipline was undermined. The Luftwaffe High Command was understandably outraged and slighted, even though Generals Stumpff, Schmid, and Weise had been present at the symposium. Mistrust and confusion were rife. Morale was weakened. Galland emerged from the infamous "Luftwaffe Parliament" convinced that his days as General of the Fighter Arm were numbered. The Big Blow therefore became of supreme importance to him. He would end his tenure with a major victory.

LT. GENERAL JOSEF KAMMHUBER
Josef Kammhuber became General of the Night Fighters and led the enlargement of the whole night fighter program. He was banished to Norway in November 1943 and headed Luftflotte 5 there until the end of the war. Kammhuber became the first Commander in Chief of the new Luftwaffe.

On 12 November 1944, Galland notified Goering and the High Command that the reconstituted Fighter Arm was ready for action. An incredible resurrection had been achieved. Eleven massive *Gefechtsverbände* were poised under the command of I.Fighter Corps. JG 2, JG 26, and JG 53 in the West, under II.Fighter Corps, would harry the heavies on the way in and on the way out as weather permitted. Airfields in western Germany were ready to support fighters flying multiple missions. 80-100 night fighters would attack crippled heavy bombers staggering to Swiss or Swedish sanctuary.

All that was now necessary was for a major American formation to head for central Germany on a clear day. Galland estimated that the Big Blow would bring down between 400 and 500 heavy bombers for the loss of about the same number of German fighters. Perhaps 150 German pilots would be lost. He expected that the material damage to the Eighth Air Force would be accompanied by an equally powerful blow at morale – a psychological shock. 4,000 to 5,000 aircrew lost in one mission would shake even the Americans. The weather remained maddeningly unfavorable, and the Fighter Arm waited.

Unknown to Galland, just two days before he pronounced the Fighter Arm ready for the Big Blow, Hitler had conceived a big blow of his own. The Fuehrer decided to make a massive surprise thrust through the Ardennes. Momentum would be sufficient to carry his armies to Antwerp. Hitler envisioned another Dunkirk.

To dupe the Allies into thinking that the German Army was preparing defensive operations along the Rhine near Cologne, the code name "Watch on the Rhine" was chosen. Everything was organized in deepest secrecy. Rigid security excluded even Galland from knowledge of the plan until early December. Two Panzer armies, with two more armies in support, were moved into position by night under total radio silence. Only top commanders and staff officers knew the secret. Motorcycle dispatch riders carried the most vital orders, to preclude Allied eavesdropping. The same weather that was delaying Galland's Big Blow also imposed an Allied reconnaissance blackout on German Army concentrations.

Sudden large demands were made for transfers of fighters to *Luftwaffenkommando-West*, the rump command left in the West after retreat from France. Galland and others involved were told that the Allies were mounting a major offensive. Large fighter forces were therefore required for tactical support of the defending German armies. 1,200 of the Big Blow fighters were now moved to the Vechta-Arnhem sector in late November.

A controversial and unwelcome presence amid Ardennes preparations was Major General Dietrich Peltz, a brilliant bomber pilot and Goering favorite. He emerged as C.O. of II.Fighter Corps in the West. This political appointment outraged the experienced Fighter Arm Kommodores. They deemed Peltz completely unqualified for fighter command. Events would soon prove them correct. Over 2,000 aircraft were eventually involved in the Ardennes thrust. Galland was stripped of his Big Blow forces, so arduously assembled.

Allied intelligence and the Allied commanders were this time completely deceived. The radio blackout had silenced Ultra. Attack by the German Army at dawn on 16 December 1944 took the Allies by surprise, throwing them into confusion. Galland's realization that the force he had built was being committed to a nonsensical, all-or-nothing gamble, caused him to follow events with anger and fury.

Despite hundreds of ground attack and fighter sorties, the Panzers ran out of fuel after by-passing Bastogne. Their fuel never came. As soon as the weather cleared, Allied air power came instead, in all its awesome might. Air superiority was rapidly wrenched from the Luftwaffe. "Watch on the Rhine" was over, famous in history only as one of the war's greatest surprise attacks.

LT. COL. HEINZ BÄR
Bär scored 220 victories and was the top ace flying the Me 262 jet with 16 victories. His warm personality bolstered his expert professionalism and resulted in making him one of the most liked. He died in a light airplane crash in April 1957.

Painfully gone forever was Galland's vision of the Big Blow. Fighter losses in the West rose steeply, due largely to the inexperience and ineptitude of Peltz and his staff in commanding fighter operations. These losses were for no return. Crowning the Ardennes disaster was a climactic brainchild of Peltz and Hajo Herrmann, Operation "Groundplate" (*Bodenplatte*). This desperation strike was to be launched against a dozen Allied airfields in Holland and Belgium.

Over Galland's vigorous objections, low-level surprise attacks were planned. After two delays, the strike went in at 9:20am on New Year's Day of 1945. Most of the participating German pilots had been trained for Big Blow operations against bomber boxes. They were minus the special expertise required for ground attack. Results were accordingly erratic. Some Allied airfields suffered heavily, and others escaped almost unscathed. RAF losses were 144 aircraft destroyed and 84 damaged. The USAAF lost 84 destroyed and 62 damaged. This one-time loss of aircraft could be easily absorbed by the Allies. Peltz gave the Luftwaffe a truly Pyrrhic victory, because the damage to the Fighter Arm was mortal.

237 German pilots were killed, missing, or captured. Many of them were downed by their own flak. 2 Kommodores, 6 Gruppenkommandeure, and 10 squadron commanders were lost in Groundplate, irreplaceable formation leaders. They all went in one day. For Galland, it was like seeing a fine rapier used to cut sugar cane, an appalling example of misuse. Fighters were a deadly yet delicate instrument of war, and Peltz had proved himself even more inept in their handling than his patron, the Reich Marshal, in 1940. Galland would always regard Groundplate as the final stab in the back for the Fighter Arm.

At New Year of 1945, Galland found himself significantly changed. All the heart to lead the Fighter Arm had gone out of him. Only his immense fortitude brought him through the mindless waste of the reconstituted fighter force. Small men in high rank who were now machinating for his dismissal hardly even bothered to conceal their scheming. The monumental damage to the Fighter Arm even seemed to bring them perverse pleasure. Galland had always stood firm for the Fighter Arm in the past, based on his own professional competence combined with the loyalty of the fighting pilots and their leaders. Now he wanted out.

Ready to relinquish his heavy responsibilities, he wished to return to a fighter unit as a honorable soldier. He yearned for the primal simplicity of a fighter pilot's life, the black-and-white of battle aloft. Girding himself for his terminal struggles in the increasingly political ant hill of Luftwaffe command, he knew his dismissal was imminent.

TWENTY-FIVE

Suicide and Salvation

The slaughter of irreplaceable combat leaders in the reckless Bodenplatte gamble on New Year's morning climaxed for Galland a period of almost unbearable frustration. Bizarre command arrangements blocked his knowledge from application to the defense of Germany. These strictures also denied him the power to prevent gross wastage of the Fighter Arm. Machinations against him by Bomber Arm leaders who sat at Goering's table became steadily more open. Tapping of his telephones and other intrigues entered his strained life as a wearying nuisance that he could not eliminate. Capping it all was the imminence of his own dismissal, which precluded effective action.

The young general was like a man with his head locked in the stock of a guillotine. Certain of his end, he was uncertain of the precise moment at which the blade would fall. No rational officer could have wished to preside over the disintegration everywhere evident at New Year 1945, but still there were those who lusted for Galland's job amid the advancing shambles.

Galland's staff soon became aware that certain clerical workers who were transferred by higher authority into Galland's office were actually spies. A close surveillance of his daily routine and activities was being conducted. Galland's office and home telephones were both tapped. His coming dismissal created an anxious and oppressive atmosphere in his office.

Goering's kindergarten was especially eager to see Galland ousted. The forceful and outspoken young fighter general had stepped on many toes since 1942, and lesser men often reacted with ill-concealed jealousy to Galland's success, fame, and high rank. In Goering's circle, the young sycophants asserted that Galland had "too much influence in the Fighter Arm" – their perverse evaluation of the loyalty he received from his troops.

Several officers were rumored to be replacing Galland, but hardly anyone knows their names today. The truth in the clear light of history is that Galland's replacement could be little more than a caretaker, as the Luftwaffe descended to final collapse. No officer in sight could ever fill Galland's shoes, or remotely rival his inspirational image among the troops.

The fighting pilots and crews seemed to draw limitless energy and power from Galland. Materializing among them on whirlwind and often surprise visits, he was like a Martian god incarnate. Huge sunglasses spreading across his battered nose, his crushed cap at the rake and always with a long Brazil in his hand, he exuded leadership and drive, will power, and personal force. When this figure departed, trailing cigar smoke, he left behind among his men a psychic electricity that brought out their best.

This leader had grown up with the Luftwaffe from its birth, and became not only its youngest general, but also its *enfant terrible*. He had, without knowing it, etched himself into aerial history for all time. Only Goering among all Luftwaffe personalities would survive as well in public memory. Galland's numerous mistakes as General of the Fighters hardly counted against the sound measures he took and the wise counsel he gave. Little wonder is it that in Germany's terminal throes, when her best officers were most needed, there was so much hesitation and uncertainty about replacing General Galland.

Galland had his confidants and friends at Hitler's HQ. Through these officers, he learned that *Reichsführer* Himmler of the SS was suggesting to Hitler that he appoint Colonel Gordon Gollob as General of the Fighter Arm. Himmler's meddling in Luftwaffe business was an escalating irritation to Goering. Himmler had ambitions regarding the Luftwaffe, and one of them was to give SS divisions their own jet fighter units. *Kommando Nowotny* had been set up earlier by Goering in response to Himmler's prodding for jet fighters to go into action.

Himmler's suggestions to Hitler about Gollob soon resulted in the Fuehrer's tackling Goering, and eventually the Reich Marshal ordered Galland to prepare a detailed special report on the proposed successor. Galland compiled the report as ordered. Gollob had originally been a Galland protegé, and as a brave and capable fighter ace he had been the first pilot in history to shoot down 150 aircraft. He had also won the Diamonds to his Knight's Cross, only one of nine fighter pilots to do so in the entire war

Galland had proposed his then-protegé to be Kommodore of JG 7, a significant promotion. Galland later proposed him for an even more responsible post, that of Jafü 5 at Bernay. Since mid-1942, the Personnel Department of the RLM had depended almost entirely on Galland for such recommendations concerning the Fighter Arm. From the Jafü 5 appointment onwards, the relationship between Galland and the officer proposed as his successor began changing. Galland's conclusion in his 1945 report was that his proposed replacement required supervision in a responsible post. Goering was anything but responsible in the way he handled this report.

Adroit at setting subordinates upon each other like dogs, the Reich Marshal had given a destructive demonstration of this talent by staging the Luftwaffe Parliament, at a time when unity was imperative. Goering now summoned Galland's proposed successor to Karinhall and read out to him selected excerpts from Galland's report. Gollob was incensed. By such incredible and malevolent mischief did Goering himself dissipate what little remained of the Luftwaffe's once legendary morale.

Several bomber pilots favored by Goering had also been in the running for Galland's job, but when Hitler suggested Gollob to Goering, the Reich Marshal quickly agreed. Hitler wanted a new Supreme Commander for the Luftwaffe, as well as a new fighter general, and Goering knew this. For months the Reich Marshal had been in total and sometimes abusive disfavor with Hitler, and would do anything to placate his master. Galland was finally out.

Goering now ordered the dismissed Galland to Karinhall, and regaled him with another tedious monologue. This one laid out the reasons for Galland's dismissal. As the Reich Marshal droned on, silencing Galland's efforts to Justify his actions, one thing emerged clearly: *Goering had no coherent idea of why he was axing his young general.*

Superficialities, excuses, trivia, notions, lies, and fantasies were interwoven in a rambling discourse. Moderate in his tone for once, Goering stumbled to the end of his "reasons" for the dismissal. The Reich Marshal knew in his core that he had been served with competence and dedication, for years and through terrible times. Suddenly, Goering's facade just fell away, and the true man spoke:

> "I am much obliged to you, General Galland, for all your good advice, and your services in your post. Thank you for all you have done. As soon as you have had a vacation, I will put you in an important, leading position."
>
> "I am sorry, Herr Reich Marshal, but I cannot accept such a position."
>
> Goering's blue eyes widened.
>
> "Why not?"
>
> "Considering the influence of the officers who have urged my dismissal, sir, and the imminent collapse of the Fighter Arm, I wish only to be an Me 262 fighter pilot."
>
> "I could put you in command of ..."
>
> "Thank you, Herr Reich Marshal, no! I do not want to command anything. I just want to be a simple combat soldier doing my duty. That is what I request of you, sir."

Goering waved him out, insisting that a decision would be made after Galland's vacation. The young general felt cleaner when he left Karinhall, but four grueling years could not be waved away with the Reich Marshal's baton. The Fighter Arm was in his blood.

He feared in his heart for the brave fighting pilots whose fortunes and fate he could no longer influence in the slightest way. He also knew that a storm was brewing in the Fighter Arm, with himself at its eye. His forthcoming dismissal had been common knowledge down to the humblest NCO pilot and the ground crews. Goering's rumored intention to pitchfork one of several famous bomber pilots into Galland's post was viewed by the pilots and combat leaders as the ultimate insult – eclipsing all the other Goering slurs through which they had suffered. Loyalty and allegiance to Galland were well-nigh universal in the Fighter Arm. Military forces anywhere in the world have always sought to evoke this kind of spirit.

Luftwaffe fighter pilots were enraged as the Me 262 fiasco continued. Priority assignments of jet fighters as bombers, and to hybrid formations designated KG (J) under Peltz, caused anger and frustration. The fighter pilots rightly regarded the Me 262 as the weapon for which they had waited amid hails of tracer, while their comrades died by the hundreds attacking enemy heavy bombers.

Bad weather operations were still continually ordered, with heavy and needless losses to weather rather than enemy fire. These losses disgusted the experienced Fighter Kommodore. They knew that these futile operations were urged by the Goering kindergarten, as part of the "advice" they gave the Reich Marshal. Goering's prestige within the Fighter Arm had sunk to an all-time low, but he continuously worsened the situation by harping on fighter pilot cowardice.

These massive currents of discontent and mistrust, washing away morale and efficiency, had brought some of the Kommodores and Division Commanders to Galland's office before he was dismissed. He was fully familiar with their grievances, but he was on a tightrope himself. All he could do was listen sympathetically. His responsibilities precluded his becoming directly involved with the highly decorated aces and old comrades who sought his ear and his aid in their extremity.

The Kommodores were seeking an audience with Hitler. They intended to ask the Fuehrer to make the drastic changes that they deemed essential to the restoration of morale and combat effectiveness. Removal of Goering as Luftwaffe Supreme Commander was at the top of their proposals.

Before going to Hitler, these disillusioned officers on 13 January 1945 sent Colonel Guenther Luetzow and Colonel Johannes Steinhoff to see Generaloberst Ritter Robert von Greim, the senior World War I fighter pilot. Von Greim was a

Hitler favorite, and the Fuehrer was already considering him as a replacement for Goering. Von Greim's advice and influence were sought by the frustrated fighter leaders.

The World War I ace listened to Luetzow and Steinhoff. The next day, von Greim called General Karl Koller, Chief of the Luftwaffe General Staff, and reported on the interview. According to Koller's diary, von Greim was sympathetic to the honest search of the Kommodores for a way out of their difficulties, but calmed them down and advised them to see Koller first.

Koller was already aware of what was afoot. He had received informally on 13 January 1945, Major Gerd Müller-Trimbusch, who was Galland's operations officer and practically his Chief of Staff. Without Galland's knowledge or authorization, Müller-Trimbusch had asked to discuss Fighter Arm problems with Koller on a man-to-man basis, all rank being temporarily set aside.

As a result of Müller-Trimbusch's indiscretion, which the Kommodores would regard as treachery, Koller was aware that the combat leaders wanted to brief Hitler without going through Goering. The Kommodores all knew Goering's ways. The Reich Marshal would block them from seeing Hitler.

Koller understood the situation. Loud and bitter talk resounded through the Fighter Arm that Goering should retire. Koller nevertheless correctly emphasized that enforced retirement of Goering could only be regarded as mutiny, when he saw Steinhoff and Neumann on 17 January 1945.

Koller now informed Goering, in writing, of the potentially catastrophic foment in the Fighter Arm. He suggested that the Reich Marshal receive a Kommodores' delegation for frank discussion of their proposals and requests. Koller gently inferred that if Goering could not straighten things out, then perhaps the Reich Marshal could secure an audience with the Fuehrer for the Kommodores.

Goering immediately saw Steinhoff and Neumann at Karinhall. Their visit and views convinced Goering that he had a major crisis on his hands. The Reich Marshal thereupon called a meeting of all available Kommodores at the House of Pilots (*Haus der Flieger*) in Berlin. Colonels Luetzow, Steinhoff, Roedel, Trautloft, and Neumann; Lt. Colonels Graf, Bennemann, and Priller; and Majors Michalski and Aufhammer were available to attend. Galland was not invited. Trautloft and Luetzow nevertheless kept him informed on events.

Luetzow had assembled all the Kommodores' requirements into a comprehensive proposal. He was appointed by the combat leaders as their spokesman. All the officers present were highly decorated aces, but Luetzow was something much more. A man of high intelligence, outstanding leadership gifts, and noble character, Luetzow was not over-awed by the Reich Marshal's rank, reputation, or charisma. A tall man of distinguished lineage, the blood and iron in *him* contrasted starkly with Goering's decadence. The Reich Marshal may have been his superior officer, but Luetzow was the superior human being. Everyone present knew that.

Luetzow read out the proposals. All causes of friction and inefficiency in the Fighter Arm were covered, including Galland's dismissal. The Kommodores stated that Galland had the trust and confidence of the entire Fighter Arm. They requested that he be retained as General of the Fighters.

Vigorous arguments ensued for the next four hours. The Me 262 and its assignment to the Bomber Arm, new tactics, new operational controls, and the unacceptable presence of Bomber Arm officers in command of fighter units were all ventilated. Forthright objections were voiced to Goering's incessant allegations of fighter pilot cowardice. Goering got the worst of these encounters. The Reich Marshal's staple response was to blame Galland, infusing the arguments with further heat. Goering became steadily angrier as Luetzow applied inexorable logic, finally asking Goering to resign. Crimson-faced and boiling with rage, Goering blew up.

"This is *mutiny*" he bellowed. "There are going to be arrests!"

Flinging out of the room, Goering turned at the door and glared back hatefully at the upright and honest Luetzow.

"You, you, you ... I'll have you shot!"

Thus ended the Kommodores' Revolt, but bitter feelings remained high. Arrest warrants were issued that evening for Galland and Luetzow. Goering had kept insisting all through the revolt that Galland was the instigator despite the Kommodores' denials. Ordering Galland's arrest was a serious step. General Karl Koller persuaded Goering not to proceed this way against his former fighter general or against Luetzow, for the good of the Luftwaffe.

Luetzow was ordered to leave Germany within 48 hours. He was to take over Colonel Eduard Neumann's post as *Jafü* Italy. Luetzow was forbidden to have any visitors in Italy or to communicate with Galland or any of the "mutineers." This was *Reichsverbannung* – banishment from Germany. The Swords to the Knight's Cross hung at his throat – Germany's second highest decoration for valor.

Galland reported next morning to General Meister, now Chief of Luftwaffe Personnel. From this officer he learned of Goering's rage against him for "masterminding" the Kommodores' Revolt. Galland made it clear to Meister that he had neither initiated nor participated in the Kommodores' actions. Their wish to approach Hitler directly was also their own. Galland further emphasized that he had already been dismissed and was without any position or influence in the Fighter Arm.

Orders issued to Galland required him to leave Berlin within 12 hours, notify General Meister of his destination, and to stay under house arrest wherever he went. He chose the Giant Mountains, and left Berlin for Oberwiesenthal. All fighter units received a Goering telex: General Galland had retired for health reasons.

With their former boss removed from office and under the disgrace of house arrest, Galland's entire staff wished to resign simultaneously in protest. While Galland personally appreciated their loyalty, he would not condone such an action. On the contrary, he pledged his staff to continue in their posts and give of their best. The well-being of the Fighter Arm had to be placed first, especially continued staff support of the combat pilots who were fighting and dying each day.

Galland's dismissal and arrest nevertheless left almost all work in his office effectively paralyzed. First there was the emotional shock and a wave of resentment. Then his staff was appalled as swarming security agents and others disloyal to Galland rummaged through official files. A search was on for evidence of Galland's "corruption." Alleged evidence of gambling and the private use of official cars was pounced upon. Such trivia were accompanied by openly bandied assertions of Galland's "disloyalty to the Nazi Party." The young general's well-known apolitical stance was reflected in Fighter Arm leaders who were notoriously unconvinced by Nazi propaganda. Only one officer ever to reach the status of Kommodore had swallowed and spouted the Nazi Party line.

While all this energy was being poured into incriminating, humiliating, and degrading Galland, proper direction of the dying Fighter Arm steadily declined. Germany's civilians were wide open to both day and night attack by ever-mounting numbers of bombers. General Doolittle was dispatching upwards of 1,000 heavy bombers every day that weather permitted. More than 300 heavies winged in daily from the Fifteenth Air Force in the south. Additional hundreds of Ninth Air Force medium bombers roamed over the western Reich with impunity. The RAF made the nights hideous.

Amid this pervasive misery of the German nation, the Supreme Commander of the Luftwaffe was urgently seeking a scapegoat for the escalating terror from the skies. The Reich Marshal remained a politician to the last gasp. He figured that he could lumber Adolf Galland with all the blame for the Fighter Arm's collapse. Goering intended to do such a thorough job of blaming his dismissed fighter general that his own political hide would remain intact.

Goering quickly appointed an investigating commission that he could control, consisting of Chief Luftwaffe Judge von Hammerstein and two other general officers. The SD, or *Sicherheitsdienst* – the secret service of the SS – went into vigorous action. They arrested Major Rolf Meinardus, Galland's adjutant, and threw him into jail to await trial. Close surveillance was placed on Galland. The SD brutally grilled his trusty batman, Sergeant Benno Reiske, and forced him to spy on his chief in the mad scramble for evidence.

All of Galland's staff, from the decorated combat veterans down to the secretaries, were intensively questioned. Through his former staff and other sympathetic friends in high posts, Galland learned of Goering's plan to assemble an air-tight case against him. On top of defeatism, he would be charged with serious breaches of duty. Collapse of the Fighter Arm would be sheeted home to him in an ostentatious legal proceeding. General Galland would end in national disgrace.

When Galland returned to Berlin, his personally-owned car was confiscated. His every move was watched. His telephone was tapped. The SD investigators turned up some people who had heard Galland say that the military situation was hopeless. Doubts were raised by the SD about his political views. Although he had avoided politics all his life, his relationship with Monica and the anti-Nazis in her circle came in for scrutiny. Tremendous energy was expended in digging out of Galland's past anything that could be used against him in his projected trial.

KRUPINSKI JOINS JG 26
Transferred from the Eastern front to support the "Battle of the Bulge" in January 1945, "Count Punski" reports to Colonel Josef "Pips" Priller who survived the war and had 101 victories. Krupinski also survived and had 197. On the left is Major Gotz (63 victories) who became Kommodore of JG 26 on 28 January 1945.

The young general was operating almost completely in the dark. He had only snippets of information, sneaked to him by friends at risk of their own liberty. The entire apparatus of the SD and the Nazi Party was being used to frame him. The odds against him were long. He had no means of fighting back in the political arena, where he was a novice. Galland the fighter was at bay. He thought fast. He had not dodged hostile lead in hundreds of combats, nor suffered wounds, nor worn the Knight's Cross with Diamonds, to end up being humiliated in a kangaroo court owned by Hermann Goering. There would obviously be no justice. He was driven into a corner.

He considered escaping to the Allied forces, but after six years of war, he knew he could not live with that course of action. Goering would have him convicted *in absentia*. His parents and surviving brother would be called to account. He could not escape, nor could he stay.

His only option was the ultimate way out – suicide. Galland disclosed his intention to shoot himself that night to Monica and a small group of his friends. He even mused grimly that Goering might mouth lardy platitudes over his grave, as the Reich Marshal had done with Udet. His decision to kill himself left Monica appalled. She took action.

Risking her own personal freedom, and after many difficulties, she finally made contact with Albert Speer, late in the night. She told him of Galland's intentions. Alarmed and concerned for the young general, Speer went personally to Hitler, despite the late hour. The Fuehrer knew nothing about Goering's legal vendetta against Galland, but he did know Goering. He took immediate action.

Hitler promptly called in the SD in the middle of the night and demanded a briefing. He quickly saw through Goering's plan to make Galland into a national scapegoat. Hitler would not tolerate such an action.

"This nonsense is to be canceled immediately" he ordered.

Before Galland could shoot himself in the small hours of the morning as planned, he received two highly improbable phone calls. One came from Ernst Kaltenbrunner, head of the dreaded Reich Security Service. The bulky and much-feared Kaltenbrunner, whose orders had snuffed out many lives, smoothly explained to Galland that there had been a mistake in his case. That was being put right. General Galland was therefore, please, not to kill himself.

A few minutes later came a second calming phone call. This time it was Gestapo Chief Heinrich Müller, no doubt rousted from bed at Hitler's orders. Again it was smoothly emphasized that there had been a mistake. Another plea was courteously made that he not commit suicide, since there was now no need for such an act. Galland counted himself lucky never to have had prior dealings with these two sinister personalities. He put the phone down after talking to Müller, incredulous that both of them were intent on saving his life. They even assigned a young Luftwaffe officer to watch over him until dawn.

In the morning, a telephone call from Hitler's Luftwaffe aide, Colonel Nicolaus von Below, summoned Galland to see the Fuehrer. At the Chancellery, von Below, in the name of the Fuehrer, advised him that the pending trial and all attendant matters had been canceled. Galland was relieved. He was also irritated by the needless ordeal that Goering had forced him to endure.

"The Fuehrer is still fond of you, General Galland" said von Below. "He did not want a public scandal at this time such as your trial would create."

Goering's investigation promptly collapsed. Major Meinardus was released from prison, although Goering vindictively transferred him to the paratroops. Galland was summoned to Karinhall two days later. The Reich Marshal was flanked by stacks of thick files created by his investigation.

Goering made many accusations based on these data. Galland was forbidden to respond. The Reich Marshal was grasping at straws. With typical dishonesty and cant, he asserted that because of Galland's past services to the Luftwaffe, he had ordered the investigation terminated.

Goering added magnanimously that he had also canceled the pending trial. The Reich Marshal was unaware that Galland already knew, through von Below, that his trial and all other proceedings had been quashed by Hitler's personal order. Galland stood before his old adversary, imperturbably listening to one more Goering lie.

The Reich Marshal then told him that Hitler had withdrawn his prohibition on further combat flying for Galland. The Fuehrer had directed that Galland was to form a small unit of approximately squadron strength and prove that the Me 262 was a superior fighter aircraft. More was not to be expected of Hitler.

More? What more was there for a German fighter pilot doing his duty than to be given an Me 262? Galland's spirits rose. Even though he realized that his superiors expected him to be killed – with fate replacing legal judgment – he could not suppress his excitement. *He would lead a jet fighter unit*! His stony expression creased into a slight smile.

There was still more. Goering told him to select the pilots he wanted, and to send him their names. Glaring at his one-time protegé, the young man he had promoted from Kommodore of JG 26 to General of the Fighters, Goering made him a gift.

"If you want them, you can have that dismissed Colonel – that Steinhoff – and that mutiny leader Luetzow. I certainly don't want them." Goering despised both these officers.

Galland swelled with elation. Jet fighters and the best pilots in the Luftwaffe to fly them with him. His wild excitement resembled what he felt in combat, but as in combat he kept a cool head. He pointed out to Goering the awkward situation with his successor. He added that he could only form his jet squadron if were under independent authority. Goering immediately agreed.

"Your unit will not be under your successor. Nor will it be under the command of any Air Fleet, Division, or Fighter Corps" said Goering. "You alone will decide where and how operations are conducted. You are also not to come into contact with any other fighter or jet fighter unit. I'll issue orders to that effect."

In the dying days of the Fighter Arm, here at last was freedom to act as he alone judged fit. He could now implement personally what he had urged on his superiors since he first flew the jet in May of 1943. Hitler's action that had made this final throw possible was not born of any benevolence, but rather of the certainty that the young general would die in combat. The embarrassing "Galland affair" would thus come to a clean end. Combat hazards did not deter Galland. He would gladly take his chances aloft as always.

Rising from the depths of despair and the brink of self-destruction, he had soared in a few days to new heights of hope and opportunity. Never again would he see the doomed Fuehrer, but it was the strangest twist of Galland's life that Hitler's personal, vigorous intervention had taken him from suicide to salvation. Few indeed there would ever be who could make that claim.

TWENTY-SIX

Back to Battle

According to Sir Isaac Newton, what goes up must come down, and the law applies to pilots as well as planes. The General of the Fighter Arm was back down to a squadron commander early in 1945 – the same assignment he held during his Spanish Civil War service eight years previously. A lieutenant at that time, he had risen to Lieutenant General. His piston-powered biplanes of 1937 were replaced now by a squadron of the fastest fighters in the world – Me 262s powered by twin turbojets. All in all, for Adolf Galland it had been a hell of a ride, a career having no counterpart in the armed forces of any other belligerent power.

He was probably now the most enthusiastic squadron commander in the Luftwaffe, for everything he had pleaded for during the bitter years was suddenly granted to him in miniature and under his personal control. A combat command after years of frustration was like a redemption. A hectic week followed his "appointment" as a squadron commander.

He went to officers he knew well on the Operations Staff and in the Quartermaster-General's office to begin organizing his unit. Aircraft, pilots, ground staff, spare parts, equipment, motor vehicles, and a long list of other items had to be procured and assembled. *Jagdverband Galland* had to be created from absolute zero.

Initially established at Brandenburg-Briest, the new unit expected to be able to draw upon the nearby resources of JG 7, also equipped with the Me 262. JG 7 was Steinhoff's last command before his dismissal by Goering. Despite this connection, Steinhoff found that JG 7 was reluctant to assist. The Reich Marshal had issued orders that JG 7 was not to come into contact with the new jet squadron.

Galland's requests for pilot transfers from other units were blocked and delayed by his successor. Complaints by the new jet squadron commander to General Meister's Personnel Department went unheeded. Galland was not going to be denied his final throw by this kind of silent sabotage. Needing "juice" to clear the blockages, he telephoned Colonel von Below at Hitler's HQ. Through the highest channels Goering quickly got the message, just as he had over Galland's proposed kangaroo trial.

Immediate orders were issued by Goering to fill up Galland's unit with the requested pilots and material forthwith. Word of this elite "turbo" unit had swept through the Fighter Arm, igniting new enthusiasm. Successful aces vied with each other to experience once more the half-forgotten thrill of air superiority. Sensing the historic nature of this jet squadron, they wanted the honor of such an assignment. Captains, Majors, and Colonels requested to fly as ordinary pilots.

Trautloft at the 4th Division of Fighter Pilots Schools had already sent Galland some of his best instructors, aces with extensive combat experience, when the Personnel Office was blocking other transfers. More pilots came to the new squadron on their own initiative, disdaining all higher authority. Most of them did not even stop to check with the Personnel Office. Some rode to Brandenburg-Briest on bicycles. Legendary pilots began gravitating to Galland's squadron.

From the Russian Front came Major Gerd Barkhorn, credited with 300 victories. Major Walter Krupinski, the fabled "Count Punski," with 197 victories, was coaxed out of the hospital, as were Erich Hohagen and "Bubi" Schnell. Guenther Luetzow returned from exile in Italy to find fellow "mutineer" Johannes Steinhoff, credited with more than 170 victories, in charge of conversion training and operations. Lesser-known aces from the war's first days added their experience and skill to Galland's roster of pilots.

Galland had requested the transfer of Captain Erich Hartmann, the most successful fighter pilot in the Luftwaffe, with nearly 350 victories. Hartmann made check flights in the Me 262, but his wish was to return to his old comrades in JG 52 on the Eastern Front. His request for transfer back to JG 52 was granted, but led to the personal disaster of ten years in Soviet captivity for Germany's greatest ace.

In the history of aerial warfare, there had never been such an elite fighter squadron. The Knight's Cross could have served as its badge. Almost all the pilots had won this decoration or its higher orders. Their commander was a Lieutenant General. Steinhoff and Luetzow were both Colonels. Heinz "Pritzl" Baer, a Luftwaffe legend with 220 victories since 1939, was a Lieutenant Colonel. Krupinski, Hohagen, and Barkhorn were all Majors. These aces and their illustrious squadron commander had almost 900 victories between them. When the numerous captains, lieutenants, and Sergeants who were aces were included, the squadron became the only one in the world whose personnel had downed over 1,000 aircraft!

Ranks rapidly blurred into insignificance, as the most distinguished ace leaders in the Luftwaffe did the work of junior officers and NCOs in ordinary units. The designation JV 44 (*Jagdverband 44*) was chosen by Galland and approved by Goering. The Reich Marshal was not told that the double F in forty-four was a play on words – a pilots' jibe at the Fuehrer, single F. The two F's symbolized in their own circle that they were now going to try two Fuehrers, since twelve years with one Fuehrer had got them nowhere. The 44 designation also harked back to the highly successful J/88 of the Condor Legion, where Galland had gone into combat for the first time. He hoped that JV 44 would be half as good as J/88, for that would be significant success.

Chief of the Luftwaffe General Staff Karl Koller asked Galland to transfer JV 44 to southern Germany, to provide at least some protection for the Me 262 factories. General Koller suggested Lechfeld. After a rapid check, which disclosed overcrowding at Lechfeld air base, Galland chose Munich-Riem. Plenty of room was essential for successful Me 262 operations, including dispersal space as an anti-strafing measure. Transfer went forward against tremendous Allied opposition. Bombers were roaming in droves far into Germany every day. Hundreds of long range American fighters hunted their adversaries and strafed airfields wherever they were found.

These realities stood starkly against high-level German charades that continued as though it were the spring of 1940. Highly-placed people still thought in terms of promotions, organizations, and appointments. As JV 44 was coming to combat readiness despite incredible difficulties, General Kammhuber was ordered back from Norway and his command of Air Fleet 5. Goering appointed him as his Commissioner for Jet Fighter Operations. This was Goering's last attempt to counteract the SS, made in response to Hitler's appointment of SS General Hans Kammler as Commissioner for Jet Aircraft Op-

JV 44 PILOTS WOLF DOWN LUNCH
With no time for formalities, harried pilots of Galland's JV 44 unit eat their lunch. 1945 was a time of near desperation for the jet pilots.

erations. Goering saw this correctly as Himmler's takeover stratagem.

Galland the squadron commander was asked by Kammler and Kammhuber for his advice on what actions should be taken on the jet fighter situation. Galland's suggestions were:

1. Terminate "Blitz Bomber" missions by the hybrid KG (J) 51 using the Me 262, and concentrate on fighter missions.
2. Disarm KG (J) 6 and KG (J) 27, and give their Me 262s to KG (J) 54 and JG 7, which were already operational. At the same time, stiffen these Geschwader with the most successful fighter pilots from all fighter wings.
3. Provide immediate jet-conversion training for the most successful fighter pilots from all Gruppen.
4. Assign all available towing tractors, tank trucks, and ground support equipment to the jet fighter units.
5. Stop all other Me 262 operations and tests, in favor of fighter missions.

Galland held that these steps would keep almost three powerful Me 262 Geschwader, as well as JV 44, operational until the final days of the war. By concentrating this force geographically, possibly 150 jet fighters could have been put up daily against the daylight bombers. This would be a relatively formidable air defense, right to the last. Events would soon prove, furthermore, that the 5cm R4M rockets were especially effective against tight formations of U.S. heavies. This was the last recommendation Galland made to higher authority in his military career. There is little doubt of its soundness, within the limits of conditions then prevailing.

SCHALLMOSER ON THE CARPET
Eduard Schallmoser, an Me 262 pilot in JG 7 gets a reprimand for ramming an American bomber for the second time. Kommodore Heinz Bär scolded him for losing one of their few remaining Me 262s. The laughing blond is Erich Hohagen who had 55 aerial victories.

ME 262 JET PILOTS
The ex-General of the Fighters and Colonel Lützow stride towards their new jets at Munich/Riem in late April 1945. Both are very serious at the moment.

Past patterns were repeated, No action along the recommended lines was ever taken. Physically achievable despite difficulties, a final fierce stand by massed jet fighters required agreement among too many disintegrating commands. Such a final resistance was never mounted by the Luftwaffe. Already being described as the Squadron of Experts, JV 44 carried the torch.

The inspirational force that had previously emanated from Galland's HQ to the entire Fighter Arm, was now concentrated on one squadron. Spirit and morale were unquenchable. Prodigious efforts by all personnel pushed the squadron through complex organizational difficulties. On 31 March 1944, JV 44 formations took off from Brandenburg-Briest on their first ferry operation. Led by Colonel Steinhoff, this dawn sweep covered 300 miles in 42 minutes. All landed safely at Munich. The Squadron of Experts was a reality.

Operational difficulties seemed endless. Jet fighters were revolutionary. With them came technical, tactical, and logistical problems of an entirely new character. These problems had to be tackled and solved amid fighter strafings and frequent bombing attacks. Allied air intelligence knew through Ultra intercepts that Germany's downfallen fighter general was going back into battle. Life was accordingly made as hot as possible for the Squadron of Experts.

Highly decorated aces with their Knight's Crosses and jet fighters were also now armed with shovels. Each man was made responsible for preparing and maintaining his own foxhole. All of them made the breathless sprint from the cockpit of the world's fastest fighter into these shallow sanctuaries – including General Galland. No more Reichs Chancellery, Luftwaffe HQ, or the Fighter Control Centers with their glittering officers and luminous displays of enemy activity. Now it was a foxhole at Riem, with bomb splinters and bullets clanging and pinging on its improvised steel lid.

Luftwaffe radar and tracking facilities, as well as communications, were approaching their final breakdown. Galland therefore had to depend mainly on the limited-range radar installed at JV 44's own small command post at Feldkirchen for making interceptions. Pilots and dedicated crews toiled feverishly amid the shambles, and JV 44 slowly became airborne against the Allies. Usually dispatching a *kette* of three jets, JV 44 pilots rarely returned without downing Allied aircraft.

Around 10 April 1945, Galland was ordered to meet with Goering at the Reich Marshal's Obersalzburg villa near Berchtesgaden. The sorely-tried commander of JV 44 half-expected another blast of blame, or more of Goering's dilettantism. The Reich Marshal received the surprised Galland with an almost exaggerated courtesy. This civilized and paternal side of Goering had not appeared to the young general for a long time.

Goering questioned him with great civility about the first victories of JV 44. The Reich Marshal then surprised Galland further, pursuant to these questions and answers, by fully acknowledging the Me 262's value as a fighter. Goering's admission was hedged with politician's reservations, but he admitted that Galland had been correct in urging full-scale use of Me 262 fighters against the Allied bombers. The war seemed strangely remote as they talked this last time amid the peaceful grandeur of the Obersalzburg.

Goering was too intelligent not to know that he was personally doomed. Galland guessed that with his extreme courtesy and civility the Reich Marshal was trying to make amends. Goering stumbled and waffled to the brink of an outright apology, but in the end could not cross the ethical gulf between the upright young general and his corrupt self. This awkwardness was especially evident as Galland departed.

"Someday, Galland, you will realize what I have done for you by dismissing you as General of the Fighters. Now you return to combat, as you always wanted. I envy you. I only wish that I could myself fly into combat beside you. Auf Wiedersehen."

There was a final handshake. Galland never saw the Reich Marshal again. Heading back to his embattled mini-command, Galland reflected on the obstruction and wasted lives that had stemmed from Goering's unwisdom. He had been a terrible antagonist to face for years.

Goering would soon be telling his captors and Allied interrogators how fortunate he had been to have had General Galland's expert advice. He would omit from his confessions and interrogations that he had joined with Hitler and Himmler in sending Galland to JV 44, in the full expectation that his troublesome young general would be killed in combat.

JV 44 kept operating. Allied bombers kept going down from their attacks. JV 44 took heavy casualties of its own. When engine failures or Allied hits took out one of the Me 262's jet engines, performance fell below that of a P-51. Most JV 44 casualties and losses were suffered during landings, takeoffs, and taxiing, when the jets were especially vulnerable to fighter attacks.

Pilot losses rose. On 18 April 1945, Galland led into the air what was probably the most elite formation in Luftwaffe history: himself, Gerd Barkhorn, Macky Steinhoff, Klaus Neumann, Lt. Faehrmann, and Sergeant Eduard Schallmoser. All aircraft were carrying a full load of 24 R4M rockets. Steinhoff's fighter dropped one wheel into a poorly patched airfield crater. With insufficient speed to become airborne, the stalling aircraft crashed in a pall of fire. Out of the inferno reeled the stricken Steinhoff, clothes smoldering, his face seared. The burns would mark him for the rest of his life. Galland had lost a close friend and his staunchest aide in organizing and operating JV 44.

BLACK FOREST HIDEAWAY
The Me 262s, as well as many other types of aircraft, sought refuge from the marauding allied fighters and bombers by concealment in the forests alongside airdromes and autobahns.

Six days later, on 24 April 1945, "Franzl" Luetzow downed a Marauder bomber near Augsburg in the morning. That same afternoon he flew his last mission and went missing west of Donauwoerth in Allied territory. His actual fate remains unknown to this day. Neither his aircraft nor his body were ever found. In Galland's eyes, Luetzow was the quintessential fighter leader, brave, honest and capable. He had become passionately devoted to proving the Me 262 fighter in the final weeks of his life.

Despite his long experience on every front, Luetzow had almost despaired in his efforts to close correctly with the bomber formations he was intercepting. The jet fighter's speed made all their past reactions and actions out of time in the new era. Virtually all the JV 44 aces experienced this difficulty to some degree, until they forced themselves to think and act faster. Late though all this had come, it was the fiery proving of all that Galland previously said about the unsuitability of bomber pilots to fight with the Me 262. Few bomber pilots ever became successful fighter pilots even in piston-powered fighters. Jet fighters belonged in the hands of only the best aces.

The day after Luetzow's death, American and Russian forces met on the Elbe river. Galland called his pilots together for one last talk.

"Militarily speaking, the war is lost. Our action here cannot change anything, but I shall continue to fight because operating with the Me 262 has got hold of me. I am proud to belong to the last fighter pilots of the Luftwaffe. Only those who feel the same are to go on flying with me."

Two pilots asked to be excused from further flying duties for family reasons. They were allowed to remain with the unit. Everyone else wished to go on to the end. As long as Allied bombers came over to attack Germany, JV 44 would fight back.

Installation of wooden rails on the Me 262 permitted up to 12 R4M rockets to be carried under each wing. These 5cm projectiles were spin-stabilized and could be launched from beyond the effective range of defensive fire from the bombers. A hit with such a single rocket usually destroyed any heavy bomber.

Flying in a rapidly scrambled formation with Eduard Schallmoser, Walter Krupinski, and Klaus Neumann, Galland made his first interception with R4M-equipped jets near Landsberg. A tight formation of Martin Marauders opened fire on the jets. Their tracer could be seen curving downwards when Galland released a salvo of twenty-four R4M rockets. Two bombers were mortally hit, one exploding in mid-air, the other spinning down minus its tail.

Galland's talent as a marksman had been carried into the rocket era. Forty years later, Krupinski would describe his witnessing of Galland's first air-to-air rocket attack in one word, "fantastic."

All this vindication of technical viewpoints and tactical advice expressed for years was occurring in the twilight of the Luftwaffe. Theory and argument became old history, as in Steinhoff's words, "The rockets roared among the bombers like a shotgun into a flock of ducks." The Lord of Battles had not smiled on Adolf Galland for many moons, but his war ended with at least an amiable grimace. JV 44 won its way to aviation immortality.

OBERST JOHANNES STEINHOFF
"Mackey" Steinhoff, a very intelligent and forceful leader scored 176 victories, 6 with the Me 262 jets. He was flying Galland's wing on 18 April 1945 when his Me 262 disintegrated on takeoff. Steinhoff was badly burned but survived the war and became C-in-C. of the new Luftwaffe. He passed away on 21 February 1994.

Albert Speer had made Galland aware that it was his intention to capture Germany's top leaders in April, 1945. He asked the former fighter general to join him. Galland agreed. When the time came, his assignment was to capture Goering. Nothing came of this plan because of the unexpected rapidity of Germany's final collapse, which included Goering's abortive effort to take over from Hitler in the last week in April. This resulted in Goering's arrest by the SS in the villa where Galland had bid him farewell scarcely two weeks earlier. Speer could only therefore alert Galland to prevent any possible escape by air that Goering might attempt.

Galland's last aerial battle took place on 26 April 1945. Again it was a formation of Marauder bombers, with six Me 262s under Galland's command making an interception near Neuburg. Closing from astern with at least a 200 mph speed advantage over the bombers, the distance diminished like lightning. Galland armed his four 30mm cannons and took the safety catch off his rocket switch.

His tenseness over the interception and his high excitement made him forget the *second* safety catch fitted to the rocket switch. In firing position and with perfect aim, the great marksman pressed his rocket switch. Nothing. No whooshing sound, no twenty-four trails of fire and smoke, no hits. In a fraction of a second, he lined up a Marauder, and his four cannons flamed the rearmost bomber. Attacking another at the head of the formation as he raced rapidly through, Galland saw heavy hits on the bomber as American bullets began thudding into his jet. Passing closely above his target at high speed, he could not judge if the bomber was finished.

Turning away from the bombers to the left, he was preparing to observe the final effects of his attack on the last bomber he had hit. Machine gun fire suddenly hailed down on his Me 262, shattering his instrument panel, cracking the canopy, and slamming into his right knee. More hits smashed into his right turbine with mortal effects, and the faring swung open to trail in the wind. The lethal fusillade hammered into his left turbine, which began running out of control, but at least it was running.

An American fighter pilot that he would identify and meet decades later had caught him with a blast of fire. His stricken Me 262 was still flying, and he did not want to risk parachuting and landing as a corpse. Jet pilots were regarded as valuable targets by the Allied commanders, although most Allied fighter pilots disagreed with the principle of shooting at parachuting enemies. Galland took no chances, and went diving down in his soggy Me 262 through a cloud layer to evade his tormentors. Spotting the autobahn leading to Munich, with Riem airfield ahead to the left, he nursed his battered fighter back to base with his radio dead.

Seconds later he came whistling downwind to the field, his one damaged engine running wide open. Right at the field boundary he had to cut this single turbine completely. Pouring smoke out behind him, he began easing his stricken aircraft down. Intent on getting home in one piece, and minus radio, Galland had not seen that Riem was under attack by strafing Thunderbolt and Lightning fighters.

Excitedly intent on beating up JV 44's base at low altitude, the American fighter pilots did not see the incoming jet in their midst in time to fire on Galland while he was landing. Down he came on an already rough field, to land on a nosewheel whose tire had been shot out. Jarring, jolting, and rattling along at a too-fast 140 knots, Galland the hunter became the hunted, as around him rockets and bombs roared and thundered.

Wounded knee hurting abominably, he sprang out of his Me 262 like a jack-in-the-box. Hurling himself into a bomb crater, his thoughts amid the hellish din ran his long struggle for the jet fighter past him in seconds. Moments before, he had been flying the world's fastest fighter. Now he crouched bleeding in a crater. The rise and fall of the Fighter Arm were contained in his plight, no less than in his person.

Galland's two victories in this final battle were supplemented by three more scored by his fellow pilots. They lost no pilots in the encounter. Galland's wrecked Me 262 might have been a serious loss a few weeks previously, when he had to scrounge for fighters. Now it could be replaced readily from dozens of jets that were donated to JV 44 by units that never should have been equipped with them in the first place.

Research units, test commandos for night fighters and ground attack, reconnaissance, and bomber outfits landed almost daily at Riem and handed over their Me 262s. Soon the field and its environs were sheltering more than 70 of the revolutionary machines. The wounded Galland felt like a beggar suddenly admitted to a banquet.

For him, there would be no more war. Splinters in his knee could not be removed from the joint capsule, and his leg was therefore put in plaster. With both Steinhoff and Luetzow gone, Lt. Colonel Heinz Baer assumed direct operational command. The unit soon had to be moved to Salzburg airport, with a small detachment flown out to Innsbruck. Galland followed these moves from the Luftwaffe hospital at Bad Wiessee, and then from a private villa at Tegernsee. From this latter makeshift HQ, he maintained contact with Baer and JV 44 at Salzburg by telephone, Fieseler Storch courier plane, and motorcycle dispatch riders.

Immobilized by his wound, Galland reflected upon the most constructive and purposeful means of concluding the war for JV 44 and its personnel. Strong rumors had circulated in Germany, originating with Hitler, that there were mortal differences between the western Allies and the Soviet Union. The belief was widespread that it was only a matter of time before the west and the world revolution of Soviet Russia would be at loggerheads. Some said there would be armed conflict immediately, with prostrate Germany as the battlefield.

Galland had brought JV 44 to operational status from nothing and created a functioning model of a modern jet fighter unit. All nations would inevitably acquire jet fighters. Why cast away, he reasoned, the decisive advantage of keeping intact an operational jet fighter unit in which all essentials had been worked out? These aircraft, pilots, and ground crews were not only formidable despite the small size of JV 44, but formed a cadre around which larger units could be built rapidly.

Whatever jet combat might become in the future, JV 44 was a microcosm of that tomorrow. Galland reasoned that his squadron had a military value beyond price at the dawn of a new era. If the west and the world revolution were to clash militarily in the near future, JV 44 could play a role out of all proportion to its size.

At Tegernsee on 1 May, he accordingly prepared in secret his attempt at a special surrender of JV 44 intact, for such later use as the U.S. authorities might determine. Despite the imminent end of the war, Nazi fanatics still abounded. Such people would execute Galland immediately if they heard of his surrender offer to the Americans. Caution was also warranted because even some decent Luftwaffe officers might not understand the scope and direction of his reasoning. May of 1945 was a chaotic and desperate time. The full story of JV 44's end has not been told until now, with the perspective provided by four decades.

In careful confidence, Galland commissioned Major Wilhelm Herget to fly by Storch from Tegernsee to Schleissheim. Herget was an outstanding night fighter ace who had transferred to JV 44, and a fine officer. With Herget went Galland's personal aide, Captain Hugo Kessler. These officers made contact with HQ of XV Corps, U.S. Army.

Galland's special surrender effort came to nothing. The original documents in the Appendix tell the story. U.S. field commanders had no authority to make exceptions to the unconditional surrender orders issued by General Eisenhower's HQ. Those on the spot lacked the necessary insight into air power to appreciate the prize they were offered.

When it seemed that surrender in the air for JV 44 might eventuate, with the jets airborne without ammunition and their landing gear lowered, word of this possibility galvanized the 64th Fighter Wing of the USAAF. Every available P-47 was to be put into the air for this dramatic airborne surrender scenario. Galland rejected this course. Captain Dick Perley, meanwhile, was awaiting re-assignment at 50th Fighter Group HQ when the electrifying teletype came through. He was immediately put in command of a pick-up section of P-47s that had been operating in close support of the U.S. 7th Army.

Reading the teletype, Perley felt the hair raise up on the back of his neck. A whole squadron of German jets was nothing to fool with, especially if they took off *with* ammunition. In appalling weather, Perley's section milled around in the soup, while a sort of blow-by-blow on the jet surrender rasped in his earphones. "They are getting ready to take off" came the word. "Be alert." Perley strained his eyes through his streaming windshield. No Me 262s.

The attempt at intact surrender of JV 44 was to have a startling echo for Perley, 38 years later and half a world away in Los Angeles, California. Adolf Galland was the 1983 Thanksgiving dinner guest of North American Rockwell executive Ray Heman and his wife, Lesley Lewis. The former Captain Dick Perley, now a greying and sixtyish electronics executive, was also invited by the Hemans. They knew he had been a WWII fighter pilot in Europe and might enjoy meeting the famous German general.

While Perley knew Galland's name well, he was unfamiliar with the details of his career. Perley casually opened conversation by harking back to May of 1945, when "there was some jet outfit in Salzburg that wanted to surrender." Now it was the hair on Galland's neck that stood up. "That was my unit" he said, eyes wide with astonishment. The two former foes ended their encounter marveling at the smallness of a world that had brought them face to face after nearly 40 years.

WAITING TO SURRENDER
Heinkel He 162 pilots standby at Lech/Holstein to surrender themselves and their new fighters to American troops. They are discussing what the future may hold in store for them. The date: 8 May 1945.

Perley had sought Galland in the "soup" near Salzburg in 1945, and found him in the sunshine of Los Angeles in 1983. In the spirit of Thanksgiving, they were both grateful that they had never been required to exchange fire. Exchanging reminiscences in peace was better.

Failure to accomplish the special surrender of his jet squadron was the war's last bowl of bitter rice for Galland. His attachment for JV 44 was intensely personal. He hated to let go of what had been created amid the Luftwaffe's terminal ordeal by the individual sacrifices of JV 44 personnel. Inexorable and charged with emotion, the moment came when he was compelled to issue his last significant order as a Luftwaffe general.

"Blow up all JV 44 jet fighters on the ground."

Just as they had built JV 44, unit personnel placed the charges and destroyed the Me 262s for which they had been willing to give their lives. A cause of gnawing regret at the time, destruction of JV 44 was actually Galland's definitive severance from a military era that was ending.

TWENTY-SEVEN

Prisoner of War

An armed American sentry at his door in Haus Kathrein at Tegernsee was final proof that World War II was over. Galland had gone down fighting, consumed by his passion for the jet fighter. His realism had for years made him aware of looming defeat, and he had tried to prepare himself psychologically for this moment. Finally falling into enemy hands nevertheless still packed a smashing emotional punch.

All the sacrifices, hopes, battles, and labors of the terrible recent years had shrunk to nothing. Before his mind's eye passed the long parade of fighter pilots lost since 1939 – expended like ammunition. Now they were only names in Luftwaffe records and phantoms in the memories of their devastated families. The tragedies of his own family, with the battle deaths of his brothers Wutz and Paul, were repeated a millionfold throughout the German nation.

Guarded now by American soldiers, he had seldom felt more downcast. The encumbering plaster on his leg further contributed to his dejection. He was nevertheless aware of his rank and position and put the best possible face on his captivity. Outwardly his usual imperturbable self, he was inwardly consumed by wretched feelings inseparable from defeat.

He was taken to Bad Tolz in an ambulance for his first interrogation. Never again would he ride in the Luftwaffe staff cars that for years had whisked him from one important meeting to the next. Months of interrogations began. At Heidelberg he met his first capable interrogator, Major Max van Rossum-Daum, USAAF. Trained in his task and with fluent German, Van Rossum-Daum was C.O. of the Air Prisoner of War Interrogation Unit (APWIU). This able officer quickly established rapport with Galland and obtained for him, through the USAAF command, confirmation of his last two aerial victories over the Marauder bombers. A friendship developed between Van Rossum-Daum and Galland that was to endure for the rest of their lives.

As an important prisoner, detailed interrogation was scheduled for Galland. Flown to England on 14 May 1945, he was taken to Camp 7 at Latimer, on the estate of Lord Chesham in Buckinghamshire. A leading Allied interrogation center, Latimer had Wing Commander King of the RAF as its C.O.

The Chief American Interrogator was "Major Emery," a pseudonym for Major Ernst Englander USAAF. Among his assistants was "Captain Todd," the pseudonym of Captain John M. Whitten. In this man, the former General of the Fighter Arm found one of the greatest friends he would ever know. Difficult months lay ahead. The worst of it all would be softened by Whitten's humanity. The two men were to examine, analyze, and set down all Galland's experiences. Rare personal accords developed during these labors.

Whitten was temperamentally and educationally well suited to the Galland interrogation. His work became an important contribution to air history. This book has also taken its main direction from Whitten's massive interrogation monograph, on which the two men worked for many months. The intelligent Whitten was much more than just an expert interrogator, with qualities that inspired Galland's confidence.

Jack Whitten is the particular kind of decent human being that springs so often from American service families. Born into a U.S. Navy family in 1920 with all-American lineage on both sides back to Puritan pioneers, he had a world-wide schooling. Finishing head of his class of 441 at the University of Maryland in 1941, his major was German. This put him on an interception course with Adolf Galland.

After drafting in 1942, basic training, and Officer Candidate school, he was sent to the Interrogation Training Center at Camp Ritchie. There he was turned into a POW interrogator and order of battle expert. His talents soon led his superiors to throw him in with the real POW "toughies" that nobody else could break. Shunning violence, he broke them all, in his own words, "by boring them to death."

Jack Whitten makes light of himself in this way, but like Galland, he is a man of wit and humor. Educated, cultured, and kind, and minus any rancor toward a beaten foe, he had everything he needed to persuade a prisoner. He also had character, something Galland valued in both friend and foe. When the former fighter general arrived at Latimer, Whitten had already been interrogating Luftwaffe prisoners there since September of 1944. For nine months prior to that, Whitten had been interrogating German POWs in the U.S.

Known as the Combined Services Detailed Interrogation Center (CSDIC), Camp Latimer authorities had already interrogated numerous Luftwaffe fighter pilots. Galland's reputation had preceded him. His new hosts received him with respect, for his pilots had all described him as a "very good man." When the Latimer C.O. reported this to Galland, it injected some warmth into his barren world. His worldly goods were now contained in two suitcases and a few cigar boxes, the latter the last of his free wartime stogies.

Since Allied interest in jet fighters remained high, Galland was first interrogated about the Me 262, as were other pilot POWs who had flown the jet. A special report on the Me 262 was compiled at Latimer. Famous American aces like Colonel David Schilling and Colonel John C. Meyer came to interview Galland and other Me 262 pilots. Whitten interpreted for these early meetings with senior USAAF officers and found that Galland always made an excellent impression, pilot-to-pilot and man-to-man. He was clearly an officer who knew his profession thoroughly.

"Galland was modest, confident, and extremely well-spoken," Whitten recalled. "His answers to complicated questions were 'ready to be set in type.'"

Whitten's interrogation experience made him adroit at gauging a POW's capacities. In Galland he knew quickly that he was dealing with a man of exceptional mentality. Only the sharpest mind can think through, and then speak out in perfect form, the answers to complex technical questions as Galland consistently did. Whitten's interest in Galland grew accordingly. Although Whitten was also interrogating dozens of Luftwaffe intelligence officers at this same time, to compile other major reports, he welcomed the order to prepare a major report on Galland.

Before all this, and toward the end of May, Galland was contemplating his fate in his small Latimer room, when the door suddenly swung open and admitted Field Marshal Erhard Milch. Both were astonished and momentarily speechless. Milch had been through hard times, including severe physical abuse by his British captors. Suddenly the Field Marshal found himself facing the young general he had always trusted without regret. Out of the man who had built the Luftwaffe for Goering came a veritable verbal torrent.

Galland had assumed all along that his room had hidden microphones, which it did, and Milch was oblivious to his warnings that they were being overheard. While the Field Marshal rambled about their mutual experiences, Galland stepped around thumping the thin partition walls. He was told later that this countermeasure defeated the eavesdroppers.

Milch's presence had one serious drawback. He kept "borrowing" cigars. Without any means of paying back the cigars he "borrowed," Milch's impact on Galland's meager stock became dismaying. Field Marshal and fighter general came to a trade agreement. Milch had a new hunter's pipe, and both could get tobacco. Galland got the pipe, and Milch continued his inroads into the remaining cigars.

About two weeks later, Milch was transferred to another room. When he packed his kit, he reached over and took the hunter's pipe from beside Galland's bed without saying a word. As Milch closed the lid of his suitcase, the hunter's eyes were on him and the air became charged.

"That wasn't our agreement" said Galland.

Milch hesitated. Galland's gaze in such circumstances acquired a searing quality. Milch opened his suitcase and gave back the pipe. That same hunter's pipe is displayed today in Galland's trophy hall at his home in Oberwinter, near Bonn.

During his early confinement in England, Galland was held for a while at the Beaconsfield interrogation center. He was roommate there to General Franz Halder, former Chief of the Army General Staff. Sacked by Hitler in September of 1942, and in a concentration camp since the attempt on Hitler's life in July of 1944, Halder knew plenty about the excesses of the Nazis since 1933. He was now casting himself in the role of a victim of Nazi politicians. Galland had experienced a chilling brush with Nazi methods during his dismissal ordeal.

The professorial Halder now detailed for him some of the high intrigue and ruthless policies of Germany's political leadership. The elderly general gave Galland a crash course in what the Nazis were really like. Such things as Hitler's intention to exterminate the Polish nation in 1939, in which Halder had acquiesced, left Galland stunned.

Halder's stories dragged Galland down out of the clean blue sky. The airman's war that he had fought with honor had no correspondence with the revolting labyrinths that Halder described with firsthand knowledge. He began wondering what he had been fighting for – willing even to sacrifice his life. For Germany? The embittered Halder was not talking about the Germany of Westerholt, hospitality, decency, and goodwill.

When he next sat down with Jack Whitten to begin their joint account of his life, Galland first interrogated Whitten. From the American he received basic confirmation in outline of what Halder had told him. His devotion to the Fighter Arm, and the immense range of his responsibilities, had separated him from politics – which he disliked in any case. His capabilities alone had carried him through his military career. Other young German generals at Latimer, who had not risen to the command hierarchy, had similar rude awakenings at this time, according to Jack Whitten. They learned for the first time, for example, about the unconscionable murder of Anglo-American POWs in the "grand escape" at Stalag III.

Intensive work began on the Galland report, uniting the two men through their common wish to make the report as complete as possible. Whitten went through all the secret Air Ministry Intelligence Summaries circulated during the war. He selected material that could be included in the report after confirmation or amplification by Galland.

Detail in this material on Luftwaffe organization, tactics, developments, equipment, personnel, and all other aspects was incredibly comprehensive. Galland was dumbfounded. Why had the Allies wanted to know all these things? More was in these reports on the Luftwaffe than he had himself known. Whitten also thought it strange that the Allies had been able to obtain such detail on the Luftwaffe. He attributed it largely to expert espionage.

The Air Ministry material that Whitten and Galland were using was actually compiled from sanitized Ultra decrypts. All linkage to mastery of German war ciphers was eliminated from this material. Such carefully edited information could be circulated to levels below the exclusive upper circle that received pure Ultra – Churchill, Eisenhower, Doolittle, and other high commanders.

More than 30 years later, when the Ultra secret was made public, both Galland and Whitten realized whence came the comprehensive detail that had astounded them in 1945. Ultra material is still being released. Many years will pass before most of the material enters the public domain, and some of it will be hidden forever. Enough is available now to convince Galland that the Allies continuously looked over the shoulder of the General of the Fighter Arm.

Around 9 July 1945, Galland was taken by an RAF interrogator to visit the RAF station at Tangmere. In a two day stay, he met many high Fighter Command officers and numerous British aces. All of them were anxious to talk to the Luftwaffe's most famous ace and general. Since Galland had held the Luftwaffe post most closely approximating their own AOC Fighter Command, he was especially intriguing to pilots who had flown against him.

At the gate of the Tangmere base, who should come stumping out of a group leaders' conference but the onetime Stationmaster of Tangmere himself, Wing Commander Douglas Bader. Here again was a full circle. Bader now had the cigars and Galland was the prisoner. Bader was spick and span, and Galland was the rumpled one. Bader concerned himself with Galland's comfort, even though he had to make a fast departure next morning – just as he had done in France four years previously. From this short second meeting, a warm friendship flowered that endured until Bader's passing in 1982.

By mid-August the Galland report was completed, officially known as ADI (K) 373/45. As a rare privilege, Whitten was permitted to sign this report with his true name over the typed name of the Latimer C.O., Wing Commander King, RAF. The report ran in a series of installments in Air Ministry and USAFE Intelligence Summaries. Galland would later use material from this book for his memoirs, published a decade later.

POW ADOLF GALLAND
Exiting from a B-17 which flew him from England to Kaufburen, Galland was surprised to see a cameraman. Galland had just undergone interrogations at Latimer in England and was returning to Germany for further questioning by American Intelligence Officers.

On 24 August 1945, a B-17 Fortress took off from Bovingdon loaded with the very people it had recently been trying to bomb. Field Marshal Milch sat in the bombardier's seat. General Galland sat with Colonel Werner Baumbach, the famous bomber pilot and onetime General of the Bomber Arm. Colonel Edgar Petersen, the last C.O. of the Luftwaffe's Rechlin Test Center, was also aboard, with another dozen German pilots and Jack Whitten.

Over the roaring engine noise, excited reminiscences were exchanged as they flew over Germany in perfect weather. Each city had its memories. A refueling stop in Schweinfurt unleashed a flood of recollections. When the B-17 touched down finally at Kaufbeuren in Bavaria, it had been a remarkable flight.

At Kaufbeuren they were quartered in a large, three-storied villa, the Landhaus, outside the grounds of the county mental hospital. Commanding this facility was Major van Rossum-Daum, Galland's first competent interrogator after the surrender. Staff studies on fighter control were to be carried out here, in an atmosphere much more relaxed than at Latimer. There were no guards. The POWs were asked to give their parole and none violated this undertaking.

A week after arrival at Kaufbeuren, Whitten and Galland drove to Hohenpeissenberg, beginning the search for his guns that would end in California nearly forty years later. Galland was shocked to learn that his cache of prized shotguns and hunting rifles had been looted by a Lt. Colonel of the U.S. Army. Whitten readily learned his identity, but in the climate of those times, nothing could be done.

Further disappointment awaited at Tegernsee, when they visited Haus Kathrein shortly afterwards. All of Galland's personal belongings and papers had been looted from his final command post-cum-hospital by Counter Intelligence Corps personnel. His Knight's Cross with Diamonds and Award Certificates were gone – souvenirs that nobody could show to this day without embarrassment. His files of Tactical Regulations, invaluable to the current APWIU project and worthless to anyone else, had also been plundered.

APWIU prisoners were officially denied mail privileges. Whitten and his fellow officers nevertheless allowed Galland and the others to write letters, and mailed them privately in town. Incoming mail was diverted around officialdom by having it all received by Colonel Walter Dahl, late of the Assault Fighters as a Kommodore, who had been released and resided at nearby Bad Wörrishofen. Families of POWs were traced and re-settled near Kaufbeuren.

The Luftwaffe's last General of the Ground Support Arm, Colonel Hubertus Hitschold, was among Galland's fellow prisoners. His captors found him to be a fine man. They obliged Hitschhold by locating his wife, bringing her to Bad Worrishofen, and letting him spend the weekend with her. Such favors were appreciated by POWs living in an emotional desert. Trautloft was located in Munich and put on the APWIU payroll as a consultant. Similarly hired was Galland's wartime staff officer and almost constant traveling companion, Major Hans Schmoller-Haldy.

This improving scene was suddenly wrecked by orders to return Galland, Hitschhold, and Schmoller-Haldy to Camp Latimer. The German Air Force Personnel Holding Unit had taken over Latimer, which now housed almost the entire Luftwaffe High Command, including secretaries and office personnel. Staff studies continued at Latimer, a boring ordeal for Galland.

The kindnesses of Jack Whitten continually stretched and bent regulations, and often broke them entirely. Walks around Latimer Park helped offset the oppressive prison psychology inseparable from any confinement. Whitten went even further. The APWIU had a huge command and reconnaissance car. On the bumpers, Whitten had emblazoned MILITARY INTELLIGENCE SERVICE in letters eight inches high. This guaranteed free parking anywhere, anytime, even in front of Military Police HQ.

CLOSE FRIENDS
USAAF Captain Dr. John Whitten was Galland's interrogator while Galland was a POW after the war. Galland was being questioned by numerous interrogators and finally asked that the nonsense be terminated. Request was granted and Whitten became the sole inquisitor.

On 22 October 1945, Whitten dressed Galland and Hitschhold in civilian clothes, and they went jolting into London in the towering vehicle. They made a sightseeing tour and lunched at the Cumberland Hotel with American fighter pilot Lt. Colonel Fred Kirtley. Afterwards they visited Selfridges, where Galland and Hitschhold bought coffee and tobacco. Clambering down out of the enormous car and strolling into Selfridges with the British public – who were now assuming he was with the Military Intelligence Service – was a caper that appealed to Galland. Something like the lobsters and champagne flight of a few years back, it lifted his spirits.

The Nuremberg Tribunal "war crimes" indictments were in progress at about this time. Many officers from the command hierarchies of all three German services were being indicted. Galland grew increasingly depressed. In the atmosphere of vengeance that prevailed at this time, he felt he might be indicted for doing his duty as a soldier.

The High Command of the Luftwaffe (OKL) was among the organizations indicted, and was permitted to prepare an answer to the Tribunal's charges. The Judge Advocate of the Luftwaffe High Command drew up a massive document that was passed around for all officers to sign. Eventually this document was brought into the room where Hitschhold and Galland were working, by a high-ranking OKL delegation. Word had gone around that the former General of the Fighter Arm had been disgusted and disaffected by what he had learned of Nazi excesses from General Halder, Whitten, and other sources in the postwar months.

The copy of the OKL response handed to Galland had already been signed by several high-ranking officers. Puffing on his cigar, Galland quietly read the document while the delegation waited. He then stood up, tore the document in half from top to bottom, and handed them the pieces.

"I personally welcome this trial, because from it we may learn who was responsible for these scandalous happenings."

Whitten learned of this incident from Hitschhold. Galland never mentioned it, and to protect Hitschhold's confidence, Whitten never revealed to Galland that he knew of the former fighter general's "response to the response." Galland forgot it as well, until it surfaced again after forty years in the draft of this book, the authors having obtained it independently from Jack Whitten.

By early December of 1945, Galland was back at Kaufbeuren, still working on the staff studies. Whitten brought him news of his parents, whom the kindly American had visited in Westerholt. They were well, and news of their famous son relieved them greatly. Life at the Landhaus was more tolerable than at Latimer, and in January of 1946, everyone skied frequently on the slopes behind the building.

Numerous U.S. fighter pilots came to visit. Lt. Colonels Fred Kirtley and Bob Delaney assisted for a time with the studies, and Colonel Ed Giller of the 55th Fighter Group became a frequent visitor, sometimes bringing young pilots with him. The staff studies served one good purpose for Galland. The systematic review of so many aspects of the war, conducted over such a long period, served to give him an organic grasp of the events and processes in which he had participated in high rank. For the remainder of his life, he would be able to discuss these matters in amazing detail.

On 21 January 1946, Galland and Whitten visited Herr Vollmer, one of the three cigar suppliers in Germany to whom Galland had granted "exclusive" rights to specially-manufactured *General der Jagdflieger* cigars.

Vollmer had also served with JV 44 as a Reserve officer doing staff work. He had owned a cigar factory in Karlsrube, but was now located at Hohenpeissenberg. A few boxes of the special cigars were still available, which pleased the man whose rank was on the label.

Through Jack Whitten's kindness and aid, he established a correspondence with the Baroness Gisela von Donner, widow of his former aide and friend, 1st Lt. Baron Conrad Hinrich von Donner. The latter had died in combat with U.S. heavy bombers in March of 1944. This attractive lady lived on the von Donner family farm in Schleswig-Holstein. She braved Germany's horrific postwar transportation system to make visits to see Galland. Whitten arranged for them to meet in town privately on weekends, a gesture of humanity best appreciated by those who have experienced protracted confinement.

Whitten' s last extracurricular act with Galland as a POW was a visit to Counter Intelligence Corps HQ in Tegernsee. They were seeking a lead on Galland's missing property. They ran into a dead end. The NCO who had done the looting had been sent back to the U. S., probably taking his loot with him. Three days after this, Captain John M. Whitten was advised that he was going back to the U.S., and ten days later was on a train out of Fürstenfeldbruck.

Losing his good friend reduced Galland's remaining POW time to a dreary routine. Whitten kept in touch by mail from the U.S. and sent his favorite POW food packages. Correspondence continued, but they did not meet personally again until 1950 in Frankfurt. Whitten was by then with the Military Government, and Galland was a prosperous consultant on vacation from the Argentine.

Throughout 1946 and into 1947, Galland worked for the Historical Division, U.S. Forces, European Theater. He was kept busy at Kaufbeuren, Oberursel, and Allendorf until practically everything he knew had been pumped out of him and put down on paper. There were scores of interrogations behind him by 28 April 1947, when he was finally released in Heilbronn. Only now was his military career and the war itself concluded. He walked out into a Germany that was decisively changed – especially for former generals.

TWENTY-EIGHT

Expatriate and Prodigal

Although Galland had never at any time been mistreated while a POW, Allied occupation policies in postwar Germany were designed to make life hard for former high-ranking officers. Severe restrictions were imposed everywhere on these capable, trained leaders. Former generals were denied even middle-level posts in civilian life. Many high-ranking Allied officers were strongly opposed to this victimization of military professionals. They considered such actions to be wrong, shortsighted, and likely to boomerang – which they did in Korea and Vietnam. Politically conceived and imposed, the policies had to be enforced by the occupying military.

Renascent German life took its theme from the occupation policies with their central theme of vengeance. As a beaten, ravaged, and forcibly divided nation sought to recover, professional officers were excluded from any kind of management, denied trade union membership, and barred from the universities. Outstanding Luftwaffe aces who had so recently won Germany's highest battle decorations in many cases lived from hand-to-mouth under these unfair policies. Doors were often slammed in their faces by their own countrymen as they sought employment. They were turned away as "militarists." Many of them had suffered serious wounds serving Germany. Allied politicians responsible for this punishment of honorable combat soldiers ignored the strict pre-war prohibition against German officers joining political parties – including the Nazi Party.

The higher the former officer's rank, the tighter were the restrictions. Ex-generals who found employment with the occupation forces and in historical projects were the lucky ones. The others could live in relative peace if they became truck drivers, sold advertising, labored on farms, or otherwise worked far below their administrative and intellectual abilities. Galland had no intention of diminishing himself this way. Once discharged in Heilbronn, he headed for Schleswig-Holstein in northern Germany and the large country estate of the Baroness Gisela von Donner.

Gisela had shown a remarkable devotion to Galland during his two years as a POW. She had ridden freight trains, sometimes loaded mainly with coal, to visit him in various POW camps. Car or passenger train travel was not available to ordinary Germans in those years. The attractive noblewoman endured the worst in his behalf. She was a primary force in strengthening Galland's spirit and morale. His prompt departure for her farm at Lehmkublen was therefore no mere whim, but a well-considered and practical step.

Gisela was raising her three very small children on her own, like thousands of other war widows. As General of the Fighters, Galland had opposed fighter pilots' marriages because of this precise situation: a widow with no father for her children. Galland could personally alleviate the problem in this instance, with the widow of his former friend and aide. Listing himself as forest help, his profile sank low enough for him to be left alone by the occupation authorities. He helped Gisela run the farm, drawing on his own early years at Westerholt. He was at home in the country. An added joy was filling in as surrogate father to Gisela's children, who would love him all his days.

As "forest help" he did little in the forest except help himself to game. This was strictly forbidden, as were all kinds of guns and ammunition. Galland hid a shotgun deep in the woods, wangled ammunition, and banged away out of official earshot. Even if he had to take constant care not to be caught, shooting game was infinitely preferable to the endless interrogations and soul-corroding confinement. As a lifelong hunter and woodsman, he found these daily forest forays cleansing him of the prison psychology, and they were otherwise highly useful

Even on a farm, food was short, and meat was hard to obtain all over Germany. At night he would return to the house laden with game. To eat what he had hunted and killed was an article of hunter Galland's faith. This fitted well with his current situation. Surplus game was excellent for trading, at a time when money was worth nothing. Other secret activities of the former general were growing and fermenting tobacco and distilling his own schnapps. He recalled that "both tasted terrible."

This life in Schleswig-Holstein had many idyllic aspects, but the man of action began chafing for a wider challenge. Activities of former generals were still restricted, and Galland began to think of going abroad, illegally if need be. Air forces were developing overseas in many nations. Training assignments had been obtained by former German aces in countries like India, Egypt, and Syria. He felt that his speaking knowledge of English and Spanish might help him find similar work. Others in Germany were thinking and planning along the same lines.

Professor Kurt Tank contacted Galland in the summer of 1948. The former Focke-Wulf chief designer was living in an old castle near Minden and invited the former General of the Fighter Arm over for a visit. Three days of intensive discussions with Tank ensued, in which he detailed his plans to build a new fighter aircraft in Argentina under contract to the Argentine Air Ministry. Galland agreed to become part of the overall package that Tank was to offer the Argentines. "It is going to be many years" said Tank, "before things are anything like normal in Germany again."

Tank worked through a German named Siebrecht, who lived in Buenos Aires and knew his way around the Argentine Air Ministry. Always a man who favored direct action, Tank suddenly slipped out of Germany via Denmark, in defiance of Allied restrictions. Once in Argentina, Tank got things moving. A second group of engineers followed him, but they were intercepted on the Denmark route and sent back to Germany. Galland was in a third group, dispatched via Austria and Italy and thence by sea to Buenos Aires, that evaded the Allies.

Argentina was humming with action. Commercial life was booming. A new jet fighter force was in the making. As a recognized authority on jet fighter operations, Galland was given a three-year contract, with two extension options. He was to work under Brigadier General Juan Francisco Fabri, C.-in-C. of the Argentine Air Force. Fabri turned out to be a fine gentleman, as well as a skilled general and pilot.

Galland quickly developed a strong liking for the Argentine people, especially those who lived in the countryside. They were honest, open, hospitable, and friendly. Life here was uncomplicated and pleasant. When the Baroness von Donner joined him in due course, bringing her three children, life became thoroughly enjoyable. Social life, family picnics, and beach and country sightseeing tours became part of their life style. The Argentine Air Force (AAF) found him a pleasant and roomy house, with servants' quarters and spacious grounds, outside Buenos Aires in the garden town of El Palomar.

The children went to school and rapidly acquired fluent Spanish. They were an integral part of Galland's happy scene. He watched over them, raising them as though he were their natural father, and forging a bond of enduring love between them all. They are now grown, married, and have families of their own.

GALLAND IN ARGENTINA - 1953
Adolf Galland helped Argentina develop their Air Force in the early 1950s. With him here are former bomber general Werner Baumbach and Stuka pilot Hans-Ulrich Rudel.

Galland's Spanish was passable for conversation, but was inadequate for the considerable paper work involved with his job. An interpreter was assigned to him, to help him with his paper work and serve as an escort. Captain Luis Grieben was a native speaker and writer, with total fluency in Spanish and German. He was to stay with Galland until 1953, at which time Grieben became accidentally involved in a plot against Peron and was jailed.

Galland was to use his war experience to set up a modern jet fighter force for the AAF. About 100 British Gloster Meteor fighters had been acquired, but the Argentines did not know how to use them properly. There is a substantial gulf between the handling and servicing of piston-powered fighters and jet formations. Bridging that gulf was the essence of Galland's assignment. He was one of the few men living who had operated jets and jet formations in combat. He showed his hosts how to use the Meteors in formation flights and in combat and shooting exercises.

LOHR 1957
Werner Streib, Hannes Trautloft, Werner Andres, Adolf Galland and Johannes Steinhoff occupy the head table at a meeting of the German Fighter Pilots associations.

GALLAND AND USAAF AEROJET TEAM LEADER
Mike Smolen and Adolf Galland exchange pleasantries with actress Liesal Bach looking on. The Aerojets were a USAAF stunt or acrobatic team which toured Europe but were based at Furstenfeldbruck.

"EVERYTHING IS HAND MADE - EVEN THE SIGNATURE"
Hitler told Werner Mölders the certificate was valuable. Jack S. Jenkins (right) bought the plaque in London at the end of WWII and on 8 May 1961 presented it to the German Fighter Pilots Assn. for return to the Mölder's family. Accepting the certificate are Adolf Galland, Gerhard Gobert and Werner Andres.

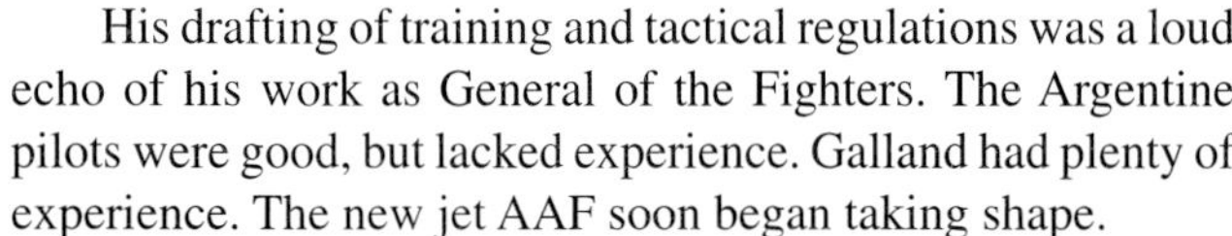

His drafting of training and tactical regulations was a loud echo of his work as General of the Fighters. The Argentine pilots were good, but lacked experience. Galland had plenty of experience. The new jet AAF soon began taking shape.

Galland was asked to give lectures on his war experiences. Flying personnel in all ranks responded enthusiastically to the reports and descriptions Galland gave. They gained some idea of what it was like to be in the hot seat – in the air and on the ground. This enthusiasm for sound, solid guidance worked wonders. AAF efficiency rose.

A vast and pleasant difference between this work and his tasks as General of the Fighters impressed Galland deeply. The AAF eagerly took up his recommendations. There was no Reich Marshal, no Reich Marshal's Kindergarten, no High Command to buck and battle. His proposals and recommendations were accepted and transformed promptly into workable regulations and procedures. Virtually everything Galland suggested was adopted and implemented in due course. He became, in effect, the father of the new AAF fighter force.

The Air Defense Command had many radars in storage, expensive, sophisticated units that were not being used. Over a period of several months, Galland showed them how and where to install these units, to monitor national borders and provide fighter control. He also established the organization necessary to man and maintain these facilities.

This radar defense net and fighter control system required a comprehensive upgrading of communications. Galland's advice was again accepted. Within a short time, the AAF had dramatically improved its communications overall. Efficiency rose in consequence. The Air Defense Command was able to live up to its name and carry out its mission.

Great prestige and status came with Galland's unintentional role as father of the modern Argentine Air Force. When this force did so well against the British fleet in the Falkland Islands war, their good showing was not Galland's direct doing. The officers he had trained were by then retired. Several revolutions had also occurred in the interim, changing the AAF structure and hierarchy. The foundations of the modern AAF jet force, including its doctrine, spirit, and efficiency were nevertheless laid in Galland's time and rested mainly on the bedrock of his advice and guidance. Sound beginnings have enduring effects. No one would doubt that "Boom" Trenchard's vision lived in the RAF of World War II, even though the distinguished father of the RAF had left the scene.

Working with the Argentines was pleasant. Their cooperation and trust naturally produced harmony and progress. His professional life bordered on the joyful, without any of the pressures, intrigues, egotism, and ambition that distorted action in the high ranks of the Luftwaffe. Opportunities were plentiful to fly jet fighters and cross the country by air. Galland enjoyed this to the full, comforted by the absence of projectiles in the air that might carry his name.

His job allowed him to take time off almost as he wished. This brought him full circle to sailplaning and his own beginnings as an airman. Sailplaning was an active sport in Argentina, and it was primal joy for Galland to soar again without an engine, casting himself on the bosom of the wind.

Social life in Buenos Aires was also relaxed and enjoyable with his many Argentine friends. Galland made a special point of entering fully into Argentine life. He wanted to understand not just the customs and ways of Argentina, but also the essence of contemporary Argentine thinking. Most of his friends during these years were accordingly local people.

Although he was among the most famous Germans in Buenos Aires, he avoided meeting too many German friends. He stayed out of organized German circles and clubs, because he was gratified by the rapport he had built with the Argentines. He did not wish to disturb such a constructive process.

THE BEGINNING OF A FRIENDSHIP
In May 1961, the German Fighter Pilots Assn. invited some American fighter aces to attend the dedication of the Memorial to the fallen fighter pilots of WWII. At Hahn Airbase are Walker M. Mahurin, James L. Brooks, Werner Andres, Jack S. Jenkins, Adolf Galland, Eugene A. Valencia and Raymond F. Toliver.

THREE FIGHTER PILOTS
At Galland's home in Oberwinter on 15 December 1967, Erich Hartmann and Ray Toliver visited Galland to set the stage for the writing of this book as well as one about Erich Hartmann (The Blond Knight of Germany).

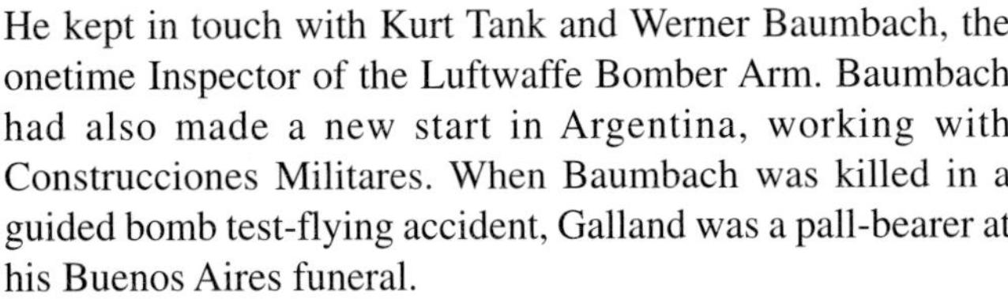

He kept in touch with Kurt Tank and Werner Baumbach, the onetime Inspector of the Luftwaffe Bomber Arm. Baumbach had also made a new start in Argentina, working with Construcciones Militares. When Baumbach was killed in a guided bomb test-flying accident, Galland was a pall-bearer at his Buenos Aires funeral.

The AAF remained highly appreciative of his competence and wisdom. Twice his contract options were picked up. He felt like a member of a military family, with uniformed friends everywhere. In this spirit, he was invited to the Great Ball of the Military Club in Buenos Aires. His hosts asked him specifically to please wear his highest decoration with his tuxedo. Galland duly arrived at the ball wearing his Knight's Cross, with its Oak leaves, Swords, and Diamonds. Everyone was happy – except the Soviet military delegation.

The warriors of the World Revolution were presented by the Russian Ambassador, who glanced at Galland's decorations with diplomatic disdain. The Russian officers were not diplomats. They scowled and glared angrily at the shiny Knight's Cross on Galland's neck. They did not believe that he would dare show himself with the highest German battle decoration.

Russia was talking peace in the world, but still refused to end World War II. Scores of thousands of German officers and soldiers were still illegally imprisoned in Russia – including many hundreds of Galland's fighter pilots. To the Russian officers in Buenos Aires, Galland thus was still an enemy and the focus of their hostile glares and remarks.

Galland had been glared at – and barked at – by the most terrible German personalities in the twentieth century, so the Russian officers' conduct did not perturb him. Their open anger simply bespoke their social illiteracy and their cloddish lack of self-control. The Argentine officers all rallied around their trusted German friend, supported him warmly, and soon calmed down the teacup tempest.

Galland had no illusions about himself as a partner for any woman, describing himself even in his 74th year as "a difficult and often terrible man in a marriage." His relationship with Gisela von Donner had been a good one, and in the Argentine they actually planned to get married. To Gisela's dismay, she was apprised of provisions in the late Baron von Donner's will that pertained to control of his estate in the event of her remarriage. Gisela found these severe restrictions unacceptable, and she and Galland were never married. Her decision to return to Germany with her children in 1953 meant the end of their de facto marriage, but their friendship continued warmly on through the decades.

Galland's Argentine years provided him with sufficient leisure to tackle writing a book about his war experiences. General Fabri and others whose views he respected predicted that such a book would be widely read in the world, and encouraged him. Galland had many doubts that a book by a high-ranking German fighter pilot would be welcome at this time. Using Jack Whitten's material and his war notes as a guide, he assembled *The First and the Last*, an autobiographical account of his war experiences.

Although familiar with report writing and accustomed to composing directives and other official documents, writing a commercial book was a new field for the former general. He was helped by Captain Grieben, Gisela von Donner, and later by Captain Erich Bindert and Franz Schneekluth in Germany. Galland referred to the latter three as "my brain trust." Franz Schneekluth published *Die Ersten und Die Letzen* in Germany in 1953.

The book was well received, despite the strong anti-military tenor of postwar German life. As a straightforward soldier's narrative, devoid of political justifications or propaganda, the book described the war from both fighter cockpit and high command. This uniquely broad perspective attracted the attention of British and French publishers. Translations were produced in 1955.

The British public has a strange and enduring passion for honorable enemies. *The First and The Last* became a big success in the British Commonwealth, and was soon on its way to becoming an international classic. U.S., French, and Spanish editions followed. Galland's personal story was eventually translated into fourteen languages. Sales eventually reached almost 3 million copies worldwide. The expatriate general's memoirs made him internationally famous.

After Gisela's return to Germany in 1953, Galland felt her loss sharply. He did some sailplaning in his leisure time, and while pursuing this hobby, made the acquaintance of the Countess Sylvina von Donhoff, an expatriate German noblewoman. From their common passion for sailplaning they quickly developed a passion for each other. Sylvina had been born in East Prussia and grew up partly in Bombay, where her father served as German Ambassador. Sylvina's mother was Argentine-born and of landed lineage.

Galland married the Countess in February of 1954, thereby beginning his official experience with marital blitz. He had always been drawn to pretty women, and they to him. To the astonishment of his numerous friends, he finally tied the knot with *one* lady – with whom he apparently expected to live happily ever after. In the Galland tradition, the Countess was a beauty. He always went first class.

His Argentine idyll came to a close in 1955. His affection for the country and its people would last his lifetime, but all good things have a natural span. On 7 February 1955, the Argentine government invested him by Presidential Decree with the title of Military Pilot, *Honoris Causa*. A certificate of appreciation for his services in the birth of the new Argentine Air Force was presented to him in a big ceremony at Air Base Moron at Buenos Aires. His expatriate years ended on a high note.

The prodigal was returning home at a propitious time. Another new jet air force was about to be born, this one in his own country. Through his vacation visits to Germany and correspondence with old comrades, Galland was aware of this important development. Steinhoff, Panitzki, and others were laying the groundwork for the Bundesluftwaffe in Chancellor Adenauer's office.

Immediately upon his arrival in Germany, Galland was asked to see Herr Blank, later to be Germany's first postwar defense minister. Blank told him that those working with him on air force matters had recommended that Galland be appointed *Inspekteur* – the title the Bundesluftwaffe was according its Commander-in-Chief. A similar recommendation had been made by his chief advisors, Generals Speidel and Heusinger.

Galland was eminently qualified for this post. His competence and capabilities were a matter of record. He was politically clean. Since the war, he had played a central role in creating a new jet air force for Argentina, the same task that was now to be carried out in Germany. No officer in Germany could

OLD COMRADES
Galland maintained a lively friendship with former Luftwaffe leaders. Here at his home in Oberwinter near Remagen are General Krupinski, Galland, Colonel Falck, General Hrabak and General Rall. These five logged 708 confirmed victories in WWII.

match either his war record or this significant recent experience. Former Luftwaffe generals were aging. They had been idle or inconsequentially employed since 1945 in non-military jobs. None had flown jets, organized them into modern formations, or organized a modern aerial defense system. Crowning all his other attributes, Galland was still a young man as generals go, being only 43 years old.

Blank asked for Galland's reaction to his offer of command of the new Luftwaffe.

"I cannot decide here and now, Herr Blank. I must think it over completely, and also examine what has been planned and done thus far. I want to know all the intentions in organization, personnel, and techniques – a complete briefing."

"Very well, General Galland. I will let you get a full briefing, and give you a week to decide. You can let me know."

As Galland walked out of Blank's office, he realized that a new zenith of his military career could lie ahead. Every young professional pilot dreams of one day becoming C.-in-C. of the air force. That is true all over the world. Blank's offer had not come as a surprise, but the actual event still carried an impact. Being offered the post of Commander-in-Chief produced a certain elation, like a sip of grand fine champagne cognac. He spent most of the next seven days at Macky Steinhoff's house. His old comrade from JV 44 had been extensively involved with air force preparations for many months. In his analytical and methodical fashion, Steinhoff knew the bright spots and where all the knots and blocks lay. They talked, and Galland studied shoals of documents. His final decision was to tackle the job. He let Herr Blank know of his acceptance and awaited developments.

The new German forces shadow organization had been keyed to participation in the European Defense Community. France suddenly balked at this concept. France wanted its own national forces, and this became firm French policy. Another full year was accordingly required to prepare the political situation and reorganize the acceptance of the planned Bundeswehr forces.

During this additional year of preparations, political wheels kept turning. Herr Blank was replaced. When Franz Josef Strauss took over as Defense Minister, the latter claimed that General Josef Kammhuber had already been selected as the new Inspekteur of the Bundesluftwaffe. Surely this was a strange choice. Kammhuber's service dated from World War I, and Germany was about to enter the era of modern jet aviation.

When Kammhuber surfaced as the new C.-in-C., Galland could not help recollecting his many acrimonious wrangles with Kammhuber during the war. There was no possibility of serving under him now. Through politics and internal intrigue, the Adenauer government managed to rid itself of Germany's outstanding and best-qualified air general. Adolf Galland would never hold another military appointment.

Galland suffered severe disappointment over losing out to Kammhuber. This did not last long. Events quickly proved that the former General of the Fighters was better off out of the Bundesluftwaffe than in. Politics were plentiful. The pre-war traditional law that kept politics out of the military was gone forever. Kammhuber had a rough time midwifing the Bundesluftwaffe, despite his remarkable organizational talents. Galland was glad the difficulties were descending on Kammhuber instead of on himself. He preferred that Kammhuber should have such troubles.

To rearm from the deepest national defamation, without a substantial period of rehabilitation, is an awkward procedure with inherent handicaps. German political leaders regarded the new forces as a *necessary evil*, and some said as much publicly. From all this, Galland had been delivered.

"I never cease to thank the French," he told the authors. "Without the delay they caused, and the reorganization they forced, I would have become the C.-in-C. I probably wouldn't have lasted 60 days in that political mill-race. I wouldn't have been able to stand it. Yes, I am very grateful to the French."

Shunted clear of military life forever, he was able to steer a completely different course. As a retired and famous general, he knew personally every significant officer in the Bundesluftwaffe. His competence and technical abilities were established. Soldiers and politicians alike showed him the greatest respect. He was therefore in an excellent position to build himself a business career. Equipment of all kinds was going to be purchased by the Bundesluftwaffe, most of it from abroad. All he had to do was organize himself.

A gratifying extra dimension to his life was developing from his memoirs. Further military service would probably have cramped this unfoldment and blurred the clarity of his wartime achievements. His status among those who studied and relived aviation history was soaring like a sailplane. This international and worldwide community esteemed him as an historical figure. His former enemies clamored to meet him. His new life would send him traveling among these admirers. Between history and commerce, he was about to embark on a fulfilling, thirty-year joyride.

THREE MEMORABLE WARRIORS
General Adolf Galland, General Curtis LeMay (USAF) and RAF Wing Commander Robert Stanford-Tuck were feted by owner Wilbur Bettis at his restaurant "Nieupont 17 " at Santa Ana, California on 20 August 1979. Galland and Tuck actually got LeMay to smile.

TWENTY-NINE

Globetrotting Businessman

During the year that passed between Theodor Blank's proposal that Galland head the new Luftwaffe, and the surprise emergence of Kammhuber as the actual appointee, Galland kept busy. Knowing what vast tasks awaited in building a new German Air Force from nothing, he turned his enforced wait to good account. Joining a private company in Düsseldorf that was already doing consulting and representative work for foreign armament firms, he took his first plunge into commercial life. Leasing a pleasant apartment across the Rhine in Neuss, he settled down happily with Sylvina. He was a businessman temporarily – or so he thought at this time.

Galland judged that insight into modern weapons procurement, from a commercial viewpoint, would help him when he assumed his new military role. Without realizing it, he was embarking on the kind of business life that would occupy him for the remainder of his career and give him all the action he could handle. Having just recently beaten Germany to the ground, and stripped her of all armaments, the Western Allies soon found themselves in a peculiar predicament. Naive wartime expectations as to the altruism and rectitude of "Uncle Joe" Stalin became a gross political embarrassment. The Soviet world revolution rapidly proved itself the most relentless political movement in planetary history. Russia stood fully armed on the frontiers of Western Europe.

Soviet intransigence and political aims made the rearmament of West Germany strategically essential. Since even the manufacture of rifles had been prohibited in Germany during the postwar vengeance period, initial arms procurement for the Bundeswehr was to come from outside Germany. America donated the first aircraft weapons, obsolescent equipment from its own stocks. Arms makers of the western world saw German rearmament as a business bonanza. All they had to do was gain access to this massive new weapons market.

Sellers of defense equipment did not know the procurement procedures of the Bundeswehr, or the special needs, requirements, and specifications of the new services. Overseas manufacturers did not know the key personalities of the new Luftwaffe, which was to be reconstructed from training planes upwards. A man with Adolf Galland's experience, contacts, and demonstrated capabilities fitted into this situation perfectly. Armaments suppliers overcame their marketing problems by using consultants – experienced, capable, and connected men who would provide the necessary liaison.

Through the contacts they had already developed, overseas and European manufacturers of aircraft and associated equipment knew that Galland was the proposed key man in the new Luftwaffe. This put him in demand. Extensive travel was required. He went all over Europe, and to Canada, Australia, South America, and the USA. His role was to keep abreast of aviation's rapid progress, to make recommendations and suggestions, and bring together the corporate and governmental people who signed the actual contracts. Months raced past as Galland's workload approximated that of wartime days, until public announcement of Kammhuber's appointment upset Galland's vision of his own future.

Disappointment was quickly crowded out of his life by new offers of consulting contracts from numerous defense hardware firms. Once they knew that he would not be going back into the new Luftwaffe, they competed with each other for his consulting services. Prosperity loomed. He had already come to enjoy his far-and-wide business travels, with their inevitable personal diversions into hunting and sport flying. Losing out on the Luftwaffe was setting him free, but there was a discordant personal note.

Galland had always wanted children of his own, which was part of his traditional outlook. With his forties now draining away, it was time for a family. Unfortunately, he could not have children with Sylvina. As long as he was anticipating joining the Bundesluftwaffe furthermore, he did not consider divorce. Once the command assignment evaporated, he began to feel that he should take action toward having the family that he so much desired.

18 MAY 1983
After the German Fighter Pilots Assn meeting in 1983, these pilots repaired to Galland's home in Oberwinter. They are (l to r): Otto Stammberger, Gerhard Schöpfel, Hartmann Grasser, Dr. H. Lange, Hans-J. Jabs, Walter Krupinski, Galland, Hannes Trautloft, Ray Toliver, Dieter Hrabak, Trevor Constable, Robert Stanford-Tuck (RAF), Alick Grant (RAF), Hans Schmoller-Haldy, and Günther Rall.

Substantial changes ensued in this period. His personal and business lives both took new turns. He resigned from the Düsseldorf company. Taking up numerous offers to consult independently for substantial British, American, French, Italian, Canadian, and German companies, he opened his own office in Bonn. In that city, he would be on the scene of all major defense decisions in West Germany.

With him he took his secretary from Düsseldorf, Hannelies Ladwein. A tall, dark, and charming brunette, her efficiency, thoroughness, and ability to handle people had been a tower of strength to him in his first commercial activities. She was now to help significantly in his personal business success. They set up offices in a rambling, high-ceilinged house on the Koblenzerstrasse, since renamed Adenauer Allee, a few minutes drive from the defense offices of the Federal Republic.

In addition to his consulting services, they made office space available, together with secretarial services, to representatives and visitors from various aerospace companies. For a period in the 1960s, Galland had "Onkel Theo" Osterkamp – his old comrade of the champagne and lobsters incident during the war – as one of his tenants. Galland went from one success to another.

His memoirs had by now been read all over the world, and new translations were being made almost every year into yet another language. He enjoyed special fame in the aerospace field, where ace fighter pilots have always been accorded legendary status. Overseas aerospace companies were eager to have such a man represent them in the huge new German armaments market.

Galland's book had another unusual consequence, unforeseen at the time he set down his memoirs. Businessmen in other countries recognized his direct soldier's narrative as the work of a man of integrity. Adding this quality to Galland's known capabilities, connections, and status in Germany made him the perfect representative. Because of his integrity, competing companies hired him as a consultant without misgivings.

His former enemies paid him a practical compliment with this kind of trust, but for those who knew his character, it was really no risk. Any man who had stood his ground before Hitler and Goering on matters of principle would never compromise his integrity for mere commercial gain. As his friend Edu Neumann put it, "Galland was a man of courage before the Thrones of Kings." His courage guaranteed everything else in his character.

Galland admitted to the authors that it was "sometimes a delicate balancing act" to avoid conflicts of interest with the companies he represented. He nevertheless served them all well. His activities were lucrative. His personal life changed after his divorce from Sylvina, and he married Hannelies on 10 September 1963. After years of living in rented apartments, they built a splendid new hilltop home in suburban Oberwinter in May of 1965. Each working day thenceforth opened and closed with a pleasant thirty minute drive along the Rhine.

English language capability beyond that acquired from Jack Whitten and others in POW days was essential to Galland's consulting work. He soon made the necessary improvements. He spoke accented English with the oft-voiced claim, "I didn't learn English, I only spoke it." The authors discovered in compiling this book that Adolf Galland was capable of grasping even the subtlest nuances of the English language, and especially the written language. He missed nothing in conversation. He was sufficiently fluent to address seminars in America and England, including the give-and-take of question and answer periods.

He referred to it all slyly as "my Oxford English," but it carried him to business and social success. He was an excellent technical advisor on this biography. With colloquial Spanish at his command as well, he experienced few language problems in his decades of world travel.

Since boyhood Galland had dreamed of one day owning his own aircraft. His dream finally came true on his 50th birthday in 1962, when he purchased a Beechcraft Bonanza, Registration D-EHEX and nicknamed "Die Dicke" – the Fat One. The plane got the name because it was more portly than the planes he flew in WWII, as was Galland himself.

Reveling in the flying qualities of the Bonanza, he flew it all over Europe for both business and pleasure. Often he flew in Rallies, sometimes with Erich Hartmann, the world's most successful fighter ace, as his copilot. They did well. When Galland took breaks from his consulting business, the Bonanza would be waiting to speed him to Austria or some other choice hunting site. His friends often flew with him.

On one business trip, he gave a lift to a Jewish fighter pilot from Israel. The youngster was a typical fighter jockey, boiling with gaiety and enthusiasm. He told Galland surprising tales of his aerial adventures in Israel's early struggles, when that country had to really scratch for armaments. "Believe it or not, General Galland, we got all your old ammunition from World War II, and we made good use of it. It was excellent ammunition, and we also made good use of your tactical combat advisories from 1942 through the end of 1944." Galland wondered at the twists of fate that would see the Israeli Air Force using tactical advice often resisted by the Luftwaffe High Command.

His Bonanza served him faithfully for 18 years. Failing vision forced him to give up piloting himself, after more than half a century in the pilot's seat. Turning away from the Bonanza for the last time was one of his hardest moments. Owning and flying "Die Dicke" had brought him the greatest joy of his life as a pilot.

Another joy had flooded in on him when Hannelies finally presented him with a son on 7 November 1966. Andreas Hubertus Galland provided his illustrious father with one of life's most exultant moments. Dolfo was now in his 55th year. Late though it was to be a Daddy, the whole event recharged him with enthusiasm and *joie de vive*. On 29 July 1969, when Galland had already turned 57, Hannelies presented him with

A GATHERING OF FIGHTER EAGLES IN THE USA
On 24 May 1984, these four retired Luftwaffe Lieutenant Generals participated in a seminar at Atlanta, Georgia. (l to r): Adolf Galland, Johannes Steinhoff, Walter Krupinski and Günther Rall. all were top fighter aces with, respectively, 104, 176, 197 and 275 aerial victories, for a total of 751. Photo by D. R. Sharpe

a daughter, Alexandra-Isabelle. His children were thenceforth the source of more late-in-life joy and fulfillment than any man can rationally anticipate. By the time this book was written his children had grown up into young adults.

Alexandra grew up favoring her mother's looks. "Andus," as his son is known, strongly resembles his famous father, and carries the signature of that same thick, helmet-like head of black hair. He acquired excellent English by working as a swimming pool serviceman in Florida one winter, and has been a comfortable visitor to America on many occasions. With British ace Bob Stanford-Tuck as his godfather, and the immortal fighter general as his Dad, Andus embarked on basic Luftwaffe training in 1985 with a heavy tradition to uphold. He did not choose to continue in military life.

When Hannelies retired from business to raise Andus and Alexandra, a replacement was necessary. This was a tall order, because Hannelies knew every business detail, and her services had figured crucially in his success. Galland's lifelong good luck held. He acquired the services of Frau Anne-Marie Drinhausen, who proved quick, capable, and precise. Single-handed she almost equaled the efforts of his wartime staff for the remaining years of his business career. Fluently tri-lingual, Frau Drinhausen daily gave mind-boggling exhibitions of unusual expertise, talking on the telephone in German, shooting asides in English to an office visitor, and reading a fax message all at once. Her greatest talent was to deal successfully on a daily basis with her famous boss, often a difficult man. Every businessman should be so lucky as to find such a dedicated aide.

Interspersed with Galland's frequent business travels abroad were increasing numbers of invitations to attend reunions, seminars, and historical celebrations around the world.

He was so mobile on business for 25 years that he became an international roving ambassador for the German fighter pilots of World War II. He enjoyed this "assignment" and represented Germany's airmen ably. Among German pilots in Germany, whether they were in Bundesluftwaffe uniform or civilian life, he remained The Boss. As former Colonel Wolfgang Falck expressed things, "I never knew any German general who so vigorously stood up for his troops." Galland was honored, respected, and revered by the men he led in World War II. For those who rose to become generals in the Bundesluftwaffe, the ultimate honor remained an invitation to a social gathering at Galland's home in Oberwinter.

Galland developed a close personal friendship with retired RAF Wing Commander Robert Stanford-Tuck, credited with 30 victories im World War II. Galland and Stanford-Tuck were both master marksmen and hunters. Both were known for hoisting a few cocktails. On this basis, and because of their status as famous aces, they enjoyed a rollicking good time together down through the decades. They made great foils for each other, refighting the Battle of Britain and in hilarious after-dinner joshing.

Galland's best after-dinner story dealt with his Diamonds decoration, Hitler, and Goering, and never failed to delight guests. Galland's humor and German accent, combined with his abilities as a raconteur, gave the story full flavor utterly beyond the written word. The tale began some time after Galland's Diamonds award, when he was sitting across from Goering in the Reich Marshal's personal train "Asia."

Goering suddenly leaned forward, peering intently at Galland's decoration. "Tell me" he said, "are those the Diamonds the Fuehrer gave you?" Assured that they were, Goering then asked Galland to take off the decoration so that he could examine it more closely. The General of the Fighters kept the decoration around his neck with a lady's garter. He handed the Reich Marshal the decoration, garter and all. Goering held the decoration up to the light, and turned it back and forth with a look of disdain.

"The Fuehrer knows a lot about tanks and guns, General Galland, but he doesn't know anything about diamonds. Why, these are just *chips*."

Galland knew nothing about diamonds, either, but he readily accepted the Reich Marshal's offer to have a superior copy of the decoration prepared by his personal jeweler. Goering appreciated jewels. The numerous rings encrusting his fingers attested to his passion. The Reich Marshal believed that the highest decoration should be of the highest quality. He promised to return Galland's decoration together with the superior Goering version in a few weeks.

The call duly came to visit Goering's HQ, and the beaming Reich Marshal met him with the new Diamonds decoration in one hand and Hitler's Diamonds in the other. Holding them up to the light, he turned on his heel and let the stones shimmer back, the decorations side by side in his hands.

"You see the difference, Galland? You see it?"

Galland had to agree that the Reich Marshal's Diamonds were bigger and much more brilliant and beautiful than those he had received from Hitler. Goering gave him both versions, so now he had a spare.

Goering and Hitler had a strange rivalry. There is no doubt that Hitler respected Goering's cultivated background and subtly tried to outdo him. Evidently Goering had said something to Hitler about improving the quality of the Diamonds to the Knight's Cross, for soon after Galland had collected the Goering Diamonds, he was summoned to Hitler's HQ and was personally met by the Fuehrer.

"I can give you your proper Diamonds to your Knight's Cross now, General Galland," said Hitler. "The decoration you have was just a temporary copy. Would you take off your decoration, please?"

To Galland's amazement, Hitler took out a jewel case and produced *another* set of Diamonds. Taking Galland's decoration in one hand, the Fuehrer took his new Diamonds in the other and held them up to the light side by side, turning on his heel as he did so, and just as he had seen Goering do.

"You see the difference, General Galland? You see it? You see that the diamonds in your temporary decoration are just *chips*!" They were Goering's own words, but they shocked Galland, because the "temporary" set of Diamonds he had just handed Hitler were the Reich Marshal's custom-made Diamonds. Galland thus finished up with three sets of Diamonds to his Knight's Cross. One set was destroyed in Berlin, but replaced by Hitler, and Galland was able to retain this one set. The two other sets were stolen by an American NCO of the Counter Intelligence Corps at Tegernsee at war's end. Those decorations are no doubt somewhere in the USA today.

The former General of the Fighter Arm was several times the guest of NASA in the USA and at numerous USAF bases and facilities both in America and in Europe. In May of 1974, he gave a speech to the American High School Air Force Junior Reserve Officer Training Corps, on the occasion of their first annual dining out – at Bitburg. The U.S. Marine Corps invited him to Yuma, Arizona, in 1979, to join their Weapons and Tactics Instructor Course. Bob Stanford-Tuck went with him. So did General Gerhard Barkhorn of the Bundesluftwaffe, who had flown with Galland in JV 44 equipped with the Me 262 jet fighters.

The war days came closest of all in the years 1967 through 1969, when he was hired as a consultant by Spitfire Productions of London. They produced the epic film "The Battle of Britain," released through United Artists. Many of the sequences in this film were shot in Spain. In addition to returning to familiar and little-changed scenes at Sevilla – including the Christina Hotel – Galland had the chance to once more fly the Me 109. Spain had built and used its own variants of the Me 109 long after World War II. Galland did not fly in scenes for the film, but for an old fighter pilot of 56, tooling around one last time in a Me 109 was an adventure in nostalgia.

Characters in the film were largely fictionalized. Representing Galland was the fictional "Major Falke," played by Manfred Reddemann. Dolfo's contemporaries chided him that it was indeed fiction, because he wasn't as handsome as Reddemann. A consoling factual touch was that Reddemann has a slightly bent nose. Heinz Riess as Goering was not as great in girth as the original Fat One, but well resembled him facially. The first time Galland saw the actor in the resplendent Reich Marshal's uniform, it was as though his old antagonist had been suddenly reincarnated – evoking memories of their wartime clashes.

Galland's lectures and appearances at seminars increased his popularity as the years passed. Nowhere was he more enthusiastically received than in Ireland. He was the honored guest of the Royal Aeronautical Society in Dublin, in March of 1980. His lecture subject was the Channel Dash, the breakout of the German battleships from Brest in 1942. Galland had given a similar lecture in both the USA and Canada in earlier years. While his trans-Atlantic audiences were interested in the subject, his Irish hosts were openly enthusiastic.

Delivering his lecture in the direct, factual, and soldierly way normal to him, Galland was astonished by the mounting applause as he recounted the breakout details. As he told of each British error, miscalculation, or oversight, his Irish audience began reveling in the succession of British mishaps and failures. By the time Galland told of the successful return of the battleships to Germany, the Irish were on their feet. Twisting the British lion's tail was something that aroused their greatest enthusiasm and admiration. That night, he was one of the most popular men in Ireland.

Audiences never seemed to tire of Galland, or of the other distinguished airmen who shared the podium with him in various countries. On the contrary, people with an historical bent realized increasingly how precious the sight and sound of these legendary warbirds in the flesh was becoming. When Galland appeared at a Long Beach seminar in California, in December of 1983, his fellow panelists were America's General Jimmy Doolittle, and Air Vice-Marshal "Johnny" Johnson, the RAF's top-scoring ace of World War II. The auditorium was packed, the audience almost reverentially mindful that they may never again see so much living aviation history in one place.

Galland found a lifelong friend in Sir Douglas Bader when he treated his fallen foe chivalrously in 1941. Bader was a man of renowned wit and humor. Quick with a quip and brilliant with badinage, Sir Douglas was ready for Galland in September of 1971 at the 1st Commonwealth Wartime Aircrew Reunion. Galland had been invited as a honored guest. The reunion was held in Winnipeg, Canada, a major center of the enormous Empire Air Training Scheme in World War II. This project had produced a flood of aircrews for the British bombing fleets, as well as many thousands of pilots.

During the introductory speeches, Bader officially greeted Galland and outlined for his audience how the organizers of the reunion had consulted with him about the propriety of inviting a former Luftwaffe general as a honored guest. Bader assured them that it was all perfectly proper.

"After all," said Bader artfully to his audience, "if it weren't for chaps like him, we never would have had an Empire Air Training Scheme."

Roaring laughter from the assembled veterans took ten minutes to subside, and Bader finally introduced their German guest. No one present enjoyed the joke more than Galland. The true measure of a man is always revealed when a public joke is on himself.

Galland's business life was punctuated by numerous similar gatherings. Former foes like the Pathfinders Association, the men who marked targets for the RAF night bombers, felt honored to invite him. The Royal Australian Air Force Europe reunion also welcomed him as an honored guest. An especially vibrant echo of the past came when Galland was the guest of the RAF Officers' Mess at No. 11 Group RAF. He sat down at a dining table in Bentley Priory at Stanmore, where Dowding and Park had out-generaled Goering, Kesselring, and Sperrle.

PROUD PAPA
Galland was immensely fond of his two children, Andus and Alexandra, seen with him here in 1983.

PERSONAL MAGNETISM
Many more handsome men than Adolf Galland envied his ability to attract beautiful women. Never more was this evident than when he married Heidi Horn, with the looks and demeanor of a movie star. She proved a valiant comrade in his final decline.

Galland was a frequent guest and often a participant in all kinds of fly-ins, rallies, and aviation social events. He unfailingly remembered his own past. Always he found time for world youth interest in aviation. Wherever he went his was a respected voice of encouragement. He was a pilot who had started at the bottom in aviation, in a sailplane built with his own hands and those of other air-minded youngsters. He had flown on into history. He signed hundreds of thousands of autographs. Requests continued to reach him from many countries until the day of his passing.

In September of 1969 he was the Honorable Guest at the German Lady Pilots' Fly-In at Ludwigsburg – a fateful occasion. The lady pilots were duly charmed and fascinated by their famous and still-magnetic guest. Galland only had eyes for one.

Retired Luftwaffe Colonel Wolfgang Falck, then president of the German Fighter Pilots' Association, was with him on that occasion. Galland began nudging Falck, directing his attention to a tall and stunning brunette. Tugging on the tail of Falck's coat, Galland whispered an urgent request, using Wolf Falck's nickname.

"Falkchen! Falkchen! You must introduce me to that girl."

"That girl" was Frau Heidi Horn, a successful Münster businesswoman. Falck's introduction began a long and sometimes rocky romance, destined for a poignant end. Those who knew Dolfo best were soon of the opinion that he had at last been "shot down" – fatally smitten by a woman. Galland and Hannelies were in due course divorced, but remained warm friends. These accords continued over the raising of Andus and Alexandra, and their joint parental responsibilities. Galland remained alone after the divorce, living in baronial solitude on his Oberwinter hilltop for many years. Heidi presented him with Arrax, a scrappy wire-haired dachshund, for company.

One May night in 1983, co-author Constable sat with Galland discussing his attitude toward the fair sex throughout his life. "After the heat has died down" said the former general, ''I like to have friendship." No sooner had he said this than his telephone jangled, and he withdrew for a few minutes. Returning with the broadest of Galland grins on his face, he was exultant.

"You see what I was just telling you? That was a girlfriend of mine from 1927, just telephoning to see how my health is."

History never ceased poking at him while he lived. In 1979, largely through the efforts of American aviation buff and historian Henry Sakaida, Galland was finally put in touch with the American P-47 pilot who clobbered him on his final Me 262 mission. Former Captain James Finnegan of San Rafael, California, was positively identified as the pilot who had fired on Galland's jet fighter and put him out of the war with fragments in his knee. On one of Galland's subsequent visits to California, and later again in Oberwinter, they met in person and in friendship. The kindly Finnegan took no pride in injuring another human being, but putting General Adolf Galland out of the war was the high point of his military career, and an historic distinction.

1990 AT CARMEL, CALIFORNIA
Visiting famed General James H. Doolittle are Gen. Günther Rall, RAF Gp. Capt. Donald E. Kingaby, Doolittle, Gen. Galland, Gen. Dietrich Hrabak and Gp. Capt. Peter Townsend of the RAF.

In 1983 Galland attended to another unsettled historical matter. Always he had wished to see again his crew chief Gerhard Meyer and his armorer Heinrich Olemotz. Both had been dedicated perfectionists in his glory days. Galland deeply appreciated the work of all ground crews and their indispensable role in the whole air effort. For Meyer and Olemotz there was a special place in his heart.

Attempting to trace Meyer through Fighter News (*Jagerblatt*), the magazine of the German Fighter Pilots' Association, he received replies from eighteen Meyers. All claimed to be his former crew chief. None of them was the real Meyer. By mid-1983 Galland finally traced both crewmen. They held a reunion at his office in Bonn, and later at his home in Oberwinter. The two veterans entered their evening with the warmest respect and regard for their former C.O. Both became members of the Fighter Association, attending all important meetings, but their pilot-and-crew reunion with Galland crowned their memories of military service.

The sudden passing of Sir Douglas Bader in 1983 saddened the world aviation community, Galland included. Their friendship had covered more than 42 years since Bader was brought down by JG 26 over France. Although he was in California on business at the time Bader died, Galland made sure to attend personally the later London memorial service held for the British ace at St. Clement Danes church in the Strand. The retired Luftwaffe general was hardly prepared for what happened, as described by Peter Tory in his *London Diary* newspaper column:

> "A curious and rather disturbing scene was enacted outside a London church yesterday, following the memorial service for our greatest derring-do air ace, Sir Douglas Bader.

"There was nothing untoward about the buzz of excitement over the presence of Maggie Thatcher and such Battle of Britain legends as Bob Stanford-Tuck and 'Laddie' Lucas. But the feverish attention paid by the public to a mustachioed, elderly man wearing a drab, black raincoat was just a little unsettling.

"So who was this figure receiving such star treatment at an event which at once was mourning the death of an English hero, and celebrating our glorious victory over Germany in 1945? The stranger was none other than World War II Luftwaffe ace Adolf Galland, who scored an astonishing 104 victories over our own lads in the RAF.

"General Galland, now 70, won Germany's highest decorations, most of which were pinned personally on his chest by the Fuehrer. Yet it was he more than any other celebrity at yesterday's service whom the public wanted to meet.

"Almost pushing aside old British air force types bent low under the weight of their DFCs and Bars, the crowds assaulted the old hun with their requests for autographs. He signed his signature a dozen or more times and shook a hundred hands. One dignitary, with a glittering shield of medals, snapped testily, 'Perhaps when the admirers have finished, we might move on.'

"Certainly Bader, had he been present, would have instantly recognized the stranger in the dark raincoat. Stomping over to his side, he would have banged him on the back and bellowed: 'Bloody good show, glad you could come!"

Galland entered his seventies with every material comfort a man could desire. His home in Oberwinter underwent successive expansions and additions, including a magnificent trophy hall reminiscent of the one at Goering's estate on the Schorfheide. Galland had to suffer hearing his beautiful room called "Karinhall" by old comrades and friends.

He enjoyed sojourns at the apartment he owned at St. Gilgen on Lake Wolfgang in Austria. An attractive summer villa in Spain near Benidorm provided him with a luxurious retreat. What else could his heart desire in the evening of his life, with his children grown and his life's work essentially concluded? What else? "That girl" Heidi to whom Wolf Falck introduced him in 1969, still as stunning as a movie star.

On 10 February 1984, Adolf Galland and Heidi Horn were suddenly married. All their friends were astonished. This final foray into marital blitz did wonders for Galland's morale as he battled against serious health problems and was hospitalized several times – a portent of the years ahead.

At the wedding reception they gave in Oberwinter, among old war comrades, friends, and dignitaries invited there, was also his first wife, Sylvina. Upon seeing the former fighter general together with Sylvina and Heidi, several old fighter pilots could not resist the obvious wisecrack based on the title of his book: "Aha Dolfo, the First and the Last."

British ace Bob Stanford-Tuck, prior to his 1987 death, couched Galland's career in the cricket vernacular, "Dolfo's had a bloody good innings, you know." Military men who have meteoric careers in youth seldom survive the burnout that usually follows early brilliance. Galland's career became long and brilliant, both military and civilian. Anton "Tonius" Weiler, the able head of the German Fighter Pilots' Association, captured the essence of the Galland mystique in a publicly delivered 70th birthday message in Cologne:

"Glory and inactivity don't mix, and Galland has acted accordingly. He always left the slow ones behind and never looked back."

The remaining Galland years until his passing in 1996 were difficult indeed for such a man of action. His health gradually went into decline, and the vibrant hunter, fisherman, ambassador, and nonstop world traveler found himself battling progressive physical limitations, harassments, and embarrassments. Life wound downward into medical tedium. For Adolf Galland, the glory had gone.

The glory that remained was unseen and silent, and belonged to "That Girl" Heidi, to whom he had been so powerfully attracted. His legendary luck had not left him. His beautiful lady proved to have supernal powers of endurance and love in sustaining him during his final difficult decade.

Close friends, like the ever-loyal Tonius Weiler, aware of the burdens Heidi bore for so long, developed a profound respect and admiration for her. Galland's friend of more than sixty years, Wolf Falck, said that "without Heidi, we would have lost Mufti years ago. I honor and admire her." The German fighter pilot community has an unwritten, spiritual pantheon for those it most esteems. Heidi Galland now belongs there.

When Adolf Galland left this life on 9 February 1996, the international aviation community lost a titan and a legend. His funeral on 21 February, Ash Wednesday, took place in terrible weather, with grey skies, rain, snow, and a cold wind. Hundreds of old fighter pilots and dignitaries braved the freezing elements to honor an historic personage.

As the Bundesluftwaffe honor guard carried General Galland's Knight's Cross with Oak Leaves, Swords, and Diamonds on a cushion, with Heidi and Galland's children following, snow swirled around the somber procession. Icy gusts were appropriate for the final rites of a general who had served his country and his people nobly in the foul weather of the war's darkest days.

Thus ended a legendary life, but Adolf Galland left a legacy of inspiration for the young. Inspired by him to be "number one," no matter what their station or nation, youngsters will through their drive to achievement elevate the human condition. Such inspired young people will grace and not disgrace the earth. So be it with them, as it was with him.

Appendix 1
Germany's Aces with One-Hundred or More Aerial Victories

Name	Rank	Unit(s)	Born	Died	Score
Hartmann, Erich	Major	52	19.4.22	19.9.93	352
Barkhorn, Gerhard	Major	6, 52, 44	20.3.19	6.1.83	301
Rall, Günther	Major	11, 52, 300	10.3.18		275
Kittel, Otto	lst.Lt.	54	21.2.17	16.2.45	267
Nowotny, Walter	Major	54, 7	7.12.20	8.11.44	258
Batz, Wilhelm	Major	52	21.5.16	11.9.88	237
Rudorffer, Erich	Major	2, 54, 7	1.11.17		224
Bar, Heinrich	Lt.Col.	51, 1, 3, 77	25.3.13	28.4.57	221
Graf, Hermann	Colonel	52, 53	24.10.12	4.11.88	212
Ehrler, Heinz	Major	5, 77	14.9.17	4.4.45	208
Weissenberger, Theo.	Major	5, 7	21.12, 14	10.6.50	208
Philipp, Hans	Lt.Col.	54, 1	17.3.17	8.10.43	206
Schuck, Walter	Lt.	5, 7	30.7.20		206
Hafner, Anton	lst.Lt.	51	2.6.18	17.10.44	204
Lipfert, Helmut	Capt.	52, 3	6.8.16	10.8.90	203
Krupinski, Walter	Major	52, 11, 26, 44	11.11.20		197
Hackl, Anton	Major	11, 26, 300	25.3.15	9.7.84	192
Brendel, Joachim	Capt.	53, 51	27.4.21	7.7.74	189
Stotz, Max	Capt.	54	13.2.12	19.8.43	189
Kirschner, Joachim	Capt.	3, 27	7.6.20	17.12.43	188
Brandle, Werner	Major	3	19.1.12	3.11.43	180
Josten, Gunther	Lt.	52	7.11.21		178
Steinhoff, Johannes	Lt.Col.	7, 77, 52, 44	15.9.13	21.2.94	178
Reinert, Ernst-W.	Capt.	27, 77, 7	2.2.19		174
Schack, Günther	Capt.	51	12.11.17		174
Schmidt, Heinz	Capt.	52	20.4.20	5.9.43	173
Lang, Emil	Capt.	52, 53, 26	14.1.09	3.9.44	173
Adameit, Horst	Major	54	8.2.12	8.44	166
Wilcke, Wolf-Diet.	Lt.Col.	53, 3	11.3.13	23.3.44	162
Marseille, Hans-J.	Capt.	51, 27	13.12.19	30.9.42	158
Sturm, Heinrich	Capt.	52	12.6.20	22.12.44	158
Thyben, Gerhardt	lst.Lt.	3, 54	24.2.22		157
Beisswenger, Hans	lst.Lt	54	8.11.16	6.3.43	152
Düttmann, Peter	Lt.	52	23.5.23		152
Gollob, Gordon	Col.	3, 77	16.6.12	17.9.87	150

Name	Rank	Unit(s)	Born	Died	Score
Tegtmeier, Fritz	Lt.	54, 7	30.7.17		146
Wolf, Albin	Lt.	54	28.10.20	2.4.44	144
Tanzer, Kurt	Lt.	51	1.11.20	25.6.60	143
Muller, Friedrich, K,	Major	53, 3	25.12.16	29.5.44	140
Gratz, Karl	Lt.	52	24.1.19		138
Setz, Heinrich	Major	52, 77, 27	12.3.15	13.3.43	138
Trenkel, Rudolf	Capt.	52, 77	17.1.18		138
Wolfrum, Walter	Lt.	52	23.5.23		137
Fonnekold, Otto	Lt.	52	15.2.20	31.8.44	136
Weber, Karl-Heinz	Major	51	30.1.22	7.6.44	136
Muncheberg, Joachim	Major	26, 77	31.12.18	23.3.43	135
Waldmann, Hans	Lt.	52, 3, 7	24.9.22	18.3.45	134
Grislawski, Alfred	Capt.	52, 1, 53	21.11.19		133
Schall, Franz	Capt.	52, 7	1.6.18	10.4.45	133
Wiese, Johannes	Major	52, 77	7.3.15	16.8.91	133
Borchers, Adolf	Major	52	10.2.13		132
Clausen, Erwin	Capt.	51	5.8.11	4.10.43	132
Dickfeld, Adolf	Major	52, 2, 11	20.2.10		132
Ihlefeld, Herbert	Col.	52, 11, 77	1.6.14	8.8.95	132
Lemke, Wilhelm	Capt.	3	27.9.20	4.12.43	131
Hoffmann, Gerhard	Lt.	52	6.11.19	11.4.45	130
Sterr, Heinrich	Lt.	54	24.9.19	26.11.44	129
Eisenach, Franz	Major	54	11.8.18		129
Dahl, Walther	Col.	3, 300	27.3.16	25.11.85	129
Dorr, Franz	Capt.	5, 77	10.2.13	13.10.72	128
Oesau, Walter	Lt.Col.	51, 3, 2	28.6.13	11.5.44	127
Zwernemann, Josef	Lt.	52, 77, 11	26.3.16	8.4.44	126
Hrabak, Diether	Lt.Col.	52, 54	10.12.14	15.9.95	125
Ettel, Wolf-Udo	Lt.	3, 27	26.2.21	17.7.43	124
Tonne, Wolfgang	Capt.	53, 27	28.2.18	20.4.43	122
Leie, Erich	Lt.	2, 51, 77	10.9.16	7.3.45	121
Marquardt, Heinz	Sgt.	51	29.12.22		121
Schnaufer, Heinz-W.	Major	NJG 4	16.2.22	13.7.50	121
Weiss, Robert	Capt.	54	21.4.20	29.12.44	121
Obleser, Friedrich	Lt.	52	21.2.23		120
Beerenbrock, Hans	Lt.	51	9.4.20		117
Birkner, Hans-J.	Lt.	52	22.10.21	14.12.44	117
Norz, Jakob	Lt.	77, 5	20.12.20	16.9.44	117
Wernicke, Heinz	Lt.	54	17.10.21	27.12.44	117
Lambert, August	Lt.	SG 2, SG 151	18.12.16	17.4.45	117
Mölders, Werner	Col.	51, 53	18.3.13	22.11.41	115
Crinius, Wilhelm	Lt.	27	2.12.20		114
Schroer, Werner	Major	27, 3	12.12.18	10.2.85	114
Dammers, Hans	Lt.	52	8.12.13	17.3.44	113
Korts, Berthold	Lt.	52	21.5.12	28.8.43	113
Lent, Helmut	Lt.Col.	NJG 3	13.6.18	7.10.44	113
Buhligen, Kurt	Lt.Col.	2	13.12.17	11.8.85	112
Lützow, Gunther	Col.	3, 44	4.9.12	24.4.45	110
Ubben, Kurt	Major	53, 77	18.11.11	27.4.44	110
Woidich, Franz	Lt.	27, 53	2.1.21		110
Seiler, Reinhard	Major	54	30.8.09		109
Bitsch, Emil	Capt.	3	14.6.16	15.3.44	108
Hahn, Hans "Assi"	Major	54, 2	14.4.14	18.12.82	108

Name	Rank	Unit(s)	Born	Died	Score
Vechtel, Bernard	Lt.	51	31.7.20	21.8.75	108
Bauer, Victor	Capt.	3	19.9.15	13.12.69	106
Lucas, Werner	Capt.	3	27.12.17	24.10.43	106
von Boremski, Eberhard	Capt.	77, 3	24.9.19	16.12.63	104
Sachsenberg, Heinz	Lt.	52	12.7.22	17.6.51	104
Galland, Adolf	Lt. Gen.	27, 26, 44	19.3.12	2.8.96	103
Grasser, Hartmann	Major	51, 1, 210	23.8.14	2.6.86	103
Freytag, Siegfried	Major	77, 7	10.11.19		102
Geisshardt, Friedrich	Capt.	54, 26	22.1.19	6.4.43	102
Mayer, Egon	Lt.Col.	2	19.8.17	2.3.44	102
Ostermann, Max, H.	Lt.	54	11.12.17	9.8.42	102
Wurmheller, Josef	Major	53, 2	4.5.17	22.6.44	102
Miethig, Rudolf	Lt.	52	17.10.21	10.6.43	101
Priller, Josef	Col.	51, 26	27.6.15	20.5.61	101
Wernitz, Ulrich	Lt.	54	23.1.21	23.12.80	101

Note: According to sources available, no pilots were credited with exactly 100 victories. At least six could have scored 100 but sufficient evidence is unavailable. They are: Paul-Heinrich Dahne, Hans Schleef, Friedrich Wachowiak, Ulrich Wohnert, Diethelm von Eichel-Streiber and Wolfgang Späte.

Appendix 2
Surrender of JV 44

To: Toliver and Constable,

Here is the correct course of events: As you know, I was wounded in my last JV-44 mission and combat, on 26 April 1945, when I had downed two B-26 Marauders. Taking off from Munich-Riem, Col. Steinhoff crashed and was extremely badly burned. (Please see photo in my photo-book page 103).

Soon thereafter my JV-44 moved from Munich to Salzburg, and a smaller part of the Me-262 was flown to Innsbruck. Since Col. Luetzow was missed, Lt. Col. Heinz Bar represented me as commander in the meantime. Two provided runways at the Autobahn Munich to Salzburg weren't used anymore because of the fast advancing Allied Forces. The Autobahn south of Munich and Ottobrunn crossing the Hofoldinger Forrest were used only for parking camouflaged Me-262 and He-162 in the woods. Here they were captured by the U.S. troops.

The main part of the JV-44, with most of the personnel, aircraft, and equipment, was thereupon stationed at Salzburg Airport, commanded by Lt. Col. Heinz Bär.

I transferred myself to the Luftwaffe-Hospital at Bad Wiessee, having my right leg in plaster. I was treated there and moved to a private villa at Tegernsee. From there I was in contact with my JV-44 at Salzburg and Innsbruck by means of telephone, Fieseler-Storch, and Motorcycle messengers.

On the first of May I decided to make a last and desperate attempt to save and maintain – at the last possible instance – this unique and advanced operational jet fighter unit for a later use to be decided by the U.S. authorities. I was completely aware of the highest danger and risks involved in case this action became known to any German military, SS, police, or political NS-party authority. This fact and the possibility of a misinterpretation of my final actions as commander of JV-44 (betrayer, deserter, etc.) prohibited me and a few involved offficers around me to speak or to write about this attempt in any detail at a later time.

Up to now the whole correct historical story of this last minute action has remained virginal.

After some last-minute-consultations Major Wilhelm Herget volunteered to take-off with a "Storch" from a small spot next to my villa in order to cross the allied advanced troops and to land at Schleipheim. He was accompanied by my personal aid, Captain Hugo Kessler. They managed to land safely at the former Luftwaffen-airfield Schleipheim, north of Munich.

The following actions on both sides can best be seen and explained by the attached copies and translations in the correct temporal order:

1. My first message dated 1st May 1945, 0.15 hours,
2. The answer of Brig. General Pearson Menoher, dated 1st May 1945, with annexes 2a, 2b, 2c, 2d and 2e (drawing for marking our Me-262),
3. My answer to Brig. General Menoher dated 2 May 1945.
4. Report of my first interrogation by Col. Newton, dated 6 May 1945 at Bad Tolz,

I believe this makes a very interesting story which has never been published before. When I was a P.O.W. I have been told that unfortunately the U.S. Army officers approached by us did not understand the importance of my offer. All experts know that the operational jet-fighter-experience could only be gained by successful fighter-pilots and a highly skilled technical staff supported by a sufficient stock of manifold spareparts and specialised ground support equipment. All this was contained in the JV-44 and subject to my offer. Without a slightly satisfying response from the U.S. side I did not have any other alternative but to give the order for demolition, destruction, and dissolution of the JV-44.

Best wishes, yours,

Adolf Galland
Lt. General

I have sent Major Herget, as well as my personal aide, Captain Kessler, to the Commander in Chief of the Allied Forces, in order to discuss with him the possibilities and terms of a special surrender for the last entire and fully operational jet-fighter-unit. I therefore kindly ask you to have me approached in this regard at the earliest possible time without any delay, since the destruction of the aircraft and special equipment, as well as the disbandment of the unit, must be expected every hour.

The couriers have been informed with regard to further details.

signed Galland
Lt. General

Tegernsee, 2 May 1945
0.15 hours

sent with this order: signed: Herget (Major)
signed: Kessler (Captain)

Headquarters

XV Corps United States Army

1 May 1945

MEMORANDUM: TO: Lieutenant General Adolf Galland.

I have authority to accept the surrender of Jagdverband 44, in accordance with the Rules of Land Warfare as prescribed by the Hague and Geneva Conventions.
I am returning Major Herget and Captain Kessler to you with details of surrender attached. It is expected that they will return at 6PM, this date, with your decision. I will arrange for their return air escort at that time.
I am open to suggestion as to the surrender of the personnel other than pilots that you indicated in the attached memorandum.

PEARSON MENOHER
Brigadier General. GSC,
Chief of Staff.

Incl. 2

The following were present at the conference between American and German representatives for the surrender of "JAGDVERBAND 44" at 45th Infantry Division Command Post, at FELDMOCHING, at 1100, 1 May 1945:

American Representatives.
Brig. Gen. Pearson Menoher, 0-3805, C/S XV Corps.
Brig. Gen. Jesse Auton, 0-3798, 6th Fighter Wing, Eighth Air Force.
Col. Dorr E. Newton, Jr., 0-3396, Deputy Commander, XII TAC.

German Representatives.
Maj. Wilhelm Herget, Jagdverband 44.
Capt. Hugo Kessler, Jagdverband 44.

Interpreters.
Capt. Rupert W. Guenthner, O-1302642, 45th Division CIC.
1st Lt. John H. Brunswick, 0-552530, G-2 Section, Hq XV Corps.
Mr. Leonid Ruminoff, Special Agent, CIC, attached to 45th Infantry Division.

Stenographer.
M/Sgt. Samuel L. Sack, 33314260, C/S Section, Hq XV Corps.

Incl. 1

45th Infantry Division
FELDMOCHING, GERMANY
(815645)
01 1300B May 1945

Notes On Conference With Emissaries of General Galland.

Q. When was this letter (letter brought by emissaries) written?

A. Last night about 12:15 (300015B).

It was explained to the emissaries that according to the rules governing Land Warfare, when a man or a unit surrenders, neither the man nor the unit, or any of their equipment, is used against their own people. All surrenders are governed by the provisions of "Land Warfare" as set down by the Geneva Convention. The emissaries stated that this was fully understood.

Q. Does General Galland have the authority to surrender the "JAGDVERBAND 44"? What are the supporting units?

A. General Galland has that authority. It is a specialized unit; all 50 planes and all the personnel are one unit.

"As a subordinate commander, I have no authority to accept anything but a surrender as a prisoner of war. SHAEF policy is "Surrender"; all personnel become POWs. Would General Galland surrender?"

A. We would have to ask their Supreme Commander if Gen Galland would surrender. We would like to take this message to the general and come back. Could we do that'?

Yes. And we would like to give you the details for bringing in the planes in the event General Galland accepts the surrender. How long does it take to fly to your place ... is it at the field?

A. It would take about 45 minutes. It is not at the field as the general has been wounded and is in bed at a private place. We have no communications with the field, but we have a motorcycle.

Q. How long would it take General Galland to say "Yes" or "No"? If you were to get back to him by 1530B, could you be back here by 1730B?

A. That is too quick. We could be back before dark tonight.

Details of Surrender

I. Marking of aircraft will be in accordance with the attached diagram.
2. One-half the aircraft will be landed at an airfield 8 kilometers Northwest of DARMSTADT (This will be the aircraft from INSBRUCK). The other one-half of the aircraft will be landed at GIEBELSTADT. (This will be the planes from SALZBURG). Alternate airfields will be LEIPHEIM and SCHABISH HALL.
3. Planes will proceed two at a time, five minutes apart, starting at 0700, May 1945, weather permitting, or if not, as soon thereafter as possible.
4. A direct course from base to destination at 3000 meters altitude, or at 150 meters under any solid cloud layer, will be flown.
5. American fighter escort will patrol on either side of the two courses to be flown and will be above their aircraft.
6. German aircraft will not carry ammunition, but will leave guns and other equipment in the planes.

PEARSON MENOHER
Brigadier General,
GSC Chief of Staff.

Incl. 3

The following discussion was made by the general and colonel from the Air Corps:

Q. Do the planes fly in formation?

A. No, only 2 or 3 together.

Q. Is it possible for the planes to reach the Rhine River?

A. I don't know. There is a shortage of fuel.

(Then followed a discussion of possible fields. The final decision was:) We would like the planes at Innesbruck to go to the field 8 Kms N.W. of DARMSTADT; the planes at

SALSBURG will go to GIEBELSTADT. Alternate fields would be at LEIPSHEIM and SCHWABISCHALL. Start at 0700B tomorrow, weather permitting, or as soon thereafter as possible. Fly at 3000 meters or 150 meters under solid cloud cover. We will have a patrol escort along both courses and your planes will fly between them. (Other points, such as markings, etc., were also discussed.)

Emissary: If only unconditional surrender is acceptable. General Galland may order the planes destroyed on the ground. We also request that you do not use radio in discussing these details as they will be intercepted and the planes will be destroyed by the SS.

Gen Menoher: That is his decision to make. Surrender is all I have the authority to offer. We will comply as far as possible in not using radio. We are giving you these details for bringing in the planes in the event General Galland accepts.

I expect to send these two men back in their own plane. I will put 2 "Stork" type (Cubs) planes on each side of them as they take off. I would like General Galland to let us know today as to the acceptance or the rejection of this plan. Our escort will go as far as the front line. If we can agree on a time, we will have 2 Cubs rendezvous at the place we leave them in order to pick them up when they come back.

A. We could do that. 1800B would be a good time for the rendezvous.

X X X X X X X X X X X X

Incl. 4

Translation

2 May 1945

To Brig. General, GSC
Chief of Staff
Pearson Menoher

I thank you for the receipt of my couriers and for your declaration.

The required execution of the action, however, does fail because of the very bad weather conditions, the lack of fuel and additionally because of the technical problems with many Me-262 aircraft.

I therefore rather suggest to again fix the terms for the special surrender of the whole unit (aircraft, spare parts, special ground support equipment, pilots, and specialized personnel.)

I am at your disposal in that regard.

signed: Adolf Galland
Lt. General

the following was written by hand below the text:

"Copy of General Galland's reply to surrender terms sent back to XV. Corps by the General. Courier pilot, Major Herget was shot down, captured, and evacuated through Army Medical channels to the rear having been burnt in the crash.

P. E. Menoher, GSC"

Headquarters
XII Tactical Air Command E-N-X

APO 374, US Army, 6 May ~945

INTERVIEW WITH GENERAL GALLAND, CONDUCTED BY COL. NEWTON. Xll TAC, THRU AN INTERPRETER, AT XXI CORPS C.P. AT BAD TOLZ, ON 5 MAY 1945.

My name is General Galland and I am from the Air Corps. My unit is Jagdverband 44.

Q. In view of your sending an emmisary to us on 1 May. we wonder if any of your unit is still in this area and if there is any that is not yet captured?

A. l don't know because I have had no communications since 1 May.

Q. Did your unit have instructions to evacuate the fields at Innsbruck and Salsburg, or did they destroy their planes.

A. I did not give any instruction to anyone. I sent two officers to you on 1 May and they came back. They had until 1800 to give an answer. It was impossible to give an answer at 1800 because I could not get my plane off the ground because of heavy snow. The stipulations could not be carried out because most of the planes had no gas. On account of weather, in general, they could not get off the ground. The next day, I sent the same major back again with orders from me but he was shot down. The front moved so close to Salsburg that the conditions set forth made no further sense. I decided to stay right here where I was until I was overrun and then start communications again. I stayed of my own accord because I wanted to take up these communications – otherwise I could have gone back. I would like to know if you want to hear some of my personal feelings as to why I started these meetings.

Q. I was at the original meeting with General Menoher and know about your feelings. I also know the reply that was written to you in answer to them.

A. I am the outstanding specialist in jet-propelled aircraft and would like to assemble all the known lights in this subject and go on working on this with you.

Q. Any decision of that nature would have to be reached by a Commander of Higher Authority than me, but would you care to mention what would you do with the results of such work?

A. I am of the opinion that Germany has lost the war but the future of all Europe lies in the hands of the Allies.

Q. What units make up Jagdt 44?

A. That was a special unit put together in February this year by crack pilots.

Q. Was it made up of KG 51, 54 and JG 7?

A. No, they were different from them. That was the second largest that was left.

Q. Where are these other units now?

A. Around Prague. I don't know whether any of my pilots left the field to join them but they had very little gas. I have here a copy of the letter I transmitted with the Major who was shot down, in reply to your surrender terms. Translated, it reads:

"I thank you for your reception of my courier and your acceptance of him. The carrying through of the stipulations was impossible because of weather and gasoline and the fact that a certain number of the planes were not usable. I propose, however, that the transfer of all planes, troops and surrounding installations will be carried forward immediately. In this respect, I am at your command.

Q. What is your address?

A. 147 Neureut Street, Tegernsee. This is Dr. Ernest S. Schubert, my physician. He is staying at the same address.

Q. If we permit you to return and remain, at least temporarily, would you give your parole to stay and remain at our disposal until we want you again?

A. Yes. You may post guards but it won't be necessary. I have to report to the hospital near there every day. I only have to report twice weekly, but I go every day.

Q. Our main mission at present was to find out about your unit and where they were. If you will give us your word to remain, we will send others to return there and they will take up the matter of your specialty and other details.

A. I gladly give my word because I have no place to go and no desire to go anywhere. I will be at your wishes at all times.

Above is a literal translation of the interview as cited.

DORR E. NEWTON JR.
Colonel, G. S. C.
Acting Deputy Commander.

Glossary

Abitur: Examinations given when graduating to qualify a student for admission to a university.

A/B Schule: Single-engine flight training school.

B-Schule: Blind-flying school.

Barbarossa: Code name for the German invasion of Russia in 1941.

Chaff: Metallic foil strips cut to German radar wavelengths, and dropped from aircraft to corrupt radar information. Chaff caused huge echoes to appear on German radarscopes. Code-named "window" by the British. See also reference under "Düppel."

C-Schule: Multi-engine flight training school.

C-Stoff: Catalyst used in the rocket motor of the Me 163 interceptor.

DLH: *Deutsche Lufthansa*, the German State Airline, known world-wide as simply Lufthansa.

DLV: *Deutscher Luftsportverband*. The German Aviation Sport Union, governing body of sport aviation.

Düppel: A town on the German-Danish border where RAF tinfoil "chaff" for corrupting radar was first found. **Düppel** became the German term for "chaff."

DVS: *Deutsche Verkehrsfliegerschule*, the German Air Line Pilots' School.

EKdo: Abbreviation of *Erprobungs-Kommando*, a testing detachment.

Ergänsung: As in *Ergänsungstaffel*, a replacement training unit or operational training unit. Also there were *Ergansunggruppen* – replacement training Gruppen, etc.

Ersatz: Substitute. As in ersatz coffee, made from barley.

Flieger: Pilot or airman, e.g. *jagdflieger* (fighter pilot) and *kampfflieger* (bomber pilot).

Flugkapitän: A rank in German civil aviation, e.g., **Flugkapitan** Fritz Wendel, the famous Messerschmitt test pilot.

Fuhrungsstab: Operations Staff of the High Command.

General der Jagdflieger: General of the Fighter Pilots, or General of the Fighters.

General der Kampfflieger: General of the Bombers.

General der Schlachtiflieger: General of Close Support.

General-Luftzeugmeister: The Chief of Aircraft Procurement and Supply. Referred to in the Luftwaffe as the "GLM."

Geschwader: Luftwaffe equivalent, roughly, of a USAF Combat Wing. A Geschwader was commanded by a *Geschwader-kommodore* of appropriate rank.

Gruppe: The basic tactical unit of the Luftwaffe. Approximately equivalent to a USAF Group or an RAF Wing. Commanded by a *Gruppenkommandeur* of appropriate rank.

Gymnasium: A German secondary school.

Hauptmann: Captain.

Himmelbett: German night fighter control system developed under General Kammbuber, in which a single night fighter was controlled in a specified area by a ground radar. Literally, the "heavenly bed."

Jabo: Abbreviation for *Jagdbomber*, a fighter-bomber.

Jabo-Rei: A long range fighter-bomber.

Jafü: An abbreviation of *Jagdfliegerfuhrer*, or Fighter Pilot Leader. The **Jafü** was usually a Colonel or of General rank, and served as liaison between fighter units and Air Fleet or other higher HQ.

Jagd: Prefix denoting fighter, as in **Jagdstaffel** (fighter squadron) or **Jagdflieger** (fighter pilot).

JG: Denoting **Jagdgeschwader**, e.g. JG 2, JG 53, JG 77, etc.

KG: Denoting **Kampfgeschwader**, a Bomber Group in the Luftwaffe. Bomber Groups were designated KG 1, KG 6, etc.

Kette: A three-plane formation of aircraft. The kette came back into vogue with the operational advent of the Me 262 jet fighter.

Kettenfuhrer: Leader of a three-plane formation.

Knight's Cross: See **Ritterkreuz** reference.

Kommodore: C.O. of a Geschwader, usually a Major or of higher rank.

Kriegsakademie: War Academy.

Luftkriegsakademie: Air War Academy.

ME: **Maschinenkanone**. Automatic cannon.

OKH: **Oberkommando des Heeres**, the Army High Command.

OKL: **Oberkommando der Luftwaffe**. The Luftwaffe High Command.

Ritterkreuz: The Knight's Cross of the Iron Cross, Germany's premier decoration for valor in WWII. There were five degrees of the **Ritterkreuz**, ascending in distinction. After the **Ritterkreuz** came the **Eichenlaub**, or Oak Leaves, then the **Schwertern**, or Swords, and then the **Brillants**, or Diamonds. Above all stood the Golden Ritterkreuz, awarded only once – to Colonel Hans-Ulrich Rudel, the famous Stuka pilot.

RLM: **Reichsluftministerium**. The German Air Ministry.

Rotte: Two-plane formation. Two **Rotten** made up a **Schwarm**.

Schlacht: Close support.

Schlachtgeschwader: A close support Group. **Schlachtgeschwader** were denoted by the letters SG, as in SG 7.

Schwarm: Two **Rotten**, or two pairs of aircraft in formation.

Sturm: Assault. **Sturmgruppen** were formations of heavily armed fighters, with lighter escorting fighters mixed in, with which the Fighter Arm assaulted the USAF bomber boxes or **Pulks**, as the Germans called them.

Stuka: Abbreviation of **Sturzkampfflugzeug**, or dive-bomber.

T-Stoff: Rocket fuel used in the Me 163 **Komet** interceptor .

Verband: Formation, as in **Jagdverband** 44, fighter formation 44, the special jet squadron formed and led by Adolf Galland.

Wehramt: Defense office.

Wehrmacht: The Armed Forces of Germany.

Wilde Sau: Literally "Wild Sow," but referred to as "Wild Boar." Tactics originated by Major Hajo Herrmann in 1943, where fighters minus radar or ground control attacked RAF bombers at night using only their eyes, searchlights, and ground glare to find their quarry. "Wild Boar" came into vogue briefly when RAF "chaff" blinded German radar.

"X-Gerät": A target-approach and blind-flying aid used early in the war. "**Y-Gerät**" was a later blind-flying and range-finding aid.

ZG: Denoting **Zerstörergeschwader**, a Group of heavy fighters such as the Me 110, which were originally envisioned as fighter-destroyers. Such Groups were designated ZG 1, ZG 77, etc.

The Aircraft of Adolf Galland in Profile

1. July 1937 - May 1938. Heinkel He 51C, W.Nr. unknown; combat novice *Oberleutnant* Galland took command of 3./J88 during the Spanish Civil War. As of late 1937, his He 51 "2-78" would display the stylized Mickey Mouse, a creation attributed to preceding *Staffel* leader Douglas Pitcairn. Note one of a pair of 10 kg. bombs strapped to the belly tank – a crude but effective incendiary weapon developed for tactical targets.

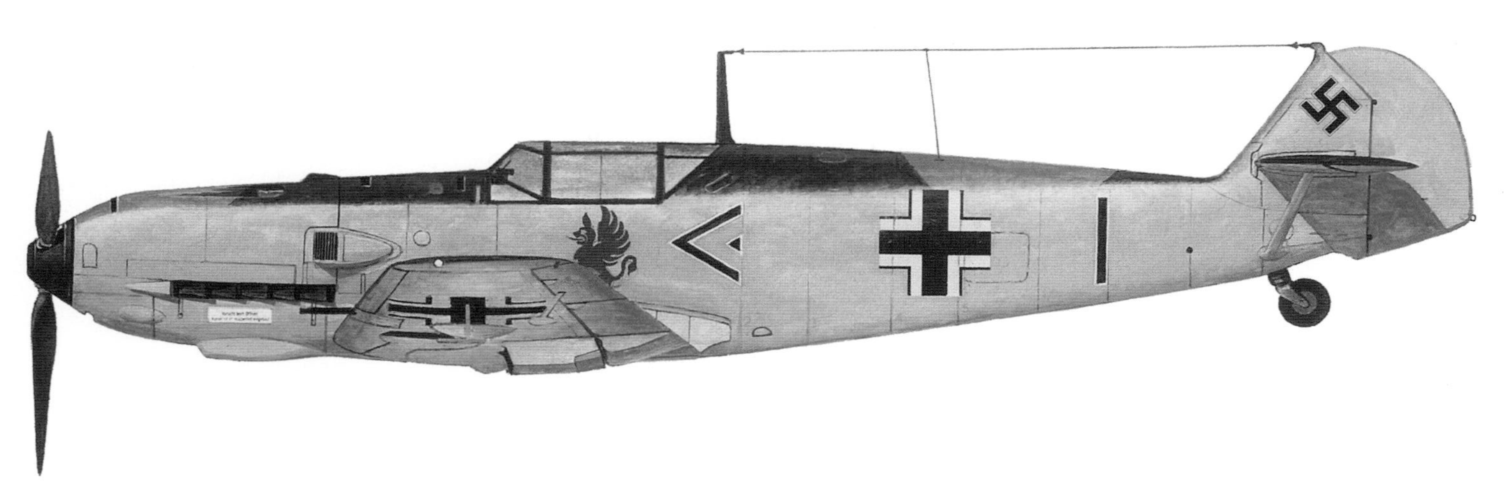

2. May - mid June 1940. Bf 109E-4, purported W.Nr.939; *Hauptmann* Galland scored his first fourteen aerial victories as Operations Officer with JG 27 in the Battle of France, then took command of III./JG 26, apparently retaining this *Emil*. Camouflaged in standard RLM 71 and 02 over 65, it displayed the *Gruppenkommandeur* double chevron (*doppelwinkel*) and vertical bar of III *Gruppe* plus the curious use of the 9 *Staffel* "hell Hound." It is doubtful victory bars were ever shown on this plane.

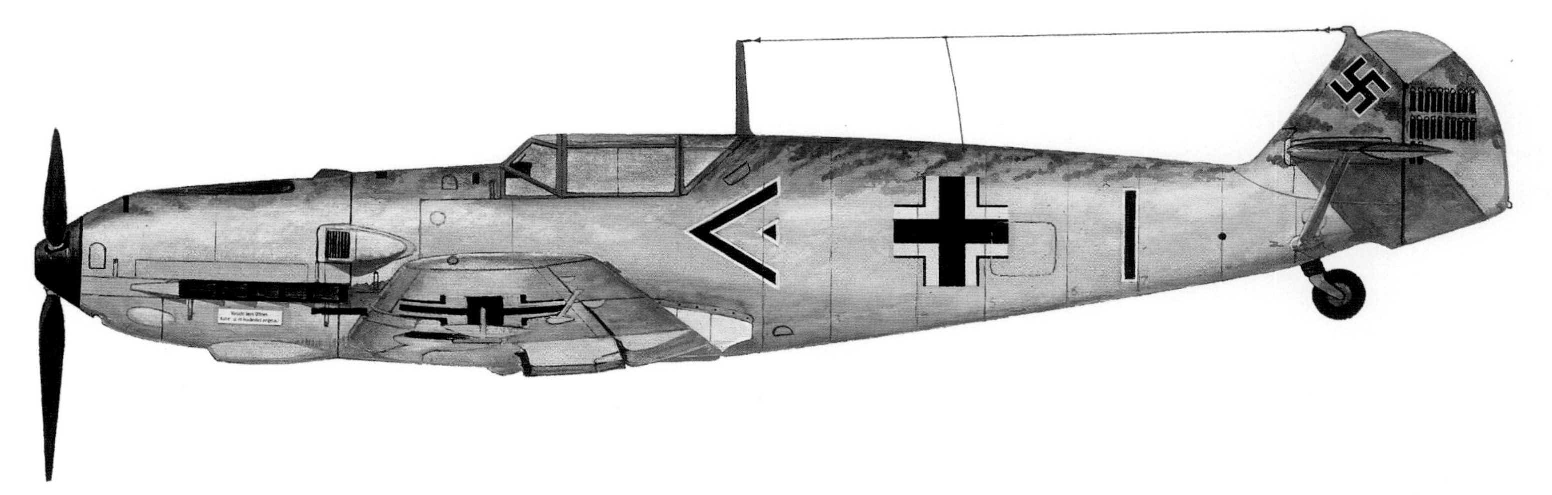

3. Mid July - mid August 1940. Bf 109E-4, purported W.Nr.2764; with the July armistice in France, newly promoted *Major* Galland flew this *Emil* in the first great air raids of England proper. Uniquely camouflaged in mottled RLM 75 over 65, it displayed twenty-two aerial victory bars, the 17th victory justifying his Knight's Cross citation. The yellow rudder tip was the early tactical marking used by many *Emil* equipped units at that time.

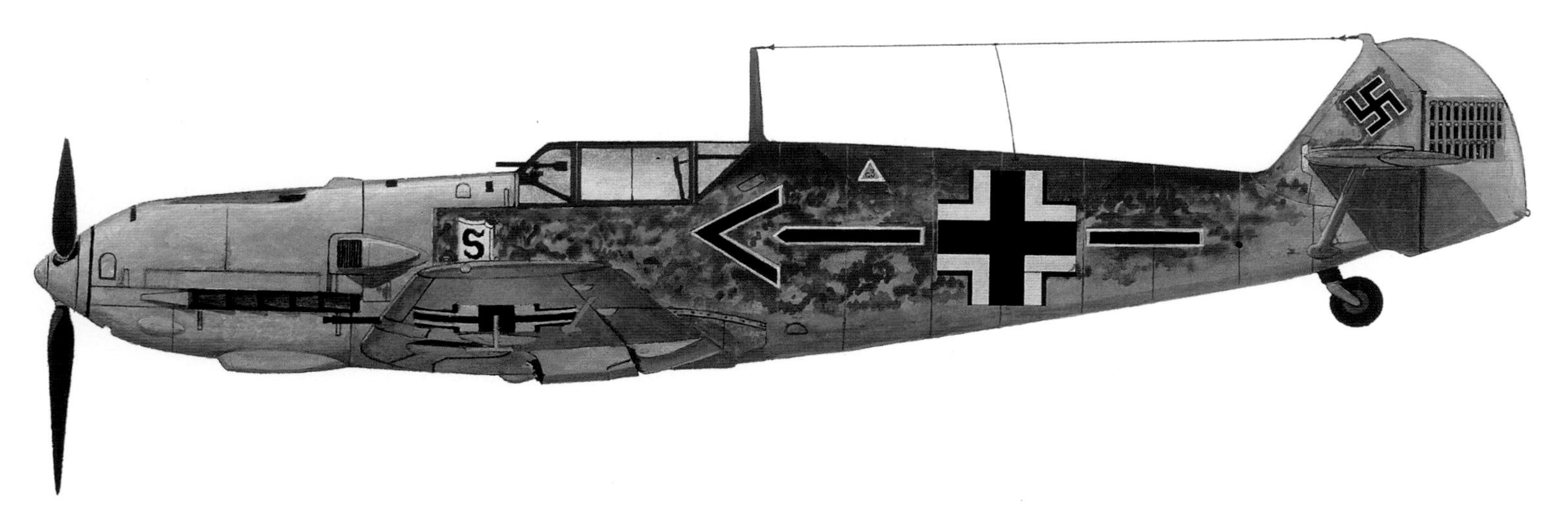

4. Mid August - early September 1940. Bf 109E-4, W.Nr.5398; Galland's first aircraft camouflaged in RLM 74-75 over 76, it displays the "arrow" chevron and bars plus 29 victory bars for the new *Geschwaderkommodore* of JG 26. The bold yellow tactical markings would identify the *Emils* now flying "free hunting" sorties over the extant of southeastern England. One final victory would be added to the rudder score board before "5398" was handed over to another pilot in September.

5. Early September 1940 - May 1941. Bf 109E-4/N, W.Nr.5819; this redoubtable *Emil* was the first to bear the infamous cigar smoking Mickey Mouse logo and gave the ace his 40th victory and Oak Leaves over his *Ritterkreuz* as of late September. Three weeks later he gained his 50th victory and was promoted to *Oberstleutnant*. On December 5th came the 57th victory to lead all *Jagdfliegern* in the Battle of Britain. During the winter furlough for JG 26, *Emil* 5819 was modified to E-7 status, and in late March of 1941, was reissued briefly to the *Kommodore*. The plane was finally turned over to a training reserve unit where a rudder tally was updated to 80 victory bars in the *Kommodore's* honor.

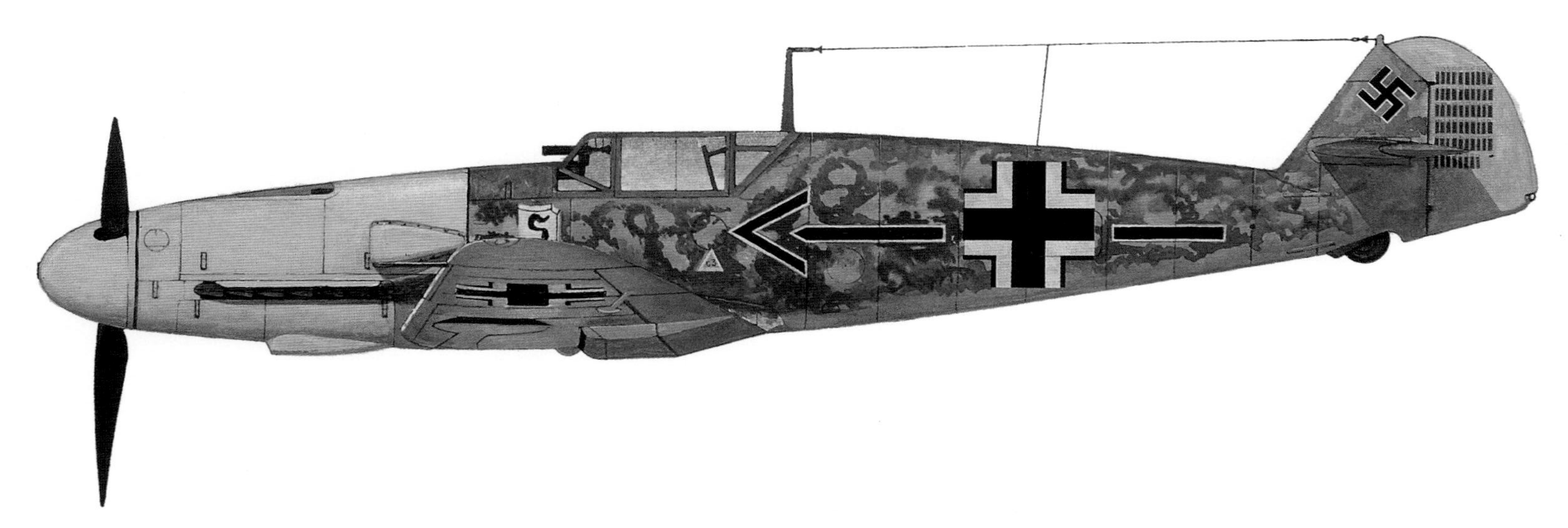

6. Late March - mid Summer 1941. Bf 109F-0, W.Nr.6714; there were purportedly two *Friedrich* prototypes and this illustration represents the one photographed at Audembert, France sporting the black and white "arrow" command insignia and possibly 58 victory bars on the rudder as of the first week of April. After an early inspection, technicians removed the useless ZFR 5 telescope protruding through the windshield, curiously repainted the command "arrow" solid white and reduced the size of the *Schlageter* shield logo. Likewise, RLM 74 was sprayed over the enlarged supercharger intake, probably to eliminate glare from the yellow cowling. *Friedrich* 6714 is recorded as the aircraft flown on the infamous "Lobster Champagne Flight" on April 15th when Galland officially scored his 59th and 60th aerial kills.

7. December 1941. Bf 109F-2, W.Nr.6750; one of purportedly three "special" weapons test bed aircraft, *Friedrich* 6750 was the first Bf 109 to mount 13mm guns beneath bulged breech housings in the upper nose. Often confused with another "special" type, photo analysis indicates that this aircraft with moderate mottled RLM 74 on the rear fuselage did not carry either the "arrow" command markings, or the Mickey Mouse logo, but did display the final score of 94 victories on its yellow rudder. How many victories Galland gained with this plane is uncertain.

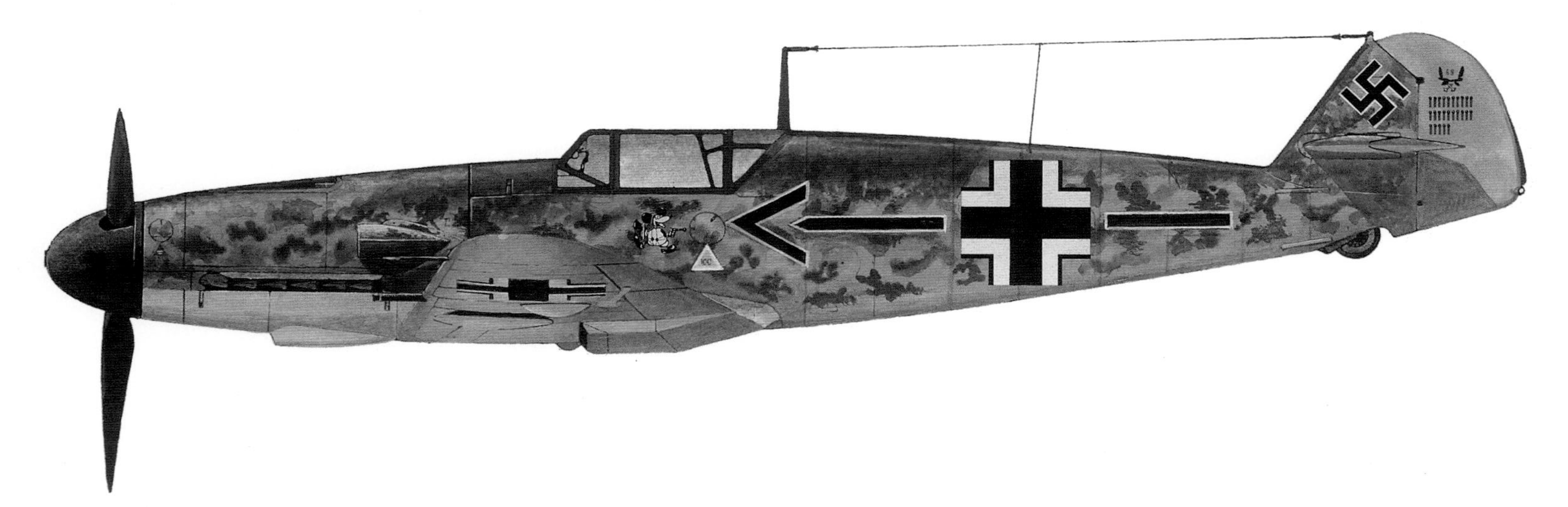

8. December 1941. Bf 109F-2/F-6U, W.Nr. unknown; Galland's "special" weapons test bed aircraft often confused with the aircraft depicted in the previous profile, this is the only *Friedrich* to be fitted with internal wing mounted 20mm cannon. This highly polished "five-gun" *Friedrich* in full command regalia, including the Mickey Mouse logo, was the aircraft used on December 5th to score his 94th victory, officially his last confirmed aerial kill. The fete resulted in his promotion to *Oberst*.

9. Early 1944. Fw 190A-6, "White 2", W.Nr. unknown; as Inspector General of Day Fighters, *Generalleutnant* Galland commandeered "White 2" from a reserve unit as his liaison aircraft to assess the best defense against the intensifying Allied air offensive. Memoirs infer Galland shot down an American heavy bomber with this aircraft in March, but mission details are vague and the victory was never officially confirmed. In April, he barely escaped in his "White 2" from a flight of 8th Air Force Mustangs in hot pursuit. The outcome of the Inspector's dangerous analysis was the establishment of a Focke-Wulf equipped *Sturmgruppe* interceptor force which by year's end was ultimately annihilated.

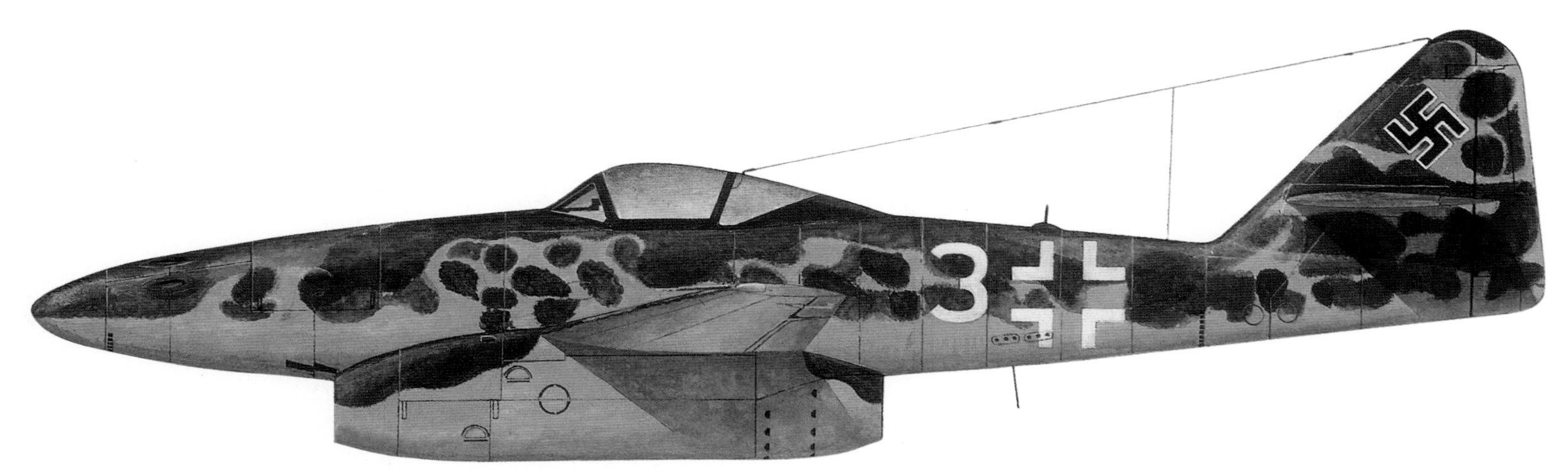

10. April 1945. Me 262A-1, "White 3", W.Nr. unknown; one of the last known fighter aircraft flown by the exiled *General* while in command of JV 44 at Munich-Reim airdrome. "White 3" is believed to be the aircraft he used to down two B-26 Marauders with underwing rockets on April 6th. Late war camouflage varied greatly on all fighter types and RLM 82-83 over 76 is chosen here as an interpolation of a single black and white photograph taken in the harrowing environment.

Index

Also from the Publisher

FIGHTER ACES OF THE USA

Revised and Expanded Edition

Col. Raymond F. Toliver & Trevor J. Constable

Fighter Aces of the U.S.A. is the most complete, full-spectrum book ever published on American fighter aces, and includes dozens of aces' combat accounts, plus capsule biographies. Evolution of aircraft, tactics and armament is seen through the eyes of the 1400 elite Americans who earned the coveted title "Ace." Comprehensive revisions and updates to this new edition include the most complete statistics of American aces ever published, and is fully current to date of publication. Authoritative and compelling narrative also presents eyebrow-raising facts on enemy aces who fought Americans in all wars and theatres. Lists include names and scores, plus intriguing data on Soviet Air Force aces who battled USAF aces over Korea. Lavishly illustrated with hundreds of photos, this book is a must reference for every historian and "buff's" bookshelf.
Size: 9" x 12", over 850 b/w photographs
400 pages, hard cover
ISBN: 0-7643-0348-1 $59.95

HERKY!
The Memoirs of a Checkertail Ace
Herschel H. Green

Here is the dramatic life story of one of the legendary USAAF fighter pilots of World War II who fought across the skies over the Mediterranean and southern Europe in the great aerial campaigns against the Luftwaffe – Herschel H. "Herky" Green. *Herky!* is the compelling story of a young man from a small Kentucky town and how he achieved fame in the reknowned "Checkertail Clan," the 325th Fighter Group. His exploits, as well as those of many of his fellow pilots, come alive as first-hand descriptions of wartime adventures show both the excitement and tragedy, success and survival, of life in the cockpits of P-40s, P-47s and P-51s. Experience the anxiety and apprehension in launching a P-40 from the flight deck of the USS *Ranger* and making a landfall at Casablanca in January 1943; feel the paralyzing terror of a first combat mission in which the pilot becomes unequivocally convinced that his life will end in just a few precious seconds; escort heavy bombers on the first "shuttle mission" to Russia; learn of heroism that was almost a routine daily occurence. Here are the electrifying exploits of Herky Green and other Checkertail Clan heroes. By the time Colonel Green was grounded by orders of higher headquarters, he was the leading ace of the 15th Air Force with eighteen aerial victories. His rise from humble beginnings to extraordinary success in both military and business careers is inspiring. His travels and adventures make absorbing reading.

Size: 8 1/2" x 11" over 150 b/w photographs
192 pages, hard cover
ISBN: 0-7643-0073-3 $45.00

GABBY: A Fighter Pilot's Life

Francis Gabreski as told to Carl Molesworth

If ever a man has earned his place in the annals of military history, that man is Francis "Gabby" Gabreski. His exploits as a fighter pilot in World War II and Korea are legendary; his rise from humble beginnings to success in military and business careers is inspiring. This is the full story of Gabby Gabreski, told in his own words. Gabreski's life is a classic American success story. Born to Polish immigrant parents in 1919, he nearly washed out of Notre Dame and then flight school. He was down to his last chance, and he made the most of it. A witness to the Japanese attack on Pearl Harbor, Gabby had his own first taste of air combat flying with a Polish RAF squadron. Shortly thereafter he joined the 56th Fighter Group of the U.S. 8th Air Force, and in seventeen months he shot down twenty-eight German planes, the highest total of any 8th Air Force pilot in Europe. He became a hero whose name was splashed across newspaper headlines from coast to coast. And then, on the very day he was to fly home to his fiancee and a hero's welcome, he took one last combat mission, crashed and, after a daring attempt to avoid capture, finished the war in a POW camp. Gabreski returned to combat in 1951, flying F-86 Sabrejets over Korea. He scored 6.5 more victories there, making him one of the few pilots ever to achieve ace status in two wars and in both propeller and jet aircraft. He retired from the Air Force as a colonel in 1967 and spent the next twenty years working in the aviation industry, sustained, as always, by his devout religious faith and his deep love for his family. Now, drawing on his private documents and photographs, Gabby, along with writer Carl Molesworth, tells his thrilling eyewitness story with a candor and a vivid style that should earn this brave pilot a whole new generation of admirers.

Size: 8 1/2" x 11" over 200 b/w photographs, eight color aircraft profiles
176 pages, hardcover
ISBN: 0-7643-0442-9 $45.00

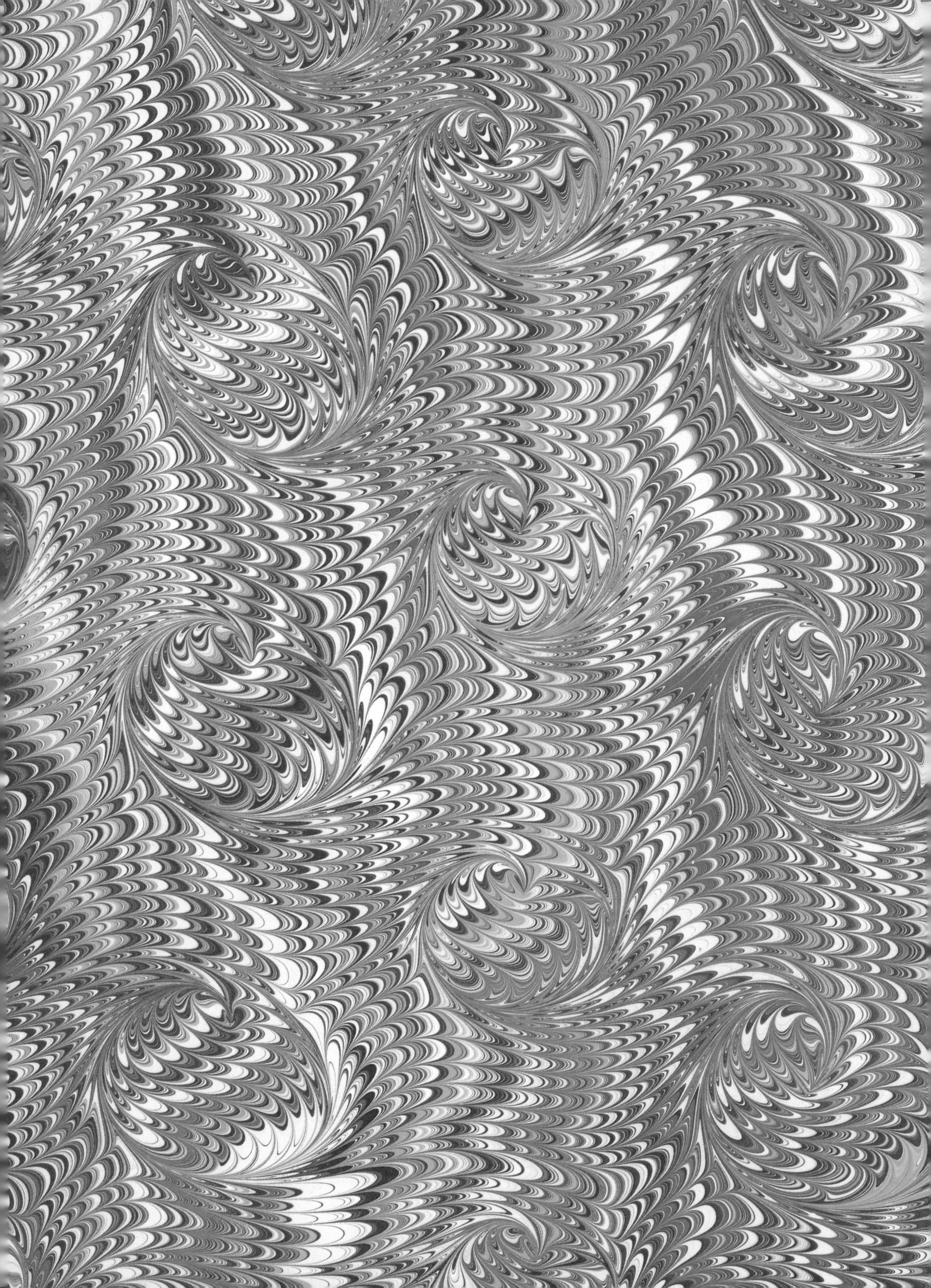